ISABELLE OF FRANCE

Isabelle *of* FRANCE

Capetian Sanctity and Franciscan Identity
in the Thirteenth Century

SEAN L. FIELD

University of Notre Dame Press

Notre Dame, Indiana

Copyright © 2006 University of Notre Dame
Notre Dame, Indiana 46556
All Rights Reserved
www.undpress.nd.edu

Manufactured in the United States of America

Library of Congress Cataloging-in-Publication Data

Field, Sean L. (Sean Linscott), 1970–
    Isabelle of France : Capetian sanctity and Franciscan identity in the
thirteenth century / Sean L. Field.
        p.cm.
    Includes bibliographical references and index.
    ISBN-13: 978-0-268-02880-0 (pbk. : alk.paper)
    ISBN-10: 0-268-02880-X (pbk. : alk.paper)
1. Isabelle, Princess of France, 1225–1270.   2. Princesses—France—Biography.
3. Blessed—France—Biography.   4. Louis IX, King of France, 1214–1270—
Family.   I. Title.
    BX4705.I79F54 2006
    282.092—dc22
    [B]   2006018595

♾ *The paper in this book meets the guidelines for permanence and durability of*
the Committee on Production Guidelines for Book Longevity of the Council
on Library Resources.

Uxori carissimae

CONTENTS

ACKNOWLEDGMENTS

A lot of debts pile up over a decade of work. My research was made possible by William J. Fulbright and Charlotte W. Newcombe Fellowships as well as grants from Northwestern University and the University of Vermont. The staffs of the Bibliothèque nationale de France, Bibliothèque Mazarine, Archives nationales de France, Institut de Recherche et d'Histoire des Textes, Bibliothèque Saulchoir, and Bibliothèque franciscaine provinciale des Capucins in Paris and the Openbare Bibliotheek in Bruges were patient and helpful. I also thank the Interlibrary Loan staffs of Northwestern University, Marquette University, and the University of Vermont and the Special Collections librarians at Northwestern, the University of Michigan, and Michigan State University. Portions of chapter 2 previously appeared in "Gilbert of Tournai's Letter to Isabelle of France: An Edition of the Complete Text," *Mediaeval Studies* 65 (2003): 57–97, and "New Evidence for the Life of Isabelle of France," *Revue Mabillon* n.s. 13 (2002): 117–31, and are used with the kind permission of the Pontifical Institute of Mediaeval Studies and Brepols Publishers.

Cecilia Gaposchkin, apparently a glutton for punishment, volunteered to read the entire book and improved it with her insights and suggestions. Lezlie Knox and Amani Whitfield read sections as well. Their comments are much appreciated, as are the criticisms of the two anonymous reviewers for the University of Notre Dame Press. A full acknowledgment of all I owe to the other generous scholars who answered my questions or provided help would stretch for many pages, so I limit myself here to a simple list of names, with the hope of not having omitted too many: Nicole Bériou, Alain Boureau, Elizabeth A. R. Brown, Louisa Burnham, Maeve Callan, Anne Clark, Jacques Dalarun, Adam Davis, Sharon Farmer, Larry Field, Thomas Hajkowski, Sandra Hindman, Elizabeth Hudson, William C. Jordan, Mark Jurdjevic, Samantha Kelly, Richard Kieckhefer, Nicole Leapley, Beth Lynn, Stefano Mula, Barbara Newman, Monique O'Connell, William D. Paden, Mary Rouse, Miriam Shadis, and Ethan Shagan. It has been a pleasure to work with Barbara Hanrahan, Rebecca DeBoer, Margaret Gloster, and Lowell Francis at the University of Notre Dame Press. Ann Aydelotte's skills as a copy editor saved me from many mistakes and inconsistencies.

By far my greatest intellectual and practical debt is owed to Robert E. Lerner. Looking back, this book had its inception when photocopies of an intriguing manuscript were conjured up from his magical, mysterious filing cabinet and handed over to my care. Not only did he subsequently provide all the guidance that one could ask for from a doctoral adviser, but he also read an early draft of this book as it was taking shape. His help, as well as that of the scholars and friends listed above, has been largely responsible for whatever strengths the book may possess. I can claim only errors and inadequacies as uniquely my own.

Finally, but most important, I thank my family. I rely on Tammy, Larry, and Nicholas Field for their understanding and support, and I appreciate their restraint in having only occasionally asked when the book would be finished. Cecilia seems happy to see me come home from work every day, an encouragement that only a three-and-a-half-year-old daughter with an irresistible grin can properly supply. Lori Elizabeth Field has stuck with me through all the vicissitudes that an academic career can produce. We were married the year this project had its intellectual genesis, and we have traveled together across two continents as the work progressed. Whether or not she ever gets around to reading the whole thing, this book is for her.

ABBREVIATIONS

AFH   *Archivum franciscanum historicum*

AN   Paris, Archives nationales de France

AS   Johannes Bolland et al., eds., *Acta sanctorum, quotquot
             toto orbe coluntur. Editio novissima* (Paris, 1863–).

BF   J.-H. Sbaralea, ed., *Bullarium franciscanum* (Rome,
             1759–1768).

BNF   Paris, Bibliothèque nationale de France

BU   Thomas of Cantimpré, *Bonum universale de apibus.*
             Ed. G. Colverinus (Douai, 1627).

DHGE   *Dictionnaire d'histoire et de géographie ecclésiastiques*
             (Paris, 1912–).

DS   *Dictionnaire de spiritualité, ascétique et mystique, doctrine et
             histoire* (Paris, 1932–).

Escritos   Ignacio Omaechevarria, ed., *Escritos de Santa Clara y
             documentos complementarios*, 3rd ed. (Madrid, 1993).

GC   *Gallia christiana, in provincias ecclesiasticas distributa*
             (Paris, 1716–1865).

Layettes   A. Teulet et al., eds., *Layettes du trésor des chartes* (Paris,
             1863–1909).

"New Evidence"   Sean Field, "New Evidence for the Life of Isabelle of France," *Revue Mabillon* n. s. 13 (2002): 117–31.

PL   J. P. Migne, ed., *Patrologiae latinae cursus completus* (Paris, 1844–1864).

RHGF   M. Bouquet et al., eds., *Recueil des historiens des gaules et de la France* (Paris, 1738–1876).

Writings of AH   Sean L. Field, ed., *The Writings of Agnes of Harcourt: The Life of Isabelle of France and the Letter on Louis IX and Longchamp* (Notre Dame, IN, 2003).

Introduction

In February 1259, Pope Alexander IV approved the first rule for the new Abbaye de l'Humilité-de-Notre-Dame, founded by Isabelle, the sister of King Louis IX of France. Though the first nuns would not enter the abbey until June 1260, the new rule had recently been composed by a team that included Isabelle and an illustrious group of Franciscan university masters. Alexander offered a preamble that justified his support for this potentially controversial new female Franciscan form of life. He began with a brilliant solar metaphor: God, "the true sun, flashing with perpetual brightness," illuminates the hearts of the faithful. But while his light shines on everyone, he often sends even more powerful rays to infuse the minds of kings and princes, so that they may "propel and lead others by their saving example towards the sweet taste and love of heavenly things." In this way, Louis and Isabelle, "suffused with this light," were leading exemplary lives—Louis ruling as the "most Christian prince . . . and illustrious king of the Franks," and Isabelle "shining with the luster of virginal modesty and powerful with the brightness of other virtues." Compelled by such outstanding piety, Alexander consented to set aside the Fourth Lateran Council's prohibition on creating new orders, "specially out of consideration for the King and Isabelle," and to approve this new rule.[1]

Alexander's rhetoric raises a number of questions that will be central to this study. They concern the development of Capetian sanctity, the institutional relationship of women to the Franciscan Order, and the nature of women's access to power in the thirteenth century.

ROYAL PIETY AND CAPETIAN SANCTITY

Just what was Isabelle's role within the intensely devout court of St. Louis? What sort of influence did she wield, and to what ends? Rarely did the medieval world witness a convergence of piety and political power as complete as that exhibited by the Capetian court in the midthirteenth century. Much of the credit for creating this climate goes to Louis, driven by his failed crusade and his sense of Christian duty to become the perfect saint-king and royal penitent. Louis IX's mother, Blanche of Castile, is usually portrayed as a stern, even domineering woman who strongly influenced the king's religious as well as political development. Yet Isabelle may have done as much as her mother or brother to set the tone of Capetian piety.

Though Isabelle of France is hardly a household name today (and not to be confused with the Isabella of France who married Edward II of England), in 1259 she enjoyed a widespread renown. She initially gained a reputation as a budding holy woman due to her successful rejection of her family's plans for her marriage. She was betrothed at a very young age to the son of a powerful noble family, and, more dramatically, in 1243, Emperor Frederick II sought Isabelle's hand for his son and heir, Conrad. But Isabelle refused to marry, preferring to dedicate herself to a life of virginity. In the 1250s, popes and friars began to note and publicize her piety. Isabelle capitalized on this growing reputation by establishing her new house for Franciscan women. The Abbey of the Humility of Our Lady, or Longchamp as it became better known, was situated just west of Paris near the Seine in the modern Bois de Boulogne (on the northern edge of the site now occupied by the Hippodrome de Longchamp). Upon founding her new abbey, Isabelle chose to remain a laywoman rather than becoming a nun. She constructed a modest residence and chapel on its grounds, where she was regarded by the sisters as a source of holiness and healing. At her death in 1270, her tomb at Longchamp became an object of pilgrimage and the site of numerous reported miracles. Pope Leo X eventually recognized her posthumous reputation for sanctity by granting Longchamp permission to celebrate Isabelle's office in 1521, from which time she has tradition-ally been known as the "blessed" Isabelle of France.

Pope Alexander's praise offers striking evidence of Isabelle's reputation for piety in 1259. Isabelle and Louis are paired together here, but it is she who is singled out as "shining with the luster of virginal modesty and pow-erful with the brightness of other virtues." Shining and powerful, *nitida et pollens*—a striking image of radiating renown and incandescent influence.

Isabelle of France's fame, I will argue, helped to create the aura of sanc-tity that increasingly surrounded the French royal house in the thirteenth century. Her career should be considered as part of the larger narrative that links the growth of Capetian power to the idea of a divinely ordained, vir-tuous, and holy royal family through an intertwining of "piety and state building."[2] Scholars interested in this notion of Capetian holiness and the promotion of French royal ideology in general have rightly pointed to the reign of St. Louis as a decisive moment.[3] But if Louis's reputation was undoubtedly instrumental in fostering this notion of the Capetians as (in Marc Bloch's phrase) a "pre-eminently holy" family, so was his sister's.

The idea of a "sacred" monarchy was gradually built upon a host of sto-ries and symbols surrounding the throne—the fleur-de-lis, the holy oil of Reims, the oriflamme, the royal touch, and the claims to the favor of the patron saints Denis and later Louis himself. The kings of France earned their "Most Christian" reputation through concrete support for the church as well, manifest in the crown's crusading activities, its frequent role as defender of the papacy and university, and its guardianship of the royal col-lection of relics deposited at the Sainte-Chapelle in Paris.[4] But this model of sacral kingship was only part of the story.[5] The idea of the Capetian line as a holy royal family also rested on a broader concept of dynastic sanc-tity—it was not just the anointed kings who were seen as holy, but also the entire bloodline, a *beata stirps*, as André Vauchez has called it.[6] This wider concept of a holy lineage needed, in turn, to be fed by publicly recognized displays of real-life devotion.[7] Visible saintly behavior was crucial to the emergence of the "reputation for outstanding piety" enjoyed by the later Capetians.[8] Indeed, it was essential for members of the family other than anointed kings to be regarded as particularly imbued with holiness, if the wider claim of family sanctity were to ring true. Certainly a number of royal family members, notably Blanche of Castile, were particularly pious.

But, besides Louis, only Isabelle was treated as a truly holy figure, credited with miracles, or seen as a saint.[9] Without her example, there would have been no real pattern of thirteenth-century Capetian holiness, and claims to the contrary would necessarily have rung hollow.

For several decades after Isabelle's and Louis's deaths in 1270, their cults ran on parallel tracks.[10] Around 1280, miracles were being recorded not only at Louis IX's tomb to the north of Paris at Saint-Denis, but also at Isabelle's burial site to the west of Paris at Longchamp. At the same time, saints' lives were being composed for both siblings, and pilgrims were visiting both sites in search of cures and other divine aid. Members of the royal family in this era considered Isabelle, as well as her brother, to be worthy of veneration. In the dreams of the nuns of Longchamp, Isabelle and Louis remained linked as saintly intercessors. Although the fortunes of the two cults diverged for a time after the early fourteenth century, the contribution of Isabelle's thirteenth-century visibility to the process of Capetian saint-building was a crucial link in constructing the French "religion of monarchy."

THIRTEENTH-CENTURY MODELS OF SANCTITY

Beyond the immediate Capetian context, as a saintly, royal woman tied to the Franciscans, Isabelle was also part of wider European trends. How does Isabelle's career fit into received ideas about thirteenth-century models of sanctity? Vauchez has shown that in the thirteenth century, sainthood was increasingly associated with the mendicants, women, lay people, and royalty, a model which Isabelle embodied as fully as any other contemporary figure.[11] But, more specifically, Isabelle exhibits a convergence between sanctity, dynastic power, and gender that is usually regarded as more typical of Central European ruling houses in this period. As Gábor Klaniczay has demonstrated, within these dynasties in the thirteenth century it "became the task of the female members to assure the halo of sainthood for the family, to ennoble them to become a *beata stirps*."[12]

The most influential of these Central European princesses was surely Elizabeth of Hungary (1207–1231), the daughter of Andrew II of Hungary and his wife Gertrude. She was raised at the court of her future husband, Ludwig IV of Thuringia. They married in 1221, and their union produced three children. Even during her marriage Elizabeth, influenced by Franciscans newly arrived in the territory, was known for her concern for the poor. Upon Ludwig's death in 1227, she devoted herself to charitable works by building a hospital dedicated to St. Francis and caring for the poor, sick, and lepers, and led a life of extraordinary asceticism under her harsh (indeed, sadistic) confessor, Conrad of Marburg. She was canonized with great speed and publicity in 1235.[13] A number of Elizabeth's female relations and followers adopted similar lives, including such well-known figures as Hedwig of Silesia (1174/8–1243), Margaret of Hungary (1242–1270), and Agnes of Bohemia (1211–1282).[14] Isabelle of France has even plausibly been treated as one of these *filiae sanctae Elizabeth* (daughters of St. Elizabeth)—women who took Elizabeth as a model.[15]

There is some reason to think that Elizabeth of Hungary could indeed have been a model for Isabelle. The names Isabelle and Elizabeth were considered to be the same, perhaps making some sort of association natural.[16] More concretely, Jean of Joinville recounts that at a celebration in 1241 for the knighting of Isabelle's brother, Alphonse of Poitiers, their mother encountered the son of St. Elizabeth. Blanche of Castile then proceeded to kiss him on the forehead out of devotion, "because she thought his mother must have kissed him there often."[17] Though it is not clear that Isabelle was actually present on this famous occasion, the incident demonstrates that Elizabeth was venerated at the Capetian court.[18] But whether or not Isabelle ever consciously imitated St. Elizabeth, she resembled her in important ways. They were both royal women influenced by the Franciscans, dedicated to charity and care of the poor, and, while drawn to a distinctly penitential spirituality, they nevertheless declined to take monastic vows.[19] Isabelle was part of a wider group of noble women who were inspired by and helped to establish this emerging model of piety.

In setting up her community outside of Paris, Isabelle had something else in common with these "daughters of St. Elizabeth." Klaniczay describes Central European princesses as inhabiting and promoting "heavenly courts"—hospitals and monastic communities where the female residents' fasting, asceticism, and devotion operated as religious critiques of their male relatives' worldly courts.[20] These holy princesses did not simply renounce temporal authority; rather, they traded it for the influence that comes with saintly prestige. But Isabelle and her foundation of Longchamp match this model only in part. She did create a "heavenly court" of sorts with her new foundation, and other Capetian princesses and noble women did eventually congregate there (though never to the extent of some of the Central European royal foundations). But her house's relationship to the Capetian court was fundamentally different, since Louis himself was a pre-eminently saintly figure, and his court "was undoubtedly the closest replica of the 'court of heaven' that thirteenth-century Europe had to offer."[21] Isabelle of France and her abbey at Longchamp must be seen as contributing to, not critiquing, the exercise of Capetian religious power.[22]

FEMALE FRANCISCANISM

A different set of questions arises within the context of Franciscan history. Why did Isabelle of France feel the need to co-author a new rule for Franciscan women? What ideals did her rule embrace? How did it differ from other contemporary forms of life? And what was its impact? By 1259 the complex relationship between women, the Franciscan Order, and the papacy had reached a delicate stage. The institutional relationship between male Franciscans and women's houses associated with the order was in a state of confusion, with multiple rules in effect and the male order generally seeking to free itself from obligations to female communities. Isabelle was therefore stepping into a veritable minefield. Moreover, her negotiations with the Franciscans and the papacy did not end in 1259, for the first rule was quickly supplanted by a revised rule that was approved by Pope Urban IV in 1263. Why was this revision necessary, and whose desires lay behind it? The impact of Isabelle's rules have generally been overlooked, or at best treated as a footnote to the history of women and the Franciscan Order in the thirteenth century. This history has recently begun to receive renewed attention,[23] and Isabelle's story offers an important vantage point from which to consider the issues at stake and how they were conceived and contested by all sides.

This story can only be recaptured through a close examination of Isabelle's rules, by reconstructing their writing process, identifying their innovations, and assessing her personal contributions and successes as well as her capitulations and compromises. Closer attention to the ideas embodied in the two rules reminds us that St. Clare of Assisi's famous battle for absolute poverty was only part of a more complex interaction between women, the male Franciscan Order, and the papal curia. Isabelle's vision of an order of *Sorores minores* (in English, "Sisters Minor," in French, *Soeurs mineures*, a title parallel to the male *Fratres minores*) reveals that in the 1250s and 1260s other models of engagement between the male Franciscan Order and the women's religious movement were possible and indeed implemented.[24] Moreover, the extent to which patrons and Franciscan women from across Europe subsequently sought to adopt Isabelle's rule for their own houses has not previously been highlighted. This process led eventually to the rule's spread from France into England, Italy, and Spain and to its influence on the lives of countless women over the next several centuries.

WOMEN AND POWER

Finally, the question of just how Isabelle achieved such notable success in negotiating with the Franciscans and the papal curia has ramifications for the wider field of women's religious history and the larger question of medieval women's ability to act as agents within political and religious institutions. Thirteenth-century women and men functioned in a culture in which status and wealth as well as gender shaped access to power and institutions. I have translated Alexander IV's Latin adjective *pollens* as "powerful," but it might be rendered more prosaically as "capable" or "potent"—in short, "able to get things done." As Pauline Stafford has put it, power at its root is "the ability or chance to realize our own will, if necessary against the resistance of others. It is efficacy, that is, the ability to act effectively, to produce effects."[25] By this practical definition, Isabelle of France was indeed a powerful historical actor who effected change and made her impact felt. Historians have recently begun to revise earlier, negative generalizations to argue that royal and noble women and their networks could play important roles in transmitting power and influence in this era.[26] Of particular relevance to the present study are the essays in the recent *Capetian Women*, edited by Kathleen Nolan, which seek "to uncover how royal women gained access to power" and to "expand our understanding of what was possible for a woman of privilege in medieval France."[27]

The collection as a whole highlights the multiple sources of authority available to women associated with the French royal family, focusing on ritual and patronage as well as on more traditional aspects of political power. But of the many Capetian women considered in this collection, Isabelle best exemplifies the coming together of religious and political power in someone who declined to marry, embraced a life of pious celibacy, but remained a laywoman.[28]

Isabelle's involvement with the composition of a rule and the process of securing its approval marks her as a woman able to exert direct influence within both religious and political spheres. By walking a tightrope between court and cloister, Isabelle retained the combination of royal influence, lay status, and Franciscan-inspired sanctity that allowed her to articulate her vision of female Franciscanism.

SOURCES

Isabelle's case for sanctity was recorded and promoted in the most intriguing item in her dossier—the contemporary *Life of Isabelle*, written by the third abbess of Longchamp, Agnes of Harcourt.[29] Agnes belonged to a leading Norman noble family. Her father, Jean I of Harcourt, and brother, Jean II, were crusading companions of Louis IX and Philip III, and her brothers Raoul, Robert, and Guy went on to enjoy successful careers in the church.[30] Agnes, probably born in the early 1240s, was most likely a lady-in-waiting in Isabelle of France's household before entering Longchamp with the first group of women to take the veil there in 1260. She served two terms as abbess of Longchamp; the first probably spanned the years 1264 to 1275, while the second lasted from 2 September 1281 to 29 August 1287. Surviving documents from the archives of Longchamp reveal Agnes to have been a literate woman and book owner as well as a leader who worked to protect her house's position, lands, and income. She died after March 1290, most likely on 25 November 1291.[31] Her first known composition was a brief *Letter on Louis IX and Longchamp*, written during her second term in office, on 4 December 1282. At the request of Charles of Anjou (another brother of Isabelle's and Louis's), Agnes began work on her biography of Isabelle around 1283 and completed it sometime before the middle of 1285.

Agnes's *Life of Isabelle* is one of the few biographies written by one European woman about another before the end of the thirteenth century, and it is probably the first substantial female-authored prose work in French. Yet in spite of the attention paid to medieval women as authors in recent decades, Agnes's work has been practically ignored by scholars. This neglect is all the more surprising because the *Life of Isabelle* is surely the most lively Capetian biography next to Joinville's famous portrait of Louis IX. Agnes's prose is animated and energetic, her text is filled with personal reminiscences and stories about the royal family and leading Franciscans, and she provides a vivid tableau of religious life around the French court in the middle of the thirteenth century. Moreover, though Agnes herself is a remarkably strong first-person presence in her texts, the *Life of Isabelle* and the *Letter on Louis IX and Longchamp* also collect the memories of others concerning Isabelle's life, character, actions, and miracles. Several members of the royal family offer their recollections, including Louis IX and his wife, Marguerite of Provence. A number of Franciscans also recount Isabelle's actions and miracles, and a total of twenty-three sisters of Longchamp are mentioned in Agnes's writings, many of them acting as witnesses to Isabelle's posthumous miracles. In Agnes of Harcourt's texts, therefore, we have a treasure trove of information about Isabelle and her relationship to her family, to her Franciscan advisers, and to the nuns of her royal abbey from a well-informed female perspective.

While Agnes's texts provide the foundation for the present work, a largely untapped body of documentary evidence also survives to complement them. This study draws on a number of recently edited papal bulls, advice literature written for Isabelle, inventories of her books and possessions, and abundant archival evidence for the princess, her biographer, and their abbey. This rich dossier allows access to aspects of Isabelle's career that necessarily remain beyond the historian's grasp for women who moved in less exalted circles.

HISTORIOGRAPHY

Isabelle of France is thus a figure of evident importance for scholars interested in Capetian, Franciscan, and women's history. But although her first printed biography appeared in 1619 and French authors have offered a steady stream of pious treatments of her life ever since, she has been the subject of very little serious study.[32] Albert Garreau contributed the twentieth century's only notable biography of Isabelle, a short book in 1943 and a slightly expanded version in 1955.[33] Since Garreau retained the edifying focus typical of hagiography and was not aware of most of the evidence for Isabelle's life, it should not be surprising that his picture of her as a uniformly quiet and humble saint is unsatisfying and incomplete. Isabelle has attracted a limited amount of attention in other scholarly works. Gaston Duchesne's survey of the history of Longchamp, now over a century old, devoted several pages to her.[34] Gertrud Mlynarczyk's thorough study of Longchamp in the fifteenth century contains a brief section on Isabelle and the foundation of her abbey,[35] and an article by Beth Lynn has rekindled some interest in Isabelle among scholars of Franciscan women.[36] Among biographers of the thirteenth-century Capetians, William Chester Jordan's work on Louis IX first pointed out the potential interest of Isabelle's career, and Miriam Shadis and Jacques Le Goff have since echoed his sentiments.[37] Most recently, Jordan has returned to the subject in a welcome article stressing Isabelle's importance to our understanding of the climate of devotion at the court of Louis IX.[38]

Even scholars as eminent as Jordan and Le Goff, however, have been limited by the lack of available and trustworthy evidence. The few recent assessments of Isabelle of France have been based almost exclusively on readings of Agnes of Harcourt's biography, while most of the additional evidence for her life has remained unexplored.[39] Until recently it has simply been too difficult for historians to separate the wheat from the chaff, to find a solid evidentiary base from which to reach conclusions. As a result, our picture of Isabelle has remained inadequate, missing some of the princess's most important aspects as a powerful royal woman, controversial Franciscan patron, and influential author of a rule.

PLAN AND SCOPE OF THE BOOK

This book generally follows a chronological outline. Chapter 1 considers the evidence for Isabelle's early life and asks how she was able to avoid marriage and find a role at court as a devout virgin, while chapter 2 analyses the contours of her youthful piety and demonstrates the spread of her reputation in ever-widening circles by the 1250s. Chapters 3 and 4 together investigate Isabelle's impact on Franciscan history by examining her foundation of Longchamp, her involvement in the genesis of its rule and its revision, and the wider significance of these accomplishments. Chapter 5 returns to Isabelle's later life at Longchamp, establishing that she did not become a nun there, but also highlighting her continued influence in shaping her house's role, and the level of saintly renown she enjoyed by the time of her death. The final chapter focuses on the ways in which Isabelle was remembered as a miracle-working source of holy power by the royal family, Franciscans, the nuns of Longchamp, and Agnes of Harcourt herself, and it concludes by briefly sketching the history of her cult's temporary eclipse and eventual reemergence.

Power and influence frame the questions that I pose. My approach addresses the world that Isabelle knew, the people with whom she interacted, the decisions she made, and the impressions she left. The larger project of writing her into synthetic histories of medieval piety and sanctity has to be left to future scholarship. This study should make the importance of that task evident.

CHAPTER ONE

The Princess and the Queen

Negotiating Virginity

Isabelle of France was probably born in March 1225.[1] The only daughter of Louis VIII of France and Blanche of Castile, if one excludes a short-lived girl born to the royal couple in 1205,[2] she was the fourth of five siblings who lived to maturity. Her brothers Louis (b. 1214), Robert (b. 1216), and Alphonse (b. 1220) were older, while Charles was probably not born until 1227, a few months after their father had died of dysentery while returning from a campaign in the Midi in November 1226.

Louis VIII's premature demise, after a reign of only three years, meant that Isabelle spent her first years in an atmosphere of political instability. Louis IX assumed the throne at the tender age of twelve, with his capable mother acting as regent during his turbulent minority.[3] Isabelle probably had few memories of a father who had often been away fighting in the south during the first year and a half of her life. Instead, it would be Blanche of Castile, among the most powerful women of her age, who would have the greatest influence on her upbringing.[4]

One of the decisions that Blanche faced after her husband's death was what sort of future to arrange for their daughter. By the spring of 1227, when Isabelle was just two years old, Blanche had already negotiated her engagement to the son of a powerful noble family. This precocious match did not come to pass, but as late as 1243 Isabelle was still being urged to marry by her family and even by the pope. Yet a decade later that same pope, Innocent IV, could praise her decision to embrace a life of holy virginity, and by the 1250s she was achieving widespread fame as a devout celibate. How did this transformation come about, and what does it tell us about Isabelle's relationship to her family?

The received hagiographic picture of Isabelle as a paragon of saintly self-effacement has tended to obscure these questions, glossing over what must have been a long-running contest of wills between the young princess and the formidable Blanche of Castile.[5] Blanche's heavy-handed approach to the marital affairs of her children is legendary. For example, Jean of Joinville's contemporary biography of Louis IX relates that Blanche interfered in Louis's wedded life with Marguerite of Provence to such an extent that the young couple was forced to surreptitiously snatch private moments together on the staircase that linked their chambers at their castle in Pontoise.[6] Isabelle would not have had an easy time in any test of wills with such a domineering mother. Yet a recent study of Blanche's marital strategies establishes that Isabelle was unique among her siblings in evading the future that her mother envisioned for her.[7] In part, this singular outcome might be linked to gendered expectations—as the only daughter of the family, perhaps Isabelle faced different demands than did her brothers.[8] But since it is a commonplace of medieval history that noble and royal women had little choice but to marry in accordance with their families' political needs, it seems unlikely that Isabelle's sex made her inherently less susceptible to family pressure.

Isabelle's youthful struggles emerge through a close examination of marriage negotiations, royal accounts, and Agnes of Harcourt's narrative. Isabelle comes into focus as a resolute young woman waging a tug-of-war with her equally determined mother over issues such as her desire not to marry, her preferred mode of dress, and her eating habits. Blanche was herself known for her austere piety and must have encouraged her daughter's devotions, but she tried to channel them into the roles she knew and understood best—those of Christian wife and mother. Isabelle eventually prevailed in this contest, but only when Blanche was convinced of the inevitability and legitimacy of her daughter's desire for ascetic celibacy. At the same time, the evidence for Isabelle's education and ownership of books casts new light on her character and intellectual development. In particular, her possession of a devotional tract that had first been written for her mother suggests that she emulated Blanche's piety, even as the two women struggled over the question of whether spiritual ideals should translate into the role of royal wife or of holy virgin.

In sum, Isabelle was an educated, literate, and determined young woman whose devotion and ideals both imitated and came into conflict with her mother's. But by the mid-1240s, Isabelle had fashioned for herself a place at court as a devout, celibate laywoman who was seen by those around her as a budding Capetian saint.

A CLASH OF QUEENS

The negotiations for Isabelle's proposed marriages offer an intriguing study in gender and power at the highest levels of medieval society, involving counts and a countess, princes and princesses, queens and kings, and an emperor and a pope. The first image we have of Isabelle of France is as a pawn in royal peacemaking efforts and marriage politics. Blanche sought to use her daughter's marriage to solidify the precarious political situation that she had inherited upon assuming power in her son's name. The queen was in a difficult situation; as effective ruler of the kingdom she was almost immediately confronted by "the most redoubtable coalition of great barons which the house of Capet ever had to face."[9] This group of disaffected noblemen, headed by Peter Mauclerc, Count of Brittany, and Hugh Le Brun of Lusignan, Count of La Marche, rose in hopes of solidifying their personal fortunes in the wake of Louis VIII's death. Henry III of England's support for these rebellious barons increased still further the danger to Blanche.

The queen's attempt to pacify the Count and Countess of La Marche entailed the settlement of her daughter's marital future. It also involved a veritable clash of political titans, since the Countess of La Marche was none other than Isabelle of Angoulême, the widow of King John of England and thus a queen in her own right.[10] As part of the Treaty of Vendôme that made peace between the two families in 1227, Isabelle of France was to marry Hugh, the oldest son of the Count of La Marche. Blanche's son, Alphonse of Poitiers, was to marry another Isabelle, the daughter of the Count of La Marche. Financial arrangements ensured that the treaty would be observed. Isabelle of France's dowry was to be at Louis's and Blanche's discretion, but if they decided not to go through with the marriages they would owe Hugh of Lusignan ten thousand silver marks.[11] Blanche and Louis thus settled the demands of this powerful and perpetually disgruntled noble family by paying them off in exchange for their loyalty. The marriages between the two families' children were intended to cement this resolution.

The provisions of the Treaty of Vendôme held up only in part. Just a year later, Blanche broke the terms of the treaty to seek the daughter of the Count of Toulouse as Alphonse of Poitiers's bride.[12] Indeed, one might wonder how concrete Isabelle's own engagement seemed to observers by this time, since Henry III of England in April 1229 instructed his commissioners charged with negotiating a peace with France to propose a marriage between himself and Louis's sister.[13] But the financial provisions of the Treaty of Vendôme were fulfilled, and perhaps for this reason the Count and Countess of La Marche remained loyal to the king and his mother during the next episode of baronial unrest.[14]

At this juncture, in June 1230, Isabelle of Angoulême wrote a letter to clarify the arrangements for her son's marriage to Isabelle of France. Though it was addressed to the king, it was certainly the result of negotiations between Countess Isabelle and Queen Blanche.[15] According to this document, Louis had given various castles and lands to the Count and Countess of La Marche, which were to be returned if the marriage went forth smoothly. If the marriage did not occur, and it was not the fault of the count and countess, they were to keep the lands. Similarly, the count and countess would automatically receive the designated lands if Louis failed to seek a papal dispensation for the marriage within two years.[16] If Louis gave Isabelle in marriage to someone else, or if he kept his sister with him until she reached marriageable age and she then refused the match, he would be liable to pay a penalty of five thousand silver marks. But if the king handed his sister over to the countess immediately, and it then turned out that Isabelle did not wish to marry when she came of age, he would not have to pay this penalty. Finally, if the papal dispensation was not obtained within two years, the marriage contract would be void and the count and countess would keep their new lands.[17]

Two noteworthy points emerge from these clauses. First, Blanche (acting in Louis's name) had the opportunity to avoid any possibility of a hefty monetary penalty by turning over her daughter to be raised at the Lusignan court, but she chose instead to keep Isabelle under her wing. Certainly, Blanche did not reject this arrangement out of any distaste for separating young girls from their families, since she herself followed this common practice of "patrilocality" several times when the tables were turned.[18] Personal rivalry between Blanche and Isabelle of Angoulême, on the other hand, must have played a role in the former's decision not to place her daughter in the latter's hands. The two women had both made their royal marriages in 1200, were nearly exact contemporaries, and had clashed a number of times. Though Isabelle of Angoulême had married the Count of La Marche in 1220,[19] she continued to style herself queen of England in her correspondence and was determined to be treated accordingly. Indeed, her pride and indignation at perceived slights would continue to cause problems for the French crown through the early 1240s. It is difficult to imagine that Blanche was entirely comfortable with the idea of allowing her daughter to fall into this woman's clutches. More generally, royal and noble mothers in this period, particularly those who had themselves wed at a very young age, often worked to postpone their daughters' marriages and to keep them at home longer.[20] Blanche herself had left Castile at the age of twelve or thirteen for a union arranged in accordance with purely political objectives.[21] Though by all accounts Blanche's marriage to Louis VIII turned out to be a happy one, she may have been reluctant to place her daughter in a similarly uncertain situation.

The second point is that the arrangement, at least nominally, enabled Isabelle herself to veto the wedding. Although Isabelle was her only daughter, and thus a unique means of widening Capetian influence, Blanche allowed her a final say in determining her future.[22] Blanche's basic willingness to take her daughter's own wishes into account is striking, especially when we think of the queen's reputation as a tyrannical mother and mother-in-law. But as a recent biographer points out, Blanche did not treat all of her children identically.[23] She seems, for instance, to have indulged her youngest son, the mercurial Charles of Anjou. Her concern for Isabelle's wishes, apparent in these early documents, indicates that this indulgence also extended to her only daughter. By declining to place Isabelle in the custody of her prospective husband's family, Blanche acknowledged her daughter's own control over her marital future. This attitude goes a considerable distance toward understanding Isabelle's ultimate success in winning over her family to her desire to avoid marriage altogether.

In the event, it is unknown which party opted out of the agreements of 1227 and 1230. The marriage may have been a dead letter by 1232, since there is no evidence that a papal dispensation was ever sought or obtained, and the engagement was certainly nullified before 1238, when the younger Hugh of La Marche married Yolande, a daughter of Peter Mauclerc.[24] But the decision not to go forward with Isabelle of France's marriage may have emanated from the Capetian camp. Hugh of Lusignan and Isabelle of Angoulême held at least some of the lands turned over to them in 1230 until 1241, when they were forced to return most of them, but they continued to hold Montreuil-en-Gâtines, "which they had as a gift from the illustrious King Louis."[25] Had Hugh and Isabelle been responsible for breaking the marriage agreement, Montreuil should have returned to Louis much earlier. So perhaps Louis, Blanche, or even the young Isabelle herself was involved in voiding the terms of the arrangement.

TENSIONS

If Blanche appears to have been surprisingly concerned about her daughter's desires in these negotiations, their relationship nevertheless was tense during Isabelle's youth. Agnes of Harcourt, our best source for Isabelle's formative years, states at the beginning of the *Life* that she will tell us "who she [Isabelle] was, and of her lineage, and then . . . will tell of her childhood and of her conversation [and] what sort of life she led."[26] After the promised brief description of Isabelle's royal lineage, between paragraphs 4 and 13 of the *Life*, Agnes employs the phrase "en sa jeunesse" (in her youth), or a close equivalent, eight times and does not repeat it after that point. Certainly, it would be injudicious to assume that the section as a whole follows a strictly chronological progression. For instance, at one point Agnes begins by saying that Isabelle had a great love of purity and innocence "from her childhood," and then goes on to give examples drawn from later life.[27] Nevertheless, this portion of the *Life* seems to correspond to Agnes's stated intention of devoting a discrete section to Isabelle's youth.

A further point can be made here on the nature of Agnes's own sources. Only once in this section on Isabelle's youth does Agnes cite herself as witness, and this in conjunction with the episode just mentioned in which she gives examples of Isabelle's later attachment to purity and innocence. Agnes's absence from this part of the text is in stark contrast with later portions of the *Life*, where she functions as a primary witness. In describing Isabelle's youth, Agnes evidently relied on what she had heard Isabelle herself say and on stories told by her family and members of her household.

How, then, did Agnes and her sources describe Isabelle in her youth? The dominant picture is of a predictably saintly childhood, of a girl who was destined to be a paragon of charity and humility from her infancy. Isabelle was beautiful and much loved by her mother,[28] but withdrawn, contemplative, and bookish. She preferred to stay in her chamber and learn Scripture rather than to go out and play with the wives of her brothers and the other girls. When she had had enough of studying, she learned how to sew and work with silk and make church vestments.[29] Several engaging *exempla* demonstrate her youthful piety and reputation. She had lovely, shiny hair, which her servants would save when they combed it. When she asked them why, they replied that they were keeping the strands so that when she became a saint, they would have them as relics. Agnes heard this tale from the girls who waited on the princess, and indeed claimed to have saved some of this childhood hair herself.[30] In another story, Agnes relates that Isabelle was accustomed to get on her knees and elbows under her covers to pray. One morning a servant came to clear away the bedclothes and unwittingly gathered them up with Isabelle still inside, but the princess yelled loudly enough that her serving girls came running to rescue her. Agnes heard this story from Louis IX as well as from Mahaut of Gondarville, who later became a sister at Longchamp, who had it from Helen of Buesemont, Isabelle's childhood nurse.[31] The latter also related that Isabelle ate very little. She would donate her food to hospitals and to religious and eat only a bit of the least savory dishes herself. And, of course, she refused to marry, since she had chosen Jesus Christ as her eternal spouse.

Thus, on one level, even before 1243, Isabelle was gaining a reputation for sanctity among the circle closest to her at court. But beneath this smooth surface, Agnes's *Life* betrays an undercurrent of conflict between a frustrated mother and determined daughter. One site for this contest was

Isabelle's eating habits. As Caroline Bynum has shown, ascetic eating practices and food redistribution could help pious girls to gain a measure of
control and autonomy within their families.[32] In this case, negotiations
between mother and daughter were explicit. According to Helen of Buesemont, Blanche would resort to promising forty *sous* to the poor if Isabelle
would take a bite.[33] The queen offered similar bribes to get her to speak to
her brother, and even then these offers did not always succeed, such was
Isabelle's love of abstinence and silence.

Another area of conflict was clothing. The royal accounts, which are
extant only for isolated years in this period, afford occasional glimpses of
Isabelle's choices in dress. Gloves and shoes were purchased for her in
1234,[34] and in 1237 she probably received a new robe for her brother Robert's marriage and knighting.[35] Two years later, when Isabelle would have
been about fourteen, she appeared in the records along with the other
young people in the household as the usual recipient of clothes and finery.
The 1239 accounts record payments for a silver belt, silk, gold thread, and
two robes as well as for a groom who looked after her horse.[36] Isabelle was
dressing the part of a princess and participating in at least some of the
sumptuous celebrations that marked her brothers' coming of age.[37]

Agnes of Harcourt confirms that Isabelle at one time had worn the court
finery appropriate to her rank, and that she later felt the need to justify
doing so. "In the time of her childhood," Agnes records, "when Madame
the queen Blanche, her mother, was alive, who loved her wonderfully and
tenderly and caused her body to be adorned with many beautiful and high
and rich ornaments, she told me with her own mouth that she had just as
good a heart and was just as devoted to our Lord when she had these rich
ornaments on her head and on her body as she had when she had more religious attire." This fact "showed that her heart was always intent on loving
our Lord and that the love of her heart was not for ornaments nor the glory
of this wretched world."[38] Even as Agnes attempts to assure her readers of
the princess's youthful piety, Isabelle's words here betray a certain amount
of guilt, an eagerness to convince herself and others that even when she
wore fine clothes, she was devoted to God. In practical terms, it seems that
Blanche insisted on dressing Isabelle in royal luxury, and Isabelle acqui-
esced up to a certain point in her youth.

READING MATTERS

Some of this tension spilled over into Isabelle's early intellectual life. She was evidently a well-educated and even bookish girl.[39] Charles of Anjou, in later testimony for Louis's canonization, specifically noted that Blanche had seen to it that his sister was taught with the same care as her brothers.[40] Agnes of Harcourt confirms that the young Isabelle was an avid reader, noting that she "very willingly stayed in her room and learned to understand divine Scripture."[41] Later, as an adult, she would customarily retire to her chamber after midday and then occupy herself until midafternoon prayers (nones) "with the study of holy writings, such as the Bible and the holy Gospels and other lives of the saints, because she understood Latin very well." Indeed, adds Agnes, she was so proficient that "when her chaplains had written her letters for her that she would have written in Latin, and they would bring them to her, she would amend them when there were any wrong words."[42] The princess's knowledge of Latin and her studious habits evidently made an impression on Agnes and helped to shape the contours of her piety. But here again, the story is more complex than Agnes's account would lead us to believe.

The surviving inventories of Longchamp's library reveal the true scope of Isabelle's youthful reading.[43] The books that are recorded as having been left to the abbey by Isabelle substantiate Agnes's picture of a literate woman with a taste for edifying Latin texts, but she was also the owner of secular works of wider interests than previously suspected. Though the presence of a few books was noted in inventories of 1287, 1294, and 1305, the first extensive survey of Longchamp's holdings took place in 1325.[44] Among those belonging to Isabelle were a "*Breviaire*," a "*Donat*," an "*Alixandre*," a "petit livre qui commence Audi domina" (little book that begins *Audi domina*), and a "*Bestiaire*."[45] One further book is added to the list in an inventory of 1339, since among those given out to the Longchamp sisters for their use in that year was a "missel qui fu madame qui nous funda" (missal that belonged to Madame who founded us).[46] The liturgical books (breviary and missal) may date from a later period of Isabelle's life and are discussed in the next chapter. The remaining four texts, however, can plausibly be thought to have helped to shape her early outlook.[47]

The *Donat* left by Isabelle doubtless refers to a copy of the fourth-century grammarian Donatus's *Ars minor*, which served as "the standard elementary text-book on Latin grammar" throughout the Middle Ages.[48] The *Ars minor* employs a question-and-answer format to lead the beginning student through the basic elements of Latin grammar. If Agnes of Harcourt's account of Isabelle correcting her chaplains can be taken at face value, then her proficiency in Latin must have attained this level. Indeed, unless these chaplains were prone to elementary errors, Isabelle's appreciation for Latin style and usage presumably extended somewhat beyond the competence of the *Ars minor*. More broadly, this evidence casts new light on the educational program for Blanche of Castile's children. Louis, for example, is commonly thought to have learned to read from a Psalter now in Leyden, thus creating the impression that only sacred texts were employed as educational materials for the future saint.[49] If Isabelle learned to read Latin at least in part by studying the *Ars minor*, then it seems likely that her brothers did too.

Isabelle's reading knowledge of Latin is further confirmed by her ownership of a Latin "*Alixandre*."[50] Tales of Alexander the Great were among the most popular of the Middle Ages.[51] Though histories, letters, and romances of Alexander circulated in too many versions to allow absolute certainty as to the specific text owned by the princess, the most likely candidate is Walter of Châtillon's *Alexandreis*, a heroic epic in hexameters written around the year 1180.[52] This "most popular of all medieval Latin epics" became a standard school text with gloss in the thirteenth century. It survives in over two hundred manuscripts, most from the thirteenth century.[53] Beyond this wide circulation, there are good reasons to think that Walter's poem would be familiar and particularly appealing to the Capetian court. It was originally written at the request of William of the White Hands, archbishop of Reims and uncle of Philip Augustus, and the poets most closely associated with Philip conspicuously took Walter as their model.[54] The author of the *Speculum anime*, a text translated for Blanche of Castile and discussed below, included a lengthy quotation from the *Alexandreis*, thus demonstrating a continuing familiarity with Walter of Châtillon among those close to the royal family.[55]

Isabelle's ownership of this book, whichever Latin version it may have been, confirms that her elementary studies in the *Ars minor* led to an ability to read sophisticated Latin works. Just as important, here Isabelle shows an engagement with the most popular secular stories of her day, contrary to Agnes's picture of a girl who only studied sacred writings. Like many other religiously minded women of her century, Isabelle must have had some familiarity with the language of love and images of chivalry found in contemporary secular romances.[56]

Isabelle's bestiary similarly demonstrates the range of her literary interest. This book was probably one of the French translations and adaptations circulating in the thirteenth century of the older Latin *Physiologus*.[57] Of the four main texts by Philippe de Thaun, Gervaise, Pierre de Beauvaise, and Guillaume le Clerc, all (except Pierre de Beauvaise's) in verse, the version of Guillaume le Clerc seems to have been the most popular.[58] These works draw theological and moral lessons from the behavior of real and imaginary animals. For example, Guillaume le Clerc's entry on the unicorn, which might have been of particular interest to a celibate woman such as Isabelle, piqued the reader's curiosity while emphasizing biblical ideals. Guillaume describes the unicorn as so fearless that it will attack an elephant, yet it may be captured by a virgin who needs only to sit near its lair and wait for it to come and lie down before her. This extraordinary beast, according to some of the biblical parallels that Guillaume then employs, is like Jesus Christ, the celestial unicorn who placed himself in the bosom of the Virgin. Indeed, God himself said, through the mouth of David, "My horn shall be exalted like the horn of the unicorn" (cf. Psalms 91:11), and this prophecy was accomplished when Jesus Christ was tortured on the cross. Thus, God showed great humility when he took human form. As he said, "Learn of me, that you see here among you, because I am simple and sweet and humble of heart."[59] In this way, Guillaume uses the unicorn to teach the values of virginity and humility, two virtues close to Isabelle's heart. In fact, Agnes's *Life* cites the same biblical quotation (Matthew 11:29): "Apprenez de moi que je sui doux et deboenneres et humbles de quer."[60]

With the record of Isabelle's ownership of these three books, the archives offer a glimpse of a young woman whose interests ranged beyond those enumerated in Agnes's *Life*. It seems likely that Isabelle would have acquired these titles early in her life, and she certainly must have possessed her Donatus since childhood. Perhaps the fact that an intelligent, literate young woman studied grammar and enjoyed reading heroic tales and the edifying but curiosity-provoking entries in a bestiary should occasion no surprise, but it is a rare chance to recover the partial reading list of a future "saint" that reveals interests beyond what her biographer chooses to stress. We are well informed, by contrast, about Louis IX's program of copying the works of the church fathers and about Blanche of Castile's ownership of religious texts, but we know very little about their secular reading habits.[61]

The final book to be considered here is in some ways the most intriguing. The "little book that begins *Audi domina*" is surely a copy of a tract entitled the *Speculum anime* or *Miroir de l'âme* (Mirror of the Soul), composed in Latin and translated into French for Blanche of Castile.[62] Although Blanche's biographers have dutifully mentioned the text since its discovery in 1888,[63] it has never been fully edited or explored.[64] Scholars until now have not been aware of the Latin text's existence or of the fact that Isabelle of France owned a copy.[65]

Unlike the version given to her mother, Isabelle's book was a Latin copy of the text, again suggesting her fluency in that language.[66] The *Speculum anime* is in large measure a reworking of a well-known, pseudo-Bernardine text, the *Meditationes piissimae de cognitione humanae conditionis*.[67] The author of the *Speculum* drew on the *Meditationes* for descriptions of the joys of heaven, the pains of hell, and the stern nature of divine justice, and he rearranged and adapted these passages to suit his purposes. He combined further material from sources including St. Augustine's *Enarrationes in Psalmos*, and more surprisingly from Walter of Châtillon's *Alexandreis*. The Latin text circulated independently, while a French translation with dedicatory prologue was prepared for Queen Blanche.

Who might the author of this work have been? The *Miroir de l'âme* and the *Speculum anime* have been attributed to very different creators. One of Blanche's recent biographers, for example, stated that the French *Miroir* was probably the work of "une religieuse" of the royal entourage.[68] By contrast, the Latin *Speculum anime* with the incipit *Audi domina* has consistently been attributed (generally sight-unseen) by Franciscan bibliographers to John Pecham, the Franciscan master and Archbishop of Canterbury.[69] Thus, depending on the language in which this tract was encountered, it has been considered either the work of an anonymous nun or of one of the most illustrious schoolmen of the thirteenth century. Neither of these attributions, however, is persuasive. The fact that we now know that the text was compiled in Latin, by someone with a good library of Latin texts from which to draw, decreases the probability that the author was a nun or abbess, though it by no means rules it out. On the other hand, the date of the text, which must have been written before Blanche's death in 1252, is too early for John Pecham.[70] The text must, for now, remain anonymous, though clearly it was the work of someone close to Blanche who had the moral authority to offer correction and advice to the queen.

Whoever may have written the *Speculum anime*, the important point for the present study is the continuity in devotional outlook that the common ownership of this text by Blanche and Isabelle demonstrates. It is impossible to know whether Blanche was responsible for giving her daughter a copy of the work,[71] whether Isabelle sought out a copy, or if the author or another third party made sure that both mother and daughter were provided with this *Mirror*. We also cannot say how Isabelle reacted to the text or even be certain whether she actually read it. But Isabelle must have known that her mother had been the original recipient of the work, and the fact that she kept her copy to the end of her life argues its importance to her.

The *Speculum* begins with a description of the joys of heaven, drawn mainly from the *Meditationes*, and then turns to citations from Augustine to make the point that such rewards are worthy of the most strenuous labors. The second broad section moves to cautionary descriptions of the pains of hell and reminds the reader that this fate may await her too, since she is a mere mortal. Here the author adapts pseudo-Bernardine prose in a scene designed to evoke the fear that the soul will feel when facing God's judgment. The Latin text reads, "If you consider how you will respond when it is said of you, 'Behold, this woman was the Queen of France!,' it would be a wonder if you did not fear, because all of your works, whether good or bad, will appear before your eyes."[72] The lesson, of course, is that she should not cling to the things of this world but strive for eternal salvation. The text then concludes with a long lament on the vagaries of the human heart, the fickleness of the world, and a closing recapitulation of the joys awaiting the pious soul in heaven.

The tract, a basic sort of Christian exhortation, combines the promise of glorious reward, the denigration of the temporal world, and the threat of eternal punishment at the Last Judgment. This outlook accords very well with the moral and spiritual direction imparted by Blanche to her children.

The dire warnings of the *Speculum anime* are in keeping with Louis IX's recollection that Blanche had told him when he was young that "she would rather he died than that he committed a mortal sin."[73] Louis absorbed this lesson, later arguing that it would be better to be a leper than to commit a mortal sin, since "when a man who has committed a mortal sin is dying he cannot know for certain that in his lifetime his repentance has been sufficient to win God's pardon."[74] Similarly, Agnes of Harcourt's *Life* preserves a later outpouring of Isabelle's own words that demonstrates a similar fear of divine judgment: "She [Isabelle] had a great reverence for our Lord, and feared him greatly; she recounted to me once secretly . . . that when she had returned from her prayer chapel, and she was leaning on her bed, she remembered the judgment of our Lord; she told me that she trembled so hard that the bedclothes and the bedstraw trembled mightily beneath her."[75] It is difficult to know how much impact this tract might have had on Blanche of Castile's own piety, but it may have served to reinforce the messages she sought to pass on to her children generally and to Isabelle specifically.

The *Speculum anime*, of course, was not the only devotional tract that Isabelle would have studied. For instance, the Franciscan master Gilbert of Tournai dedicated a rather different work of exhortation to her (discussed in chapter 2). But the fact remains that the only work of religious advice that the princess left behind at her death was not a reflection of the Franciscan or mendicant piety with which she is usually associated, but rather what might be thought of as a "family mirror," a work that demonstrates the continuity of devotion at the Capetian court as well as the spiritual influence of Blanche of Castile on her daughter. In a well-known image, Charles of Anjou asserted in his testimony for the inquiry into his brother Louis's sanctity that Blanche was the holy root from which the equally holy branches of her children sprang.[76] If so, the *Speculum anime* compiled for Blanche and passed on to her daughter surely represents a textual element in this spiritual flowering.

WATERSHED, 1243–1244

We can now picture Isabelle around age eighteen as a literate, educated young woman who was gaining a local reputation for piety while struggling to come to terms with her mother over her eating habits, her dress, and her marital future. The dissolution of the early engagement to Hugh of La Marche did not mean that Blanche had given up on arranging a union for her daughter. In the summer of 1243, powerful forces converged to promote the prospect of a dazzling political match for Isabelle. The Capetian court, Emperor Frederick II, and newly elected Pope Innocent IV—a truly unlikely trio—combined to try to convince her to marry Frederick's son and heir, Conrad (the future Conrad IV of Germany). The stakes for this proposed alliance could not have been higher. In hindsight, the importance of the moment is apparent. If Isabelle and Conrad had married and produced an heir, the outcome of the conflict between the papacy and the Hohenstaufen might well have been different, altering European history in a myriad of fundamental ways. Charles of Anjou, for instance, might never have become king of Sicily, and one can only wonder how Louis IX's prosecution of his first crusade might have been different had he sailed for the Holy Land with his sister as the wife of the titular king of Jerusalem.[77]

In June 1243 the prospect of an international marriage alliance must have struck both the Capetian and imperial courts as fortuitous. Louis had just put down the last great attempt by his rebellious nobles to assert their autonomy.[78] In March, Henry III had agreed to a peace treaty, and Louis could hope for relative quiet both internally and with England. With fewer worries from these quarters, Louis and Blanche could turn their attention to building stronger ties with the Hohenstaufen. Frederick, for his part, had high—if short-lived—hopes for better relations with the papacy. His great adversary, Gregory IX, had died in August 1241, and the moderate Celestine IV had then reigned for only a few weeks in October and November. After an interregnum caused in no small part by Frederick's machinations, on 25 June 1243, Sinibaldo de' Fieschi was elected as Innocent IV. Frederick made a public show of joy at the news, sent his congratulations to the new pontiff, and withdrew the troops that had been threatening Rome. His actions demonstrated his desire for a more congenial climate in which to negotiate an end to his long-running battle with the papacy.[79]

Frederick also had good reason to seek better ties with the Capetian court at this pivotal moment. For most of the thirteenth century the Capetians and Hofenstaufen had been on good terms, but the generally respectful relationship between Louis and Frederick had been strained in May 1241. Gregory IX had called a council to condemn and depose Frederick,

and the latter sought to prevent this by seizing a number of leading churchmen, French and otherwise, as they sailed to the council. Louis had been
justifiably outraged,[80] and Frederick was evidently trying to patch up relations in the wake of this episode.

The new pope's support for the proposed marriage, in turn, shows his
momentary belief that a peaceful solution to the imperial-papal conflict
might be at hand. Had he not thought that a settlement was a real possibility, he would not have risked promoting an alliance between the French
crown, the papacy's traditional supporter, and the emperor, its great an-
tagonist. A Capetian-Hohenstaufen marriage carried the potential to dramatically recast relations between king, emperor, and pope. At this level,
a young woman's decision to accept or reject her family's wishes regarding marriage was an issue of much more than personal importance. The
pressure brought to bear on Isabelle should not be dismissed lightly.

For pressure there was. The final clause of a letter written from Frederick II to Louis in June 1243 announced that "in order to contract and
arrange the consummation of the marriage treaty between our beloved son
Conrad, King-elect of the Romans [that is, the Holy Roman Empire] and
heir to the Kingdom of Jerusalem, and Isabelle, your sister, we have
directed that the venerable abbot of Cluny and master Walter of Ocra, our
notary and faithful servant, be designated special nuncios and legates of our
Excellency to your presence."[81] These negotiations probably proceeded to
the point where some sort of agreement was actually reached. Here is
Agnes of Harcourt's account of the matter, worth considering in detail:

> She was pledged [*jurée*] by her family [*ses amis*] to contract a marriage
> with the son of the emperor of Rome, who was to be the heir to the
> empire, but she never wanted to assent to corporal marriage, because she
> had chosen the enduring husband our Lord Jesus Christ, in perfect vir-
> ginity. Monseigneur the pope Innocent IV wrote to her and preached
> wonderfully to her to marry for the benefits that would come from the
> marriage of such a lady. We still have this letter in our abbey. And after
> he saw that he could not alter her good purpose, he wrote another letter
> to her in which he set himself as much as he could to praise her good
> purpose and the state of virginity, and this same letter we [also] have in
> our abbey.[82]

Though the first of these two letters is now lost, a later copy of the second has recently been recovered and demonstrates that Agnes was relying on documentary evidence for her description of events.[83]

A passage in the contemporary Dominican Thomas of Cantimpré's *Bonum universale de apibus* further confirms that some sort of betrothal was indeed arranged. Thomas recalls of Isabelle that "having been promised [*desponsata*] to Conrad the son of Frederick Emperor of the Romans, she preferred to remain unmarried in virginity."[84] The Latin *desponsata* agrees with the French *jurée* in indicating that an actual promise of marriage was made.[85]

Moreover, this was no fleeting proposal. To judge from Frederick II's letter cited above, it seems most likely that the initiative for the marriage came from the imperial camp. But Frederick's wording does not have the ring of an initial proposition; rather, it would appear that the idea of a marriage between Isabelle and Conrad had been raised previously, and the emperor now hoped to close the deal. More concretely, though the letter does not bear a date, it's contents show that it was written before Innocent IV's election.[86] The lapse of time needed for the pope then to involve himself in the negotiations indicates that the marriage was being considered for weeks and probably months. Isabelle, therefore, had to defend her resolution not to marry in the face of a concluded agreement and pressure from her family, friends, and even the papal curia over an appreciable stretch of time, a feat that must have called for notable determination and strength of will.

Time, however, was on her side. Serious consideration of this proposed alliance could not have extended past the first half of 1244. Hopes for peace between Innocent IV and Frederick II ran high up to the end of March 1244 and maintained some flicker of life until June, when emperor and pope were scheduled to meet in person.[87] But, probably concluding that he was being maneuvered into a disadvantageous settlement, Innocent instead fled to Genoa and then, by December, to Lyons. The atmosphere of peace-making that might have favored Isabelle and Conrad's marriage had clearly come to an end. It is thus extremely unlikely that a marriage between Isabelle and Conrad was still a subject for discussion when Louis and Innocent met at Cluny in November 1245, as Garreau has speculated.[88] Not only had Innocent declared Frederick to be deposed from his throne in July, but Conrad was known to be seeking the hand of Beatrice of Provence in late September and early October 1245 (in fact, he married Elizabeth, the daughter of Duke Otto II of Bavaria, in 1246).[89] Moreover, there is some indication that Frederick may have been looking elsewhere for his son's bride as early as March 1244, and we shall shortly see that Isabelle's family may well have become convinced by that time that she would never marry.[90]

This shift in the political climate must have been one factor in ensuring that the marriage did not come about. Once Innocent IV's relations with Frederick II degenerated into open hostility in June 1244, papal support for the marriage would have ended. Though Frederick still had reason to seek Capetian friendship, and Louis IX continued to try to make peace between pope and emperor, Louis and Blanche were unlikely to see a marital alliance with the Hohenstaufen as prudent by this time. Thus, Isabelle may have been able to wait out events with time as her ally. Furthermore, we have seen in the earlier round of negotiations with the Count and Countess of La Marche that while Blanche of Castile had no qualms about making initial arrangements for her daughter's marriage without her consent, she hesitated to take the final decision out of Isabelle's hands.

Nevertheless, Isabelle's own resolution stands out as one of the main impediments to the marriage. Agnes of Harcourt is explicit in claiming that Isabelle had chosen Christ for an eternal husband and had rejected corporeal marriage. Thomas of Cantimpré likewise points to the princess's own preference for virginity as the key factor. Isabelle's tenacity in the face of some of the most powerful men and women in Europe demonstrates that even in her youth she was an active agent in shaping her own life.

This moment was a watershed in Isabelle's career. Her rejection of Conrad as a husband must have had an air of finality in transferring her from the mental category of marriageable princess to a royal virgin irrevocably dedicated to a devout life of celibacy. In terms of simple timing, at eighteen she was nearing the far edge of the age by which royal women usually married. Expectations at the French court seem to have been that girls would marry between twelve and nineteen, to husbands in their early twenties.[91] Thus, by 1238 Isabelle would have been seen as ready for marriage, while by about 1244 she would have remained unwed so long that her continued celibacy would have marked her as someone moving out of the marriage market and into a life of virginity. Moreover, once her family had unsuccessfully thrown their support behind the marriage, they must have realized that further attempts would only produce similar results, especially since no more illustrious earthly groom could be imagined than the heir to the Holy Roman Empire.[92] Thus there is no reason after 1243 to suppose that another marriage was ever seriously contemplated. Isabelle's success in standing her ground at this pivotal moment was instrumental in crystallizing her permanent shift in status from political bride to royal virgin.

ILLNESS AND ACCEPTANCE

There is still, however, the question to be addressed of how and why Blanche, Louis, and the royal family actually came to support Isabelle's decision. Isabelle was not, of course, moving in a milieu generally hostile to religious aspirations. As William Jordan has noted, the Capetian court was an environment "in which fervent religious devotion was constantly stressed. There was tension only because people in the royal circle differed about the proper form it should take."[93] In this case, the tension centered on whether Isabelle could convince her mother that her desire for a life of holy virginity was preferable to the role of pious Christian wife.

An episode recounted by Agnes of Harcourt may reveal the moment when Blanche came to terms with her daughter's chosen life. According to Agnes, Isabelle once fell sick "in her childhood," and Blanche had had to leave her with Louis's wife, Marguerite, at Saint-Germain-en-Laye. But when Isabelle worsened, Blanche (and Louis) hurried back to find her at death's door. Blanche, "afflicted in her heart as a mother," solicited prayers, especially sending to a "very religious and contemplative person" in nearby Nanterre, "to whom she indeed revealed the affliction of her heart so that this person with her prayers would more attentively compel our Lord to aid her daughter." And, continues Agnes,

this person informed her by writing that her daughter would recover from this malady, but she was certain that her heart would never be in the world, nor in the things of the world. And this certainly came to pass, because nevermore did she put on her body any of those rich adornments, but from day to day and more and more she gave herself entirely to prayer and to works of perfection and to a religious life. And as for robes and ribbons and all the things that were suitable for her to adorn her body with, she despised all corporeal riches in order to acquire for the soul the adornments of virtue and humility.[94]

In this story, it is again implicit that Isabelle had once been more interested in the things of the world, and that she had once worn fine clothes, but that after her illness she changed her ways. In this sense it is a conversion narrative about Isabelle, at odds with the portrait that Agnes tries to paint elsewhere of the perfectly pious child progressing to saintly adult.

But even more arresting is the extent to which Agnes's treatment of this episode focuses on the experience and reaction of Blanche of Castile. Although the referent of the pronoun "she" slips back and forth between mother and daughter, the story is narrated from Blanche's point of view. One would like to know where Agnes heard this tale, but this is one occasion on which she does not divulge her source. Perhaps Marguerite of Provence is the most likely candidate, since she was present and supplied a number of Agnes's other anecdotes. But, in any case, the story is in large part a description of how Blanche reacted to her daughter's illness and of how she came to accept Isabelle's choice of a religious life. Frantic with worry, Blanche was essentially presented with a nonnegotiable deal by the mysterious holy woman from Nanterre;[95] her daughter would recover, but in consequence she would inevitably embrace a religious life and dress. This holy figure, having pleaded with God on Blanche's behalf, in turn conveys God's plan—the queen must accept that Isabelle is destined for a life removed from the luxury of the court.

When might this pivotal event have taken place?[96] Agnes says only that it occurred *en sa jeunesse*. In thirteenth-century usage, however, this phrase could certainly apply to someone in late adolescence or even to what the modern world would consider early adulthood.[97] In Agnes's story, the presence of both Louis and Marguerite puts it between their marriage in 1234 and Louis's departure on crusade in 1248. The court is known to have been at Saint-Germain-en-Laye at least five times in this period (May 1235, June 1239, June 1240, February 1244, and October 1246).[98] But a case can be made that Isabelle's illness probably occurred in late 1243 or early 1244. For one thing, if we picture a literal rejection of court finery after Isabelle's illness, then it must have been post-1239, since she was still wearing costly robes, belts, and silks in that year. Also, Agnes of Harcourt relates the story of the illness close after her description of Isabelle's rejection of the marriage to Conrad. Though Agnes does not give a single date in the course of her work, she does follow a very loose chronological organization from Isabelle's youth through her adult life to her death. Her linking of the two events may be more than coincidence. Finally, the logic of Agnes's narrative seems to demand that the illness follow the offer of marriage. If, as I have argued, the illness narrative represents the moment of Blanche's acquiescence to her daughter's resolution, then it must have been after June 1243, or else Conrad's suit would not have been given extended consideration. Of the dates when the court is known to have been at Saint-Germain-en-Laye, February 1244 is therefore the most likely.[99]

This dating, admittedly tentative, would provide a satisfying version of events. Throughout her youth, Isabelle had been determined to lead a life of religious devotion and celibacy. Blanche had, in all probability, been instrumental in inspiring these aspirations to Christian morality in her children, but nevertheless she was unwilling to accept the extent to which Isabelle took to heart her vision of a holy life. So Blanche attempted to get Isabelle to temper her devotion with a more worldly life: to aspire to the roles of wife and mother, to eat sufficiently, and especially to dress the part of a princess. Isabelle adopted the fine dress on which her mother insisted, up to a point. But in June 1243, when the most illustrious marriage possible was proposed, Isabelle rejected it, while her family, friends, and even the pope urged her to reconsider, thus bringing the issue to a head. Shortly afterward, probably while the political climate still favored the marriage, Isabelle fell ill. The threat of her daughter's death and the confirmation that both her recovery and her path of devotion were divinely ordained allowed Blanche to come to terms with Isabelle's decision. Thus, by early 1244, Isabelle's own resolution and the culmination of a long process of negotiation over food and finery had resulted in acceptance by Blanche, and by the Capetian court more generally, of her irrevocable commitment to a life of virginity.

If the reconstruction presented above is correct, Isabelle's brush with death preceded by about ten months a better known incident in which Louis IX fell deathly ill. According to Joinville's famous account, in December 1244 the king was so sick that one of the two women attending him thought that he had died, and she began to draw the sheet over his face.

When Blanche heard that he had recovered, she was overjoyed. But when Louis told her that he had vowed to go on a crusade in gratitude for his recovery, she mourned as though she had seen him lying dead.[100] Jordan has drawn attention to the parallels between the illnesses of the two siblings, noting that Isabelle's experience may have been a model at this pivotal moment in Louis's life. Louis's illness allowed him to assert his independence from Blanche by giving him a reason to embark for the first time on a project that he could fully control—the crusade. According to Jordan, "anticipating Louis, she [Isabelle] successfully opposed the plans for her future with the vow that if she recovered from her illness she would be forever virgin and dedicate her life to God."[101] Isabelle's devotion to virginity would therefore be parallel to, and part of the inspiration for, Louis's devotion to the crusade.

I fully concur with Jordan's underlying insight—that Louis in this instance was following the model established by his sister. But there were also significant differences between the siblings' experiences. Most concretely, the link between Isabelle's illness and a vow of virginity is not actually found in Agnes's *Life* or in any other source.[102] In fact, while Agnes does assert that Isabelle's illness helped her to resolve to reject court finery, she says nothing at all about virginity. Rather, she regards Isabelle as always having been firmly set against marriage. There is no single moment in Agnes's writings in which Isabelle swears off marriage, nor do we have any other evidence as to a specific occasion on which she pledged herself to virginity. Instead, according to Agnes, Isabelle "never" wanted to contract an earthly marriage. Thus, in Agnes's narrative, illness functions not as the event that causes Isabelle to make a vow of virginity, but rather as the shock that allows Blanche to come to terms with her daughter's resolve. It is a mechanism of reconciliation rather than confrontation. Louis's case was, in a sense, just the opposite; his illness did lead to a controversial new vow and thus raised a fresh dispute with his mother, who subsequently did her best to fight it. Thus, while the parallels between the two episodes are important—Isabelle and Louis reached turning points in their lives at about the same time and in a very similar manner—the differences are just as revealing.

Isabelle's actions and the evidence for her reading demonstrate that previous hagiographic characterizations of her have been grossly oversimplified. In one sense this is a question of complicating Agnes of Harcourt's own picture. Isabelle was indeed seen as a potential saint by such people as the serving girls who collected her hair for future relics, but she was also engaged in a struggle for acceptance with her family. And just as Isabelle seems to have worn more court finery and participated more fully in court life up to a certain age than Agnes and subsequent biographers cared to admit, so her reading extended beyond the Gospels and sacred texts to popular secular stories such as those about Alexander the Great. But this evidence also substantiates Agnes's testimony to the princess's command of Latin and her ownership of liturgical and devotional works. In the *Speculum anime*, we have a text that embodies the points of both agreement and conflict in Isabelle's relationship to her mother. This work was originally presented to Blanche as an exhortation to a royal laywoman, urging less attention to the "cares of the temporal kingdom" and more thought to the life of the soul to come. It was teachings such as these, if not this text itself, that Isabelle took to their logical conclusion in pursuing her own vision of what the life of a devout royal laywoman should be. Though Blanche fought her decision, the shared ground seen in their common ownership of this Capetian *Mirror* must have helped the princess and the queen ultimately to arrive at a point of mutual acceptance. With the support of her family finally assured, Isabelle could turn to other battles.

CHAPTER TWO

Virgo regia

Fashioning a Royal Reputation

In her vividly evocative *Flowing Light of the Godhead*, the thirteenth-century author Mechthild of Magdeburg included a harrowing description of her firsthand vision of hell. For Mechthild, eternal damnation seems to have been reserved mainly for men. "Of women," she recalled, "I saw there only princesses."[1] Perhaps Mechthild had her own reasons for populating her inferno with princesses, but surely one explanation for why they alone among women risked being damned must have been that they moved in powerful and highly visible circles and therefore faced the temptation to sin. Mechthild's assertion of the prevalence of princesses in hell is not raised here to suggest anything about Isabelle of France's fate in the next world, but rather as a reminder that her contemporaries recognized the extent to which royal women could wield power. In Isabelle's case, her reputation and access to influence grew hand in hand in the years after her rejection of the marriage to Conrad of Germany.

In 1244, Isabelle, at nineteen, had finally secured her family's acceptance of her life of virginity. What choices did she realistically have available to her in shaping the rest of her life? The simplest would have been to become a nun at an established abbey. If Isabelle's goal had been merely to escape the world into a life of contemplation, she had only to make her profession at any number of royal houses. Her mother's

Cistercian foundations of Maubuisson and Lys would have been obvious choices. Moreover, the sister of the king of France very likely would have been made abbess of any house she joined, had she desired to exercise a measure of traditional ecclesiastical authority. Isabelle's rejection of this path indicates that she did not covet the life of a nun or abbess. Often overlooked is the fact that she spent sixteen years as a devout presence at court between her family's acceptance of her permanent status as virgin around 1244 to the entrance of the first nuns into Longchamp in 1260. It was during these years that Isabelle's reputation as a budding saint blossomed into widespread recognition. Agnes of Harcourt affords us a thematic assessment of Isabelle's adult piety in these years, stressing her charity and penitence. But this royal devotion did not go unnoticed by others. The women of her courtly circle, then churchmen and friars, and finally even popes began to praise her life of virginity and to recognize her potential as an example to others, as a patron and as a symbol of royal sanctity.

LIFE BEFORE LONGCHAMP

Agnes of Harcourt's *Life* contains a short section that seems to describe Isabelle's adult habits before her retirement to Longchamp.[2] While Agnes is not explicit in drawing a line between the princess's daily life before and after her abbey's creation, the section in question does precede the *Life*'s depiction of the founding of Longchamp. Moreover, the nature of Isabelle's charitable acts and the presence of her brother Louis in one story fit better with a setting at court than at a monastery, and a reference to the crusade can almost certainly be dated to 1248. This portion of the *Life* is also marked by Agnes's greater presence in the text, compared to the earlier section that dealt with Isabelle's youth. Her use of firsthand observation for episodes that seem to have preceded the foundation of Longchamp substantiates the tradition that Agnes was part of Isabelle's household before becoming a nun.[3]

How, then, does Agnes describe the princess as an adult? Her portrayal is grouped around four virtuous traits: Isabelle's strict attention to the rituals of daily prayer and liturgical observance, her almost obsessive stress on confession, her mortification of the flesh, and her charity and personal attention to the poor.

First, Isabelle observed a quasi-monastic routine of daily prayer. She would rise to say matins well before daybreak and without returning to bed would remain in prayer until midday, even making her servants eat before her so that she could linger in prayer. She would not speak while saying her hours, nor before the early-morning office of prime, nor after the bedtime office of compline, unless she was ill. She often shed a great abundance of tears, so that when she came out of her oratory her eyes were enflamed and red. After midday she would enter her chamber and study holy writings up until midafternoon (nones).[4] During Lent she devoted even more time to prayer.

Here again we can refer to the evidence of Isabelle's books to verify Agnes's account. Isabelle left a missal—the words and prayers to be read or sung during mass throughout the ecclesiastical year—and a breviary to Longchamp upon her death.[5] Her ownership of a breviary confirms Agnes's description of her daily routine. In these books were the material necessary for reciting the services of the daily offices (matins, lauds, prime, terce, sext, nones, vespers, compline) that made up the routine worship of the regular clergy, or in this case of the devout laity.[6] Further evidence of Isabelle's devotion may be provided by a Psalter and Book of Hours now held by the Fitzwilliam Museum at Cambridge, since she has long been regarded as the original owner of this volume, a companion to the more famous Psalter of St. Louis (BNF ms. lat. 10525). More recently, however, scholars have argued that it was more likely to have been made for Marguerite of Provence or her daughter,[7] and thus Isabelle's connection to this book remains too much in doubt for analysis here. But even regretfully leaving aside the latter text, Isabelle's liturgical books support Agnes's portrayal. While we cannot be sure whether these two books came into Isabelle's possession before or after her retirement to Longchamp, they certainly could have helped to structure the routine of a devout laywoman at court.

Second, the princess also placed great stress on confession, to the point of appearing compulsive even to Agnes. Isabelle was representative of thirteenth-century piety in this regard. In 1215 the Fourth Lateran Council's new requirement of annual confession had created a symbiotic relationship between devout lay people—especially women—and their confessors.[8] Agnes reveals how fully Isabelle had internalized the necessity for confession and penance. Not at peace with her conscience unless she was certain that her confessor had heard her sins, she sometimes confessed every day. But her relationship with her confessor was not entirely passive. On one hand, she was humble and obedient, "as though she had been a woman of religion,"[9] but she would insist that he sit in front of her so that she could see that he was paying full attention to her. She took steps to guard against scandal by having only an elderly master of divinity as her confessor, and by always having a mature woman and a girl in attendance. In spite of this constant desire for confession, a single dominant relationship with a confessor, such as that of Elizabeth of Hungary to Conrad of Marburg, is not a major theme of Isabelle's spiritual life. Her two known confessors, Aymeric of Veire and Eudes of Rosny, were both influential men and important advisers (as we shall see), but Isabelle was in no sense under their thumb.

Third, Agnes alludes to Isabelle's mortification of the flesh. Helen of Buesemont, her nurse, would secretly administer her discipline. Indeed, Helen made a point of remarking in public that Isabelle's discipline exceeded that of other penitents, to the point of leaving her bloody. Moreover, Isabelle would undergo it not with a simple switch but with a *fracon*—apparently a daunting plant whose leaves were extremely sharp and shaped like a spearhead.[10] This sort of gruesome ascetic behavior was hardly rare in medieval saints' lives and, according to many authors, was particularly associated with women's religious expression.[11] But here this isolated incident stands out in the *Life of Isabelle* precisely because of its uniqueness; there is relatively little stress on harsh physical asceticism or dramatically somatic religiosity in Agnes's portrayal of Isabelle. There is no reason to doubt that Isabelle did subject herself to this sort of physical discipline, but for Agnes this is no more than a minor aspect of her piety.[12]

Instead, Agnes places her heaviest emphasis on the fourth theme, Isabelle's charity and attention to the poor and needy. Isabelle would visit the sick to comfort them with her holy words and advise them on the salvation of their souls. As part of her daily routine, after she had heard her office and before she dined, she would receive a great multitude of poor people and serve them bread, wine, and soup with her own hands. Her dispensation of alms rewarded both religious and lay people "beyond count."[13]

In this way, Isabelle was typical of the female and royal piety of the period, both of which emphasized feeding and supporting the poor.[14]

Two *exempla* are offered here by Agnes to demonstrate her subject's charity. In the first, a noblewoman (or girl) known as the damsel of Meru was languishing in a nearby infirmary in a miserable state. Isabelle took pity on her and sent her dishes from her table; she chose with her own hands those that would be most delicious, as diligently as though the damsel were her daughter. In the second, the princess sewed with her own hands a night-cap which King Louis then asked her to give to him. Instead, Isabelle sent the cap to a poor woman who lay in great distress, whom she visited each day. This story was apparently well publicized, since Agnes notes that later Lady Jeanne and Lady Peronelle of Montfort, nuns at Saint-Antoine-des-Champs outside Paris, heard of this affair of the cap and went secretly to the poor woman and purchased it from her. And, according to Agnes, the Cistercian nuns of Saint-Antoine continued to guard it as a relic.[15]

Moreover, with the money her father had left her, Isabelle sent ten knights overseas (presumably as part of Louis IX's crusade of 1248), placed countless people in religion, and gave goods and alms to widows and orphans. With compassion for those in pain and affliction, on Maundy Thursday she would wash the feet of thirteen poor people, serve them food with her own hands,[16] and give them shoes and thirty *sous* "in remembrance of the price for which Christ was sold."[17]

Thus, Agnes portrays Isabelle's adult piety as balanced between her own devotions, confession, and physical mortification, and a desire to extend Christian and royal charity to those in need. Even as Agnes seeks to describe her subject as humble and to a degree self-effacing, she lets us see a woman energetically engaged with the world around her. Moreover, in phrases such as "she would advise them [the sick] on the salvation of their souls," we catch an intimate glimpse of Isabelle's sense of her mission to minister to the poor and needy, to speak directly to them and offer guidance as well as material assistance. In the story of the cap, we see not only her ability to rebuff her brother if she thought it necessary in the pursuit of pious ends, but also the renown that had begun to circulate among devout Parisians. Many of her good works were highly visible and must have spread her reputation among the poor as well as among the devout, such as the nuns of Saint-Antoine.

Moreover, for those in contact with the royal court, Isabelle's religious practices must have seemed of a piece with her brother's. Like his sister, Louis served food to the poor with his own hands and commended the practice of washing their feet on Maundy Thursday. He heard the hours of Divine Office every day, confessed frequently, refused to eat extravagant dishes, and routinely fasted above and beyond the church's recommendations. His "disciplines" were administered every week (more frequently in Lent), and he was said to wear a hair shirt next to his skin (something never reported about his sister) until his confessor persuaded him to moderate the practice.[18] The question of who was imitating whom in this sibling relationship is intriguing but probably unanswerable.[19] It can be noted, however, that Louis's piety is generally said to have become much more pronounced after his return from the Holy Land in 1254,[20] by which time Isabelle was already established as a devout presence at court. But more important than the question of priority is the recognition that Isabelle and Louis together created a public image of a court dedicated to intense devotion, compassion and charity, and semi-liturgical routine.

FROM INVISIBILITY TO CELEBRITY

If Agnes of Harcourt provides our best firsthand evidence for Isabelle's life in this period, she was far from the only person taking note of the princess. Even in her youth, Isabelle was well known for her piety among the circle of women connected to court, as shown in the recollections and actions of Helen of Buesemont, Lady Peronelle of Montfort, and her servants. By the early 1250s her reputation had spilled out of this circle to a wider audience.

This transformation, however, was gradual. In the decade after Isabelle's dramatic rejection of an imperial marriage in 1243, chroniclers often mention Blanche, Louis, and the king's brothers but overlook Isabelle when describing high-profile gatherings of major religious and political significance. For instance, there is no record of Isabelle's presence at the dedications of the church at Maubuisson in 1244 and the Sainte-Chapelle in Paris in 1248, or indeed Louis's departure on crusade in the same year. It seems most unlikely, however, that she would purposely have avoided such events.[21]

The silence of the chronicles is not conclusive evidence that Isabelle had no public visibility in these years. In several cases we can glimpse her movements thanks to other evidence. For example, in September 1244, Isabelle probably traveled with her mother and brothers to the Cistercian General Chapter meeting at Cîteaux, since in their statutes for that year the order promised to offer masses for her, both then and at her death.[22] Matthew Paris's description of the 1244 meeting, however, mentions the rest of the royal family by name but ignores Isabelle.[23] But behind the indifference of the sources, we see here that Isabelle was traveling with her family and acting as part of the royal court on important occasions. Though presumably the young princess played little role in the discussions held at this meeting, she would certainly have been exposed to questions of great religious and political import. There, the grand topic of debate was whether Louis would allow Innocent IV to reside on French royal lands in order to escape the reach of Frederick II.[24] Since Isabelle had recently been in correspondence with Innocent concerning her own projected role in papal peace-making efforts, this issue would have been of interest to her.

Isabelle had occasion to meet the new pope when, at the end of November and beginning of December 1245, the royal family traveled to Cluny for a conference with Innocent IV. Here again, neither Matthew Paris nor Guillaume of Nangis mentions Isabelle, and only a later Cluniac chronicle indicates that she did indeed attend the Cluny meeting.[25] Innocent must have been interested in observing the comportment of the young woman who had rejected the imperial heir in favor of a holy life, while Isabelle, for her part, had the opportunity to initiate a personal relationship with the pontiff. The seeming cloak of invisibility that shielded Isabelle from the gaze of observers such as Matthew Paris did not prevent her from making important contacts in this period.

A Bishop, a Preacher, and a Pope

Isabelle was also present with her family for the translation of St. Edmund of Abingdon in the beginning of June 1247 at the Cistercian abbey of Pontigny. By this time the princess was being singled out for praise rather than passed over in silence. The *History of the Canonization and Translation of the Blessed Edmund*, written shortly after 1252 by Albert of

Suerbeer, archbishop of Armagh and head of the papal inquiry into Edmund's sanctity, noted the presence of "the pious King of France Louis and his venerable mother the Queen Blanche (now happily resting in the peace of the tomb) . . . and the three counts, the king's brothers, Robert of Artois, Alphonse of Poitiers, and Charles of Anjou, who afterwards was Count of Provence, and the sister of these four, Isabelle, daughter of a king and sister of a king, who was no less than a queen, because she was joined to Christ the King by the flower of virginity!"[26]

In this author's eyes, Isabelle's status as a virgin marked her as the member of the family most deserving of singular praise, the emphatic example who best demonstrated the importance of the royal presence. As the daughter and sister of kings of France, Isabelle along with her siblings and mother embodied Capetian support for Edmund's sanctity. But as a virgin, Isabelle was also the bride of Christ the celestial King. Albert effectively used her presence to signal both royal and divine approval for St. Edmund's translation. By 1252 (if not 1247), Isabelle was attracting the notice of churchmen eager for visible models of exemplary royal piety.

At about the same time, the Dominican Thomas of Cantimpré used Isabelle's example for similar ends, playing on the same themes of royalty and virginity. Thomas is well known as the author of several important *vitae* of the *mulieres religiosae* of the Low Countries as well as for his popular *Bonum universale de apibus*. It is the latter work, a massive reservoir of stories about thirteenth-century religious life, that refers to Isabelle (as already mentioned in chapter 1).[27] Thomas may have begun this book as early as 1246, was probably given new impetus in 1256 by Dominican Master-General Humbert of Romans's call for collections of *memorabilia dominicana*, and finished it by May 1263. Thomas's memories of Isabelle, however, reflect reports of her life current in the early 1250s.[28]

Recent scholarship has demonstrated that Thomas intended his *Bonum universale* primarily for a Dominican audience, as a treatise on the proper religious life and as a preaching aid for the members of his order.[29] Where, then, does Isabelle fit into a tract on the Dominican life? As the subprior of the Dominican house at Louvain, Thomas was asked by those close to him to write an outline of the duties of "prelates and subjects." Thus, book one deals with "prelates" and book two with "subjects," a designation referring to members of religious communities.[30] Book two, which concerns us here, is further divided into sections on simple religious, lay brothers, and officeholders. Chapters twenty-four to fifty-six systematically outline the functions of monastic officeholders. Among these were the instruction of the young in various virtues (chapters twenty-eight to thirty-three). In chapter twenty-nine, "On the Virtue of Chastity," Thomas offers guidance on the duty of officeholders to exhort their young charges to remain chaste. It is here that Thomas employs Isabelle as a model—in a chapter on virginity, contained in a list of virtues to be preached to the young, as part of a treatise on the responsibilities for Dominican officeholders.

The chapter is divided into forty parts, most of which revolve around the example of the Virgin Mary.[31] Thomas devotes most of the first thirty-three parts to alternately recounting miracles of the Virgin and castigating the Jews for not believing in the virgin birth, in the process retailing some of the Middle Ages' vilest imputations of Jewish ritual murders of Christians. But eventually Thomas advances to examples from his own day. Moreover, since he is still within the broader section of the work on inculcating virtue in the young, it is specifically to the theme of youthful virgins who defy parental wishes that Thomas devotes the last three examples of chapter twenty-nine. First (parts thirty-eight and thirty-nine), Thomas tells the stories of Jacqueline, the sister of the Count of Apulia, who dressed as a man and fled (by walking on water!) when her brother planned to arrange her marriage; and of Yolanda, the daughter of the Count of Vianden, who was inspired by the preaching of a Dominican to enter a house of that order, even though her parents were arranging a noble marriage for her.[32]

Finally, at the end of his chapter on virginity (part forty), Thomas comes to Isabelle:

> We have seen the daughter of Louis King of the Franks (how unjust it is for me to put her last!), that is, the sister of the most devout King Louis who happily reigns at present. She had been betrothed to Conrad, the son of Frederick the Roman Emperor, but preferred to remain unwed in virginity. Having time for God alone, she gave herself so much to contemplation and virtue that she seemed to have no care for any transitory things. And her brother, the most devout King Louis whom we have mentioned, so much esteems those embracing the modesty of virginal dignity, that he collected a great multitude of Beguines at Paris,

so that they might employ themselves in the submission and salvation of humility.[33]

Isabelle, like the Beguines, led a life of devout chastity in the world. She was thus an example not only of resolute devotion to virginity in the face of parental opposition but also of devout laywomen's ability to remain in the world.[34] Like Albert of Suerbeer, Thomas found the combination of virginity and royalty compelling, in this case because Isabelle's royal status made her rejection of her family's plans a very public affair.

Hard evidence is scanty for Isabelle's life and reputation during the period between her brother's departure on crusade in June 1248 and her mother's death in November 1252. As mentioned above, Agnes's *Life* relates that the princess contributed a portion of the funds left to her in her father's will to send ten knights on the crusade, indicating her support for her brother's enterprise.[35] A letter to Alphonse of Poitiers from Philip, his chaplain, reports that Isabelle was in good health in early 1250.[36] According to Philip, Blanche was residing at Melun, and he implies that Isabelle was close by. In a letter dated 11 August 1251 addressed to Alphonse in Paris, Louis himself asked after their sister along with their mother and brothers.[37] These meager references allow few inferences beyond the fact that Isabelle remained part of the Capetian court centered on Blanche in Louis's absence.

The death of Blanche of Castile in late November 1252 marked the beginning of a new phase in Isabelle's life. We know nothing about Isabelle's immediate reaction to the loss of her mother, though it seems safe to assume that she would have been present at her deathbed at Melun, participated in the procession that carried her body to Saint-Denis, and attended her burial at Maubuisson.[38] But as much as the princess may have lamented her mother's death, Isabelle after 1252 emerges into the light of public attention as though from out of a shadow.

Two bulls issued by Pope Innocent IV mark Isabelle's entrance onto this wider stage. As Agnes of Harcourt informs us, Innocent had written to Isabelle in 1243 to urge her to marry. But a decade later, on 22 July 1253, his bull *Sanctae virginitatis propositum* reversed his earlier advice, confirming and praising Isabelle's status as virgin.[39] Why did Innocent choose this moment to write to the princess? The pope's letter seems to have responded to a petition for recognition, indicating that it was Isabelle who renewed the correspondence. Blanche's death had created an uncertain political atmosphere. Since Louis IX was still in the Holy Land, nominal political power passed to his ten-year-old son Louis, with a council of five bishops exercising real authority.[40] The result of this stopgap arrangement has been described as "a major political breakdown in France," which may have led Isabelle to seek papal confirmation for her status. For his part, Innocent apparently tried to take advantage of this momentary confusion and ecclesiastical predominance to assert his influence.[41] To this end, he may have wished to placate the royal siblings then resident in France, since he issued a series of concessions to Alphonse of Poitiers at about the same time that he was writing to Isabelle in flattering terms.[42] Moreover, Innocent had tested Isabelle's steadfast dedication to virginity ten years before and had subsequently met her at Cluny in 1245. He presumably now saw no reason not to gain an ally by reversing himself and praising her devotion and celibacy.

While the letter is relatively short, it offers more than just formulaic approbation. The opening words, *Sanctae virginitatis propositum*, echo an early liturgy for the consecration of virgins. The prayer that this phrase was intended to call to mind reads, "Lord, look favorably upon this woman your handmaiden, so that through your guidance she may preserve the purpose of holy virginity, which she has undertaken through your inspiration."[43] After invoking this reference, Innocent professes himself overjoyed at hearing that Isabelle burns with her purpose, "in such a way that wholly rejecting alliances of carnal marriage, and pure in body and sound in mind you persistently remain steadfast, and ignorant of male company, for Him [Christ] you set virginal purity above marital embraces."[44] Thus, the pope's opening signals several levels of approval. Innocent was well aware that Isabelle's initial *virginitatis propositum* had been undertaken in the face of his own opposition, but now he subtly acknowledges it to have been through God's guidance. Similarly, by stressing Isabelle's steadfastness, the pope hints that God has indeed "looked favorably on his handmaiden." Isabelle now is fully recognized in the sight of God and man as a holy virgin.

Not surprisingly, Innocent exclaims that "it is indeed a great good and a grand gift to live in the flesh without corruption of the flesh in the love of virginity," adding approvingly that Isabelle has dedicated herself to this ideal "like a holy temple to the Most High and a sanctuary of the Holy Spirit." Yet the pope feels obliged to include a further exhortation to perseverance. To this end he cites the well-worn example of the five wise and five foolish virgins (Matt. 25: 1–13), urging Isabelle to pursue her vow so prudently "that among the ten evangelical virgins you may join yourself to the number of the five prudent ones."[45] But Innocent then pauses to caution Isabelle against feeling too much disdain for marriage, reminding her that "even though you emulate angelic purity . . . it is still fitting for the full merit of your salvation and faith that you devoutly esteem and earnestly revere the mystery of holy union which is represented by carnal marriage."[46] In issuing this caution, Innocent may have been going out of his way to warn against the heretical rejection of marriage and other sacraments propounded by the dualist Cathars, though he could hardly have thought Isabelle a likely heretic and Catharism was no longer the threat that it had been a few decades earlier. Innocent may also have been defending his own role as papal matchmaker. Having urged Isabelle to marry ten years ago, now in singing the praises of virginity he thought it wise to underline the validity of his earlier advice as well. In any case, after this rather abrupt foray into the merits of marriage, Innocent closes by returning to his main theme—for Isabelle to continue to commit herself to God and to virginity.

On 26 May 1254, still before Louis's return to France, Innocent issued another bull that reveals Isabelle's growing ties to the Franciscans. *Decens ac debitum* was addressed to the Franciscan Provincial Minister for France, Geoffrey of Brie.[47] The pope informed Geoffrey that Isabelle, "who like a particular imitator of honesty and sanctity is sometimes said to spend her time in nuns' cloisters, seeks with a longing soul some brothers of your order to stay with her for the propriety of her honesty and so that the sins of her infirmity may be confessed to them."[48] Innocent instructed the Provincial Minister to grant this wish when Isabelle asked him.[49] Perhaps Isabelle chose to reside close to her mother's tomb at Maubuisson for a time, or at Blanche's other favored abbey of Notre-Dame-de-Lys. With her mother's death, the king's continued absence, and the uncertain political atmosphere, a temporary sojourn at one of the royal abbeys might have been an attractive option.

These two bulls are revealing in a number of ways. Though Innocent and Isabelle had met nearly a decade earlier at Cluny, updates on Isabelle's reputation had evidently reached the papal curia by indirect means, since Innocent refers to "having heard" of her life and remarks that "it is said" that she lives piously. They demonstrate Isabelle's reputation not only as a devout virgin but also as an "imitator of sanctity" and a woman who liked to frequent cloisters. For Isabelle it must have been significant that the same pontiff who had once urged her to marry now confirmed the praise-worthiness of her life and could see her as an "emulator of angelic purity" rather than bait for a political marriage. *Decens ac debitum*, moreover, shows that Isabelle was able to call on the pope to use his influence on her behalf, in this case to legitimate her increasing ties to the Franciscan Order.

The Franciscans, for their part, had every reason to see Isabelle's interest as an important inroad at court. Louis had been granted the right to choose his own confessor by Innocent IV in 1243, and in 1248 he had selected a Dominican, Geoffrey of Beaulieu.[50] Isabelle was being given a similar privilege by the same pope in 1253. According to Agnes of Harcourt, at one point Isabelle's confessor was Aymeric of Veire, the secular chancellor of Notre-Dame in Paris, while later she identifies the Franciscan university master Eudes of Rosny as confessor to the princess. There is no evidence that Isabelle exchanged Aymeric for Eudes at precisely this moment, but clearly she was signaling a "transfer" to Franciscan loyalty with her request. In fact, it was Isabelle, along with Marguerite of Provence and her daughters, who initiated a long-term pattern of Capetian women employing Franciscans as confessors.[51]

A Friar's Advice

If Isabelle was gravitating toward the Franciscans, then leading members of the order evidently reciprocated this interest.[52] Probably between 1253 and 1255, shortly after Blanche of Castile's death and about the same time that Innocent IV was issuing his two bulls, Gilbert of Tournai (ca. 1200–1284) wrote a letter of religious advice to Isabelle.[53] He began by noting that he wrote in part because her "fame" had reached his ears—that is, within Franciscan and university circles at Paris. Gilbert was a well-known preacher, scholar, and moralist in his day.[54] He had studied in Paris, earning the master of arts in the 1230s, and probably taught in the arts faculty at this time before joining the Franciscan Order around 1240. It has sometimes been claimed that he participated in Louis IX's first crusade (1248–1254), but this assertion seems dubious.[55] After taking his doctorate in theology, Gilbert was Franciscan Regent Master at Paris in October 1259 when he composed the *Eruditio regum et principum* for Louis IX. The most likely dates of the full term of his regency are 1259–1261. Thus, Gilbert, a leading Franciscan figure in Paris in the 1250s and early 1260s, was not shy about addressing advice literature to royal and noble patrons.[56]

Gilbert's *Epistola ad dominam Isabellam* takes as its theme a quotation from Psalm 44:14–15: "Omnis gloria eius filie regis ab intus in fimbriis aureis circumamicta varietatibus" (All the glory of the king's daughter is within in golden borders, clothed around with varieties). Gilbert divides the passage, and hence the treatise, into five sections corresponding to *hereditas, puritas, virginitas, humilitas,* and *honestas. Filiam regis* refers to Isabelle's heavenly inheritance, *gloria ab intus* demonstrates internal purity, *aureis* signifies unimpaired virginity, the *fimbriis* represent humility, and *circumamicta varietatibus* implies propriety and exterior grace.

The first of these five sections is certainly the most intriguing. It is divided into ten steps that represent the "inheritance" of the daughter of the king. In advocating detachment from the world, section one resembles the *Speculum anime,* the tract translated for Blanche of Castile and owned by Isabelle (discussed in chapter 1). But Gilbert goes beyond the straight-forward strategy of describing the rewards of heaven and the agonies of hell employed by the *Speculum's* author to offer a more expansive and dar-ing vision of spiritual ascent.

The first three steps describe a soul weighed down with worldly con-cerns; step one is simply misery, step two is laborious servitude, while step three is the unworthy or fallen-away soul, in which desire for temporal affairs flourishes. If the first three stages do not add up to much progress, in the fourth step the soul commences its upward journey. Here one begins to yearn for celestial things, as "the hearts of those praying and contemplating are often shaken from their innermost depths to the memory of the origins of this joy above. . . . The origin of this joy, which is sometimes experi-enced here, is a drop, a tiny droplet, descending from that river of which *the stream makes the city of God joyful* (Ps. 45:5). And thus it exhilarates the mind, so that the soul feeling its force spurns the desires of the flesh."[57] At this point, Gilbert abandons the simple admonitions found in steps one through three, typical of advice literature for lay people such as the *Speculum anime*, and articulates an intellectually developed theory of the way in which the awakened soul works its way back to God.

Through this desire for celestial things manifested in step four, in the fifth the soul is able to scorn temporal adversity, for to the soul intent on heavenly matters the trials of this world are light and brief. In the sixth step an ardent love for God and heaven exceeds the strength of the body. In the seventh, the mind's eye, yearning for the Father and the Fatherland, is sharpened by the force of this fervor. Gilbert invokes the teachings of pseudo-Dionysius, saying, "And thus the heat of love, according to the blessed Dionysius, brings about a sharpening of knowledge." He develops his point by employing an explanation found in Hugh of St. Victor's commentary on pseudo-Dionysius's *Celestial Hierarchies* to draw a parallel with the Apostles. For in the Gospel (Luke 24:32), they recall, "Was not our heart burning for Jesus while He spoke to us in the street?" Gilbert echoes Hugh without directly quoting him in commenting on this passage, explaining, "Love seized their hearts through Jesus. They thirsted for Jesus, heard and saw him and yet did not know him. Hence they were called *foolish and slow*. But since they burned in this way, therefore they soon deserved to know. Since they had the heat of love, soon they gained sharpening." But to explain the difficult idea of "sharpening" (*acutum*), Gilbert turns to a definition drawn directly from Hugh: "*Sharpening* here signifies a sort of force of love and violence of burning desire carrying one into the loved one, entering and penetrating and going over into the loved one itself."[58]

The eighth step yields an initial reward for this "sharpening," when the mind longing for the sweetness of the Fatherland is refreshed by its fruits. At the ninth step, all of creation is seen to be nothing more or less than a sign of and path back to God. The tenth step will only be completed in the future, when the soul, made into the form of God, will be filled with God.

In this ten-step "inheritance," Gilbert shows remarkable confidence in a laywoman by assuming her interest in and ability to follow the difficult ideas of pseudo-Dionysius's *Celestial Hierarchy*. And although he does not acknowledge the citation, in the course of explaining how burning love leads to the Dionysian idea of "sharpening" of spiritual or inner senses, Gilbert familiarizes Isabelle with Hugh of St. Victor's explanations. Again, one need only contrast the more limited punishment-and-reward approach found in the earlier *Speculum anime* to appreciate the level of intellectual engagement assumed by Gilbert's advice.

The remaining portions of the letter are less striking. As noted earlier, section two develops a brief exhortation on purity of mind, sections three and four are intertwined discussions of humility and virginity, while section five dwells on external decorum. As Gilbert brings his letter to a close, he ends, as he began, with praise for Isabelle's renown: "it is well known (the Lord be praised!) that by no means do you need to be admonished concerning these things."[59]

What conclusions can be reached about Gilbert's intentions? The five-part division of his work indicates that virginity was only one of the topics on his mind. Section one on spiritual ascent forms 40 percent of the work, and the linked sections three and four on virginity and humility take up almost another 40 percent, leaving only 20 percent of the text to be divided between the introduction, section two on purity, and section five on external discipline. Evidently, Gilbert's main preoccupations were equally split between the importance of virginity and spiritual ascent to God.

Another way of laying bare Gilbert's intentions is to consider what use he made of the "model" letters to virgins that he seems to have consulted. His greeting, with its wish "to preserve the title of virginity, to meditate on its merits, to grasp its rewards," is a recognizable echo of St. Bernard's twelfth-century letter of advice to a virgin named Sophia. But after the greeting, Gilbert does not return to this model letter until he has completed section one and moved on to his second section on purity, where he extracts several useful passages from Bernard. Sections three and four borrow from this letter several more times, but they actually rely more heavily on a second model text, the African bishop (ca. 467–532) St. Fulgentius's letter of advice to the virgin Proba. In his final section, Gilbert turns to the works of St. Ambrose, drawing from his *Liber secundus de virginibus*, as well as from his *Libri de officiis ministrorum*.[60] Thus, in sections two through five of his letter, Gilbert has put together an effective but fairly standard exhortation to virginity and humility, adding his own thoughts but deriving his themes from well-established models. But section one represents an entirely different sort of spiritual advice not found in the letters *ad virgines* of Bernard, Fulgentius, or Ambrose. It is as though Gilbert has inserted a learned and daring mini-treatise on mystical unity with God into a more pedantic tract on good behavior. By including this dynamic vision of spiritual growth, Gilbert has gone beyond the usual boundaries of the genre of advice letters to virgins. Thus, Gilbert encouraged Isabelle to think about the nature and goals of spiritual development even as he urged her to observe strict rules of conduct.

Why did Gilbert write to Isabelle in the first place? While Albert of Suerbeer and Thomas of Cantimpré each referred to her in the third person to make a point in their narrative works, and Innocent IV probably responded to correspondence initiated by the princess, Gilbert's motivation was different. He makes it clear in his opening address that Isabelle had not requested his advice; rather, it was he who took the initiative. Certainly we should take Gilbert at his word when he says that he wrote to offer guidance and spiritual consolation to a young woman, but he also wrote to bring himself to the princess's attention, to curry favor and make his name known to a member of the royal family. Isabelle's growing fame was important to Gilbert; it afforded him an opening in which to propose himself for the role of counselor. In this light, his willingness to open his tract with an extended foray into the workings of the spiritual ascent to God has an air of deliberate showing off. Not having been asked to write, the Franciscan could hardly offer something without interest or insult his reader by focusing on the simplest sort of encouragement to good behavior. Thus, Isabelle's own status, power, and prestige can be thought of as dictating Gilbert's approach. Advice literature may seem inherently one-way, but here power flows in both directions; an implicit bargain offers religious counsel in the hope of access to royal favor. Gilbert's tract is evidence of the value that Franciscan leaders placed on cultivating their connections to Isabelle.

The New Pope Approves

Isabelle's reputation as royal virgin came to its full fruition during the pontificate of Alexander IV. As the Cardinal Protector of the Franciscans, Alexander had probably been aware of Isabelle's growing renown even before his ascension to the papal throne following Innocent IV's death in December 1254. Like Innocent's *Sanctae virginitatis propositum*, Alexander's bull *Benedicta filia tu*, dated 12 June 1256, offers approbation for Isabelle's life as a virgin.[61] Alexander, however, far outdoes his predecessor in heaping praise upon the princess. Perhaps Alexander wrote at just this moment because Isabelle had asked for renewed approval for her life as a celibate laywoman, and no doubt his letter was at least in part inspired by the political necessity to curry favor at the Capetian court. But he also seems to have sincerely viewed Isabelle as a woman whose example and influence could be spiritually and institutionally important.

Where Innocent's letter had evoked liturgies for the consecration of virgins, Alexander begins with a phrase taken from an antiphon for the Assumption of the Virgin Mary.[62] The phrase *Benedicta filia tu* in itself echoes the Annunciation's "Blessed are you among women" (*benedicta tu in mulieribus*), signaling in no uncertain terms the pope's flattering comparison between Isabelle and the Virgin Mary. An elaborate opening flourish refers to Isabelle as following St. Paul's "fitting councils of sanctity to unmarried people and widows in desiring his own likeness," praises her as humble, obedient, and prudent, and lauds her as inspired by not only the Holy Spirit but also by the spirit of royalty.[63] Whereas Innocent had urged Isabelle to make sure that she would be among the wise rather than the foolish virgins of the Gospel parable, Alexander refers to her matter-of-factly as "prudent virgin." Rather than pedantically asking Isabelle to follow his biblical example, Alexander rejoices that she has already grasped the importance of Paul's advice to widows and virgins in 1 Corinthians 7:8: "I say to the unmarried and to widows that it is good for them if they remain thus, just as I." Like Innocent IV before him, Alexander notes that both marriage and virginity are praiseworthy. But of these two options, Isabelle, as a "devoted follower of the Queen of Virgins," has chosen the second path, "judg[ing] it worthy of royal birth and distinguished conduct to spurn the servile worries of the world."[64] Evidently, Alexander was less interested in reminding Isabelle of the merits of marriage than his predecessor had been.

Alexander then returns to his comparison between the Virgin Queen of Heaven and the virgin princess, in a paragraph where he makes explicit his vision of Isabelle as sharing in the glories of the Virgin Mary:

Hail, therefore, royal virgin, and may you be filled with the plenitude of heavenly grace! You who, choosing the better part with discreet judgment, so that you may flee far from the punishing labors of the curse which the seduced and betraying Eve brought upon women, strive after the blessing of virginal integrity with Mary, with whom you certainly share the "Hail" of angelic greeting, as in your own way by an enduring vow you join with her in the purpose of spiritual and bodily sanctity.[65]

Isabelle's recognition of the importance of a firm vow of virginity also comes in for praise, providing Alexander with the means of introducing her role as an example to other women. This juxtaposition of Isabelle's approval of vows of virginity and her potential as a model of conduct strongly implies that the pope was expressing approbation for the early stages of Isabelle's plans for a new royal abbey, writing: "In this certainly you look to the interests of not only yourself but of many others who are to follow you, like a visible ideal of imitation, to the service of the Lord through praiseworthy emulation, and thus even from the merits of others you will reap a richer harvest of rewards." At this point, Alexander remarks that he has heard that Isabelle has even attracted her first "follower," whom he refers to as "Agnes the daughter of Heloise" ("Agnete Eloidis"). Emulating Isabelle, this girl "follow[s] your advances, as we have heard, in love of virginity towards the goal of a more saintly life."

Who was this Agnes, Isabelle's first follower? Among the women with this name who can be identified in circles close to Isabelle, Agnes of Anery, the first abbess of Longchamp, is a plausible candidate. But the most intriguing possibility would be Agnes of Harcourt herself. She probably belonged to Isabelle's household in the 1250s and would certainly fit as a woman who eventually followed Isabelle's lead in retiring to Longchamp. Her mother was probably Alix de Beaumont, whose name could be rendered as "Aelidis" in Latin.[66] But whether or not Agnes of Harcourt is really the woman referred to here, the passage confirms that Isabelle's aura of sanctity was increasingly recognized by women within her circle who took her as a model even before Longchamp's foundation.

Alexander here breaks into the only passage that could be described as exhortation. But rather than merely reinforcing the idea of adherence to chastity, he urges Isabelle to "encourage [Agnes] in the Lord as a pupil of your teaching, so that she should be your inseparable companion of the road to the God of life, and that in her companionship should be the more pleasant enjoyment of spiritual good, which you have received from the Lord."[67] Again, it is Isabelle's role as a teacher of others that Alexander praises.

Nearing the end of his letter, Alexander promises his support for Isabelle's future endeavors: "Since glowing accounts of your conduct are increasing, with religious men, chiefly beloved sons the brothers of the Order of Minors, supporting you, we decree that the grace and favor of the apostolic see is due to you. Wherefore confidently seek our help whenever it is expedient, since apostolic blessing in the Lord will accompany your vows."[68] It is apparent that influential Franciscans were continuing to sing her praises to the pope. Alexander responded with expressions of unmitigated support.

Finally, he expresses his confidence in Isabelle's future glory while granting an indulgence for all her sins.[69] A plenary indulgence in a papal bull directed to a single individual seems to have been rare in this period, offering another indication of Alexander's respect for Isabelle of France's saintly life.[70] Moreover, Isabelle is praiseworthy due not only to her "vow of virginal continence" but also to her "proposal of celestial service." The latter phrase may have been referring to Isabelle's plans for Longchamp, or more generally to her desire to lead other women to a holy life by example. In either case, Alexander recognized and encouraged her potential to make an impact on the world around her.

Thus, in the dozen years between 1244 and 1256, Isabelle's reputation grew by leaps and bounds. Whereas chroniclers at the beginning of this period hardly seemed willing or able to discern the princess behind the more imposing figures of her mother and brothers, by the mid1250s she had emerged as a figure worthy of notice and praise by churchmen such as Albert of Suerbeer and Thomas of Cantimpré, and Gilbert of Tournai could see her as a Capetian patron worth cultivating. Not only did Albert, Thomas, and Gilbert single her out as a remarkable woman devoted to virginity, but when Isabelle's reputation came to their notice, they also held her up in their own writings as an example to others. The letters from

Innocent IV and Alexander IV praising her vow of celibacy and her virtuous life reveal the spread of her renown to the highest levels of the church hierarchy.

These authors saw Isabelle as a specifically royal holy woman. With the exception of Innocent's letter, each text is based on the literal or rhetorical joining of the themes of virginity and royalty. Albert of Suerbeer's linking of these two was probably intended specifically to allow Isabelle to stand for terrestrial and celestial royal approval. Thomas of Cantimpré emphasized her royal status by linking her example to Louis IX's support for the Beguines of Paris. Gilbert of Tournai's entire letter is built on a biblical passage describing the glory of the king's daughter. Alexander's letter is the most exuberant in developing this link, comparing Isabelle's royal virginity to the Queen of Heaven. It would be difficult to imagine more laudatory language emanating from the very pinnacle of the ecclesiastical hierarchy. To judge by this sort of admiration for Isabelle, it is tempting to speculate that leading churchmen of the 1250s might well have proved poor prophets if they had been forced to guess which pious Capetian family member would ultimately be canonized in 1297.

This recognition was not, however, merely an end in itself; rather, it promised practical support for future projects. These important churchmen were willing to encourage the dynamic potential for Isabelle's own spiritual development and her role in influencing other women in their choice of a religious life. This remarkable aspect of the texts considered in this chapter becomes apparent when compared with Barbara Newman's analysis of a dossier of this sort of "literature of formation" drawn from forty-five texts written between 1075 and 1225.[71] Newman's work shows that when men wrote to instruct religious women, virginity concerned them far more than when writing for men. More specifically, this stress on virginity produced a static vision of women's religious and spiritual lives. Whereas treatises for men such as St. Bernard's *On the Steps of Humility and Pride* focused on step-by-step spiritual development,[72] advice to women concentrated on preserving an existing state of physical purity and perfection, thus privileging stasis over growth. The logic for this gendering of advice literature is evident; if virginity is seen as the defining characteristic of female religiosity, then simple avoidance of physical or mental corruption is the virgin's paramount lifelong goal. This was a lesson that needed constant reinforcing, churchmen feared, for the perfectly preserved female body might at any moment display its weakness and give way to corruption. Accordingly, although male authors encouraged brotherhood and spiritual friendship among monks, they strongly discouraged women from developing real friendships with either sex. The threat of the loss of virginity outweighed the potential good of mutual exhortation.[73]

The texts written for Isabelle reinforce some aspects of this picture. At the most basic level, each text is obsessed with virginity—it is this attribute that makes Isabelle worthy of notice, praise, and emulation. More specifically, several of these works demonstrate the sort of static vision of female virginity outlined by Newman's analysis. In Thomas of Cantimpré's example, for instance, Isabelle has already accomplished her virtuous act by rejecting marriage. She now devotes herself to contemplation, but it is the negative act of avoiding her betrothal rather than any positive spiritual development that makes her worthy of imitation. More explicitly, Innocent IV's letter might be reduced to two messages—praise for Isabelle's decision to embrace virginity, and an admonition not to give in to either the physical corruption of the body or the mental corruption of pride. Gilbert of Tournai's sections on virginity, humility, and exterior discipline are couched by and large in the same negative tones, though they are laced more consistently with promises of rewards in the life to come.

In several ways, however, it is apparent that Isabelle was the recipient of a more dynamic encouragement to spiritual growth and friendship.[74] The most obvious example is Gilbert of Tournai's decision to go beyond the usual genre boundaries of "letters to virgins" by devoting two-fifths of his missive to a ten-step outline of spiritual growth—his own *Itinerarium mentis in Deum*, to borrow the title of Bonaventure's more famous work. The very fact that Gilbert was demonstrably familiar with earlier advice literature to virgins means that he must have realized that his letter to the princess differed in its attention to spiritual growth and development. Similarly, Alexander IV's explicit praise for Isabelle's new influence as role model and mentor stands out. In exhorting the princess to pursue and deepen her spiritual friendship with her disciple Agnes, Alexander was urging the sort of ties of community and friendship that churchmen usually discouraged in virgins. More generally, Alexander's tone is consistently one of encouragement to future possibilities rather than reinforcement of a negative sort of passive retention of virginal virtue. Isabelle is a model for others; she is "growing from good to better" and can expect papal support "in her future endeavors."

Particularly in comparison with Innocent IV's avoidance of these themes, it is apparent that, in Alexander IV, Isabelle had not only an admirer but also a practical supporter. But just how solid would this support prove to be? As we shall see in the next two chapters, Isabelle put Alexander's promises to the test by turning her attention to one of the most controversial institutional questions of the thirteenth century—the relationship between women and the Franciscan Order.

CHAPTER THREE

House Rules

Isabelle of France and Longchamp's Rule of 1259

Denis Diderot's novel of 1760, *La religieuse*, narrates the battle of a reluctant nun named Suzanne for release from her enclosed life. Much of the drama unfolds at Longchamp, which was still very much a part of the Parisian landscape in the mid-eighteenth century. As one of the milder aspects of Suzanne's punishment for beginning a court process intended to annul her vows, Longchamp's vindictive Mother Superior orders Suzanne's cell stripped of all its images, including "le portrait de notre fondatrice" (the portrait of our founder).[1] It seems safe to assume that Isabelle of France would have been less than enchanted by the Encyclopedist's scathing portrayal of Longchamp's eighteenth-century inhabitants. But one wonders whether she might not have been equally piqued at being reduced to anonymous *fondatrice*, saintly humility notwithstanding. Diderot's nameless reference to Isabelle's image is emblematic of the way in which her wide-ranging impact as royal patron of Longchamp has been overlooked. The following two chapters seek to place Isabelle, her foundation, and her rule in a new light by piecing together the process by which she parlayed her royal status and religious renown into a role as co-author of a new form of life for Franciscan women.

The project of establishing a new monastic house was relatively unremarkable in and of itself; it followed firmly in the tradition of royal patronage as dispensed by Blanche of Castile and many others.[2] Authoring or even co-authoring a monastic rule, by contrast, was an extremely rare feat for a medieval woman.[3] Clare of Assisi's rule for her house of San Damiano, approved by Pope Innocent IV in 1253, is generally acknowledged as the first to be written by a woman and to receive papal approval.[4] It would, in fact, be more accurate to say that it was the first to strongly reflect a woman's ideas, since Clare's contributions are enshrined along with the words of St. Francis and regulations from earlier rules composed by Cardinal Hugolino and Innocent IV. But because Clare's own voice distinctly emerges from the text, historians have rightly regarded her as its primary author. Isabelle of France's collaboration with leading Franciscans on her own rule only a few years later is of comparable interest, but it has not received the scrutiny that modern scholars have accorded to Clare.[5]

This neglect is due in part to the very way in which historians tend to tell Clare's story. Her struggle is often seen as a heroic yet ultimately tragic dead end, a personal triumph but an institutional failure, since her rule was not widely adopted in the thirteenth century. A narrative of thirteenth-century women and the Franciscan Order that stresses Clare's faithfulness to Francis's original ideal of poverty reaches its logical culmination in her rule of 1253, but, after this "shallowest of victories," one must conclude that "the struggle was over."[6] This narrative would implicitly make Isabelle's life and rule a retreat from a high point of female influence and adherence to the true *vita apostolica* and Franciscan calling. Even scholars who carry the story through to Urban IV's issuance of a new rule for Franciscan women in 1263 have seen Isabelle's concurrent battles as little more than a footnote to the working-out of female Franciscan institutions. But if Isabelle's story is less dramatic than Clare's, her rule was at least as influential over the course of the thirteenth and fourteenth centuries.[7]

This chapter begins by examining the motivations for Isabelle's initial impulse to found a new royal abbey, and it then seeks to disentangle the writing process of the Rule of 1259. Chapter 4 goes on to consider the revised Rule of 1263 and its significance for our understanding of Isabelle's vision of female Franciscanism. This vision centered around her desire for an order of *Sorores minores*—a term so controversial that women, friars, and popes quarreled over its usage for decades. Yet even as scholars have begun to consider the importance of this inflammatory label in thirteenth-century Franciscan history, they have tended to view it through an Italian lens that has obscured Isabelle's central role in the debate.[8] I argue in these chapters that Isabelle's desire to implement her ideas was the strongest impetus behind the writing of her rules, and that she herself was directly responsible for much of what was new and innovative in these forms of life.

LOOKING TO LONGCHAMP

How and why did Isabelle decide to create a new royal abbey for Franciscan women? In 1256, Alexander IV had described the princess as eager to act as a model for others. But her foundation also emerged gradually out of her pious efforts to turn royal funds to charitable ends. In the *Life of Isabelle*, Agnes of Harcourt's discussion of Isabelle's largess leads directly into her description of the foundation of Longchamp. According to Agnes, it was not enough for Isabelle to contribute to the crusade, provide alms and funds for people to enter monasteries, and involve herself directly in charity for the poor. In order to give institutional form to her devotion, Isabelle began to consider founding either a hospital or a house for Franciscan women.

Immediately after enumerating the ways in which Isabelle dispensed the money that her father had left her, Agnes proceeds to recount how the princess arrived at her decision to found a new royal abbey:

> She was very anxious to do something that would be pleasing to our Lord and had a great desire to found a hospital, but did not know what she ought to make of this, whether a house of our order or a hospital. She sent to the chancellor of Paris and had him asked secretly which he thought would be more pleasing to God, whether she should found a hospital or a house of Sisters Minor (*sereurs mineurs*). The chancellor Aymeric, who was a wise man and master of divinity, who was then her confessor, wrote to her that there was no comparison with a hospital when it came to founding a house of religion, and especially of this order, because the divine praise of our Lord is carried out and celebrated there, and virginity is guarded and multiplied there, and also works of charity are done there, since the sisters serve one another. And he further said to

the messenger, "Tell her that she should not demand further counsel on this matter, but build the house of religion." And soon after she founded our abbey, which indeed cost [her] thirty thousand Parisian livres.[9]

Where did Agnes get such detailed information about this exchange? Perhaps Aymeric's written response survived (though it is not extant today). The messenger whom Agnes refers to might also have been the source, or Isabelle may have related the story to Agnes. Given the uncertain attribution of the episode, it would be unwise to place too much credence in the exact words it claims to repeat. Yet there is no reason to regard it as an outright fabrication. Agnes probably recorded at least the basic outlines of a real event.

Thus, it appears that Isabelle's first impulse was to create a *charitable* foundation, such as a hospital.[10] In this idea she was following in the footsteps of such thirteenth-century royal women as Elizabeth of Hungary and Agnes of Bohemia, both of whom linked their Franciscan-inspired piety to the building of hospitals for the poor.[11] But doubts began to enter Isabelle's mind as to whether it might not be more pleasing to God to found a house of *Soeurs mineures*, so she consulted her confessor, Aymeric of Veire, chancellor of Notre-Dame and hence of the university in Paris. In the chancellor's response he recognized the primacy of charity in Isabelle's mind, and accordingly he stressed that a house of religion would promote this end just like a hospital, since the sisters would serve each other, but an abbey would also foster the praise of God and the preservation of virginity, which a hospital could not do, and would therefore be more useful. Aymeric thereby acknowledged Isabelle's desire to employ the legacy at her disposal for charitable purposes— for what one might think of as a "socially useful" foundation—but steered this impulse toward the creation of a new religious house.

When might this exchange have occurred? Since Aymeric de Veire is referred to as chancellor, it was certainly after he assumed this title in 1249.[12] Furthermore, it seems very likely that it was only after Blanche of Castile's death in November 1252 that Isabelle would have sought a new outlet for her political and spiritual energy in the form of her own royal foundation. On the other hand, land on which to build Isabelle's abbey was actually being purchased by April 1255, so her decision must have been made well before that date.[13] Moreover, we know that Innocent IV granted Isabelle's request for Franciscan confessors in May 1254, raising the likelihood that Aymeric ceased to act as her confessor around that time and that the conversation would have occurred before then. Though Isabelle would have been aware that new building projects were not economically or politically feasible until Louis's return from the crusade, this fact would not have prevented her from mulling over her decision somewhat earlier.[14]

The evidence thus points to 1253 or early 1254 as the period in which Isabelle's plans crystallized. At the same moment that her fame reached papal ears and her status as virgin received papal confirmation in *Sanctae virginitatis propositum*, she was debating how best to channel her personal piety into an institutional form. Moreover, just as *Decens ac debitum* first reveals Isabelle's growing Franciscan proclivities, and at about the same time that Gilbert of Tournai was offering his encouragement and advice, she was also pondering whether to change her plan from a hospital to a house for Franciscan women.

After the king's return from the Holy Land in the summer of 1254, Louis and Isabelle worked together to see to the new house's material foundation as well as to secure papal recognition and privileges.[15] In her *Letter on Louis IX and Longchamp* (written in 1282), Agnes of Harcourt describes the laying of the cornerstone for Longchamp, which must have occurred after April 1255:[16] "our very reverend and holy father, Monseigneur the king Louis, founded our church and with his own hand placed its first stone at the foundation." She then goes on to relate that Louis's wife Marguerite and their oldest son Louis laid the second and third stones, and Isabelle the fourth. At that moment, three white doves appeared, causing Marguerite to exclaim to Isabelle that the birds demonstrated the Holy Trinity's presence.[17] Later authors, perplexed as to why it was Louis and not Isabelle who laid the first stone, emended the original text to read that Isabelle, "out of humility," chose to place only the fourth one.[18] In fact, the prominence of the king, the queen, and their heir in the ceremony confirmed to the public the royal family's support of Isabelle's new project.[19]

By February 1259 the construction of the abbey was nearing completion. In the space of a month, Alexander IV issued at least five bulls detailing the life to be led by the sisters. In spite of the fact that most of these letters were addressed to the abbess and sisters of the abbey, the pope must have directed them primarily to the attention of Isabelle and Louis, since there was not yet an abbess or community of nuns in residence.

On 10 February, Alexander issued by far the most important of these documents, the first rule for Longchamp, in the bull *Sol ille verus*. (This text will be considered in detail below.) On 22 February, Alexander's bull *Inter alia sacra* granted Louis special privileges: he was allowed to enter the abbey's cloister as often as he liked, in spite of the rule's strictures to the contrary. Moreover, with the consent of the abbess he would be allowed to place his daughter, together with five young women as companions, at Longchamp to be raised and educated.[20] Two days later, on 24 February, the bull *Cum a nobis* allowed the nuns to offer burial at Longchamp to anyone except excommunicates or infamous usurers.[21] On the next day, Alexander issued *Etsi universe orbis*. Among other privileges, this bull specifically exempted Longchamp from the jurisdiction of the bishop of Paris and the archbishop of Sens and placed it directly under the pope; further, it confirmed the abbey in its possessions and guaranteed the nuns the free right to elect abbesses according to their rule.[22] Finally, on 3 March, Alexander's bull *Devotionis vestre precibus* allowed the sisters of Longchamp to retain, receive, and sell the possessions that would have belonged to them in the secular world.[23]

Thus, Isabelle and Louis together worked through papal channels to cement the success of the new abbey. Louis protected his own continued ties to Longchamp and envisioned it as a place to raise and educate young royal women. The nuns were given a maximum of independence from local jurisdiction and all the material support that they could desire. Complete poverty would obviously not be a component of life of Longchamp. But the most important document—a rule for the sisters—emerged from a more elaborate set of negotiations.

The Rule of 1259

Reconstructing the Writing Process

Longchamp's rule was the result of multifaceted bargaining between Isabelle, the Franciscan Order, and the pope. The demands, compromises, and concessions made by each side of this triangle need to be disentangled. For this task we have two main sources—Agnes of Harcourt's account of the process, and the texts of the rules themselves. Both raise difficulties, but a careful investigation ultimately settles many of the uncertainties surrounding the origins of the rule and reveals the leading role played by the princess in its composition.

Immediately after her account of Isabelle's exchange with Aymeric of Veire, Agnes discusses the composition of Longchamp's rule. It is worth quoting from this crucial passage at length:

> She [Isabelle] was very diligent as to the rule, that it should be good and sure, and had it approved by Brothers Minor (*freres meneurs*) who were good people and mature and masters of divinity, such as Brother Bonaventure, Brother William of Meliton, Brother Eudes of Rosny, Brother Geoffrey of Vierson, [and] Brother William of Harcombourg, and she had put into the rule what was in the privileges, and what was doubtful or perilous in the rule she eliminated, and she had such great concern for this matter that she stayed up a large part of the nights and days. She worked and devoted herself so much to this that it can hardly be recounted. Many people were in her chamber, of which some would read the privileges and the others would note them, and there was always present a Brother Minor (*un frere meneurs*), master of divinity, to examine the matters before her in her presence. And she was so concerned that nothing should pass that would be perilous to souls that it was a wonder. And she took such great care with this matter and was so involved that she could hardly rest.
>
> And she had a wonderfully great desire that this matter should be confirmed by the pope. And above all things she desired that the sisters of her abbey would be called Sisters Minor (*sereurs mineurs*). And in no way could the rule be acceptable to her if this name was not given. Her blessed heart chose to give to her abbey this blessed name by which our Lord Jesus Christ chose our Lady to be his mother. It is the name of The Humility of Our Lady that she gave as name to her abbey, and with this name she desired that it should be named.[24]

Since Agnes then goes on to repeat a conversation that she had with Isabelle about her choice of names for the abbey and its sisters, she would seem to have been an eyewitness to at least parts of this process. Though this conversation could have taken place years later, it is more likely that Agnes would have questioned Isabelle when the name was first granted, that is, around the time of the issuance of the Rule of 1259. By this logic, her list of the Franciscans involved in creating the rule and her account of Isabelle's part in that process were probably based on her own memories as lady-in-waiting to the princess. This is not to say that her recollections should be treated as infallible (they are not, as we shall see). Nevertheless, her account of Isabelle's desires and the makeup of the group of Franciscans with whom she consulted is probably trustworthy.

This assemblage of Franciscans was indeed illustrious. Bonaventure, one of the most influential theologians of the thirteenth century, was regent master in theology at Paris from 1254 until he was chosen Minister General of the order in February 1257. He enjoyed close ties to the royal house, as witnessed by the twenty-seven sermons that he is known to have preached before Louis IX and his family between 1254 and 1270. As Minister General, he subsequently played an important role in negotiating the relationship between the male and female branches of the Franciscan Order.[25] William of Harcombourg (or Ardenboch) became Provincial Minister of the Franciscans for France in June 1257. In this capacity he attended the entrance of the first nuns to Longchamp in 1260, before holding the Franciscan chair of theology at Paris several years later.[26] Eudes of Rosny, Isabelle's confessor, was evidently a close adviser to the princess. If he was among the Franciscan confessors requested by Isabelle in 1254, then their relationship spanned a good sixteen years, since Agnes's testimony shows him in contact with the princess through the end of her life. This period would have included his regency, which must have been sometime between 1257 and 1263.[27] William of Meliton (or Middleton) was regent master at Paris from about 1248 until 1253. It is possible that he then took up a similar position at Cambridge, but if so he had returned to Paris by 1256.[28] The fifth member of this group, Geoffrey of Vierson, is otherwise an unknown, though on the strength of Agnes's characterization scholars have generally included him among the Franciscan masters of the university in this period.[29]

This assemblage, then, included the top organizational leadership of the Franciscan Order—the Minister General and Provincial Minister for France as well as some of the foremost intellectuals of the order. Every holder of the Franciscan chair in theology at Paris between at least 1248 and 1263 participated, with the somewhat surprising exception of Gilbert of Tournai. Moreover, Bonaventure, Eudes of Rosny, and William of Harcombourg demonstrably had extended contact with Isabelle, Longchamp, and the royal family, so they cannot be seen as merely distant experts called in for brief consultation. Finally, it should be noted that Agnes says that Franciscan masters of divinity "such as" (*si comme*) these men were involved in writing the rule. Therefore, she claims only to list examples of the sort of illustrious men who gathered in Isabelle's chambers, not to define an exclusive or formally appointed Franciscan delegation.

Agnes also gives us an inside look at how the compositional process progressed. As Agnes tells it, Isabelle took the active role: *she* was very concerned that the rule should be good and sure, so *she* had it approved by the team of Franciscans; *she* caused to be included "what was in the privileges," and *she* had "what was doubtful or perilous in the rule" removed. Moreover, the writing took place in *her* chambers, in *her* presence. Agnes furthermore assures us of Isabelle's passionate commitment to the process—she was so concerned that she was up all night and day, worked so hard that one could scarcely describe it, and was so wrapped up in the rule that she had difficulty resting.

Thus, Agnes allows us to envision the scene; several of the Franciscan masters, perhaps the entire group, meet in the princess's chambers. An existing text or texts (the "privileges") are on hand for reference. Isabelle acts as the driving force, setting out her ideas on what should be included or removed, while the Franciscan masters approve or counsel against proposals that they find objectionable. It should be kept in mind that, according to Agnes, Isabelle was able to read and correct Latin, a linguistic facility that would have involved her in the exact wording of the rule and not just in its general tenor.

There is, however, one great problem with the reconstruction that has been traced so far: Agnes of Harcourt entirely obscures the fact that not one but two rules were given to Longchamp in its first years of existence. The initial rule was approved by Alexander IV in his bull of 10 February 1259, while Urban IV granted a second revised one on 27 July 1263. As one of Longchamp's first nuns and abbesses, Agnes must have been aware of this fact and could hardly have forgotten it, even two decades later. We will return to the intriguing question of why Agnes might have found it convenient to present a simplified version of events in her biography of Isabelle. But, whatever her motivations, the existence of two rules and therefore (at least potentially) two discrete compositional processes raises several questions about the picture given by the *Life of Isabelle* that must be addressed before proceeding further. On which of these two rules did the Franciscan masters work with Isabelle, or did they continue to collaborate on both? Was one or the other of the rules imposed on Isabelle and Longchamp, with only the other representing her desires and her negotiations with the Franciscan Order?

In fact, the group of Franciscans detailed by Agnes of Harcourt is much more likely to have collaborated with Isabelle on the Rule of 1259 than on the Rule of 1263. William of Meliton died at Paris before 23 May 1260, so his contribution could only have been to the genesis of the first rule.[30] The chronology of Bonaventure's career points to his involvement with the earlier rule as well; he was certainly in Paris from 1254 to 1257, the years of his regency. After his election as Minister General on 2 February 1257, he left for Italy in the summer, then returned to Paris and remained there through the winter of 1257–58 before journeying back to Italy once more in the spring. He certainly was in Paris again in the winters of 1258–59 and 1260–61, but after this date he is not known to have returned until 1266.[31] Thus, while it is just possible that Bonaventure could have had a hand in discussions that took place after 1259, it is unlikely. Similarly, though William of Harcombourg lived until 1270 and hence could have participated in any later negotiations, it seems logical that his advice was particularly sought in his official capacity as Provincial Minister for France. Since he only held this position until 1261, the evidence points to his involvement in the Rule of 1259.[32] In sum, Agnes described a group of the Franciscan masters most likely to be in Paris and in close contact with the Capetian court in the second half of the 1250s. Her depiction of Isabelle working on the text in collaboration with her team of Franciscans refers to the original writing process for the Rule of 1259, not to its revision of 1263.

The text of the papal bull that approved the Rule of 1259, however, seemingly raises an obstacle to this interpretation. In 1765, J.-H. Sbaralea published the bull *Sol ille verus* in volume 3 of his monumental *Bullarium franciscanum*, in the rather awkward form of a long footnote.[33] Sbaralea stated that he edited the text "ex autographo in nostro conventus S. Crucis Florentiae Archivo sub plumbo," implying that he had found an original papal document, with the pontiff's seal, that had somehow made its way to Santa Croce in Florence by the eighteenth century. Since this copy is not known to have survived and no others have come to light, we are left to rely on Sbaralea's text and his description of the manuscript. The perplexing element is a note cited by Sbaralea at the end of the text, which would seem to identify the author of the rule not as Isabelle and her collaborators but as Mansuetus, a Franciscan confessor and chaplain to Alexander IV. It reads: *"Here ends the Rule of the Humble Handmaidens of the most glorious Virgin Mary mother of God, which Brother Mansuetus of the Order of Brothers Minor by order of the Highest Pontiff and the cardinals and with their diligent counsel composed and dictated.* This addition is read in the already-mentioned Florentine codex."[34] Since original thirteenth-century papal bulls are discrete documents issued on single pieces of parchment and sealed, they do not carry superfluous *incipit* or *explicit* indications. Thus, this concluding comment was probably a later addition to the original text. It is, in any case, misleading. Agnes of Harcourt's evidence, combined with the chronology outlined above, is sufficient to demonstrate that the Rule of 1259 was not composed solely by Mansuetus with the advice of the pope and his cardinals. The assumption made by some previous scholars, that this rule was imposed on Isabelle by the pope and his chaplain and that therefore only the Rule of 1263 represents Isabelle's wishes and her negotiations with the Franciscans, is thus unwarranted.[35]

Nevertheless, the *explicit* noted in Sbaralea's edition does argue that Mansuetus played some role in the composition and approval of Isabelle's first rule. Indeed, he was particularly well situated to have had a hand in any negotiations involving the papacy, the Franciscan Order, and the Capetian court. Mansuetus of Castiglione Fiorentino was named papal confessor and chaplain shortly after the election of Alexander IV in December 1254.[36] He seems to have been something of a specialist in conflict resolution. After a sojourn in Paris around August 1255,[37] he journeyed to Pisa early in 1257 where he settled a long-standing papal excommunication and interdict of the city. In September 1257, Mansuetus was sent to Louis IX's court and then on to England in early 1258 as the pope's representative in the negotiations that resulted in the Treaty of Paris. When these efforts met with success, he returned to Paris, where the terms of the treaty were agreed to on 28 May 1258.[38] Perhaps as a gesture of gratitude, Louis IX sent Mansuetus relics of the Crown of Thorns and the True Cross along with a letter dated 24 August 1258 at Compiègne.[39] Mansuetus may have already returned to Italy by this time; certainly he must have left by the fall of 1258, if he himself carried the text of Longchamp's rule back to the papal curia in time for Alexander to approve it on 10 February 1259.[40] Back in Rome, Mansuetus acted as procurator for Longchamp at the curia. The original bulls *Inter alia sacra* and *Cum a nobis* (dated 22 and 24 February 1259 and discussed above), were both marked on the dorse "frater Mansuetus," indicating that they were placed in his hands to be delivered to Louis IX or to the abbey of Longchamp.[41] Here the evidence for Mansuetus's involvement with Longchamp ends, though he remained in the curia of Urban IV and Clement IV until his death in June 1270.

Brother Mansuetus's participation in composing the Rule of 1259 thus fits neatly into Agnes's testimony and the chronology established above. The negotiations between Isabelle and her team of friars must have taken place around 1257–58. In the summer of 1258, Mansuetus, as both a Franciscan and papal representative, was present to add his voice to the process and then to carry the finished rule to Rome.[42]

Given this complex authorial dynamic—Isabelle of France working with a team of at least six Franciscans, of whom one also represented the papal curia—how can we decide what Isabelle's own contributions were? One aspect of this question can be answered quickly. It will be recalled that Agnes of Harcourt records Isabelle's two principal demands: that the sisters of her abbey be known as *Soeurs mineures*, and that the abbey itself bear the name of L'Humilité-de-Notre-Dame. The first of these demands was not, in fact, granted by the Rule of 1259. The end of Alexander's preface stated that the sisters were to be called "Sorores Ordinis humilium ancillarum beatissimae Mariae virginis gloriosae" (Sisters of the Order of Humble Handmaidens of the Most Blessed Glorious Virgin Mary). Isabelle's second wish was gratified, however, as Alexander named the new abbey the "Monasterio humilitatis beatae Mariae virginis" (Monastery of the Humility of the Blessed Virgin Mary).

This rule, therefore, is immediately revealed to be the result of negotiation and compromise. The name of the abbey is evidently a reflection of

Isabelle's personal intentions and demonstrates that her own wishes directly impacted the final text of the rule. But concerning one of the issues about which she cared most passionately—the name by which her sisters would be known—her desires were overruled by either the Franciscans, the pope, or both. A closer study of the rule itself and its broader context is therefore necessary in order to carry this analysis beyond these two points of nomenclature.

The Context: Franciscan Rules for Women

Isabelle, the Franciscan leadership, and the papal curia were stirring up waters already muddied by decades of dispute. By the time the negotiations for Longchamp's new rule took place, four decades of contention had resulted in three different rules for women connected with the Franciscan Order.

The most controversial issues that these rules sought to codify centered around poverty and the institutional links between women's houses and the male order.[43] Francis himself had given a primitive form of life to Clare's original community of women at San Damiano, but he did not envision the incorporation of further women's houses into his order. While Francis lived, a wave of similar but unaffiliated women's houses in central Italy were organized by Cardinal Hugolino, the future Gregory IX, and were referred to as the "Ordo pauperum dominarum de valle Spoleti sive Tuscia" (Order of the Poor Ladies of the Spoleto Valley or Tuscany). In 1219, Hugolino assigned them a short form of life modeled on the Benedictine rule and named a Cistercian as Visitor for the houses.[44] This was the first entirely female religious order ever approved by the church, but, as its name and rule indicate, it was not "Franciscan" in any institutional sense, and many of the houses it incorporated were penitential communities that may not originally have been inspired directly by either Francis or Clare. But in 1227, after Francis's death and Hugolino's ascension to the papacy, the latter was able to join approximately twenty-three of these houses to Clare's and call them the Order of San Damiano (*Ordo S. Damiani*). Pope Gregory placed them under the direct care of the Franciscan Minister General (though still with his Rule or Constitution of 1219), thereby initiating the trend toward linking the Order of San Damiano to the male Franciscans. Clare herself, however, was probably not enthusiastic about her house's absorption into this new order and was mollified only by receiving the famous "Privilege of Poverty" from Gregory in 1228.[45]

During the rest of Gregory's pontificate the number of houses of this order was not allowed to increase.[46] But, in 1246, Innocent IV responded to the demands of women's communities by incorporating a number of new ones into the Order of San Damiano. Disputes over whether Franciscans had to care for the temporal and pastoral affairs of these houses, together with the question of poverty, caused Innocent to attempt to establish uniformity of practice by issuing a new rule for the *Moniales inclusae ordinis S. Damiani*, on 6 August 1247.[47] This rule stipulated that houses should hold property and that the Franciscans should provide chaplains (though they were not obliged to actually reside on the premises) as well as appoint a Procurator to each house to oversee temporal matters. Although this rule was much more explicit than its predecessor of 1219 in spelling out the links between male Franciscans and the Order of San Damiano, it does not seem to have been received favorably by either the communities for which it was intended or by the male Franciscans. At this juncture, Clare received approval for her own rule, which applied only to San Damiano. Clare emphatically rejected property and insisted on direct Franciscan pastoral attention with brothers resident at the house. Cardinal Rainaldo (the future Alexander IV) approved this rule on 16 September 1252, and Innocent IV confirmed it two days before Clare's death on 9 August 1253.[48]

Thus, when Longchamp was being built, there were three rules concurrently in effect for "Franciscan" women: Hugolino's Rule of 1219, which made no statement on either property or pastoral care by Franciscans; Innocent's Rule of 1247, which insisted on income and property and allowed the Franciscans to delegate pastoral and temporal responsibilities to nonresident chaplains and procurators; and Clare's Rule of 1253, which refused property and required direct Franciscan pastoral attention.[49] This fractious situation presented not only obvious pitfalls but also the possibility for influential new solutions.[50]

Isabelle and her collaborators might conceivably have chosen any one of the three rules as a starting point, or to have drawn equally from all of them, or to have started from scratch. But, in fact, a close comparison reveals that Innocent IV's Rule of 1247 served as the basis for writing the new rule.[51] Identifying this text as the starting point for negotiations allows us to pinpoint the nature of alterations and new ideas that were introduced and also to assess whose desires they may have reflected.

The Content

Alexander IV himself left a strong stamp on the new rule. As Cardinal Protector of both male and female Franciscans since 1227, as a close associate of Gregory IX, as an adviser to Innocent IV who may have had a hand in the writing of the Rule of 1247, as the cardinal who had first approved Clare's Rule of 1253, and indeed as the pope who had strongly supported and recently proclaimed Clare's canonization in 1255, Alexander was probably the most knowledgeable and experienced participant in the negotiations for the new rule. He was well aware of its importance and would have been keenly attuned to any innovations.[52] The text of the rule is enclosed within a papal bull evidently written at the curia, and Alexander IV's language is clearly enshrined in the opening and closing sections.[53] The preamble, already cited in the introduction to this book, offers striking evidence for his own vision of the new document's significance, and must be considered here in detail:

> The true sun, flashing with perpetual brightness . . . , with the invisible infusion of its admirable clarity, illuminates the hearts of the faithful who dwell at the bottom of this deep and dark valley under the weight of the flesh. And it often touches kings and princes with more sparkling rays of light . . . , so that, contemplating with a more perceptive insight, they understand higher things more freely, elect the more lofty of them more discriminatingly, and embrace them more ardently. Thus they vehemently propel and lead others by their saving example towards the sweet taste and love of heavenly things.
>
> Suffused indeed with this light, the most Christian prince Louis, our dearest son in Christ and illustrious king of the Franks, and our beloved daughter in Christ the noble woman Isabelle his sister, who, shining with the luster of virginal modesty and powerful with the brightness of other virtues, spurns the spacious palace of the temporal realm [and] seeks relentlessly with a fervent spirit to make time for divine praises in the

repose of sweet contemplation, have devoutly and humbly entreated us, that we should take care to establish and concede to this same Isabelle and to all the handmaidens of Christ desiring with her to devote a noble service to Christ, some fixed rule or special form of regular living, under the saving observance of which these same women might find the strength to be more pleasing to the Lord.

Although it has been forbidden by the General Council that anyone should invent a new form of religious life, "but whoever wants to be converted to the religious life should assume one of the approved [forms], similarly whoever wants to found a new house of religion, should accept the rule and institutions of an approved religious community," nevertheless, wanting to look favorably upon the desires of the above-mentioned king and Isabelle in this matter, we grant the rule included below to this same Isabelle and to all the women wanting to flee from the world to profess it in the Monastery of the Humility of the Blessed Virgin Mary in the diocese of Paris and under this same rule to dedicate themselves to finding divine favor, in this same monastery alone to be observed in perpetuity, granting a dispensation from the General Council's prohibition in this matter specially out of consideration for the King and Isabelle. Moreover, we want this Rule to take its name from the above-mentioned place, so that those who will have professed it shall be called the Sisters of the Order of the Humble Handmaidens of the Most Blessed Glorious Virgin Mary.[54]

Isabelle's active role in lobbying for papal approval for her rule is evident here, as is Alexander's respect for the princess. But the papal language also seems to betray indecision over the issue of just how widely this rule was intended to spread. Alexander refers to the rule being observed "in this same monastery alone," but then alludes to creating a new order, thus implying the potential for a growing network of houses.

This tension may have resulted from Alexander's recognition of the novelty of this rule. Comparing his preamble with the introduction to Innocent IV's Rule of 1247 helps to highlight his purposes. Whereas the opening rhetoric of the 1259 rule focuses on royalty's potential for enlightenment and positive influence, the introduction to the Rule of 1247 had centered on the negative dangers of neglecting to follow a correct rule. In view of this peril, Innocent had announced in 1247 that he was granting to the Order of San Damiano the "observance of the Rule of St. Francis with respect to the three [counsels], namely, obedience, the renunciation of property in particular, and perpetual chastity, as well as the Form of Life written in the present document."[55] Thus, the Rule of 1247 was couched in language that sought to find safety from potential danger in an ostensible return to the Rule of St. Francis, just as the Rule of 1219 had claimed to be nothing more than the Rule of St. Benedict.[56] In 1259, by contrast, Alexander explicitly sanctioned something new. Rather than seek the cover of an existing rule, he openly set aside the Fourth Lateran Council's prohibition of new forms of religious life.

At the same time, in 1259, Alexander eschewed any mention of Francis, Clare, the Franciscan or Damianite rules, or overtly Franciscan ideals. Whereas the Rule of 1247 had been addressed to the Order of San Damiano, a name evoking both Clare's house and the early days of the Franciscan Order, the Rule of 1259 created the new Order of the Humble Handmaidens of the Most Blessed Glorious Virgin Mary, a title without specifically Franciscan connotations. When Alexander (as Cardinal Rainaldo) had given preliminary approval for Clare's Rule of 1253, he had invoked the language of spurning the world and its fickle delights in order to freely contemplate God. But he had also stressed Clare and her sisters' desire to live in poverty and acknowledged Francis as the ultimate source of the newly approved rule.[57] This explicitly Franciscan rhetoric is lacking in 1259. There is no mention of poverty in 1259, though even the 1247 Rule at least had gestured toward the nuns' desire to lead a *vitam pauperem*. It was in keeping with this attitude that Alexander refused to grant Isabelle's preferred name of *Sorores minores*, which would have explicitly designated her sisters as female analogues to the male Franciscan *Fratres minores*. Instead, the pope tried to placate the princess by calling the sisters after her chosen name for the abbey.

The Rule of 1259 also closes with a papal admonition, exhortation, and indulgence. Alexander's voice returns in a florid passage that restates the themes of contemplation and royalty found in his preamble, but it is now applied to the abbey's sisters rather than to Isabelle of France. Alexander here refers to "these beloved daughters and brides of the magnificent King . . . spurning the pomp of the empty present, despising the vanity of the florid world, disdaining cheap joys filled with mourning"; and he urges, "let nothing of an earthly quality from this time forward have any savor for them, let nothing delight them. But rather, spurning all mortal things, embracing only their Spouse . . . let them ardently strive with the fire of love to be united to Him."[58] The pope then concludes with a remarkable clause, reminiscent of *Benedicta filia tu*, in which he grants a plenary indulgence to all those professing the new rule, allows any minor vows taken in the world to be commuted by the vows of entering this order, and adds a special blessing, "so that they [the sisters] may proceed, glorified with sublime splendor, until they shall arrive at the marriage bed of brightness."[59] No similar language was included in any other rule for Franciscan women in the thirteenth century.

Thus, Alexander IV contributed his own enthusiastic voice to the text. But he also flatly refused to permit the inflammatory measure of giving the sisters of the new house the title of *Sorores minores*. We shall have to return to the issue of this label and the controversy surrounding it, but evidently Alexander's opening and closing sections carry no references to Franciscan models, preferring instead to stress the rhetoric of contemplation, bridal imagery, and detachment from the world. Aside from a possible allusion to the recently canonized St. Clare in the opening paragraph's use of light imagery ("lux quidem clarissima . . . infusione . . . claritatis"), there is little in Alexander's preamble to indicate that this rule or the new order that it creates should be regarded as "Franciscan."

Let us now turn to a closer analysis of the differences in substance and language between the Rules of 1247 and 1259. The Rule of 1259 begins with new language that gives spiritual justification for its prescriptions,[60] stating that "any woman joining this order, inspired by the divine spirit and following in the footsteps of our Lord Jesus Christ and his most holy Mother, according to the counsels of Evangelical perfection, shall always live in obedience, chastity, without property, and like the hidden treasure of a celebrated king, will remain enclosed her whole life."[61] The call to obedience, chastity, and poverty is wholly standard and is found several lines later in the Rule of 1247, but the rest of this passage is new. The 1259 Rule also introduces an important clause that permits the nuns to leave the monastery en masse, without waiting for permission from anyone once the abbess and convent have reached a decision, in the case of flood, hostile attack, fire, or other disasters.[62]

Having chosen to enter the religious life, sisters will undergo a one-year novitiate before taking formal vows. The Rule of 1247 mentions simply that novices will be assigned a *magistra*, who will instruct them in regular discipline. The Rule of 1259 replaces this short statement with a more elaborate wording: "A prudent *magistra* shall be given to them from among the more devout sisters, who will instruct them in holy ways, and inflame them in the fervor of devotion and those things to be performed according to this sacred religion, and will teach them to act in the sweetness of charity, and will diligently correct [them] in those things that must be corrected."[63] After their probationary year, they will take their vows. In the Rule of 1247 the sisters promised to God, the Virgin Mary, St. Francis, and all the saints "to observe perpetual obedience according to the Rule and Form of Life given to our Order by the Apostolic See, living all the days of my life without anything of my own and in chastity."[64] The Rule of 1259, however, omits Francis from the list of saints in whose name the vow is sworn, adds the stipulation that the vow be made in the hands of the abbess ("in your hands, Mother)," and adds the new, specific vow to live *sub claustra* (enclosed).[65] A brief sentence in both rules notes that servants will observe a similar vow. In the 1259 Rule this sentence is followed by a clause stating that if it is necessary to send servants outside the abbey, only the more mature and modest should go, and the permission of the Minister General is required for these journeys. The Rule of 1247, by contrast, does not deal with this question of leaving the enclosure until near the end of the text, but it then goes on to provide another substantial paragraph of regulations for serving sisters when they are outside the abbey.[66]

The Rule of 1259 next turns to details of daily life—what the nuns were to wear, where and when they were to sleep, how they should perform their daily round of Divine Office, what and when they were to eat, when and where they might speak. These sections of the rule may not make compelling reading, but for the nuns themselves they were the very basis for their daily existence.

The changes concerning clothing are too minor to be worth spelling out, but they were pervasive enough to show that each clause was scrutinized and carefully revised. Several passages newly expressing the purpose of the regulations and highlighting the abbess's discretionary role here are worthy of note. Both rules require that the sisters' heads, throats, cheeks, and foreheads be covered. But only the Rule of 1259 goes on to justify this requirement, arguing that "it is not fitting that the spouse of the eternal King should show herself to anyone else, nor to delight in anyone else."[67] Furthermore, in clauses unique to the Rule of 1259, the abbess is given authority to allow the nuns to go without veils, and decisions on appropriate footwear for the sisters and servants within the cloister are left up to her as well. Sleeping arrangements follow nearly identical models in the two rules, with the nuns lodged in a common room with the abbess, who was to keep watch, but the Rule of 1259 includes a unique clause that allows nap time in the afternoon from Easter through September.

The clause requiring the sisters to engage in manual labor at certain times is significant, since Isabelle's rule includes a caveat found in both St. Francis's *Regula bullata* and Clare's Rule of 1253, warning the sisters that "while banishing leisure [that is] harmful to the soul, they should not extinguish the spirit of holy prayers and devotion which temporal affairs ought to serve." Isabelle's rule goes on to further justify this exaltation of prayers and devotion, "to which the bride of Christ ought to totally give herself up, so that she may enjoy the conversation and consolation of her Spouse."[68]

At this point the Rule of 1259 inserts a clause detailing the sisters' access to the Eucharist. Usually they are to receive the Lord's body twice per month, but during Lent and Advent they may receive it each Sunday, unless they are excused by permission of the abbess. This is a significant innovation, since the Rules of 1219 and 1247 do not specify how frequently the nuns should be able to receive communion, and Clare's Rule of 1253 states seven times per year on major feast days.[69]

The Rule of 1259 also makes numerous small changes to strictures on fasting and eating. To take the single example of fast days, in 1247 the sisters were to follow a fasting diet from September 14 until Easter, except on Sundays and on the feasts of St. Michael, St. Francis, All Saints, the Nativity of the Lord and two days afterward, as well as on Epiphany and the Purification. In 1259 the dates were slightly liberalized to October 4 (Feast of St. Francis) to Easter, with the same exceptions, but omitting the two days after the Nativity. But Isabelle's rule also added a new fast during the ten-day period from Ascension to Pentecost, "so that their [the nuns'] hearts may be made fruitful by the gifts of the Holy Spirit."[70] Thus, in terms of the total portion of the year devoted to fasting the two rules are virtually identical, but in Isabelle's we again see considered innovation and the spiritual rationale behind it.

Here the Rule of 1259 inserts a unique clause that urges the abbess to lead a life in common with the sisters and to be "a mirror of charity to the others and an example to all her sisters." If she cannot or will not follow the common life, she should be removed by the Minister (whether General or Provincial is not specified) or the Visitor.[71]

The long section on speech and silence begins in a manner obviously drawn from the Rule of 1247, but then goes on to offer regulations on the physical characteristics of the grilles, doors, and veils that separate the sisters from their confessors and any visitors. These regulations were found scattered throughout the later portions of the Rule of 1247, demonstrating the way in which some of the 1259 Rule's structural reorganizations reflect an attempt to deal with logically related topics in sequence. The new rule offers significant changes here as well. Almost immediately it inserts a new clause allowing the nuns to speak on holy and honest topics from nones until vespers (midafternoon until dusk) on double feast days and their octaves. Both rules state that when anyone wants to speak with a sister, if the abbess consents she should be accompanied to the parlor (*locutorium*) by two sisters who will witness the conversation. But whereas the Rule of 1247 goes on to stipulate that when a sick sister wants to confess to a priest, she may not do so unless there are at least two other nuns present, the Rule of 1259 allows that "when any sister wants to confess, she may make her confession alone in the parlor to a lone priest."[72] The Rule of 1259 also stipulates that confessors will be assigned to the house by the Minister General or Provincial Minister. From here the Rule of 1259 moves to regulations on not speaking without good cause at the iron grille through which the sisters accept communion and hear the Divine Office and sermons.

The rule next deals with admittance of outsiders to the abbey. The rules of 1247 and 1259 agree that no one may enter the enclosure unless given permission by the Apostolic See. The latter rule actually removes the ability of the General and Provincial Ministers to grant permission while specifying that the Ministers themselves will be able to enter. The exceptions to these regulations differ considerably between the two rules. Innocent IV's Rule of 1247 adds exceptions for those given permission by the General or Provincial Minster as well as for doctors and bloodletters or for people whose assistance may be required in case of fire or disaster. Cardinals and bishops may enter for legitimate purposes with a few attendants and companions. No one, however, should speak with these visitors except in the previously described manner. Isabelle's Rule of 1259, however, allows in the General and Provincial Ministers and "those who, by order of the abbess and with the counsel and consent of the convent, [show] the evident need to do something necessary." In this case the assent of the Provincial Minister was required, if it could suitably be brought about.[73] The Provincial Minister could also enter with two honest companions for visitation or other urgent causes; cardinals now could have seven companions, and bishops three or four. In place of the simple statement that no one was to speak with visitors except in accordance with the usual regulations, Isabelle's Rule of 1259 decrees that the abbess with two discreet and mature sisters may converse with them; and if a female visitor should enter, sisters may speak with her with the abbess's permission. And so that the nuns should not be disturbed in their divine praises, anyone entering the abbey contrary to these regulations should suffer excommunication. The section of the Rule of 1259 concludes by insisting that even those who have obtained papal approval still must produce letters for the abbess and other discreet sisters of the abbey before they can gain access.

Both rules stipulate that if the house has a chaplain, he should be of suitable life and age. The Rule of 1247 goes on to regulate the chaplain's behavior when entering to hear confession or to give communion or last rites to the sick. The Rule of 1259, however, abruptly changes the subject of these regulations from the chaplain to the confessor and then proceeds to regulations concerning the main door. The Rule of 1259 here adds the unexpected stipulation that no animals are to be kept within the abbey except cats, and that a residence just inside the walls should be set up where a nurse (*nutrix*) or surgeon may be admitted with the advice and consent of the convent.

Finally, the rules arrive at the crucial issues of the Visitor, visitation, the Procurator, and use of possessions. The Rule of 1247 specified that the Visitor was to be the General or Provincial Minister or another qualified brother appointed by them in General Chapter. The Rule of 1259 makes a slight change, stating that "the Visitor should always be from the Franciscan Order and sent by the Minister General," but in any year in which this

Visitor cannot fulfill this duty, the visitation will be carried out by the Provincial Minister.[74] Concerning the actual procedure, the Rule of 1259 insists that the Visitor will first read the text (presumably aloud to the sisters). Most important, the same rule adds new language concerning the "rights" of sisters and the abbess. For instance, "when one of the sisters or even the abbess is 'visited,' let her not be present but wait outside the chapter. [And] against her nothing shall be said in public that cannot be proved as a fact or public knowledge."[75] Furthermore, "let all the sisters beware and diligently consider, especially in the visitation of sisters, that nothing other than love of God and the correction of their sisters should move them to speak." These nuns may defend themselves against accusations: "Those, however, who may not want to recognize the guilt which is attributed to them, if they want to exonerate themselves, especially if the offenses are weighty, will not be denied a hearing. Those making grave accusations, however, if they are not able to prove them, may legitimately be punished for this manner of laying blame. An excess which has been sufficiently corrected by the Visitor, shall in no way be corrected again."[76]

The Rule of 1259, moreover, contains a unique clause limiting the length of time that a visitation may take—no more than five days if the abbey has less than fifty sisters, or eight or nine days if more than fifty; and "after the visitation is over, he [the Visitor] will not afterwards have the right to enter the monastery."[77] The Rule of 1259 also requires that "if brothers will ever be staying there, or even if not staying there they hear their [the nuns'] confessions, and the Visitor finds something notable against them, he must tell it to the Provincial Minister, who ought to quickly correct them or remove them from the place."[78] Finally, an arresting clause forces secrecy upon and offers recourse against the Visitor:

> We strictly enjoin the Visitor, that what he has found in his visit must be kept secret, and in no way knowingly revealed. But rather when the excesses have been read and penalties enjoined, all writings are to be burned in the presence of the convent, unless there should be things which, by the counsel of the discreet sisters of the convent, are to be referred to the Minister General. If indeed the Provincial Minister should find anything notable against the Visitor or his associates after the visitation, he must indicate it to the Minister General of the Order.[79]

Both rules state that the election of the abbess will be the free right of the convent, and that her confirmation or removal shall be done by the Minister General or, in his absence, the Provincial Minister. The Rule of 1259 adds language reminding the abbess and sisters to be obedient to the said Ministers in all things that are not contrary to their soul and to the rule, and all sisters similarly to be obedient to the abbess. The Rule of 1259 also includes a unique clause stating that if, through infirmity or any other reason, the convent is without the leadership of an abbess, it may elect an interim president.

On the controversial issue of poverty and possessions, both rules agree that the sisters will be able to hold property in common (in distinct contrast to Clare's Rule of 1253). Both rules further stipulate that a Procurator will be assigned to take care of these temporal possessions. Neither rule insists that this Procurator be a Franciscan. However, several rhetorical and substantive changes are apparent here. The Rule of 1259 adds a unique clause stating that "neither the General or Provincial Ministers nor the other brothers of the Order shall in any way involve themselves with the care, disposition, and dispensation of possessions and temporal things."[80] The latter rule also seeks to explain the permission to own possessions and the need for a Procurator, "because indecent running about on the pretext of temporal things is to be avoided, and so that the aforesaid sisters may more tranquilly serve the Lord."[81] In the Rule of 1247, moreover, the Procurator was to be appointed by the Visitor. But in one of the most dramatic changes implemented in 1259, the Procurator was to be chosen by the abbess with the counsel and consent of the convent, and he could be removed by the abbess and convent as well.[82]

The Rule of 1259 winds down with new admonitions, stating that "since the eternal dwelling of the Fatherland of the sisters of this religion should be elsewhere, we wish them to avoid in all ways curiosity, which is hateful to God in all things and strongly contrary to piety, and excess in superfluous buildings."[83] Priests serving the house were limited in the splendor of their vestments. Finally, the seal of the abbey was to be guarded and no sister was to send or receive letters unless they were first read by the abbess or aloud in her presence. The abbess was also to gather the sisters in chapter once per week for any necessary correction or admonition.[84]

Ascribing Agency

Having carried out this detailed investigation into the innovations found in the Rule of 1259, we can now consider Isabelle's role in the creation of the document as a whole in relation to the desires of her Franciscan collaborators and the papal curia. Isabelle's own influence was first apparent in the granting of her request to have the abbey named after the Humility of Our Lady and in Alexander's deference to her wishes in his preamble. But, more substantially, the nature of many of the new elements in the rule shows that the princess's influence pervades the text. Consider the possible sources for the new clause detailing the nuns' permission to abandon their abbey in an emergency. It seems unlikely that either the Franciscan masters, the papal legate Mansuetus, or the pope himself felt it necessary to address this previously unconsidered eventuality. Almost certainly we have here a direct result of Isabelle's contribution to the writing process. As an "outsider" to monastic life, the princess was raising a practical objection and insisting on this precautionary exception to the usual rules of obedience and enclosure.

Moreover, a concern to grant decision-making authority to the abbess in relation to the male Franciscan hierarchy is apparent throughout the rule. Again, it seems virtually certain that this confidence in the role of the abbess reflects Isabelle's own outlook, since the Franciscans were unlikely to have proposed an internal check on their own authority. This goal is apparent in the clauses allowing the abbess to exercise her own judgment regarding clothing regulations and dispensations from fasting. More important, the abbess receives increased powers to regulate access to the abbey for outsiders and to speak more freely with her visitors. Perhaps most impressively, the abbess and convent, not the Franciscan Visitor, are given the new power to choose and even dismiss the Procurator. Indeed, this evident desire to bolster the abbess's authority in her dealings with ecclesiastical officials extends to a generally increased consideration for the position of individual nuns. The clauses detailing the sisters' ability to defend themselves from accusations by their fellow nuns certainly display a new sympathy for the victims of spiteful rumors. But the stipulations limiting the length of visits, enjoining the Visitor to secrecy, insisting that he publicly destroy his records, and raising the possibility of the Visitor himself being removed, are extraordinary in their success in protecting the autonomy and privacy of the abbey, the abbess, and the nuns.

These elements are not stressed in the earlier rules for Franciscan women. It seems most unlikely that the rule's Franciscan co-authors or the pope himself would have suggested this consistent direction for revision. There can be little doubt, therefore, that Isabelle of France herself secured this new level of authority and autonomy for her nuns and abbess. Her stress on autonomy may not have been intended as a specifically "feminist" stance in the face of a masculine hierarchy; it should be seen simply as a pragmatic attempt to keep as much decision-making power as possible at Longchamp. Nevertheless, its effect was undeniably to carve out space for women's control within the Franciscan world.

The reconsideration of the details of such issues as dress and fasting must also reflect Isabelle's desires, though probably as refracted through consultation with her Franciscan collaborators. It is only logical to deduce that the woman who envisioned and worked for the new abbey also asserted her opinion on such questions as whether it was more appropriate for the sisters to possess two tunics and one mantle or three tunics and two mantles, whether they should begin their fasts in September or October, whether afternoon naps were allowed, or whether they should be bled four or six times per year. It may well have been Isabelle who insisted on keeping cats in the abbey, perhaps as a check on the rodent population.

Of more interest in assessing Isabelle's religious ideas here is the clause granting the nuns frequent access to the Eucharist. This stipulation is again unlikely to have reflected papal or Franciscan priorities and represents a significant change from the previous rules. It also associates Isabelle with the Eucharistic devotion that characterized female piety in the thirteenth century, even though Agnes of Harcourt's biography omits any mention of the Eucharist in connection with Isabelle. Many *vitae* of contemporary female saints as well as writings by female spiritual authors focus attention on the importance of the body of Christ to women in the period after the Fourth Lateran Council of 1215.[85] Isabelle's institutional influence adds another dimension to this picture by writing this concern into the life of her nuns.

On the other hand, some of the changes brought about in 1259 must have reflected the will of the Franciscans involved in writing the rule.

Specifically, since Bonaventure and William of Harcombourg were Minister General and Provincial Minister of the order, clauses affecting the role of these posts are unlikely to have been directly contrary to their desires. For instance, the provision stating that the Minister General must grant a license to serving sisters to leave the abbey may show Bonaventure's attention to a point that he considered potentially troublesome. The rule grants the Ministers (or the Visitor) the power to depose an abbess who will not lead the common life—possibly a safeguard put in place by Bonaventure and William as a check on the abbess's greater powers. Similarly, the 1259 clauses reminding the abbess to be obedient to the Ministers were probably a reaction to any independence on her part. In other cases, what at first seems like a diminution in the Ministers' power may have been welcomed by these men. For instance, in the Rule of 1259 the Ministers are no longer given the authority (along with the pope) to grant special entry licenses. This change may have been part of Isabelle of France's campaign to keep Longchamp's affairs in the hands of the abbess and sisters, but it may also have met with the approval of the Ministers, who did not particularly wish to be responsible for these issues. Along the same lines, in 1247 one of the Ministers was expected to act as the Visitor, whereas in 1259 he was explicitly allowed to assign another brother to this post. Though this change lessened the direct control of the Ministers, it was likely seen as the lifting of an unwelcome burden. This is presumably the reason as well for the clause specifying that neither the Ministers nor the brothers of the order were to involve themselves in the temporal affairs of the abbey, though the Ministers were nevertheless to reform and correct whatever was necessary in both temporal and spiritual matters.

The clause allowing nuns to confess alone to an unaccompanied priest is intriguing as well. If this is thought of as a measure protecting the sisters' privacy, then Isabelle might have been behind it. But Agnes of Harcourt emphasizes Isabelle's own practice of always having two women present when she confessed (as earlier Franciscan rules for women had insisted was proper), so she would not seem to have leaned in this direction. Perhaps, though, she might have believed that safeguards proper for a laywoman were superfluous for enclosed nuns.

Finally, the Rule of 1259 offers new rhetorical explanations for its provisions, which are difficult to assign to an author. But it is at least possible that Isabelle, so passionately committed to her new house, according to Agnes of Harcourt's vivid description, sought to make sure that these values were stressed. It might, for instance, be reasonable to hear Isabelle's own ideas in the language that hopes that the sisters will be "inflamed with the fervor of devotion" by the *magistra* and be taught "with the sweetness of charity." At the very least, even if these phrases were dictated by Isabelle's Franciscan collaborators, they probably can be said to have received her approval. Similarly, although it is possible that one of the ecclesiastical officials involved would have invoked the Virgin Mary and the example of Evangelical perfection in the rule's first sentence, given Isabelle's fervent desire to dedicate her abbey to the Virgin's example of humility, her ideas may have been behind this language as well.

This passage also hints at a second influence dimly at work—Clare's Rule of 1253 and the language in which its official approval was expressed. The passage cited above concerning the utility of manual labor may have been drawn from Clare's rule (though it may also have come directly from Francis's *Regula bullata*), and the provision for weekly chapter meetings may also echo provisions in Clare's rule (though the tone of the two clauses is quite different).[86] Isabelle's rule, moreover, begins by referring to sisters "Domini nostri Jesu Christi et eius sacratissimae Matris vestigiis inhaerendo" (adhering to the footsteps of our Lord Jesus Christ and of his most holy mother). Clare's rule began not only with a preface expressing the approval of Innocent IV but also the original approval given by Cardinal Rainaldo, which alludes to the sisters of San Damiano as "Christi eiusque sanctissimae Matris sequentes vestigia" (following the footsteps of Christ and of his most holy mother). Thus, there may be an echo here not of Clare's own language but of Cardinal Rainaldo's, now that he had assumed the papal throne as Alexander IV. Clare's rule was certainly not a major influence on the Rule of 1259, but Alexander's role in both texts links them together on the level of curial language and imagery.

The attempt to separate the different demands of princess, friars, and pope should not be carried too far, since many of the ideas here may have enjoyed acceptance on all sides. The issue of enclosure, for instance, seems to reveal a negotiated compromise. For the first time it is made a part of a Franciscan nun's formal vows. The rule seems to glory in the rhetoric of enclosure, describing the sisters as "enclosed like the hidden treasure of a celebrated king," and stipulating that "indecent running about on the pretext of temporal things" must be avoided. Since the papal curia (with the support and at the urging of the male Franciscans) had been seeking tighter enclosure for Franciscan women for decades, this vow and its accompanying rhetoric probably came from papal and Franciscan influences.[87] Indeed, the Rule of 1259 reflects wider fears among churchmen concerning religious and semi-religious women's mobility and lack of material support.[88] The vow to live *sub claustra* was an important milestone on the road to *Periculoso*, the bull issued by Pope Boniface VIII in 1298 that required strict enclosure of nuns no matter what rule they professed.[89] Yet, at the same time, the newly concrete specificity of the vow of enclosure seems to have called forth Isabelle's response identified above: if enclosure was to be a formal vow, then there must be a formal exemption in case of physical danger to the sisters, even if it was not feasible to consult the Minister General first. The Franciscan hierarchy, the pope, and the princess reached a mutually acceptable consensus on this issue.

ROYAL POWER AND PATRONAGE

The foregoing analysis of the text of the Rule of 1259 substantiates Agnes of Harcourt's picture of Isabelle of France as an active agent—indeed, the driving force—behind many of the new ideas contained in Longchamp's rule. In concluding this chapter, we must ask how Isabelle was able to negotiate with such success.

I have been arguing that her royal influence and personal reputation allowed her to bargain with the papacy and the Franciscan Order from an enviable position. After about 1244 she had her family's support for her life of holy virginity, and by the early 1250s she was being praised by friars and popes and sought out by university masters such as Gilbert of Tournai. Alexander IV's bull *Benedicta filia tu* of 1256 is enough to demonstrate the importance of her reputation as a devout royal woman. Alexander saw Isabelle as an example to other women, pointing the way to a pious life dedicated to virginity. It was for this reason that he promised papal support for Isabelle's endeavors in 1256 and lived up to his word in 1259. In turn, much of Alexander's high opinion of Isabelle seems to have been based on reports from Franciscans who had his ear. There emerges a circular flow of influence whereby Franciscans recognized Isabelle's importance as a royal patron and sang her praises to the pope, who was sufficiently impressed to put her in a strong bargaining position even when her ideas may have conflicted with those of the very friars who had first brought her to Alexander's attention.

A brief comparison with the negotiations of another contemporary royal woman helps to clarify several aspects of Isabelle's relationship to ecclesiastical power. Agnes of Bohemia (or Prague) had a great deal in common with Isabelle of France. Indeed, in some ways their careers are uncannily similar.[90] The daughter of Ottokar I of Bohemia and Constance of Hungary, Agnes was born in 1211 and sent at the age of three to live with her intended husband, the son of Duke Henry of Silesia and his saintly wife, Hedwig. Two years later, however, at the death of her fiancé, Agnes returned to her father's court. Around 1219 her family betrothed her to Emperor Frederick II's eldest son, Henry, and now sent her to be raised at the court of Leopold VI of Austria. But when Henry married one of Leopold's daughters, Agnes returned once more to Prague in 1225. After her father's death in 1230, she rejected marriage proposals from Henry III of England and Frederick II himself, and in 1233 she founded at Prague a hospital for the poor, a male Franciscan priory, and the first female Franciscan house in Central Europe. Agnes entered this house in 1234 and in the same year became its abbess and began her famous correspondence with Clare of Assisi.[91] After battling with Pope Gregory IX, and supported by her brother, Wenceslas I of Bohemia, Agnes in April 1238 gained a papal privilege of poverty, such as that secured by San Damiano, guaranteeing her house the right to be free of any possessions. In May, however, Gregory categorically refused to approve her request for a rule modeled after the primitive form of life given by Francis to Clare.[92] The house thus continued to follow Cardinal Hugolino's Rule of 1219, specifically reissued to Agnes in 1238.[93] Agnes enjoyed a long life at her abbey, dying only in 1282. But though her skirmishes with the papacy over the privilege of poverty reemerged sporadically in later years, the events of 1238 determined her institutional legacy.

Though it hardly does justice to Agnes of Bohemia's historical interest, this short sketch sheds light on some of the ways in which Isabelle of

France achieved her objectives. On one hand, the similarities between Agnes and Isabelle bring out the wider pattern of royal power exerted by devout princesses. Their lives ran almost in parallel; daughter and sister of kings, betrothed to a noble at an early age, sought in marriage by the Hohenstaufen, founder of a new abbey, inspired by Franciscan ideals, correspondent of popes—this description could fit Agnes or Isabelle equally well. Both these women, like Elizabeth of Hungary and others, combined royal power and patronage with mendicant piety. Their influence from the top of the social scale helped to determine the form of female Franciscan institutions as they spread outside Italy.

The differences, however, are equally instructive. First, Isabelle never abandoned her position as laywoman to adopt a formal position within the church hierarchy, as did Agnes. When Gregory IX denied Agnes's request to approve the rule she had drafted, he reminded her in no uncertain terms of her vows of obedience. Though her position as abbess gave her substantial local power, it also relegated her to a subordinate place within the larger church hierarchy. By contrast, as a laywoman, Isabelle preserved the full weight of royal independence. Second, Agnes of Bohemia's insistence on poverty as the central virtue of a female Franciscan life placed her firmly in the mold of Clare, who was clearly her inspiration and guiding light. But this stance made her fervor suspect in the eyes of churchmen who regarded temporal support as essential to enclosed nuns. While Gregory was willing to grant Agnes a rare privilege of poverty, he would not enshrine this concession in a formal rule that might then be transplanted to other communities. Isabelle of France, by not making poverty an issue, probably gained legitimacy in papal eyes and was able to secure concessions on other questions.

In addition, the greater importance of the French crown to the objectives of the Franciscan hierarchy and the papal curia may have given Isabelle more leverage than Agnes. Isabelle's negotiations with the Franciscan Order were intertwined with larger issues that pushed the order and the crown toward each other. The Franciscans were particularly keen to assure themselves of the political support of the Capetians in the 1250s during the conflict between the mendicant and secular masters at the University of Paris.[94] The chronology of this dispute is telling. In 1253 the seculars' resentment erupted into open conflict when the mendicants refused to join in a general strike called to protest ill treatment at the hands of the Parisian authorities. Then, in 1254, Innocent IV sharply reversed the papacy's traditional favor toward the mendicants. The bull *Etsi animarum* of 21 November has been described as reducing the friars "to being supplements to the secular ecclesiastical structure, whereas previously they had been its competitors."[95] But just sixteen days after issuing *Etsi animarum*, Innocent died and the College of Cardinals elected Cardinal Rainaldo, the Protector of the Franciscans, as Alexander IV. The election itself sent a message of support for the friars, and Alexander quickly restored their privileges. Yet the grievances of the seculars remained, spurred on by the publication of *De periculis novissimorum temporum* by the secular master William of St. Amour in late 1255. This work accused the friars of heresy and hypocrisy and questioned their very right to exist. Louis IX's position in the dispute up to this point had been relatively neutral,[96] but this ambivalence must have been sorely tried when William preached a sermon in Paris on 4 June 1256 that accused the king of insincerity and weakness in his admiration for the mendicant way of life.[97] Louis can hardly have been pleased with this outburst, and he must have been gratified when the pope condemned William's tract in October, deprived William of his offices, and exiled him from France the following August. There can be little doubt that June 1256 brought the mendicant-secular controversy squarely home to the Capetian court.[98]

Isabelle's founding of a Franciscan house at Longchamp intersects with this narrative in obvious ways. The object of Innocent's praise in *Sanctae virginitatis propositum* just as the dispute broke out in 1253, she was moving closer to the Franciscans, as evidenced by Innocent's bull *Decens ac debitum* of May 1254. Plans for Longchamp were under way by April 1255 when Alexander was swinging papal support back behind the friars. His bull *Benedicta filia tu* praising Isabelle came barely a week after William of St. Amour's attack. The royal family's very public laying of the first stones for Longchamp may have come at that time.[99] Moreover, Isabelle could hardly have been unaware of the importance of the events against which the founding of Longchamp was set, or of the opinions of men such as William who saw royal affinity for the Franciscans and Dominicans as dangerous. Not only did her brother have an important role in the affair, but also, of her two known confessors, Aymeric of Veire was the chancellor of Paris (and hence titular head of the faculty of theology) and Eudes of

Rosny was a leading scholar at Paris who would shortly occupy the Franciscan chair of theology. One of Isabelle's collaborators on her rule, William of Meliton, was the Franciscan master whom the seculars expelled at the outset of the conflict in 1253, and another, Bonaventure, was the man who took his place. These Franciscan masters must have appreciated royal support wherever they could find it, and the sister of the king would not have been unmindful of this fact.

Moreover, Longchamp occupies a surprisingly distinct place in royal patronage of the Franciscans at this moment. Particularly after his failed crusade, Louis poured his resources into founding new mendicant houses, establishing six in the years 1255–59 alone, while his brothers Alphonse and Charles endowed their own foundations in this period.[100] In this sense, Longchamp was part of a larger pattern of renewed royal patronage for mendicant houses. Yet the striking aspect of Louis's postcrusade patronage was his support for the lesser-known mendicant orders such as the Sack Friars, Pied Friars, and Crutched Friars. Longchamp was, in fact, the last royal Franciscan foundation of Louis's reign, though the king continued to give generously to existing houses.[101] From the perspectives of both the Capetian court and the Franciscan hierarchy, Isabelle's royal abbey for Franciscan women was an important creation that afforded its founder a wide latitude of influence at just the moment when French royal support was indispensable.

Finally, Alexander may have been looking to Isabelle's experiment as a solution to the long-standing problem of women and the Franciscan Order. Isabelle was bringing a female Franciscan form of life to the environs of Paris for the first time. The precedent set by such a centrally located house, one backed by the royal family and tied to the most important Franciscan figures at the University of Paris, could not help but be influential. From the papal perspective, the dilemma had always been how best to incorporate mendicant-inspired women's communities into the ecclesiastical hierarchy while satisfying both the women's desire for a mendicant identity and the male orders' reluctance to be tied to these communities. Alexander may have hoped that a new rule associated with the prestige of the French court—one that sidestepped the controversial issue of poverty and granted closer ties to the Franciscans without actually calling the women "Franciscans" or *Sorores minores*—might open up a widely acceptable solution to this difficult situation. He was hardly advancing this hope explicitly; his caution is evident in the tension found within his preamble to the rule, noted above, where he seems undecided as to whether the rule will apply to a single house or to a wider order. But since the text of the rule refers repeatedly to an order, and indeed includes provisions such as accommodations for cardinals that seem more appropriate to an entire order than to a single house, Alexander may well have been contemplating the rule's potential to apply to a large number of communities.

It was thus the combination of Isabelle's status as royal laywoman, her esteem in the eyes of Alexander IV, Franciscan desires to develop and maintain allies within the royal court, and the fluid nature of relations between male and female Franciscans that explains Isabelle's ability to negotiate with the Franciscans and the papal curia. Yet her vision remained only partially fulfilled in 1259, since Alexander would not allow the title of *Sorores minores* for the sisters of the new abbey. It was this check to Isabelle's ambitions, perhaps more than any other issue, that sparked her push for a revised version of the rule in 1263.

CHAPTER FOUR

A *Minor* Triumph

The Revised Rule of 1263 and Its Impact

F rench scholar Jacques Dalarun has recently ruminated over a paradox inherent in the career of Francis of Assisi. In order to found a new form of religious life that valorized humility, Francis had to be arrogant enough to think that God had chosen him for this mission, that existing forms of life were insufficient, and that his innovation was worthy of papal approval.[1] Perhaps true humility would not have permitted him to confront authority in the ways necessary to achieve these goals, yet, without steadfast resolve, the institutional forms establishing the humble path of the *Fratres minores* could not have been secured. Isabelle of France exhibits the same paradoxical juxtaposition of humility and resolution. In order to follow her own vision, she had to assert herself against reluctant ecclesiastical authorities in a most unhumble manner. The results of this paradox are displayed nowhere so clearly as in Longchamp's revised Rule of 1263.

The first rule of 1259 did not hold sway at Longchamp for long. Only four and one-half years after its approval, and only three years after the entry of the first nuns to Longchamp, a revised rule was granted to the abbey by the new pope, Urban IV, on 27 July 1263.[2] What factors could have led to such a speedy revision? We have already seen that Isabelle of France's collaboration with her Franciscan co-authors was part of the negotiations for the original Rule of 1259. There is no reason to think that

Bonaventure and his fellow friars played a direct authorial role in the revision of 1263 or that their wishes were behind the specific changes that it instituted.

Instead, the revised Rule of 1263 probably resulted from two facts. First, the Rule of 1259 had not satisfied Isabelle's vision for her abbey and had led her to continue to fight for the elements that she thought were lacking. Second, the debate over the relationship of women to the Franciscan Order came to a head after Alexander IV's death in 1261. New protests by the male Franciscans at the beginning of Urban IV's pontificate raised the possibility that all relations with female communities would be renegotiated, perhaps to Longchamp's detriment. But this reopening of the question also offered Isabelle the possibility of securing new concessions in a moment of uncertainty. Both because the original rule had left Isabelle frustrated and because she feared that sweeping changes in the Franciscan Order would place her house's institutional status in jeopardy, she secured the revised Rule of 1263.

This success necessitates a reassessment of the importance of Isabelle of France's impact on Franciscan history. Just as Francis and Clare were as important for their institutional influence as for their personal struggles, so did Isabelle's intervention leave a substantial, if underrated, legacy. Isabelle's rule and its formation of an order of *Sorores minores* encapsulated a vision of female Franciscanism that resonated widely with thirteenth- and fourteenth-century women. By putting this vision into institutional form, Isabelle gave a voice to these women's demands and ideals.

ISABELLE, LOUIS, AND LONGCHAMP, 1260–1263

By early 1259, Longchamp had its first rule, strong royal support, and papal privileges—all it needed was residents. The first nuns took the veil on 23 June 1260. The earliest evidence for the date and circumstances of this ceremony comes from the introduction to the abbey's first necrology, compiled in 1325, which recorded that "in the year 1260 the day before the feast of St. John the Baptist, which was on a Wednesday, the convent of *Soeurs mineures* of the Humility of Our Lady of Longchamp was veiled and enclosed. Present were Monseigneur Saint Louis who was then the King of France, Madame Isabelle his sister who founded the said church from her own funds, and brother William of Harcombourg, who was then the [Franciscan] Minister of France, and many other people not named here."³

As with the initial laying of the first stone for the abbey, Louis IX appeared as prominently as Isabelle on this important occasion. Agnes of Harcourt's *Letter* confirms Louis's presence at the entry of the first nuns and goes on to detail his continued attention to the abbey in its early days. "Soon after" the initial enclosure, Louis and Isabelle together attended a chapter meeting, where the king emphasized his own humility by "seat[ing] himself right down on our level." The scene recalls Louis's penchant for taking a place among the brothers during monastic gatherings, as described by contemporaries such as Salimbene and Guillaume of St. Pathus,⁴ but here it is a community of nuns rather than monks. In spite of (or perhaps capitalizing on) this humble posture, Louis proceeded to take center stage and assumed the role of preacher. According to Agnes, "he gave the first sermon and teaching that we had had since we had entered there, and he said that we ought to take as our example Monseigneur Saint Francis and Madame Saint Clare and other saints who lived with such sanctity and perfection, and that we should begin so high that the others who would come after us would not be able to equal us, and that we should be a mirror to all the other women of religion and lead such a life that the others could take it as a good example."⁵

Louis's assumption of the role of preacher here is striking. Though he liked to moralize in public and may have occasionally functioned as an informal "preacher" for his own crusade efforts, this seems to be a unique episode that highlights the depth of his personal investment in the foundation of Longchamp.⁶ Just as noteworthy is his pointed reference to Francis and Clare. For all Louis's well-known attraction to the mendicant orders, there is little evidence for his own thoughts on Francis, let alone on Clare. Thus, the rituals surrounding the first days of Longchamp took on great importance for both Isabelle and Louis. As Agnes's *Letter* puts it, the royal sister and brother were Mother and Father to the nuns. Nor did Louis's support for the abbey stop at ritual and ceremony. Again according to Agnes, Louis made a habit of checking up on the nuns' well-being, of visiting the sick on his trips to the abbey and seeing that they had enough to eat. He gave the nuns a sliver of the True Cross and one of the precious thorns from the recently acquired Crown as well as rents, money, and firewood.⁷

While Louis had urged the sisters of Longchamp to set an unparalleled example to the world, practical guidance and internal leadership were still needed for this undertaking. Accordingly, some experienced sisters from the Franciscan house at Reims came to instruct the new nuns of Longchamp in the religious life. In a bull dated 20 November 1261 the new pope, Urban IV, directed the guardian of the Franciscans in Paris to absolve these sisters of their vows to Reims so that they could remain at Longchamp permanently, since the king had asked this favor of him.[8] Five of these sisters can probably be identified through the 1325 necrology: Sisters Gile of Reims, Étienne of Reims, Ade of Reims, Angre of Reims, and Isabelle of Venice of Reims, "who was president in the first year that the convent was veiled, because there was no abbess in that year." Thus, Louis's intervention, very likely reflecting his sister's wishes, secured the permanent residence of these sisters as well as the community's first leader.

Beyond these women from Reims, there is little evidence as to how the new nuns of Longchamp were recruited. The necrology of 1325, taken together with other documents, allows ten additional women to be identified as among the first to take the veil.[9] Though the evidence is sketchy, most of these fifteen women would seem to have been drawn mainly from the middle and upper nobility, and several must have come from Isabelle of France's household.[10] On the other hand, Longchamp was not peopled with princesses; no royal women entered Longchamp until Blanche of France, the daughter of Philip V, in 1319, nor indeed did any women of the highest level of nobility until Marguerite and Jeanne of Brabant in 1301 and 1303.[11]

What of the princess herself during these years? Isabelle certainly had not elected to become a nun or the abbess of Longchamp. This point will be considered more closely in chapter 5, but we can note here that Agnes of Harcourt's description of the entrance of the first women to Longchamp has Isabelle arriving at the sisters' initial chapter meeting with Louis, obviously not as a common nun. But if she did not take the veil, Isabelle almost certainly moved her residence from the royal court to the grounds of Longchamp at this point. Though direct evidence is surprisingly scant, Isabelle probably constructed her own living quarters and a chapel adjacent to the abbey.[12] The surviving descriptions and depictions of Longchamp in the seventeenth and eighteenth centuries are not detailed enough to allow any confident identification of original elements in its architecture, but there is no doubt that accommodations for royal lay people existed at Longchamp from as early as the thirteenth century, and that these chambers were consistently said to have originated as Isabelle's private residence.[13]

Isabelle's position before 1263 is further revealed in two letters from neighboring monastic houses that addressed or referred to her. In March 1262, Emeline of Fleury, abbess of Montmartre, directed a letter concerning lands and rent to "the noble and wise lady Madame Isabelle, sister of the king, and to the religious and honest lady the humble abbess of the *cordelières*."[14] Similarly, in September of the same year, Thomas, abbot of Sainte-Geneviève, issued a document that made it known that his abbey had possessed rights over lands of "the new abbey of the illustrious Lady Isabelle, sister of the most excellent King of France," but at the request of "the Lord King and the Lady Isabelle," he allowed the abbey to buy out these rights.[15] In the first years of its existence, heads of neighboring religious houses thought of Longchamp as "Isabelle's abbey" and addressed petitions and correspondence to her attention as its acknowledged lay patron. It is also clear from Abbot Thomas's letter that Isabelle continued to join her brother in actively working to secure Longchamp's material status and financial well-being.[16] These two documents show Isabelle's willingness to use her influence within the monastic world of the Île-de-France, her ability to work with her brother in securing her ends, and her position at Longchamp. She was equally adept at continuing to negotiate on a wider stage.

THE REVISION OF 1263

Assessing Isabelle's Role

Several initial indications might seem to lead away from Isabelle as the principal actor behind the revised Rule of 1263. First, much as with Mansuetus's role in the genesis of the Rule of 1259, the pope in 1263 credited Simon of Brie, Cardinal of St. Cecilia, sometime papal legate to France and the future Martin IV, with having corrected the new rule.[17] That Simon would have played an advisory role is likely, given his enjoyment of royal favor and his path of advancement through the church's ranks. He had studied in Paris, then been named archdeacon of Rouen in 1254, treasurer of Tours in 1256, and counselor and keeper of the great seal to Louis IX in 1259.[18] He was elevated to cardinal on 24 December 1261, but he did not depart for Rome until 22 March 1262.[19] This interval would have given him ample opportunity to consult with Isabelle in Paris and then to have been involved in final papal approval at the curia before the new rule was issued in July 1263.[20] But Simon was hardly the real force behind the changes implemented in this rule. Indeed, as "a Frenchman whose career owed much to royal favor," it has been suggested that he was Louis's "life-long protégé," and in his subsequent papal career he has been called "the most French of thirteenth-century popes."[21] At this juncture he was acting essentially as the conduit for Capetian requests to the pope.

A second factor that tends to obscure Isabelle's role in the revision of 1263 is the language of Urban's preamble to the rule itself. Unlike Alexander's bull approving the Rule of 1259, Urban's 1263 preface makes no mention whatsoever of Isabelle. Addressing the abbess and sisters, Urban states that before any nuns had actually moved into Longchamp, Alexander had granted to the sisters of the monastery of "The Humility of the Blessed Mary" a rule "to be known with the name of *Sorores inclusae*." Urban continues:

> In turn, it has been humbly asked of us on the part of the said king [Louis], that, causing the said rule to be corrected in some chapters, we should deign out of apostolic kindness to add the word *minores* to its name. Therefore, moved by the prayers of this same king, causing this rule to be corrected by our beloved son Simon, Cardinal of S. Cecilia, so that in deed as well as in name it should be distinguished with the advances of humility . . . [and] adding to the name of this rule the said word *minores*, we have decided to establish that this may henceforth be called the rule of the *Sorores minores inclusae*, and that it be maintained as thus corrected in perpetuity in the aforementioned monastery, and in other monasteries hereafter to be founded or created by others, in which it shall happen that the sisters profess this rule.[22]

In spite of Isabelle's absence from this papal version of events, when Agnes of Harcourt's evidence that "above all things [Isabelle] desired that the sisters of her abbey would be called *Soeurs mineures*" is recalled, the princess's own desires are clearly discernible behind these passages. Isabelle—not her brother and not Simon of Brie—was the ultimate source of the request conceded in Urban's preface. A preliminary conclusion about the reasons for the revision of 1263 is thus apparent: the Rule of 1259 had not been fully acceptable to Isabelle because her chosen name was not granted to her sisters. Refusing to be thwarted, she had bided her time until the opportunity to reopen negotiations presented itself.

Given this evidence, additional testimony by Agnes as to Isabelle's comportment and to Louis's role as negotiator on her behalf falls into place. After noting Isabelle's insistence that her nuns be known as *Soeurs mineures* and that the abbey be named "The Humility of Our Lady," *The Life of Isabelle* goes on to provide more details about Isabelle's state of mind regarding the rule. The princess was "gravely ill" before it was confirmed, "so that it was as though she were languishing in her heart until this affair was accomplished." But "out of great sense and great humility," Isabelle did not want herself to request anything of the pope, and instead "all these things she would cause to be requested by Monseigneur the king Louis, her brother, whom she made chief of all her affairs, and he would do it most courteously and would send his letters and his own messages."[23]

As we have already seen, the great difficulty with Agnes's entire version of the genesis of Longchamp's rule is that she conflates the two rules of 1259 and 1263 into one. This description of Isabelle agonizing over papal approval and insisting on acting through her brother cannot apply to the Rule of 1259. Alexander's preamble to that document makes it perfectly clear that Isabelle had taken a leading role in seeking its confirmation. Agnes's portrayal of Isabelle as modestly letting her brother handle all the arrangements with the papal curia is therefore deceptive—the Rule of 1259 was granted explicitly at the request of both royal siblings. Moreover, we have clearcut evidence from *Benedicta filia tu* that Isabelle was well aware that she could expect full support in her endeavors from Alexander.

Agnes of Harcourt's description must therefore refer to the negotiations for the revised Rule of 1263. Isabelle was overwrought and unwell specifically because she was anxious to see the previously rejected name *Sorores minores* acknowledged by the pope. Lacking confidence in her influence with a new pope with whom she may not have yet developed a personal relationship, she asked Louis to exert the pressure necessary to sway the curia. Indeed, this was apparently not an isolated incident but part of a pattern of making requests of the new pope through Louis, since Urban's bull of November 1261, which granted permission for nuns from Reims to stay at Longchamp, also refers only to Louis's request as a motivating factor, though Isabelle's desires must surely have been at the root of the royal action.

The wisdom of Isabelle's strategy may be apparent in the way that Urban rewrote history in his preface of 1263, referring to the original Rule of 1259 as though it had been issued at the request of Louis alone and removing any trace of Isabelle's influence. Moreover, Urban's revisionism extended to the original name given to the nuns. He referred to them as having previously been known as *Sorores inclusae* (enclosed sisters), when in reality Alexander's preamble had called them the "Sorores Ordinis humilium ancillarum beatissimae Marie virginis gloriosae." This was a clever rhetorical gesture that allowed a difficult issue to appear less problematic. On the one hand, Urban thereby asserted that he was doing nothing more than adding a single word to an existing title, rather than instituting a wholesale change. And since the title *Sorores inclusae* had previously been used by Pope Gregory IX to refer to other "Franciscan" women,[24] Urban was subtly de-emphasizing the novelty of the Rule of 1259. But on the other hand, the word *inclusae* was crucial in saving face for the papacy and for the male Franciscans. Isabelle's request was granted, but with an explicit caveat—that her *Sorores minores* were not to evoke the wandering life of the *Fratres minores* but were to be enclosed by both vow and name. By asserting that the word *inclusae* had already been part of the nuns' title, Urban smoothed over what must have been the fundamental compromise in the revised rule—papal recognition for the name *Sorores minores* in return for Isabelle's acceptance of the qualifier *inclusae*.

In 1259, as was generally the case, the papal and Capetian courts had been engaged in multiple questions of mutual importance. The involvement of the papal legate, Mansuetus, in 1259, for instance, connects Isabelle's rule to negotiations brokered by the papacy between Louis IX and Henry III of England. By 1263, however, the political dynamic was significantly altered, with more intense papal interest focused on the French royal family. The new pope, Urban IV, himself a Frenchman (Jacques Pantaleon), had been educated in Troyes and Paris before his election to the papal throne on 29 August 1261.[25] One of the most pressing challenges of his papacy was to find a new champion to wrest the crown of Sicily from Manfred of Hohenstaufen. Attempts to get Henry III's son Edmund to pursue this task had failed, and now Urban turned to Charles of Anjou (Louis and Isabelle's younger brother). Louis had at first been against the idea but granted his sanction in May 1263. In June and July, Urban was deeply involved in negotiating Charles's acceptance of his terms for the enterprise. It was at exactly this moment that he approved Longchamp's revised rule. Simon of Brie was sent back to Paris in early 1264 to continue the negotiations with Charles, which were finally concluded by July.[26] As controversial as the title *Sorores minores* was within Franciscan circles, Urban may have decided that yielding to Isabelle and Louis was a small price to pay if this concession helped to solidify support at the French court for papal objectives in southern Italy.

Isabelle took advantage of this moment, working through the very legate who would handle negotiations on the Sicilian question, to gain papal acceptance of her remaining demands. Moreover, she made the politically astute decision to let her brother approach the pope on her behalf, thereby assuring her cause of the best possible reception while allowing Urban to concede gracefully. Historical arguments from silence always call for caution. But, in this case, Isabelle's apparent invisibility in Urban's preface to the Rule of 1263 may demonstrate her ability to test the political waters and marshal her resources in the most effective manner.

The Revisions

If one of the main reasons for the revision of 1263 was Isabelle's continuing insistence on papal approval for her chosen name for the sisters of Longchamp, what other changes did the new rule introduce, and whose desires did they reflect? Fortunately, having already subjected the language of the Rule of 1259 to detailed investigation, we can assess the modifications made in 1263 in more summary fashion.[27] Though many smaller alterations were implemented, the main changes tended to increase the autonomous power of the abbess, to allow a wider influence for the rule, and to form tighter bonds between the male Franciscan Order and the Order of *Sorores minores*.

First, the revised Rule of 1263 reflects a certain number of alterations in mundane daily regulations that must have resulted from practical difficulties discovered after three years of life at Longchamp. Urban's preface hints as much by noting that no one had yet been living at Longchamp when the Rule of 1259 was issued. Experience had led to requests for minor modifications, such as granting a lower door through which heavy items could be brought (the Rule of 1259 unrealistically envisioned a door reached only by ladder). The king is now given explicit permission to enter the abbey with up to ten associates, though this clause merely confirmed the right granted by Alexander IV's bull, *Inter alia sacra*, of 22 February 1259. The clauses from 1259 that forbade animals except cats and set aside an area within the walls for a nurse and surgeon are also removed.

More important are a whole series of small changes that continue the trend toward granting the abbess greater discretionary powers. Regulations on minor issues such as haircuts and bloodletting include new clauses permitting dispensations at the discretion of the abbess. Of greater significance are revised regulations on speech. The abbess may now allow additional days during which speech on holy and legitimate topics is permitted, and the hours may be extended on those days. Furthermore, the abbess may relax the rules requiring the veil to remain on the window of the *locutorium*, and the closing and locking of the small door through which the sisters receive communion and confession. Most clearly, a new clause is inserted specifically allowing speech with the sisters' confessors and other honest people, at the discretion of the Ministers *or* the abbess.[28] In a change summing up this explicit increase in autonomy, Alexander's paragraph enjoining the abbess and nuns not to seek dispensations or relaxations of the rule without proper permission is now altered to threaten that no Visitor or Minister should try to make changes without the approval of the nuns.[29]

Second, the new rule adopts several clauses that more clearly envision its application to multiple houses beyond the original foundation of Longchamp. For example, in the section describing the process of profession, a clause is added clarifying that it refers to everyone wanting to join this "religion in the above mentioned monastery or in others to be newly founded in which this rule will be professed."[30] If Alexander IV exhibited a certain reluctance in 1259 to specify that Longchamp's rule might apply to other houses, in 1263 this caution is thrown to the winds.

Third, the most significant alterations concern the relationship of male Franciscans and the Franciscan Order to the abbey. Though the language concerning the contentious issues of the Visitor and Procurator remains unchanged from 1259, the link between the order and Longchamp is tightened in several other ways. On a largely symbolic level, the vows of the nuns now include a reference to St. Francis (though not to Clare), the first time the *poverello* is mentioned by name in the two rules (except for a passing reference to his feast day). More concretely, all references to the existence of a chaplain are entirely omitted in the Rule of 1263. The Rule of 1259 had already reduced the importance of the chaplain compared to Innocent IV's Rule of 1247, preferring to refer to confessors, but now the term is entirely suppressed. Though this change might at first seem mainly cosmetic, the complete effacement of the position of chaplain, in fact, was almost certainly the result of a desire to eliminate a role that could be filled by non-Franciscans. This assertion is borne out by new regulations that call for Franciscan confessors in the place of chaplains. For example, the 1259 clause regulating the entry and actions of the chaplain during the burial of a sister is replaced by the stipulation that Franciscans will handle this task.[31] Similarly, within the section on visitation, the language that allowed the Visitor to correct confessors who may be living at Longchamp is rearranged and expanded into a new insistence that confessors *will* be Franciscans and *must* live at Longchamp.[32] Moreover, an earlier stipulation that confessors are to be assigned by the Minister General or Provincial Minister now omits a loophole that allowed these confessors to appoint others to act in their stead.[33] In a final change indicative of the closer relations envisioned with the order by the new rule, the clause found in the Rule of 1259 stating that neither the Ministers nor other brothers will involve themselves with the "care, disposition, and dispensation of possessions and temporal things" is removed in 1263. This move may have been intended to permit Franciscans to licitly act as Procurators.

Why, then, were these changes made? It has long been suggested that life proved too difficult for the delicate aristocratic women of Longchamp.[34] There is little basis for this claim, though some of the more quotidian alterations may well have been suggested by the nuns themselves. It is not difficult to imagine exasperated sisters wondering how to work out the practical aspects of using a door that could only be reached by a ladder!

But the most important revisions of 1263 were essentially the result of pressure from Isabelle of France. The strengthening of the abbess's discretionary powers is in keeping with the trend already evident in 1259 toward securing maximum autonomy for the abbess and sisters of Longchamp. I have argued in chapter 3 that these demands must have emanated from Isabelle in 1259; continuing changes in this direction in 1263 were therefore probably her work as well. Though no evidence exists to demonstrate the source of the new willingness to see Longchamp's rule serve as a blueprint for additional houses, this impetus is more likely to have come from Isabelle and Longchamp than from the Franciscan Order or the papacy, for reasons that will become more clear momentarily. Finally, the express desire to secure Franciscan confessors and ensure that non-Franciscan chaplains could not be foisted on Longchamp is distinctly in accord with Isabelle's passionate desire to see the explicitly Franciscan name of *Soeurs mineures* granted to the nuns, and just as distinctly contrary to the way that male Franciscan desires were running in 1263 (as we shall see). In sum, the Rule of 1259 had been a compromise between Isabelle, her Franciscan advisers, and Pope Alexander IV. The revised Rule of 1263 represented Isabelle's successful attempt to see her own ideas more fully instituted.

1263: A Climactic Moment

To understand the full significance of Isabelle's success in 1263, it is necessary to situate it as part of the climactic moment in the thirteenth-century history of rules for Franciscan women. The death of Alexander IV in 1261 provided an opportunity for the male Franciscans to attempt to weaken or even sever their ties to the women's houses.[35] As Protector of both the Franciscans and the Order of San Damiano (and its predecessor, the Order of the Poor Ladies of the Valley of Spoleto) since the 1220s, Alexander had long been able to keep personal control of the situation. But upon Urban IV's ascension in 1261, Cardinal John Gaetano Orsini (the future Nicholas III) became Protector of the men, and Cardinal Stephen of Hungary Protector of the women. When Stephen tried to insist that Franciscans continue to provide spiritual care to the women's houses, the friars protested and asked Pope Urban to allow them to relinquish all responsibility for the female communities. In August 1262, Urban arranged a temporary truce whereby the Franciscans' relationship to the women's houses was to be left intact until the Franciscan General Chapter to be held in Pisa beginning on Pentecost (20 May) 1263.[36] If a settlement was not reached by that time, then the friars could end their relationship to the women's houses. In anticipation of this deadline, Urban wrote on 15 May 1263 to Bonaventure and the chapter urging the order to take responsibility for their Franciscan sisters. This letter may even have contained an oblique reference to Isabelle of France, since it exhorted the friars to consider how scandalous it would be to neglect their female counterparts after they had encouraged "daughters of kings and other magnates" to embrace the order.[37] In the event, no specific agreement was reached at the General Chapter, but neither were any drastic measures taken by the order to assert its rejection of responsibility.[38] Trying to breach this impasse, on 14 July Urban reunited the two Protectorships in the hands of Cardinal Orsini and directed him to ensure that Franciscans offered spiritual care to the women's houses.[39] Cardinal Orsini and Bonaventure then agreed that the Franciscans would continue in their roles as pastoral caregivers and Visitors, but only on a voluntary basis.[40]

Bonaventure's own attitude at this juncture is made clear in a letter to the Provincial Minister of Aragon, dated 27 September 1263, wherein he complains "just how much our Order has been plagued up to now with threats, troubles, and litigation occasioned by the monasteries of the Order of St. Clare." Bonaventure sums up the situation by stating that the sisters were alleging "that the customary services provided for them by our brothers are in fact prescribed by law; thus our brothers have proposed having nothing more to do with them unless they first recognize our complete freedom by public written documents sent to the said Holy Father." But Bonaventure thought that he could announce victory, crowing that "now, through the favor of our Lord Jesus Christ and by the strenuous effort and considerable pains of our venerable father, the Lord John [Orsini], . . . we have fully achieved independence." Given Orsini's concessions, it is "entirely right that we trouble ourselves to assist our venerable Father in providing spiritual services for the monasteries of the said Order as a special favor, at least until the next general chapter." But to be certain that the voluntary nature of this decision was clear, Bonaventure stipulated that "to better safeguard our independence, it is the wish of the Lord Cardinal and myself that the above services are to be conceded only to those monasteries which will give letters or public documents stating that they accept all these services from the brothers only as a special favor."[41]

On 18 October 1263 Urban confirmed his new rule for Franciscan women, which embodied this compromise.[42] This rule transferred responsibility for the nuns directly to the Cardinal Protector rather than to the Franciscan Minister General, thereby inherently weakening the internal link between Franciscan men and women. The Protector was not required to use Franciscans as Visitors, and confessions would be heard by Franciscans or "others" deputed by the Cardinal.[43] Furthermore, the rule formally renamed the Order of San Damiano as the Order of St. Clare.

The confirmation of Isabelle's revised rule on 27 July 1263 thus came at a critical juncture in the history of the relationship between Franciscan men and women, and it secured exactly the type of relationship that the male Franciscans were fighting to avoid. Bonaventure's language in his September letter to the Provincial Minister of Aragon makes the contested nature of Isabelle's achievement abundantly clear. She had trumped the Franciscan hierarchy by committing them to pastoral care for Longchamp on a definite rather than on a voluntary basis. What seems at first to be an unremarkable continuity in the role of the Visitor between Isabelle's two rules was indeed a fundamental concession to Longchamp, and the measures in her rule that actually strengthen her house's ties to the male order ran directly against the stated goals of the friars in 1263. Given these facts, the newly raised possibility that other houses might adopt Longchamp's rule cannot have pleased the male Franciscans and therefore probably demonstrates Isabelle's widening vision of the potential influence of her form of life.

Moreover, even the majority of Franciscan women who ultimately followed Urban IV's Rule of 1263 felt the impact of Isabelle's ideas. There is no doubt that Urban's rule continued to be heavily based on Innocent IV's Rule of 1247, and not primarily on Isabelle's Rule of 1259 or 1263. But in specific areas, Isabelle's innovations seem to have been acknowledged as improvements and thus included in Urban's rule. For instance, the clause in Isabelle's rules that allows the sisters to pack up and move in case of true emergencies is reflected in a briefer acknowledgment in Urban's text that nuns might leave during "unavoidable and dangerous necessity, such as fire or hostile attack."[44] I have argued that the original clause was almost certainly a reflection of Isabelle's personal concerns. If so, they evidently made their way into Urban's rule. Similarly, the vows in the new rule follow Isabelle's by including the abbess (though called *domina abbatissa* rather than *mater*) and the vow to live *sub clausura*.[45] The thoughtful provision of naptime is also adopted.[46] The passage describing the reasons for manual labor, previously unique to Isabelle's rule, is included in Urban's, and the more liberal clause allowing speech on honest topics during certain feasts is retained.[47] The unique clause on the convent's seal is preserved with small changes in language.[48] Most striking, the abbess and sisters, rather than the Visitor, continue to be able to remove the Procurator.[49] Moreover, the structure adopted by Isabelle's Rule of 1259 and followed by her Rule of 1263 has been found more logical at times, since Urban's Rule of 1263 occasionally adheres to it, for instance, in discussing the Divine Office following clothing regulations. Undoubtedly some of these innovations that were retained by Urban's rule were the result of compromises or the desires of Isabelle's collaborators. Nevertheless, the process of writing Isabelle's rules for Longchamp led to specific changes that were then incorporated in the most widely followed rule for Franciscan women.

THE SIGNIFICANCE OF SUCCESS

Longchamp's rule attracted both attention and adherents in the aftermath of the events of 1263. Its appeal is most dramatically described in a letter that Pope Clement IV sent to Cardinal Orsini on 31 May 1266. Clement had recently been confronted by a group of Franciscan nuns who had journeyed to the curia at Viterbo to voice their demands. It had been three years since Urban IV had issued his new rule and created the Order of St. Clare, but many of the nuns were refusing to adopt his rule, thus leaving Clement, his successor, in a trying situation.[50] As he reported to Cardinal Orsini, a group of "sisters of the Order of St. Clare came to Viterbo on behalf of the sisters of many lands, whose lingering at the curia previously did not please you and which does not please us now! They all agreed on this proposition, that they would not receive your rule, but would observe either their pristine state or, if this seemed doubtful, they would accept the form of life that our beloved daughter in Christ the sister of the King of France has."[51] Clement seems to have been at a loss as to how to deal with this rebellious delegation, and he asked Cardinal Orsini to send him his thoughts on the matter without delay.

This episode raises questions of importance beyond Clement's sputtering surprise at such female effrontery. Why would this group of women, claiming to represent Franciscan sisters "of many lands,"[52] specifically demand to be given the rule negotiated for Isabelle of France's abbey of Longchamp? What was it about this rule that made it more desirable than Urban's Rule of 1263 to the sisters themselves?

Isabelle's passionate insistence on securing her favored name for her nuns offers clues to the nature of her rule's wider appeal. The name *Sorores minores* had never before been officially sanctioned.[53] Indeed, Francis himself was said to have explicitly rejected it.[54] For its part, the papal curia had been steadfast in refusing to acknowledge the legitimacy of this title since at least the 1240s. As early as 1241, Pope Gregory IX decried the sight of women wandering barefoot through the cities, wearing the habit of the nuns of San Damiano without permission and calling themselves *Minoretas*.[55] In 1246, 1250, and 1251, Innocent IV complained to the bishops of Lombardy, France, and England about the "usurpation of the name of *Sorores minores*, which is not even due to the sisters of the Order of San Damiano." By this usurpation, moreover, Innocent lamented that "the purity of the beloved Order of *Fratres minores* is darkened with the cloud of infamy."[56] The language here is striking—not only are these women unsanctioned in and of themselves, but the coveted title of *Sorores minores* is also so far beyond the pale that not even proper Franciscan nuns may adopt it, and so dangerous that its invocation by uncloistered women threatens to sully the reputation of the male Franciscans. In 1257, at about the time when Isabelle was negotiating her first rule with her team of Franciscans, Alexander IV directed one of these denunciations to Gascony and Aquitaine, and as late as 1261 the same pope sent a similar bull to the bishops of Germany.[57] Small wonder, then, that Alexander was unwilling to grant this title to Isabelle's nuns in spite of his evident respect for the princess.

But, as these bulls themselves demonstrate, there is overwhelming evidence that female communities sharing Franciscan ideals chose this name almost from the beginning of the mendicant movement and continued to do so through Isabelle's day. For instance, in his famous letter of 1216 describing the early religious movement in Italy, Jacques de Vitry referred to seeing "many wealthy lay people of both sexes who flee the world leaving behind all things for Christ, who were called *Fratres minores* and *Sorores minores*."[58] Also in Italy, a community at Verona was made up of *Sorores minores* in 1224, as was a group in Milan in the 1240s. The bishop of Asti referred between 1236 and 1244 to a new monastery living "in habitu sororum minorum," and the *Sorores minores* of Novara enjoyed the support of the local bishop in 1252.[59] In Northampton, England, a community of five *Sorores minores* is mentioned in the same year.[60] In France, when Thibaud V of Champagne (husband of Isabelle of France's niece Isabelle) made his will in 1257, he left a legacy to "nostre abbaie de Provins de Serors Menors."[61] The Provençal *Life of St. Douceline* refers to "las Sorres Menors de Jenoa" (Genoa), probably before 1240.[62] Undoubtedly, further examples could be gathered.[63]

Indeed, the sisters of Longchamp were commonly referred to as *Sorores minores* even before Urban approved this appellation in 1263. Documents recording transactions with the abbey showed some uncertainty about the proper name for the sisters before 1262. For instance, in May 1261, still in the first year of the house's existence, the instrument by which three novice sisters made over all their worldly possessions to Longchamp referred to "the monastery or church newly founded near the village of Saint Cloud of the Order of Saint Damian and Saint Elizabeth."[64] But at least four documents dated between February and September 1262 (new style) refer to the abbey as the "Monasterium Sororum Minorum Inclusarum Humilitatis Beate Marie iuxta Sanctum Clodoaldum."[65] Evidently, Isabelle and her community had not waited for formal papal approval before adopting this title.

Isabelle's championing of this name, therefore, represented a push for explicit recognition of a title that many women across Europe had wanted to claim for themselves for decades. It was an attempt to appropriate and legitimate a forbidden label. Small communities of women with little influence could not realistically hope to counter the refusal of the male Franciscans and the papal curia to accept a religious identity centered on this term. The sister of the king of France could.

The title *Sorores minores* must have appealed for two reasons. First was its explicit assurance of a place for women within the Franciscan "family." Words such as *frater* and *soror* necessarily imply family relationships.[66] One can, of course, have only brothers or only sisters. The designation *Fratres minores* could evoke the single-sex link between brothers, as in a "band of brothers." Isabelle's term *Sorores minores* no doubt had a similar resonance— the women were to be sisters to each other. But the protracted struggle of women's communities to adopt this contested term underscores the importance of another sibling relationship, that of the sisters to their brothers. In the context of thirteenth-century Franciscan history, the title *Sorores* was more than a monastic commonplace. It was a claim to membership in the Franciscan family.

It seems likely that the women who came to Viterbo in 1266 saw the insistence on the title *Sorores minores* in this light. More specifically, women who were looking to return to their order's "pristine state" probably understood the title as evoking the roots of the religious movement of the thirteenth century, when Jacques de Vitry could write of "*Fratres minores* and *Sorores minores*" working side by side.[67] In terms of formal recognition of gendered equality within the Franciscan world, Isabelle's rule imagined both a step forward and a symbolic return to the ideals of the early mendicant movement.[68] Isabelle wanted to be certain that her sisters were *Franciscans*, that they were recognized as such by the society around them and especially by the male order.

Moreover, the Franciscan identity promised by this title was buttressed by the very real institutional measures implemented in Isabelle's rule. For the Order of *Sorores minores*, the Visitor would be a Franciscans, resident confessors would be Franciscans, and the Franciscan Minister General would remain responsible for the sisters; none of these things was assured for the Order of St. Clare. At the same time, the increased discretionary authority placed in the hands of the abbess by Isabelle's rule ensured that the sisters would have maximum opportunity to protect their own views on day-to-day affairs. Iron-clad links to the male order, combined with practical autonomy—these were undoubtedly attractive attributes for other women's communities faced with a choice of accepting the new Order of St. Clare or looking for alternatives that better matched their ideals.

The second aspect of the rule's appeal involved Isabelle's focus on the Franciscan virtue of humility, as evoked by the word *minores*.[69] In this regard, one might view Clare and Isabelle as effectively splitting Francis's legacy of poverty and humility between them. Though it is perhaps a bit of a caricature, it is commonly said that Clare herself narrowed her idea of a Franciscan vocation to a single-minded adherence to the ideal of poverty, clinging to the aspect of Francis's legacy that she thought that cloistered women could embrace. For Isabelle, by contrast, poverty was not a particularly important issue. In her own life, she used her money and resources for charitable purposes and for the founding of her abbey. She lived simply but retained the means to distribute alms to the needy. A complete rejection of all association with money and possessions was not at all her ideal.

Instead, Isabelle imagined a female Franciscan identity rooted in humility. Besides her insistence on the title *Sorores minores*, the most obvious evidence for the conscious promotion of humility in Isabelle's mind is her choice of the formal name of her abbey. The significance of the unique title of L'Humilité-de-Notre-Dame becomes apparent in comparison with the official name given by Blanche of Castile to her Cistercian monastery of Maubuisson, Notre-Dame-la-Royale. Isabelle opted to emphasize the Virgin Mary's humility where her mother had thought to stress her royalty. Longchamp's seal also associated Franciscanism, the Virgin, and humility,[70] as seen in a well-preserved example attached to a document issued by Agnes of Harcourt as abbess in 1266. At the bottom is St. Francis, with stigmata, preaching to the birds, and above him is the Virgin holding the Christ Child in her arms. The legend around the outside reads: "Convent[us] Sor[orum] Minor[orum] I[n]clusar[um] Hu[m]ilitat[is] Be[atae] Ma[riae]."[71] The image of Francis together with the words *Sorores minores* seeks to legitimate this title as a female Franciscan inheritance, while the juxtaposition of Mary and Francis links the virtue of humility to the imitation of both figures.

Agnes of Harcourt's testimony, moreover, emphasizes Isabelle's conscious cultivation of humility at every turn. In the opening to the *Life* she portrays Isabelle as especially learning the biblical lesson to be "humble of heart." She ties Isabelle's humility to her ultimate rejection of finery, her obedience to her confessors, her visits to the sick, and her reason for not writing to the pope directly. Indeed, Agnes says that Isabelle ended her life "in great humility and charity." Some of these descriptions may tell us more about Agnes's image of Isabelle than about the princess herself and may be problematic attempts to shape the reader's perceptions. Nevertheless, Isabelle's clear statement in choosing the name of her abbey and the title for her sisters allows us to give general credence to Agnes's picture. Isabelle consciously projected herself as a woman who prized humility above all else.

In part, this identification of humility as the supreme virtue of female Franciscanism may have been encouraged by Franciscan advisers such as Gilbert of Tournai. Gilbert, in his letter of advice to the princess, did not choose to mention poverty in any context. Instead, he made humility (in conjunction with virginity) one of his main themes. The consciousness of his choice is more apparent in contrast with several of his model sermons on female saints associated with the Franciscan Order. For instance, in a sermon on St. Elizabeth of Hungary, Gilbert describes her as a "noble woman" who "suffered poverty for Christ and lived by manual labor."[72] In his same collection of sermons *de sanctis*, Gilbert authored one of the earliest and most widely distributed sermons on St. Clare. Here, Gilbert considers Clare as the Bride of Christ, a betrothal "initiated in her virginity, ratified in the poverty of religion, and consummated in humility."[73] Thus, while Gilbert saw poverty as a key attribute for these established (and dead) female Franciscan saints, he chose instead to push the sister of the king of France toward a focus on humility as the center of her spiritual life. Humility was also one of Bonaventure's favorite topics when preaching to Franciscan women, though we cannot be certain exactly how he might have tailored this message to Isabelle when preaching in her presence.[74]

To this extent, Isabelle's focus on humility rather than on poverty as the most important Franciscan virtue probably pleased friars such as Gilbert and Bonaventure. But Isabelle interpreted the humble life by incorporating elements typical of the royal piety of her mother and brother rather than by simply following Francis's model. It has recently been emphasized that Francis, in effect, passed over the part of the Gospels' message found in Matthew 25, which promised that at the Last Judgment eternal reward awaited those who had fed the hungry, clothed the naked, and cared for the sick. Instead, Francis was inspired by biblical passages that emphasized

Jesus' voluntary poverty as an end in itself; he chose to give up all possessions as an example of perfect poverty rather than to use money and material goods to care for the poor.[75]

Agnes of Harcourt gives us very little information about Isabelle's reading of the Bible. She does tell us, however, that the princess "strove greatly to accomplish the words of the Gospel, especially those works of mercy that our Lord says in the Gospel he will praise at the Last Judgment."[76] Isabelle presumably had Matthew 25 or a similar passage in mind. For the princess, then, the preeminent command of the Gospels was to carry out works of mercy toward the poor. Thus, many of the actions in the *Life* that define Isabelle's sanctity link humility with concern for the needy. Humility held a paradoxical appeal for devout royal figures such as Isabelle (or Louis) as a way of emphasizing the depth of their piety.[77] It was perhaps natural for the princess to embrace this element in Francis's legacy. But in doing so she offered a version of female Franciscanism that emphasized identification with the "lesser" elements of society more than with poverty for its own sake.

Thus, part of the appeal of Isabelle's rule must have rested on its insistence that a female Franciscan identity could be grounded in humility, rather than in absolute poverty. "Lesserness"—or *minorité*, in the useful French formulation—as Francis's original ideal embraced both poverty and humility.[78] Where Clare of Assisi and some communities influenced by her chose one path, Isabelle emphasized the other. Neither adherence to Clare's model nor the single issue of absolute poverty can be assumed to be the uniquely distinguishing attribute of all Franciscan women in this period.[79] Scholars such as Maria Pia Alberzoni have effectively pointed out the amorphous nature and varying backgrounds of women's communities associated with Franciscan ideals at this time.[80] Women's communities inspired by the *vita apostolica* worked out the institutional aspect of their lives within the uncertain atmosphere engendered by the papacy's recurring struggle to define their relationship to the mendicant orders.[81] Clare's insistence on absolute poverty made her a controversial and influential figure, but perhaps one more often admired than imitated by the second half of the thirteenth century.

In practical terms, moreover, Longchamp's rule was an alternative not to Clare's own vision but to Urban IV's newly instituted Order of St. Clare.

Clare's Rule of 1253, only grudgingly granted to San Damiano, was not a viable option for most women's communities in the later thirteenth century. As important a figure as was Clare in her own right, her fame also made her a symbol to be manipulated and promoted in accordance with papal desires. As early as 1227, when Gregory IX created the Order of San Damiano, the papacy was already trying to employ Clare's community as a nominal model while sharply limiting the application of her own desires for strict poverty.[82] Urban's creation of the Order of St. Clare in 1263 was an attempt to use the recently canonized saint as a symbol for a newly homogenized order, to insist by a sort of sleight-of-hand that Clare's model was normative, even as the rule for this new order rejected her prized privilege of poverty. The label "followers of Clare" was blanketed upon Franciscan women at the same time that the link between her name and poverty was broken. It should not be surprising, therefore, that many women might have thought that an Order of *Sorores Minores*, grounded in the ideal of Franciscan humility, claiming affiliation with and inspiration from the *Fratres minores*, and guaranteed institutional incorporation into the Franciscan family, came closer to their religious goals than did the Order of St. Clare.

THE SPREAD OF ISABELLE'S RULE

The Franciscan women who besieged the curia at Viterbo in 1266 were not the only ones who found Isabelle's rule enticing. Royal women and other female patrons frequently chose to request Longchamp's rule when founding new Franciscan houses in the later thirteenth and fourteenth centuries.[83] Not surprisingly, Isabelle's rule had its first successes in France, particularly with houses closely associated with the royal family. The first community besides Longchamp to receive permission to follow Isabelle's rule was Sainte-Catherine of Provins. This house had been founded by Thibaud IV of Champagne (also known as Thibaud I of Navarre) and his wife Marguerite around 1247. It is not clear what rule this community originally followed, but Urban IV's bull of 22 June 1264 granted the request of Thibaud V of Champagne (Thibaud II of Navarre), that the house be allowed to follow Longchamp's rule.[84] Provins was thus the only other house to adopt Longchamp's rule during Isabelle of France's lifetime. Since

Thibaud V was married to Isabelle, the daughter of Louis IX, the connection of Longchamp's rule to his wife's aunt would have been well known and must have been part of its attraction.

A second French community to follow Longchamp's rule was, if anything, even more closely tied to the royal family. The house that became known as Saint-Marcel (or Lourcine) seems to have been founded originally at Troyes by the same Thibaud V and his wife around 1268 (shortly before both of their deaths) with the support of Louis IX.[85] The first abbess is said to have been Giles of Sens. This woman had been governess to Louis's daughters, retired to Longchamp in the 1260s, and then took four sisters from that house with her when she went to Troyes.[86] The house was refounded between 1284 and 1289 on the outskirts of Paris in the Faubourg Saint-Marcel thanks to a gift of new residences by a canon of Saint-Omer named Galien of Pise.[87] Marguerite of Provence (Louis IX's widow) helped to arrange the refoundation, and she and her daughter Blanche then retired to Saint-Marcel and became its major benefactors.[88] Pope Honorius IV referred to Saint-Marcel following Longchamp's rule as early as 1287, though the nuns do not seem to have entered their new residence until 1289.[89] The grant of the rule was confirmed by Pope Nicholas IV in 1290 at the request of the royal family, especially the three living queens of France.[90] Here again the spread of the rule was a family matter, but we also see evidence of the sisters of Longchamp playing the role of "ambassadors" for their rule and physically moving to the new house.

At about the same time, the abbey of La-Garde-de-Notre-Dame at La Guiche (in Blois) was founded by Jean of Châtillon, Count of Blois, his wife Alix, and their daughter Jeanne, the wife of Louis IX's son, Pierre of Alençon. Plans for the new house were put in motion by 1277, and in 1285 exemption bulls and Longchamp's rule were granted by Martin IV.[91] Once again the sisters of Longchamp were involved in transplanting the rule, since Julianne of Troyes, one-time abbess of Longchamp, became first abbess at La Guiche.[92]

At the end of the thirteenth century, Blanche of Navarre, the daughter of Robert of Artois and therefore the niece of Isabelle of France and St. Louis, founded the royal abbey of Nogent-l'Artaud in 1299. Blanche donated a substantial endowment to her new house and was probably instrumental in selecting Isabelle's rule for the abbey.[93] She had become queen of Navarre through her first marriage to Henry the Fat of Navarre (the brother of Thibaud V of Champagne) and was subsequently the wife of Edmund, Earl of Lancaster, the brother of Edward I of England.[94] Somewhat later, in 1309, Philip IV began the foundation of the female Franciscan abbey of Moncel.[95] Benedict XII granted Longchamp's rule to the abbey in 1335, and several of Longchamp's nuns are known to have gone to Moncel to help get it off the ground.[96] In the south of modern-day France, the female Franciscan abbey at Toulouse has been referred to as following Longchamp's rule. Founded by 1247, it is not clear when or under what circumstances the sisters of Toulouse adopted Longchamp's form of life.[97] Finally, Longchamp's rule continued to attract adherents in France after the fourteenth century. The house of Reims may have adopted it in 1507, and a daughter house of Saint-Marcel, the Petites Cordelières of Paris founded in the seventeenth century, probably followed it as well.[98]

Thus, Longchamp's rule was spread to other French Franciscan houses associated with the royal family, particularly through the agency of its women. It seems likely that Isabelle's personal example was important here; these royal women themselves had often known Isabelle and wanted their new foundations to follow their kinswoman's form of life. Marguerite of Provence's close association with the founding of Longchamp will be recalled. Now, two decades after Isabelle's death, not only Marguerite but also her daughters Isabelle and Blanche, her niece Blanche of Navarre, and her daughter-in-law Jeanne of Blois chose to associate themselves with new Franciscan abbeys and to ensure that they professed Isabelle's own rule. It is possible to discern here a distinct shift in the patronage of French royal women. Without unduly oversimplifying the picture of royal monastic patronage in the period, Blanche of Castile is well known as a consistent supporter of the Cistercians, having founded the royal abbeys of Maubuisson and Lys in the first half of the thirteenth century. As the evidence given above shows, however, the next two generations of royal women often chose to favor Franciscan foundations. A shift toward the mendicant orders would undoubtedly have occurred in any case, simply as a sign of the times, but Isabelle's example and the availability of her rule also provided women such as Marguerite of Provence with a model for their own patronage.

As important as Longchamp's rule was in France, it had its greatest geographic success in England. Though there is evidence for the existence of women claiming affiliation with the Franciscans in earlier decades, the first formal communities of Franciscan women were not founded in England until 1293–94, at London (known as Aldgate) and Waterbeach (near Cambridge).[99] The house at London was founded by Blanche of Navarre, the same woman who would found Nogent-l'Artaud.[100] The foundress of Waterbeach was Denise of Munchensey. Whether she herself had previous contacts with abbeys inspired by Isabelle's rule is not clear, but the first four nuns of her house came from France, very likely from Longchamp. Indeed, the first abbess of Waterbeach was almost certainly Jeanne of Nevers, fifth abbess of Longchamp.[101] Later houses were founded at Denny (a manor situated near Waterbeach; the two houses existed side by side for a time before Waterbeach's disappearance) around 1342 by Marie of St. Pol,[102] Countess of Pembroke and a descendant of both Blanche of Navarre and Denise of Munchensey, and at Bruisyard in Suffolk between 1364 and 1367 by Maud of Lancaster, Countess of Ulster and a granddaughter of Blanche of Navarre. These were the only medieval houses of Franciscan women ever founded in England, and all followed Isabelle's rule before they were dissolved in Henry VIII's reformation.

Thus, the history of Franciscan women in England further demonstrates the way in which royal women advanced the spread of Longchamp's rule. In particular, Blanche of Navarre emerges as a sort of godmother to Isabelle's rule—not only did she found one of the French houses that followed it, but she also oversaw its implementation in England. Moreover, for several decades in the late thirteenth and early fourteenth centuries, sisters from Longchamp were traveling as far as England to help found new communities, with least two abbesses transferring to other houses directly upon finishing their terms at Longchamp.

Longchamp's rule was followed farther south as well. In Italy, at least one house's adoption of this rule is well documented. This community was first founded by Margherita Colonna (sister of Roman Senator Giovanni and Cardinal Giacomo Colonna) near Palestrina, and after her death in 1280 the women moved to San Silvestro in Capite in Rome. In 1285, Honorius IV granted Longchamp's rule to the newly transplanted sisters.[103] Moreover, one recent scholar adds San Lorenzo in Panisperna (Rome), Giovanizza, and Cuneo to the list of Italian houses following the rule.[104] Finally, at least one house in Spain adopted Longchamp's form of life. In

November 1290, Pope Nicholas IV granted to the house of Allariz in León (Galicia), founded by Alfonso X's estranged queen Violante of Aragon, the rule that he had already given to the house in Blois—which is to say, Isabelle's Rule of 1263.[105]

All told, at least twelve and perhaps as many as fifteen houses across Europe are known to have been following Longchamp's rule by the mid-fourteenth century, and this list is unlikely to be complete. By way of comparison, only a handful of houses adhered to Clare of Assisi's rule in this period.[106] It was Isabelle's rule, and her order of *Sorores minores*, that provided the main alternative to Urban's Order of St. Clare until the fifteenth-century Observant and Colettine reforms placed new emphasis on returning to Clare's form of life.

Chapters 3 and 4 have explored Isabelle of France's relationship with the Franciscan Order and have sought to demonstrate both the nature of her own ideas and her impact on the institutional history of women's Franciscanism. Isabelle turned the support and encouragement provided by her royal status and reputation into the ability to negotiate a new rule, a singular achievement for any medieval woman but especially significant given the fierce battle over the institutional links between men and women in the Franciscan Order. But if Isabelle's greatest institutional impact was in the realm of Franciscan history, she also continued to play a role as a specifically royal figure. Let us turn to the last years of her life, to her death and the miraculous events recorded around it, to reconstruct the final flowering of her reputation as a royal saint.

CHAPTER FIVE

Between Court and Cloister

Life and Death at Longchamp

Sometime between 1260 and 1270, Sara of Houpelines, one of Longchamp's nuns, became ill with a mysterious disease that left her skin covered with blotches, causing her sisters to despair for her life. But all was not lost, for, according to Agnes of Harcourt, "Madame our holy mother came among us and looked pityingly at her and touched the malady with her blessed hands, and soon after the sister was entirely cured."[1] The "mother" was, of course, Isabelle of France. Agnes's rather terse account of Sister Sara's recovery demonstrates Isabelle's developing role not only as royal patron to the nuns of Longchamp but also as "saint-in-residence," an immediate source of holy comfort. Indeed, Agnes's depiction focuses less on belief than on power. Isabelle seems to sweep into the room, coming "among us" apparently unbidden, to intervene with miraculous efficacy. To judge from this portrayal, Isabelle herself was willing to play the role of saintly intercessor in a very visible fashion. But such moments did have their effect, since Agnes's later accounts of Isabelle's posthumous miracles repeatedly stress the nuns' growing devotion to Isabelle's cult.

Chapters 5 and 6 address the final decade of Isabelle's life and the early development of her cult. Rejecting the role of simple nun, to the end of her life Isabelle straddled the line between court and cloister, working to make Longchamp a center of pilgrimage and a site for royal burials and remembrance. By the time of her death, Longchamp was very much part of the mental map of pious people around the north of France who were seeking access to spiritual power and miraculous cures. And as Isabelle may well have anticipated, her ultimate contribution to Longchamp's attraction for pilgrims would be the reputed power of her own body and tomb.

Did Isabelle of France Become a Nun?

Isabelle's importance as a specifically royal and Capetian saint was enhanced by the fact that she remained a laywoman, that she kept one foot at court even as she planted the other firmly at Longchamp. Chapter 4 has already noted evidence indicating that after 1260 Isabelle was living as a laywoman on the abbey grounds and had not taken the veil. Specifically, letters written to her or mentioning her in the first few years of Longchamp's existence do not refer to her as a nun, but instead treat her as resident royal lay patron.

This was the position she maintained until her death; Isabelle never did become a nun. But the truth of this assertion is in need of definitive corroboration, since even careful modern scholars refer to her as having been a sister at Longchamp or as having served as abbess.[2] The evidence, however, is clear. No document from Isabelle's lifetime refers to her as ever having been a nun or even suggests the possibility in any serious way. Papal bulls (discussed below) addressed to her in 1267 and 1268 do not offer any hint that she was a religious. The abbey's earliest necrology, composed in 1325, invokes Isabelle's memory in its preamble as the house's founder but does not list her among the deceased nuns. It is inconceivable that in only sixty-five years after Isabelle's death, the nuns of Longchamp could have forgotten that she had been one of them, nor is it likely that they would have found it somehow to their advantage to obscure the fact of her profession. By the same token, neither any extant manuscript produced at Longchamp or commissioned by its nuns nor any printed biography associated with Longchamp ever claimed Isabelle as a sister. In addition, the 1325 necrology and other supporting documents from Longchamp's archives provide the names of all the early abbesses of Longchamp, leaving no doubt whatsoever that Isabelle did not serve in this capacity.[3]

Agnes of Harcourt certainly does not relate that Isabelle ever became a nun, but neither does she make a definite statement to the contrary. In spite of this reticence, a close reading of Agnes's works does further confirm that Isabelle remained a laywoman to the last days of her life. For instance, when reporting the princess's early battles with her mother over finery, Agnes mentions that "she told me with her own mouth that she had just as good a heart and was just as devoted to our Lord when she had these rich ornaments on her head and on her body as she had *when she had more religious attire.*"[4] Agnes could have explicitly contrasted Isabelle's youthful clothes with her later nun's habit, had she ever worn one, but she mentions only a subsequent, "more religious" mode of dress. Similarly, in describing Isabelle's obsession with penance and confession, Agnes says that she "would be very obedient to him [her confessor] *as though* she were a woman of religion."[5] Here the conclusion is even more clear-cut: Isabelle was humble and obedient *like* a religious, but she was not one.

Agnes's *Letter* does reveal, however, that Isabelle was buried in the habit of the Longchamp nuns. According to Agnes, at her funeral, when Louis "saw the body of Madame his sister in our church, dressed in our habit, he kneeled and bowed deeply as a sign of great devotion."[6] If the sight of Isabelle in a habit was worthy of note to Agnes and particularly moving to the king, it was because this vision was something new. Presumably, Isabelle's burial dress was the result of her own wishes, just as her mother had chosen to be interred as a Cistercian. It is unclear, though, exactly when she was actually clothed in nun's garb. The habit might have been put on her body only as it was prepared for burial, or Isabelle might have donned it just before her death. It is possible that she took formal vows on her deathbed, as Blanche is said to have done, but this seems unlikely, since Agnes of Harcourt would have mentioned such a momentous event. In any case, Isabelle remained Longchamp's lay patron up the last moments of her life.

The nature of her burial attire helps to explain subsequent claims that Isabelle had been a professed nun at Longchamp. The well-informed contemporary chronicler of Saint-Denis, Guillaume of Nangis (ca. 1250–1300), was the most important of the early authors who seem to make this assertion. A close look at Guillaume's text demonstrates the way that confusion about Isabelle's status began to spread at an early date. Here is the relevant entry from his *Chronicon*, given in both its first redaction, written by

Guillaume before 1297, and the second redaction by a continuer in the early fourteenth century:[7]

ORIGINAL REDACTION

m.cc.lix:
  Fundatum est cenobium sororum minorum iuxta sanctum clodoaldum super secana[m] a religiosa et illustri domina Ysabelle sorore Ludovici regis Francorum, ipso rege eidem monasterio redditus et possessiones congruas assignante.

SECOND REDACTION

m.cc.lix:
  In episcopatu Parisiensi fundatum est cenobium sororum minorum iuxta sanctum clodoaldum super secanam a religiosa et illustri domina Ysabelli *virgine* sorori *Sancti* Regis Francie Ludovici, ipso rege eidem monasterio possessiones et redditus *in sustentationem sororum* congruos assignante. *Que Ysabellis habitum sororum ibidem suscipiens religiose vivendo vitam suam fine laudabili terminavit.*

In the Year 1259:
  The convent of "Sorores minores" was founded near St. Cloud on the Seine, by the religious and illustrious Lady Isabelle, sister of Louis the king of the Franks, with this same king assigning to this monastery incomes and suitable possessions.

In the Year 1259:
  In the bishopric of Paris the convent of "Sorores minores" was founded near St. Cloud on the Seine, by the religious and illustrious Lady Isabelle, *virgin* sister of the *holy* King of France Louis, with this same king assigning to this monastery possessions and incomes suitable *for the sustenance of the sisters. This Isabelle, taking the habit of the sisters there, living religiously, made a praiseworthy end to her life.*
  [Italics indicate changes to the second redaction.]

  Only the later redaction included the final sentence that has sometimes been taken to indicate Isabelle's profession. Guillaume of Nangis, however, did not comment on whether she ever took the veil. The later redactor, to add a few more words about Isabelle, tacked on an ambiguous line about her praiseworthy death and religious life. Indeed, it is far from certain that even the second redaction referred to anything other than a deathbed donning of the habit.

Similarly, an anonymous fourteenth-century *Beati Ludovici vita* says of Isabelle that "she elected to stay there [Longchamp], so that she would more freely have time for contemplation. There at last she donned the habit of the sisters, and just as she had lived in a saintly way, she ended her life in a most saintly way in Christ."[8] This passage even more clearly portrays Isabelle as living at Longchamp as a lay woman until taking the habit "at last" on her deathbed.

This distinction, however, between a woman who had merely been buried in the habit of a nun and one who had actually led a professed life was increasingly obscured in both royal and Franciscan sources. Thus, a *Chronique anonyme des rois de France*, written between 1286 and 1314 and closely related to the Saint-Denis chronicles, refers to her as a *cordelière*—the common French term for a nun wearing the Franciscan cord, or belt.[9] And a now-lost life of Isabelle that was found in the royal library in the late fourteenth century was entitled *La vie de suer Ysabeau de Longchamp, qui fu suer S. Loys* (The Life of Sister Isabelle of Longchamp, who was the sister of St. Louis), indicating that Isabelle was thought to have been a "sister" not only of St. Louis but also of Longchamp.[10]

Based on these sources, perhaps, though more likely out of a general proprietary impulse, early modern Franciscan authors with no connection to Longchamp seized upon the idea that Isabelle had been a nun, just as they began to insist in this period that St. Louis had been a Franciscan tertiary.[11] Since Isabelle was undeniably a patron of the Franciscans, it may have seemed natural for Franciscan writers to assume her formal membership in their order, but their claims were based more on a mix of confusion and wishful thinking than on any hard evidence.[12]

Isabelle never became a nun, and there is no reason to think that she ever seriously intended to follow this path. Rather than adopt the role of sister or even abbess, Isabelle preferred to shape Longchamp's function and future through her less formal position as lay patron.

LIFE AT LONGCHAMP

Agnes of Harcourt provides only a partial picture of Isabelle's life at Longchamp. Her description of Isabelle's involvement in the process

of composing a new rule shows beyond doubt that the princess cared passionately about the lives of Longchamp's nuns and their institutional ties to
the Franciscan Order. But aside from this issue of the rule's genesis, only
three paragraphs of Agnes's *Life* and the first three of the miracles that
she records deal specifically with aspects of Isabelle's daily existence at
her abbey.

In these paragraphs, Agnes emphasizes her own contact with Isabelle
and her responses to her actions and statements. Agnes first links Isabelle's
customary silence with penitence. She relates that when the princess's confessor, Eudes of Rosny, would ask Isabelle why she was so quiet, she would
reply that it was in penance for having said so many frivolous things in the
past. This spirit of repentance in turn was motivated by fear of divine judgment. According to Agnes, as already related in chapter 1, Isabelle once told
her "that when she had returned from her prayer chapel, and she was leaning on her bed, she remembered the judgment of our Lord; she told me
that she trembled so hard that the bedclothes and the bedstraw trembled
mightily beneath her."[13] To this extent, Isabelle conceived of her life at
Longchamp as one of repentance and atonement.

The penultimate paragraph (before the *Life* moves on to Isabelle's miracles) is a touching testimonial by Agnes to the power of Isabelle's holy
example. She would sometimes see Isabelle reprimanding people who had
not adequately carried out the good works that she had asked them to do,
but then Isabelle would repent of her sharp words and admit her fault to
Agnes.[14] Moreover, Agnes reports that Isabelle suffered from "great mal-
adies" for two years before she died, which "she received from her sweet
groom [Jesus Christ] very sweetly and bore in great patience." At last,
"very devoutly her life ended, in perfect virginity and in very great humility
and charity."[15]

This brief sketch seeks to portray Isabelle as absorbed in a penitent piety
in her last years, but it also contains tensions and contradictions. Agnes had
earlier presented Isabelle as leading a particularly saintly youth, yet here we
see her implying that her move to Longchamp was to atone for previous
transgressions. Agnes works to create a portrait of Isabelle as devoted to
silence and penitence at Longchamp, but it is apparent that the princess was
still involved in perpetuating "good works" in the world and could lose her
temper when these tasks were not carried out satisfactorily.

Isabelle in her last years was not only a model of holiness for Agnes, but she was also a source of saintly healings, a woman who could cure through her prayers and even her touch. Of the forty miracles recorded by Agnes in the *Life*, the first three occurred while Isabelle was still alive.

In the first miracle, one of Louis IX's sergeants approached Isabelle and begged "on his knees with great tears and with joined hands" for her to pray to God for his sick child. Isabelle indeed offered her prayers. When the father returned home, he found that the boy had regained his health. Rushing back to Isabelle, he insisted that the cure had been her doing. She modestly refused to acknowledge her role in the child's recovery and made the father promise not to reveal the incident during her lifetime. He later recounted it to Queen Marguerite of Provence, who in turn related it to Agnes.

The second miracle gives a vivid impression of the princess's physical and spiritual relationship to her house. When Alice of Mucedent was suffering from a fever, she asked Agnes of Anery, the first true abbess of Longchamp, if she would ask Isabelle to pray for her recovery. Since Agnes of Anery was abbess for no more than three years beginning around June 1261, this episode occurred at the outset of Longchamp's existence.[16] The abbess refused Sister Alice's request out of reverence for Isabelle. So Alice turned to Agnes of Harcourt, who approached Isabelle, with the happy result that Alice was healed.[17] Isabelle's presence at the abbey was as an awe-inspiring and somewhat intimidating source of holiness who came among the sisters periodically. The third miracle, in which Sara of Houpelines was cured of the *orguelleux* through Isabelle's touch, has already been related at the beginning of this chapter.[18]

The first of these miracles might plausibly have taken place before Longchamp's foundation. But even if it may have had a courtly rather than a monastic setting, the story certainly shows the way in which Isabelle was seen as a woman who had special access to God and who attracted lay people in search of divine aid. The latter two miracles clearly reveal her place at Longchamp as powerful royal patron and saintly protector. Not only did nuns such as Alice of Mucedent believe that Isabelle's prayers could heal them, but also that she was imbued with the power of effecting cures through physical contact.

Isabelle herself took a visible and active role in the proceedings. Though afterward declining to take credit, she offered her specific prayers on behalf of others. If Isabelle really asked the father of the recovered boy to remain silent about her role only "during her life," then she apparently anticipated that stories about her cures would circulate freely after her death. Perhaps she even realized that someone such as Agnes of Harcourt would eventually want to gather up this testimony. More directly, on at least one occasion she engaged in a semi-public display of her healing powers, inducing a miraculous cure by laying hands upon the affected area of a sick sister.

A close reading of Agnes's account thus shows Isabelle in her last years as a woman consciously projecting the image of a taciturn penitent but still wielding practical authority and, indeed, beginning to be seen (and perhaps even to see herself) as a source of divine power. But since this portrait remains rather sketchy, it is fortunate that we can augment it with additional sources.

The surviving inventories of Longchamp's goods and assets record some of Isabelle's material possessions. As discussed in chapters 1 and 2, these registers list the books that Isabelle left to her house at her death, but the nuns also preserved luxurious items more obviously worthy of a princess. Most striking, Isabelle left a number of precious stones to Longchamp that the nuns carefully guarded and catalogued. The earliest surviving inventory, which records the abbey's possessions for 1281–1287, notes that the treasury contains "two sapphires set in gold that were Madame's."[19] Later inventories of 1305 and 1325 mention not only Isabelle's sapphires but also a silver and gold drinking cup that she had bequeathed to Longchamp.[20] The sacristy, too, held an ivory box, leggings, a down pillow, and a Veronica (an image of Christ's face, perhaps painted on leather or parchment) that had belonged to Isabelle. Other items, including an "amber apple" and an *Agnus Dei* (a wax circle impressed with the figure of a lamb) may also have been hers, though the list leaves room for doubt.[21] Vestments sewn by Isabelle herself even remained.[22]

Precious stones, golden goblets, and down pillows are not the stuff on which Franciscan hagiography thrives, but neither are they posthumous indictments of Isabelle's piety. These possessions merely confirm that she remained a princess to the end of her life. Isabelle, no doubt, cultivated a studied simplicity, and we see evidence here that she devoted herself to the task of sewing priestly garments, just as Agnes of Harcourt claimed that she had learned to do in her youth.[23] She did not, however, lead an existence of extreme deprivation or of abject poverty.[24]

Moreover, at least one item on this list—the Veronica—hints at otherwise hidden aspects of Isabelle's devotional life. Beginning in the thirteenth century, these images were popular objects for meditation, especially for enclosed women. They served as tangible reminders of Christ's passion, and as representations of his body they were connected to the rise of Eucharistic devotion in this period.[25] Perhaps this gives us some indication of how Isabelle focused her attention during those long hours of prayer described by Agnes of Harcourt.

Beyond this evidence for Isabelle's material possessions, several papal bulls issued to Longchamp or directed to Isabelle in the 1260s reveal the ways in which she sought to shape her abbey's role and reputation in a wider context. On 8 November 1266, Clement IV issued *Devotionis vestre promeretur*, which allowed the abbess and nuns of Longchamp to offer burial freely to "any heir of our beloved son in Christ the illustrious king of the Franks, or of his successors, who out of devotion may choose ecclesiastical burial at your monastery."[26] This concession must have pleased the abbess (Agnes of Harcourt at the time of this bull) and nuns, but almost certainly the princess's wishes can also be discerned behind Longchamp's request to be recognized as a site for royal burials.[27]

Isabelle's continuing ties to her family are further demonstrated by Clement IV's bull *Digne nos agere*, issued on 10 September 1267. Clement praised Isabelle for "scorning the earthly and loving the heavenly kingdom," and granted that upon her death, "your nephews and nieces, relatives, relations and kin shall freely be able to approach your tomb . . . and these same shall be able to be present personally at your burial, any customs or statutes of the place or order to the contrary notwithstanding."[28] Perhaps by the fall of 1267 she already felt herself to be nearing the end. As her thoughts turned to her approaching death, Isabelle planned to be buried at Longchamp, and she wanted to be certain that her entire family would be able to attend her funeral and to visit her tomb.

A later inventory of Longchamp's papal bulls and privileges, recorded in 1472,[29] summarizes one more concession granted by Clement to Isabelle. It would seem that Longchamp's church was not officially dedicated until 17 November 1267, since in the third year of his pontificate (begun

15 February 1267), "at the request of Madame Isabelle of France," Clement granted three years and three forty-day periods of pardon to anyone truly confessed and penitent who should devoutly visit the church and monastery of the Humility of Our Lady of Longchamp on the day of the dedication of its church or within eight days thereafter.[30] And for anyone visiting the abbey on anniversaries of this date, one year and forty days of pardon were granted. Though the lack of any surviving copy of this bull calls for caution, such indulgences were commonly granted by thirteenth-century popes, and there is no compelling reason to suspect a later forgery.[31]

A final papal letter, though hardly approving in its tone, most fully underscores the scope of Isabelle's ambition for Longchamp as a center of pilgrimage. Clement's bull of 18 April 1268, *Scias filia apostolorum*, rebuked Isabelle for mistakenly believing that she had acquired a relic of the head of the Apostle Paul, saying, "If indeed the Greeks at some time have said that they had this [head], you need not wonder; for hating the Latins it would have been easy enough for them to lie to you! . . . Therefore you will do well, if in our name you will give back what you have to our beloved son Simon the Cardinal of S. Cecilia, legate of the apostolic see, to be sent to us through him; lest if it should fall into other hands, scandal could be aroused from this with danger of error."[32] There is no record of Isabelle's response or any other indication of how she came to have this relic, though Clement evidently was under the impression that she had acquired it from Constantinople (the so-called Latin Empire had recently been reconquered by the Greeks). Perhaps it was among the items that had arrived in France after the crusaders' sack of Constantinople in 1204, making its way to Paris along with the numerous relics acquired by Louis IX in this period.[33] Whatever this skull's provenance, the news of Isabelle's claim had filtered back to the curia in Rome,[34] indicating a significant amount of publicity for Longchamp's collection of relics. Moreover, Louis IX had helped to make Longchamp a pilgrimage site by donating fragments of the true cross and the crown of thorns.[35] These items alone made the abbey worthy of any pilgrim's time and travels, but perhaps Paul's skull was intended to lure relic-seekers to Longchamp from among the sacred sites surrounding Paris.[36]

These papal bulls help to establish the nature of Isabelle's relation to her abbey and her vision for its future. Her continued ties to the court were important to her in her final years, as was the idea that she would remain in the memory of the royal family after her death. Moreover, like Blanche of Castile's foundation of Maubuisson, Longchamp was intended as a site for Capetian burial and memorial, as an auxiliary to the established royal necropolis at Saint-Denis. But Isabelle's plans to make Longchamp a center of spiritual influence sought to draw in a wider public as well. Her attempt to collect impressive (if dubious) relics such as the head of St. Paul must have reflected a desire to promote her abbey as a destination for pilgrims. Her successful petition to reward visitors with papal indulgences demonstrates even more clearly her wish to make Longchamp a magnet for the devout. As late as November 1267 Isabelle was actively using her influence to secure papal favor in this regard.

Isabelle is often described as "withdrawing" or "retiring" to Longchamp. No doubt there is an element of truth to this view. Life there afforded the princess leisure for contemplation, piety, and penance. But Isabelle did not seek to leave the world entirely. Rather, she worked to attract both her family and pious Christians to her new center of Capetian and Franciscan devotion and influence at Longchamp.

The Death of a Princess and the Birth of a Cult

Isabelle of France died during the night between 22 and 23 February 1270.[37] As the end approached, she was given the last rites by an assembly of Franciscans, including Denis of Étampes, who was resident at the abbey to administer the sacraments.[38] It is clear from the nuns' stories to Agnes that the princess's death took place at the abbey but not actually in the presence of the sisters of Longchamp. Four different nuns told of waiting anxiously on this Saturday night for word of Isabelle's fate. Sister Erembour of Cerceles heard an angelic voice proclaiming *in pace factus est locus eius* ("in peace her place has been prepared," a reference to Psalm 75:3), so she went to the abbess, Agnes of Harcourt, and learned that Isabelle had died. Sister Jeanne of Louveciennes claimed to have heard the same voice. The same night, Sister Clemence of Argas opened the window by her bed a little before the dawn office of matins, to see if she could detect anything in the courtyard that would tell her of Isabelle's fate, and she also heard "a very sweet and melodious voice above the house where she was lying." Sister Aveline of Hainault, too, perceived what the nuns held to be the glorious song of angels as they came to take the soul of Isabelle away.[39] Evidently, Isabelle's deathbed was within the grounds of Longchamp but inaccessible to the sisters of the abbey. Just as clearly, the sisters were deeply affected by her death, which was accompanied by all the signs and portents appropriate to the demise of a saint.

As she had wished, Isabelle was buried at the abbey. Her interment at Longchamp, however, is more striking than it might appear at first glance. Isabelle's father, mother, brothers, and many of her nieces and nephews followed contemporary fashion by having parts of their bodies interred at different locations.[40] Isabelle's intact burial thus emphasizes her attachment to Longchamp as the single locus for her veneration by the royal family, the nuns of Longchamp, and the wider public.[41]

Agnes of Harcourt's *Letter on Longchamp* records details of the events around Isabelle's initial burial. If Louis was not present at the moment of his sister's death, he certainly hurried to Longchamp in time to view her body before it was placed in the tomb.[42] Agnes depicts the king as watching over the nuns' private grieving: "And when Madame Isabelle, his good sister, passed away, he himself in his own person guarded the door of our enclosure so that no one entered there who should not enter," and "he kneeled and bowed deeply as a sign of great devotion, and afterwards he comforted us very sweetly and charitably."[43] Agnes's reference to "devotion" suggests that Louis, like the women of the abbey, saw his sister's death as the passing of a saintly figure. It was probably during this emotional visit to Longchamp that Louis entered the nuns' chapter and implored them to pray for the success of his second crusade, for which he was shortly to leave Paris on 15 March.[44] Indeed, anxiety over Louis's impending departure may have intensified reactions to Isabelle's death and subsequent translation.

Almost immediately, nuns and friars began to treat Isabelle as a true saint—someone who, after her death, could serve as a conduit to divine power, healings, and help. While Denis of Étampes was administering the last rites to the princess, he was suffering from a recurring fever, but he was cured "by the merits of the holy lady" and afterward described the miracle to the sisters. It was probably also Brother Denis who related a more dramatic episode. Eight days after Isabelle's death he was covering the altars of the church for Lent when a large table toppled over on him. He was not able to free himself until he invoked Isabelle's aid, but then arose easily.[45]

Denis of Étampes thus had good reason to be among the most fervent participants when Isabelle's body was translated amid great public spectacle at the beginning of March 1270.[46] Agnes's *Life* vividly records the interest and devotion that Isabelle's reburial aroused in noble women, Franciscans, and the townspeople of Paris. After "our holy Lady" had been in the tomb for only nine days, "she was raised" and put in "another coffin more suitable than the one in which she was." While Agnes does not employ a vernacular equivalent of the Latin term *translatio*, her text strongly asserts that this was indeed a translation, or transfer, of saintly relics. For like any true saint, Isabelle's body emitted no unpleasant odor, and, according to Agnes, her limbs were so pretty, plump, and flexible that she could merely have been sleeping. Indeed, at one point, as the body was being moved, the princess's eyes actually opened, yet they did not appear "dimmed by death." The nuns then removed her burial dress, since "we wanted to have this robe as a relic," and gave her new attire for her reburial.

The simple act of reburying Isabelle's body was actually an audacious statement by the women of Longchamp. By translating Isabelle's remains and treating her possessions as holy relics, Agnes and her nuns were publicly declaring her sanctity. Since the Carolingian era it had been forbidden to venerate new relics or translate a saint's body without the permission of a bishop or prince, so that the act of translation had long functioned as a semi-official legitimization of a new saint's cult.[47] By the early thirteenth century, however, the papacy had successfully reserved to itself the formal right to canonize saints, and Gregory IX in 1230 had insisted that only the pope could authorize translations of saints' bodies. Unofficial translations nevertheless continued to occur, which gave an ambiguous status to the act of moving a saintly body. While it no longer signaled official approval of a saint's cult and technically was not even a true translation of recognized relics unless formal papal canonization was involved, in the popular imagination such a moment was a visible acknowledgment that veneration was due to the translated "saint."[48] The mendicant orders, in particular, were known to employ unapproved translations as an effective means of promoting saintly status outside official ecclesiastical channels.[49] Cults begun in this manner might then generate the levels of veneration that would later lead to formal canonization.

The events of early March 1270 were carefully orchestrated by the nuns of Longchamp, their abbess Agnes of Harcourt, and probably their Franciscan advisers. A translation after only nine days was unusual; even for widely acknowledged saints a wait of a few years was expected.[50] Perhaps this speed seemed advisable in order to ensure that a bishop or other outside churchman would not get involved. But the ritual must have attracted advance publicity, because a large number of men and women arrived at Longchamp on that day. According to Agnes, the translation was witnessed by

> Madame the countess of Flanders Marguerite, and Madame Marie, her daughter, who is a nun, and the Lady of Audenarde, and many other people, and Lady Heloise, the bourgeois widow of Paris, and Monseigneur William of Quitry, canon of Vernon, who was her chaplain, and the two masons who were there to set the coffin, and all these people were in the enclosure. Outside at the window were so many people who saw her that we could not count them, both religious and secular, among whom were Brother Eudes of Rosny, master of divinity, who was her confessor, Brother Pierre of Meureville, Brother Thomas of Plexi, Brother Giles of Sally and many other Brothers Minor. And there was Madame the daughter of the Count of Flanders, who was the duchess of Brabant, and many other ladies and knights and city people and common people. We opened the window of the monastery and lifted the chest [coffin] and showed them the holy lady like an infant in its cradle. They strove as best they could to dangle their caps, their rings, their brooches, their hats, their belts, their purses to touch the holy body through great devotion, and what had touched it they kept as relics.[51]

Louis, perhaps preoccupied with preparations for the crusade, does not seem to have attended. This Lenten gathering was nevertheless notable, in particular the presence of four noble women from the Low Countries. In addition to the "Lady of Audenarde," Agnes refers to three generations of women from the ruling house of Flanders: Countess Marguerite was ruler in her own right (though sharing power with her son Guy); her daughter Marie was a Cistercian nun perhaps best known as the dedicatée of Gilbert of Tournai's *Tractatus de pace*; and the "Duchess of Brabant" was most likely Marguerite's granddaughter, also named Marguerite.[52] These women's presence not only lent an air of celebrity to the proceedings but also demonstrated the extent of Isabelle's reputation at the moment of her death. Similarly impressive is the number of Franciscans who were there, including the university master Eudes of Rosny, Isabelle's confessor. Denis of Étampes is not mentioned by name, but it is hard to believe that he would not have attended; after all, Isabelle had miraculously come to his aid only days before. Technically, these friars should have frowned on such an unapproved translation. Their presence, therefore, indicates not only a personal belief in Isabelle's sanctity but also an attempt to give legitimacy to her nascent cult. They must have been pleased by the way that the crowds of onlookers touched their possessions to Isabelle's body to create instant relics, which they could then preserve as reminders of the saint and her tomb.

Moreover, this translation served another strategic purpose. It was probably at this moment that Isabelle's tomb was oriented in such a manner as to place it half within the choir, accessible only to the nuns, and half out into the public area of the abbey's church.[53] With this positioning, Isabelle's resting place was graphically designated as both a site for the devotion of the nuns of Longchamp and a destination for pilgrims and those looking for miraculous cures. Isabelle herself had worked to make Longchamp a pilgrimage site; her abbess, nuns, and Franciscan associates were now building on this desire not only by carefully orchestrating her very public translation but also by turning her tomb into a space designed to draw miracle seekers.

The excitement surrounding Isabelle's translation did not dissipate immediately; rather, expectations rose and experiences of miraculous happenings multiplied. One of Ade of Reims's fingers had once been injured and subsequently had lacked a nail for twenty years. When Isabelle was buried, Sister Ade took some earth from around the saint's body and applied it to her wound for nine-days, producing a "pretty and entire nail." If she began this treatment on the exact day of Isabelle's first interment, then the nine-day interval would indicate that her final cure was made manifest on the occasion of Isabelle's translation. Giles of Sally, one of the brothers who had attended the translation, had kept the sweat-stained cap that Isabelle had worn during her final illness. Suffering from a fever, he put on this cap "out of devotion" and was cured. Agnes relates this story directly after the translation, and it seems likely that not much time had elapsed.

At about the same moment, "just after" Isabelle had passed away, Sister Ermesent of Paris was alone in the abbey church without permission when she suffered a great pain in her head and an accompanying wave of over-whelming fear. She was about to join the other sisters in the refectory when suddenly it seemed that a voice was speaking to her heart, saying, "Do not do it, but rather go to your holy lady and ask her for help!" So she went and pressed her cheek to the ground over Isabelle's tomb and prayed to her and fell asleep. When she awoke, she was cured. And finally, in one of the more unsettling images found in Agnes's work, a nameless sister had lost her wits; if not restrained, she would climb the walls and crawl under tables to catch and eat spiders and ants. Isabelle, before the end of her life, visited this unfortunate woman and showed great compassion for her. Then, three and one-half months after Isabelle's death, the sister was brought to Isabelle's tomb to spend the night in vigil and prayer. On the next day she, too, was cured.[54]

Thus, in the days and months after Isabelle's death, the Franciscans and sisters at Longchamp began to treat Isabelle's tomb as a locus of saintly power and to regard Isabelle posthumously as an intercessor who would help those who prayed to her or had faith in relics of her life and death. They kept her possessions as sources of divine aid, they called out to her when faced with sudden peril, and they came to her tomb to be healed or calmed. Just as many people, without waiting for official papal confirma-tion, began almost immediately after his death to voice the belief that Louis IX had been a saint, so, too, did those around Isabelle treat her as an example of Capetian sanctity.[55]

Isabelle of France devoted much of her energies during the last years of her life to making Longchamp a place where pious pilgrims would desire to travel, where the royal family and others would visit and perhaps be buried. She did not wish to become a nun or abbess at her foundation but rather chose the more ambiguous role of lay patron. From this position, while straddling the line between court and cloister, she accomplished her goals by securing papal concessions, working closely with her brother the king, collecting relics (to the pope's dismay), and building her own reputation as a saintly woman. She was at once an imposing and comforting presence to the sisters of the abbey and others. She lived apart, yet she came among the nuns to effect healings and offer compassion. The nuns, and even laymen such as Louis's sergeant, sought her out when in need of divine intervention. Her own death and translation, as managed by Agnes of Harcourt and her nuns, cemented these achievements and made Isabelle's tomb an attraction that drew the pious to Longchamp. The stage was set for Isabelle's final ascent to popular acclamation as a royal saint.

CHAPTER SIX

Notre Sainte Mère

Making a Capetian Saint

O n the first of November 1272, less than two years after Isabelle
of France's death, Eudes of Rosny preached a sermon on the theme *Beati
qui habitant in domo tuo Domine* ("Blessed are they who dwell in your house,
Lord," Psalm 83:5). He delivered it in either the small church or the open
market found near the cemetery of Les Saints-Innocents in Paris (near the
current Forum Les Halles). We have a very good idea of what Eudes said
and how his words were received, since an avid student named Raoul of
Châteauroux happened to be taking notes. Apparently it was quite an effective presentation, because Raoul made a point of jotting down "it
pleased me very much!" (*placuit mihi multum*). Perhaps Raoul was impressed by Eudes's deft use of illustrative examples. Midway through
his sermon, Eudes began to develop the rather predictable theme that those
who would dwell in the house of the Lord should not be overly concerned
with the riches and vanities of this world. To bring home his point, the
Franciscan university master recalled that "I had a spiritual daughter who
was such that she would not regard her face in a mirror for a hundred *livres*,
or for any great reward!"[1] There is now no way to be completely certain as
to the identity of this exemplary woman, but it is at least quite likely that
Eudes was referring here to his most famous "spiritual daughter," the
recently deceased Isabelle of France, whose confessor he had been. Eudes

was probably invoking the image of the woman whose humility had only been amplified by her royal status and whose memory was still fresh in the minds of his listeners. Indeed, Eudes, who had himself been present at Isabelle's translation, had good reason to expect her example to move his hearers.

If, as I believe, Eudes really had Isabelle of France in mind, this appearance as a preacher's *exemplum* nicely demonstrates the way in which her cult took hold. In the years between Isabelle's death and translation in 1270 and Agnes of Harcourt's composition of the *Life of Isabelle* in about 1283, interest in the princess grew at a steady pace, often mirroring the progress of public devotion to her brother's memory. Miracles were being recorded at both saints' tombs, and saints' lives were composed for both siblings. In the past there had been brief and quickly aborted attempts to promote veneration for other Capetians, most notably efforts emanating from Saint-Denis earlier in the century to proclaim Philip Augustus a saint.[2] But for only two members of the royal family were saints' lives composed; for only two members of the royal family were miracles gathered and attested to; to the tombs of only two members of the royal family did pilgrims travel in search of cures and divine aid in the later thirteenth century—Louis and Isabelle.[3] In the 1280s their parallel cults were part of a developing vision of Capetian sanctity. If, by the middle of the fourteenth century, interest in Isabelle's cult had begun to be eclipsed by her brother's, it did not entirely disappear and would ultimately be rekindled in the later fifteenth century.

This final chapter deals with memories of Isabelle and argues that after her death she was regarded as a Capetian saint by a wide range of people in the later thirteenth and early fourteenth centuries. My approach to the evidence is twofold. First, I analyze the miracles described in Agnes's *Life of Isabelle* in order to reveal the extent of interest in Isabelle as a source of miraculous power in the decades after her death. Second, I take a wider view. How, within the *Life*, *Letter*, and other relevant texts, did royal, Franciscan, and monastic witnesses remember Isabelle? And how did Agnes herself construct and promote her subject's claims to sanctity? Finally, the concluding section of this chapter offers a sketch of Isabelle's later cult. It is hardly a definitive treatment of the subject, but it aims to establish the contours of Isabelle's reemergence as a Capetian saint.

MAKING MIRACLES

The spread of belief in Isabelle's saintly status in the dozen years or so after her death is most clearly seen in the miracles recorded in Agnes of Harcourt's *Life of Isabelle*. These stories confirm that people ranging from the royal family to criminals fearing for their lives, coming from an area centering on Paris and its environs but stretching to Flanders and Tournai in the north, saw Isabelle as a source of miraculous aid after her death. Her tomb demonstrably did function as the magnet for cure-seekers and pilgrims that it was intended to be.

These miracles fall into a number of clusters, each concerning a distinct social group. I have already discussed in chapter 5 the miracles that were attributed to Isabelle during her lifetime (miracles 1–3) and those that surrounded her death and translation (miracles 4–13). Most of these concerned sisters of Longchamp and Franciscans close to the abbey. But the mob scene that Agnes describes at Isabelle's translation also reveals the way in which noble women, townspeople, and common folk sought contact with Isabelle's body and relics in their search for access to divine power.

The next eighteen miracles in the *Life* (miracles 14–31) occurred between late 1270 and approximately 1283, the date of the *Life*'s composition. With one exception, these stories all concern nuns at Longchamp. Many are short accounts of healings. Some, such as Sister Julienne's recovery from a fever (miracle 14), were brought about by a devout desire to touch an object that had belonged to Isabelle, in this case to drink out of the princess's goblet.[4] Other objects vested with this sort of healing power included her clothes (miracle 18), her pillow (miracle 20), earth from around her tomb (miracle 21), and indiscriminate "things" (*choses*) that had been hers (miracles 22, 23, 31). Sisters also often offered giant candles to Isabelle when seeking cures, as when Ermengare of Chartres took a candle of her own height to the princess's tomb and was cured of a tertian fever (miracle 16). In other cases devout prayer at Isabelle's tomb sufficed, as when Marie of Cambrai's hearing was restored after nine days (miracle 19). Of course, these methods of supplication could be combined. Sister Alice of Mucedent had been suffering from a contorted face and impaired speech for nearly a month, presumably as the result of a stroke. Leaving nothing to chance, she placed some of Isabelle's "things" on her neck, prayed at

Isabelle's tomb for eight days, and offered her a candle the size of her head. She was duly rewarded with a full cure (miracle 23).

Other miracles were more idiosyncratic. For example, Marie of Tremblay was saved from drowning in the abbey's pond when she called out to Isabelle (miracle 24). Even more dramatically, this same sister was once fetching water from the pond (apparently a perilous place), when she was attacked by the devil in the guise of a green dog with red eyes as wide as a cow's; she was so afraid that it seemed to her "that someone had pulled her hair straight up!" The demonic dog was driven back when Marie cried out to God, but it subsequently returned, and she was saved only when she appealed to Isabelle for help (miracle 25). Sister Sara of Houpelines was likewise attacked by a dog, though it was not of the demonic variety. Not only was she saved by invoking the aid of Madame Isabelle, but when the severe bite wounds on her thigh became dangerously infected, she prayed at Isabelle's tomb and was cured (miracle 28). In a miracle with a literary bent, the breviary of Sister Agnes of Paris was miraculously dried out and restored to a readable state after it had fallen into some water, but only when placed on Isabelle's tomb for three hours (miracle 30). Indeed, one of Isabelle's specialties appears to have been as a restorer of damaged or lost books.[5] Sister Julienne (she who had been cured by Isabelle's goblet) had misplaced a book that had once belonged to Isabelle and cried over her tomb for its return. While Julienne was sleeping, Isabelle appeared to her and instructed her to pray to her brother for its restoration. This she did, for good measure promising Louis a pound of wax, and the book was found forthwith (miracle 15).

The latter miracle also highlights the association of Isabelle and Louis as a sibling team of miracle workers. Two miracles were reported by Jeanne of Louveciennes (miracles 26 and 27, so similar as to make one suspect that the second might be a rewriting of the first). In the first story, Sister Jeanne had been suffering from a severe malady for three months, and she appealed devoutly and repeatedly to Isabelle. One night the princess appeared to Jeanne, so she prayed to Isabelle on her knees. Isabelle, however, offered a concise directive: "Go to my brother." Then it seemed to Jeanne that she saw pilgrims proceeding to Louis's tomb at Saint-Denis, but as a cloistered nun she could not go herself, so she cried out to him and thought that she was carried there. Isabelle was present as well and asked the king to heal

Jeanne. He made the sign of the cross over her and promised that she would be cured within eight days, which indeed she was. In the second miracle, Jeanne's illness is said to have lasted for three years, and she grew frustrated after fasting on bread and water for three Saturdays and appealing to Isabelle without result. Again she fell asleep and seemed to be borne to Isabelle's tomb, where she saw Isabelle sitting. When Jeanne asked her to intervene with God on her behalf, she again replied, "Go to my brother." Then "it seemed to the sister that she saw a procession of kings most nobly appareled, and all crowned, and at the end of this procession was Monseigneur the king Louis."[6] And once more Isabelle asked her brother to heal Jeanne, which he did. But here one would very much like to interrogate Jeanne about her vision. Was this a line of holy Capetian kings with Louis as the culmination of a sacred dynasty? Did this image place Louis as the successor to the biblical kings such as David and Solomon? Or did Jeanne's imagination fuse the two together? In any case, Jeanne's dreams certainly stressed Isabelle's association with Louis's royal status and his growing cult, making her something of a Marian figure interceding with the more Christ-like Louis.[7]

If nuns such as Jeanne of Louveciennes and Julienne tended to link Isabelle and Louis, members of the royal family themselves could approach the princess directly when faced with a crisis. Miracle seventeen of Agnes's *Life* (the exception mentioned above) offers a striking example of Isabelle's role as a saintly intercessor for her own family. Marguerite of Provence, the widow of Louis IX, had known Isabelle since the early 1230s, when they were both mere girls. Now she turned to her sister-in-law for divine aid. Her grandson, the future Philip IV, was suffering from a fever, so Marguerite brought him to Longchamp in hopes of finding a cure. She had him laid by Isabelle's tomb, and indeed he recovered. Moreover, Philip later told several nuns about this episode. We see in this story not only the faith displayed by a member of the royal family who had known Isabelle in life, but also the way in which this faith was transmitted to a new generation of Capetians.

The final nine miracles in Agnes's *Life* mark a distinct shift signaled by "miracle" thirty-two, which is merely a simple statement: "We would not be able to recount in a few words the spiritual good and consolations that she has provided to people who have devoutly requested her aid. In any tribulation and unhappiness in which she is asked for help, she promptly aids and comforts whoever prays to her with a true heart."[8] Here, Agnes not only asserts that the number of miracles attributable to Isabelle is growing too large to record systematically, but she also shifts her claims into the present tense to emphasize Isabelle's ongoing presence at Longchamp as a worker of cures. The miracles that follow, moreover, move away from the nuns of Longchamp to pilgrims who have come from farther afield. Thus, this section of the *Life* demonstrates Isabelle's appeal outside the walls of Longchamp.

Miracles thirty-three to thirty-five concern women from the area who were in danger or seeking miraculous help. A woman from Paris named Agnes "the chest maker" had a seriously ill child who was on the point of death. Waiting for the child's end, she fell asleep and heard a voice that said, "Agnes, dedicate your child to Madame Isabelle, near St. Cloud, and offer her the cup that your father gave you, and your child will be cured." Indeed, Agnes carried out these instructions and the child lived (miracle 33). Similarly, another woman named Agnes from the nearby town of Suresnes lost her eyesight, but after traveling to Longchamp, dedicating herself to Isabelle, and offering two eyes made of wax, she was able to see (miracle 34). In a more dramatic episode, a maiden (*pucelle*) who lived not far from Longchamp was about to yield to the entreaties of some would-be paramour. But the night before the lovers' tryst, Isabelle appeared to her in a dream: "Get up, go to my abbey, which is near St. Cloud, and you will be delivered!" The maiden arose early and ran to the abbey with such alacrity that she lost her coat, and from then on she lived a good and honest life (miracle 35). Isabelle's example of pious virginity evidently preyed on the troubled conscience of this young woman.

Miracle thirty-six is particularly striking, not only because it involves men instead of women but also because of the distance from which they had come. The nuns of Longchamp must have been surprised one day to find at their door two ex-convicts who had traveled all the way from Tournai. Demanding to be shown Isabelle's tomb, they said that they had been in prison and in danger of being hanged, when a voice told them to "dedicate yourselves to Madame Isabelle, near St. Cloud, and you will be delivered!" The nuns reluctantly admitted the men, who dutifully lit candles to the holy lady and then departed. Just exactly how Isabelle had come to the attention of these men in Tournai is not evident (it is tempting but probably too neat to see the influence of Gilbert of Tournai here). Nor does the text make clear how Isabelle's miraculous intervention actually saved them. Perhaps this was a version of the sort of miracle in which a saint supports the condemned man's feet or causes the rope to snap in time to prevent his death by hanging.[9] In any case, Isabelle's reputation as a source of holy power had evidently spread well beyond the Île-de-France.

The final four miracles return to men attached to Longchamp. The first offers a glimpse of the technology involved in cleaning the lofty interior of a Gothic church.[10] The abbey's sentinel was high up in the church's vaults, suspended in a basket attached to a cord worked by a machine (*par engin*), when the cord snapped and he was dashed to the floor below. He suffered a severe head wound but was cured when the sisters dedicated him to Isabelle (miracle 37). Likewise, when the valet of the chaplain of "Madame the queen" fell into a great frenzy, others had pity on him.[11] They, too, dedicated him to Isabelle and offered her a candle of his height, and he was soon himself again (miracle 38). The abbey's procurator, Philip, suffered from an intense tertian fever until he was laid on Isabelle's pillow (miracle 39). And finally, the son of Richard "the Welshman" was cured of a recurring fever by contact with some of the earth around Isabelle's tomb (miracle 40).

Thus, the many witnesses to Isabelle's miracles came from varying backgrounds. Altogether, twenty sisters of Longchamp are mentioned as either experiencing or attesting to Isabelle's miraculous intervention, and indeed many of these women testified to more than one miracle. They revered Isabelle as a royal founder and mother, usually referring to her as "mère," "madame," or "notre sainte dame"—an evocative title in an abbey dedicated to "l'Humilité-de-Notre-Dame." Nuns often cried out to "ma douce dame" or "ma douce mère," emphasizing Isabelle's compassion and gentle nature. Four different women from the surrounding area—from Lady Heloise, the bourgeois widow of Paris, to the anonymous *pucelle* in danger of losing her virginity—figure in Isabelle's miracles, while the four noble women from Flanders were sufficiently devoted to Isabelle to travel to Longchamp for her translation. A total of eight common laymen, five Franciscans, and two other religious men also appear together with the royals Marguerite of Provence and Philip IV. Only in the single episode of the *pucelle* does Isabelle's reputation as a virgin come into play as a saintly quality. Yet Isabelle may have had a particular appeal as a saintly intercessor for women. More women than men witnessed her miracles (twenty-nine to sixteen), though these numbers are skewed to some degree by the prevalence of the sisters of Longchamp.[12] By contrast, the miracles gathered at Saint-Denis for the investigation into Louis IX's sanctity recorded cures of slightly more males than females.[13] And while it is true that fewer miracles and witnesses are attributed to Isabelle than to her brother, Agnes of Harcourt and the nuns of Longchamp did not have the benefit of an extended official papal inquiry to gather their testimony.

Few of the miracles recorded by Agnes would have been out of place in any other contemporary saint's *vita*, and there are evident parallels with Louis's developing cult at this time. For instance, contemporaries also sought cures through Louis's possessions and clothing, traveled to his tomb to seek intervention for illness and insanity, and vowed candles to him in return for the healing of their sick children.[14] The point, therefore, is not that the events detailed above were unusual miracles to be recorded around a saint's tomb, but rather that Isabelle's burial place, much as her brother's, was seen as the tomb of a saint. The miraculous occurrences expected at such a holy locus did take place (or were thought to) and did draw people to the site. Devout miracle-seekers in these years had two well-publicized options from which to choose if they desired to approach a saintly Capetian intercessor.

Visions of Isabelle

Taken together, the forty miracles preserved in the *Life of Isabelle* demonstrate that contemporaries really did see Isabelle of France as a source of saintly power in the years after her death. Let us now take Agnes of Harcourt's writings as a whole and ask how certain groups remembered the princess. Various "voices," in fact, made up Agnes's raw material.[15] The abbess was not working with an entirely free hand; her task was at least in part to act as compiler of other people's testimony. If she twisted that testimony too far, she ran the risk of producing a text that readers familiar with Longchamp would reject as unconvincing. We can both isolate the categories of voices with which she worked and consider how her narrative reveals her own perceptions of the princess.

Capetians and Capetian Sanctity

Some of the most ardent promoters of the idea of Capetian sanctity were, not surprisingly, the Capetians themselves. Agnes of Harcourt's writings were in some measure a product of this drive for recognition from within the royal family. As I have argued elsewhere, the initial impetus for Agnes's writings was provided by Louis IX's canonization process and the resultant opportunity to develop a wider picture of Capetian royal sanctity.[16] The main papal investigation into Louis's saintly merits took place at Saint-Denis from May 1282 to March 1283 under the patronage of Pope Martin IV, the former Cardinal Simon of Brie, the same man who had approved the revision of Isabelle's Rule of 1263. This highly visible inquiry included the testimony of over three hundred witnesses. Agnes of Harcourt's *Letter on Louis IX and Longchamp*, dated 4 December 1282, was almost certainly inspired by these proceedings and was intended to contribute to them in some fashion. Agnes and the nuns of Longchamp evidently wanted to let it be known that Louis had been instrumental in the foundation of their abbey, that he had visited them and preached to them, showered gifts on them, humbled himself before them, and even performed miraculous healings among them. Moreover, Agnes's *Life of Isabelle* was probably begun later in 1283, still within the swirl of events surrounding the public inquiry into Louis's sanctity.[17] Agnes and her nuns were gathering stories about Isabelle at almost the same moment that a similar process was going on for Louis across Paris at Saint-Denis, within a climate that was keenly attuned to Capetian holiness.

Even more specifically, Agnes tells us that she wrote her biography of the princess at the request of Isabelle's brother, Charles of Anjou. One of the moving forces behind the papal drive toward Louis's canonization, Charles was a firm believer in a vision of a wider Capetian sanctity. He saw his family as a holy lineage—a *beata stirps*—in which the royal blood transmitted sanctity, and he actively promoted this idea.[18] For example, in his own deposition for Louis's canonization hearings, Charles went out of his way to argue that Louis, his brothers, and his sister were all saintly figures brought up by the pious Blanche of Castile.[19]

Charles's need to bolster his family's claims to sanctity was particularly intense at this moment. He had departed from France in 1265 in order to make good the papal invitation to become king of Sicily.[20] On 29 March 1282, however, Charles's Sicilian subjects rebelled against his rule in what has become known as the Sicilian Vespers. Peter III of Aragon, whose wife had inherited the Hohenstaufen claim to Sicily, took this opportunity to support the rebellion and have himself crowned king of Sicily in September. Martin supported Charles by excommunicating Peter, placing Sicily under interdict in November 1282, and releasing Peter's subjects from allegiance to him in March 1283.[21] Seeking assistance against Peter, Charles traveled north to France in April 1283, when he spent several months in Paris at the court of Philip III. Charles and Peter then agreed to settle the Sicilian question in hand-to-hand combat, with each king leading one hundred knights onto the field at Bordeaux on 1 June.[22] Following what proved to be an inconclusive encounter, Charles was again briefly at Paris at the end of the same year, but he then departed for good.[23] Since it was surely during his time north of the Alps in 1283 that Charles urged Agnes of Harcourt to begin her *Life of Isabelle*, he therefore had the immediate political incentive of strengthening the contrast between Capetian sanctity and the excommunicated House of Aragon.[24] Charles's own branch of the family would obviously benefit from a perception of general Capetian holiness; the need to legitimate and sacralize his line's threatened claim to the crown of Sicily provided a powerful motive for commissioning a life of his sister.

One of the fundamental objectives that brought Agnes's *Life* into existence, then, was the desire to create a literary case for a Capetian sanctity that both encompassed and extended beyond Louis IX. Charles of Anjou knew that his sister had been seen as a holy figure in her lifetime, and he must have realized that her posthumous cult was developing a steady local following. He sought to exploit this situation, and Agnes was apparently happy to comply.

Moreover, Agnes evidently wrote in part to encourage a new canonization process for Isabelle herself. Not only did she meticulously note the names of witnesses to events whenever possible and record the existence of physical evidence when it survived, but in one instance she also underlined the truth of an assertion by stating: "I believe that there will be others who will certainly testify to this if need be."[25] This phrase clearly envisioned future efforts to delve more deeply into Isabelle's canonization dossier.

The goal of sparking formal canonization hearings also necessitated reaching a royal audience, since only with the support of powerful figures such as Charles of Anjou would full papal proceedings go forward.[26] Some of Agnes's most compelling witnesses were royal personages whose presence in the text not only linked Isabelle to the larger question of Capetian sanctity but also lent unimpeachable authority to Agnes's account and reminded the royal family of its continuing obligations to Longchamp. Eight members of the royal family, spanning three generations, are mentioned in the *Letter on Louis IX and Longchamp* and the *Life of Isabelle*: Philip II, Louis VIII, Blanche of Castile, Charles of Anjou, Marguerite of Provence, Louis IX, his son Louis, and Philip IV (the wives of Isabelle's other brothers and Philip III are referred to without being named). However, only Louis IX and Marguerite contributed substantial testimony to Agnes's texts.

Marguerite of Provence, in particular, emerges as a woman who believed in, promoted, and benefited from Isabelle's sanctity. In spite of Agnes's statement in the *Life* that Isabelle had not wanted to play with her brothers' wives, Marguerite seems to have been close to Isabelle. In their youth (Marguerite was the older by three years), they may have spent considerable time together, and we know that Marguerite was left to comfort Isabelle in her illness at Saint-Germain-en-Laye.[27] The queen was the source for two of Agnes's more interesting tales about Isabelle—and since Marguerite was still alive when the *Letter* and *Life* were composed, Agnes would not have dared to put words in her mouth. Marguerite related the anecdote in the *Letter* that described the laying of the first stones for Longchamp's foundation, when she turned to Isabelle to exclaim, "Look, *belle soeur*, here are three white doves that show that the Holy Trinity is present at the commencement of our work!" This shared sense of mission—"our work"—was fully borne out by Marguerite's later role in refounding the Franciscan house of Saint-Marcel and helping to secure its adoption of Isabelle's rule. The first miracle recorded in the *Life* was also reported by Marguerite, when she remembered the story in which the child of one of the king's sergeants had been cured through Isabelle's prayers. Finally, Marguerite publicly demonstrated her faith by bringing her grandson to Isabelle's tomb in search of a cure.[28]

Louis IX appears even more frequently than his wife in Agnes's texts. He related one tale directly to Agnes (or at least recited it in her presence), that of Isabelle in her youth praying so intently on her elbows and knees under her bedcovers that she was nearly carried away with the laundry. Louis was likewise an actor in a number of anecdotes, such as when he unsuccessfully sought the cap that his sister had knitted. Louis's voice, as it emerges from Agnes's writings, combines a big brother's indulgence, a sibling's support, and sincere admiration. The story about Isabelle praying under the covers certainly has a lighthearted tone, and Louis's attitude in the exchange over her first effort at knitting headgear may have been more indulgent than serious. But Louis eventually regarded Isabelle as an equal, as seen in their joint appearances at Longchamp and his expressions of displeasure when Isabelle would kneel before him. Indeed, his role at her funeral and his display of devotion there show the respect he ultimately accorded his sister's example.[29]

There is plenty of evidence beyond Agnes of Harcourt's texts that indicates that family members continued to preserve Isabelle's memory and patronize her abbey. Both Alphonse of Poitiers and Louis consistently gave alms to Longchamp and remembered the house in their wills.[30] Among Louis IX's children, Pierre of Alençon made a bequest to Longchamp, the place "where our dear aunt lies."[31] Louis's daughter Blanche, who had married Ferdinand of Castile in 1269 and returned to France after his death, was allowed by Pope Honorius IV to fulfill her desire to reside for a time at Longchamp.[32] She and her sister Isabelle followed Isabelle of France's model by helping their mother to found the new house for Franciscan women at Saint-Marcel.

Philip IV contributed his own voice to Agnes's narrative by assuring the nuns of Longchamp that he "remembered well" his cure at Isabelle's tomb.[33] Perhaps in gratitude, he was a consistent benefactor of, and visitor to, Longchamp during his reign.[34] Philip actively promoted the image of his family as a holy line, particularly through his support for Louis IX's canonization and cult.[35] Isabelle's impact on him may be seen in two ways. First, and most intriguingly, Philip placed a new public emphasis on the power of the royal touch—the ability to cure scrofula through the laying on of hands, which was traditionally ascribed to anointed Capetian kings.[36] Though Louis had participated in this ritual, Isabelle was also known to heal with her touch, and Philip's own experience at the receiving end of a royal cure came not by the grace of St. Louis or any other king but through the merits of his great-aunt. Philip was a walking demonstration of the efficacy of Capetian healing power—but of Isabelle's rather than Louis's. Second, Philip's monastic patronage had ties to Isabelle. Though it was not as clear a statement about royal sanctity as his better known foundation of Saint-Louis-de Poissy for Dominican nuns, his female Franciscan abbey of Moncel adopted Isabelle's rule and helped to further her long-term institutional impact and perpetuate her memory. Thus, Philip must have counted Isabelle as well as Louis among the holy ancestors who sanctified the Capetian dynasty.

Royal memory of Isabelle and patronage of Longchamp reached their culmination in the reign of Philip V. Philip placed his youngest daughter Blanche at Longchamp around 1315, where she took vows in February 1319 at the age of eight or nine.[37] Blanche herself probably maintained a dedication to Isabelle, since her tomb at Longchamp is said to have depicted Isabelle and Louis together.[38] Moreover, Blanche's mother Jeanne, in her will of 27 August 1319, directed that her entrails should be interred at Longchamp if she died in France and Blanche was alive at the time of her death; she also left rents, relics, and books to Blanche and Longchamp.[39] Thus, Longchamp continued its strong ties to the royal family in this era both as a place of burial and as a site for the preservation of royal memory.[40]

Finally, Philip V, in his last illness, chose to be transported to Longchamp in October 1321. As Elizabeth A. R. Brown has pointed out, the king's movements in the final months of his life were not without purpose. He was seeking a place "which might promote his recovery or where, if it came to that, he might die in peace."[41] He probably chose Longchamp to be near his own daughter, but also in hopes of a repetition of his father's boyhood cure. Isabelle, her tomb, and her house drew this king to Longchamp, where he died between 2 and 3 January 1322, probably in the very lodging that had been built for Isabelle of France.[42]

Franciscan Memories

If members of the royal family considered Isabelle to have been a Capetian saint, what of the Franciscans who had known her or had been close to Longchamp? Nine Franciscans are named in the *Life*. Four—Bonaventure, William of Meliton, Geoffrey of Vierson, and William of

Harcombourg—are mentioned only as Isabelle's collaborators on her rule, though William of Harcombourg also attended the abbey's dedication in 1260 and Bonaventure preached at Longchamp in subsequent years. Two more Franciscans—Pierre of Meureville and Thomas of Plexi—appear in Agnes's narrative only as having been present at Isabelle's translation, but even this simple act may have indicated their belief in her sanctity. Denis of Étampes and Giles of Sally, two friars with close ties to Longchamp in 1270, related miracles that occurred around the time of Isabelle's death and translation (discussed in chapter 5). To these brothers, Isabelle after her death quickly became an acknowledged source of miraculous power. Denis of Étampes, in particular, came increasingly to believe in the reality of Isabelle's saintly status. Apparently surprised by the cure that he experienced at her deathbed, he quickly learned from the experience, so that when he found himself in danger of being crushed under a table only days later, he turned to her as a proven saintly protector. Giles of Sally, similarly, kept her cap at the time of her death and later invoked its aid.[43]

Only one Franciscan appears more intimately as someone whose direct words Agnes actually records—Isabelle's confessor, Eudes of Rosny. Agnes notes that "sometimes Brother Eudes of Rosny, her confessor, would say to her, 'Lady, it would be well if you spoke and amused yourself, it would not displease our Lord if you were to take a little recreation,' and he would ask her why she kept such silence."[44] The princess's confessor seems to have seen her as a figure of almost too pronounced a personal asceticism. Eudes had worked with her on her rule and watched her career unfold, and he evidently tried to get her to moderate her intensely devout behavior. But after her death he displayed the effect that her life had had on him, first by being present at her translation and lending his prestige to the proceedings. And, as this chapter began by arguing, Eudes most likely was referring to Isabelle in a sermon two years after her death as an example of modesty and humility. For Eudes, his "spiritual daughter" was a model of piety, worthy of praise and imitation.

The Abbess's Answer

In addition to their royal and Franciscan recollections of Isabelle, Agnes of Harcourt's writings can be thought of as preserving Longchamp's shared memories. A total of twenty-three sisters, including Agnes herself, appear in the *Letter* and the *Life*. The nuns, as we have seen regarded Isabelle in death, as in life, as "notre sainte mère"—our holy mother; they looked to her as their patron, as a source of protection both temporal and spiritual, as a powerful presence at her tomb, as someone who even after death returned to help and comfort them, as an associate of her holy brother in dreams and visions, and as an attraction to pilgrims who might come to venerate her and seek her aid.

But what of Agnes of Harcourt herself? As important as the nine Franciscans above may have been, the striking fact is that memories of Isabelle were not narrated by a male mendicant confessor, as was so often the case with saintly female figures of this era.[45] One may speculate as to how a biography written by Eudes of Rosny might have differed from that authored by Agnes, or why such a *vita* was never composed, but the fact remains that an abbess, not a confessor, compiled the evidence for Isabelle's life and sanctity. Agnes decided what stories were to be included, how they were to be shaped, and what morals were to be drawn. It was she who harmonized the other voices considered here.

Indeed, in a number of regards, Agnes subtly manipulated the stories at her disposal. She often seems purposely to skirt problematic issues and to remain silent on contentious areas of Isabelle's life, but Agnes's own clear voice also emerges from her text. The following analysis of Agnes's approach as an author is hardly exhaustive. It is intended only to illuminate the question of how she remembered Isabelle and influenced others' perceptions through her literary efforts.[46]

Crafting an acceptable picture of Isabelle's role as co-author of a controversial rule must have presented Agnes with her most daunting challenge; I limit my analysis here to this theme. Agnes's approach is simultaneously to insist on the importance of Isabelle's personal vision for her abbey while stressing the way in which the new foundation was shaped in harmonious agreement with other powerful forces. In setting out to smooth over the princess's rough edges, Agnes actually acknowledges just how controversial a figure Isabelle had been.

For example, Agnes introduces Longchamp's foundation with the story of Isabelle asking her confessor, Aymeric the chancellor, for his advice. It is his (supposed) words that finalize the decision to build a house for Franciscan women rather than a hospital: "Tell her that she should not demand further counsel on this matter, but build the house of religion!"[47] Thus, Isabelle is seen as merely following the advice of an imposing secular master. While she retains the credit for her good work and her status as ultimate patron, she is absolved of any suspicion of willfully embarking on a controversial project. By calling special attention to Aymeric's words (instead of Isabelle's, whatever they may have been), Agnes cloaks Isabelle's decision with her confessor's authority.

Next, Agnes moves to the rule. As I have pointed out in chapter 3, she stresses Isabelle's own agency here, recalling that the princess was "very diligent as to the rule, that it should be good and sure." But Agnes makes it equally clear that Isabelle assembled her team of Franciscan masters to help put it together. Agnes would like to have it both ways—it was Isabelle who "worked and devoted herself so much to this that it can hardly be recounted," but since a Franciscan master was always present, she cannot be accused of brazenly blazing her own trail.[48]

Moreover, Agnes had to have known that she was giving a distorted version of the composition and approval of Isabelle's two rules, since she omitted any mention of the process of revising the 1259 Rule in 1263. This elision reveals the central goal behind Agnes's treatment of the issue—to create an image of agreement between Isabelle, Bonaventure and the Franciscans, King Louis, and the papal curia. This tactic was useful in avoiding any hint that Isabelle was at odds with the Franciscan Order or the papacy. This strategy was furthered as much by Agnes's silence as by her statements—by conflating the two rules into one, she hid the fact that Longchamp's rule was the product of an extended contest between the princess, two popes, and the Franciscans. In addition, her subsequent references to Franciscans who had witnessed or experienced Isabelle's posthumous miracles furthered this goal; the legitimacy of a rule written by a saintly intercessor who had actually cured brothers of the order could hardly be doubted.

A similar process can be discerned behind the way that Agnes next alludes to Isabelle's desires for the naming of her sisters and her abbey. Only after asserting official Franciscan complicity in the composition process does Agnes mention Isabelle's absolute insistence that her nuns be known by the forbidden title of *Soeurs mineures*. But then, in an abrupt transition, Agnes recalls how Isabelle also insisted on "The Humility of

Our Lady."[49] With this juxtaposition, Agnes pairs Isabelle's stubborn adherence to her most audacious demand with her uncontroversial valorization of humility.

Agnes's final paragraph on the rule's approval continues to present a picture of a woman working within a consensus of royal and Franciscan actors. According to Agnes, Isabelle was frantic to secure papal approval for her rule, but out of humility she had Louis handle the negotiations.[50] I hope to have explicated the political realities that lay behind this misleading passage. The point here is that Agnes crafted her portrait in such a way as to obscure those realities, hinting at Isabelle's passionate involvement but then insisting on her subordination to her brother. In the process, Agnes stressed that Isabelle acted only in tandem with the king. Thus, faced with the task of painting an acceptably saintly portrait of the princess, Agnes manages to give an impression of Isabelle's personal commitment as well as her humility while also emphasizing the Franciscan, royal and ultimately papal approval enjoyed by the princess, her rule, and her house. But under the surface of her narrative, Agnes's own efforts to reshape the facts reveal a "saint" in need of reworking—the devout but sometimes difficult woman she had actually known.

Writing the *Life* also provided an opportunity to speak for and through Isabelle. Throughout the text, Agnes operates as the sole intermediary for Isabelle's voice. Though many other witnesses describe Isabelle's actions and miracles, the author cites only herself as a direct witness who can claim to specifically relate the princess's words. This control actually functions on two levels—within the text itself, Isabelle's words are always recalled by Agnes the actor; and then they are recorded by Agnes the author.

A prime example is the bargaining between Isabelle and Louis over the knitted nightcap, where the first-person referent shifts from Agnes to the royal siblings: "She did not want to give it to him, as I, Sister Agnes of Harcourt, who was present, heard from her mouth with my own ears. She responded to the king and said, 'I propose that it should be given to our Lord, because it is the first that I have ever sewn.' And he beseeched her and said, 'Sister, then I beseech you that you sew another one that I might have.' And she responded, 'I would be pleased to do that if I sew more.'" Similarly, the direct dialogue between Agnes and Isabelle on the issue of naming the abbey purports to give the princess's exact words: "And I, Sister

Agnes of Harcourt, asked her, 'Lady, tell me please, for God's sake, why you have given this name to your abbey?' She responded to me, 'Because I have never heard tell of any person who took it, which surprises me, for it seems to me that they have left out the highest name and the best that they could take, since it is the name by which our Lord chose our Lady to be his mother. And for this I have taken it to give to my house.''[51]

In three other cases, Agnes claims to recall Isabelle's words but does not repeat them in direct dialogue. Isabelle's somewhat defensive self-justification is recorded when, as we saw earlier, Agnes remembers: "She [Isabelle] told me with her own mouth that she had just as good a heart and was just as devoted to our Lord when she had these rich ornaments on her head and on her body as she had when she had more religious attire." Another time, Isabelle informed Agnes "with her mouth" how she always made sure her confessors were really paying attention to her and not daydreaming or napping. Similarly, Isabelle told Agnes (and Eudes of Rosny) secretly about her fear of the Lord and the great trembling it produced.[52]

Isabelle's own voice would seem to be most directly heard in these five episodes, but it is always filtered through Agnes's memory, choices, and goals. The two direct quotations nicely balance opposing sides of Isabelle's personality: her steadfastness in her ideals, and her cultivation of humility. Similarly, in the three additional anecdotes, Isabelle displays a mix of guilt-tinged justification, high-handed insistence that her confessors be attentive, and penitential fear of judgment. Isolating these moments reveals not only the paradoxes of Isabelle's character but also the way in which Agnes controls Isabelle's "speech."

Agnes's other appearances in the text often take the form of swearing to the truth of her story or acting as witness to those direct conversations that she has overheard, thereby offering herself as guarantor of authenticity. Indeed, she inserts her own name and first-person presence into her text far more frequently and assertively than did many thirteenth-century hagiographers.[53] Her own role in the narrative seems to grow as her text progresses.

In both her *Letter* and the *Life of Isabelle*, Agnes initially submerges herself in a collective "we" before emerging as a distinct individual voice.[54] This process is apparent first in the *Letter*, which is collectively addressed from "Sister Agnes of Harcourt, humble abbess of the Enclosed Sisters

Minor of the Abbey of the Humility of Our Lady of Longchamp, and the whole convent of this same place." The initial word in the text is not *je* but *nous*: "*We* make known to all who will see this letter that *our* very reverend and holy father, Monseigneur the king Louis, founded *our* church. . . ." Here, as elsewhere, Isabelle is always "*our* holy mother," emphasizing her relationship to the community as a whole. But by the end of the first paragraph, individual witnesses emerge: "I, Sister Agnes of Harcourt, I, Sister Isabelle of Reims, I, Sister Angre, I, Sister Julienne, I, Sister Mahaut of Gondarville, and many other sisters heard these things from the mouth of Madame the queen Marguerite." As author, Agnes determines what is represented as collective truth, what "we" remember, but as nun she is one of a group of sisters who signify their own place within the collective "we."[55]

The *Life of Isabelle* also begins with the word "we" (*nous*). "*We* have proposed to write the life of *our* holy and blessed lady and mother, Madame Isabelle of France . . . in so far as God will grant *us* his grace. . . . And first *we* will tell who she was, and of her lineage, and then *we* will tell of her childhood. . . ." The referent of this "we" is not even expressed, initially producing a vague, collective picture of authorial responsibility. But Agnes's status as author is quickly revealed. The text records that Isabelle's *desmoiselles* would keep her hair as relics when they combed her locks, and "I, Sister Agnes of Harcourt, heard these things from the mouth of the damsels who served her, and I still have some of her hairs from her youth."[56] But, unlike in the *Letter*, only Agnes is ever accorded the first person "I" in the *Life*. From here on, her voice emerges more forcefully, increasingly taking sole responsibility for authenticating information with eyewitness reports and occasionally allowing her own words and responses to creep into the text.

We know, for instance, that Isabelle would warn people who asked her for alms to be truthful, because "I, Sister Agnes of Harcourt, who sometimes carried this message, bear witness to this matter." Louis's recollections about Isabelle praying under her bedcovers reach us thanks to the fact that "I, Sister Agnes of Harcourt, heard this from the mouth of Monseigneur the holy king Louis, who recounted it to us." Presumably "us" refers to the nuns as a community, yet only Agnes's voice is offered as verification of his words (although Mahaut of Gondarville heard the same story from Isabelle's childhood nurse, Helen of Buesemont). Isabelle was proficient at reading and correcting Latin, "and I, Sister Agnes of Harcourt, saw this many times, and other people too." In at least one case, Agnes offers evidence from silence, noting that Isabelle would never say a false word, since "I never heard any oath escape her mouth."[57]

Agnes's voice perhaps comes through most clearly in the penultimate paragraph before the *Life* moves to its recounting of miracles, worthy of reconsideration here: "And sometimes I saw that for some things that displeased her she would strongly reprimand some people before me, Sister Agnes of Harcourt," because they had not accomplished the good works "with which she had charged them. And since it seemed to her that she had spoken too sharply, she would admit to them her fault before me wonderfully humbly, and she would accuse herself very much and recall the words that she had said, making them [appear] worse. It did me much good to hear her, and since then the memory has done me good many times." And, concludes Agnes, "I believe" that God would forgive any sinner, no matter how bad, if he would repent as thoroughly as Isabelle did.[58] This episode is unique in introducing Agnes's own reaction and response, but she also presents herself here as a confidante.

In the records of Isabelle's forty miracles, Agnes mentions herself less frequently but continues to be an important witness. She swore to the truth of Alice of Mucedent's cure, one of the three occurring while Isabelle was still alive. When Ermesent of Paris was cured by placing her cheek on the ground over Isabelle's tomb, we learn that "I, Sister Agnes of Harcourt, who then held the office of abbess, bear witness to this matter, since this same Sister Ermesent came right away to me." And "Sister Agnes of Harcourt" is listed along with other nuns as witnesses to Isabelle of Crécy's cure. The reference to Agnes in the third person here again indicates her ambiguous stance as both witness and author.[59]

Interestingly enough, Agnes of Harcourt did not testify to having experienced a miraculous cure herself, yet there is no doubt that she was an ardent believer in Isabelle's sanctity. At the same time, she was Isabelle's literary interpreter and promoter, putting forth a somewhat sanitized picture of the princess that sought to obscure—but often unwittingly revealed—her less saintly human qualities. For the abbess, these were also practical matters with immediate import. Isabelle's memory continued to matter, to conjure up images of Capetian sanctity that commanded respect and opened up avenues of influence. Controlling Isabelle's voice as an author was a way to shape memories of her, to speak for and through her. Positioning herself as the sole conduit for Isabelle's words and the most important witness to her sanctity reinforced Agnes's position as heir to the princess's authority at Longchamp. As both a saint and a patron, Isabelle's power continued to radiate from beyond the tomb.

The Eclipse and Reemergence of a Royal Saint

For all of the groups and individuals analyzed above, Isabelle of France was remembered as a Capetian saint. Why, then, was her sanctity not officially proclaimed? One answer is that by the early fourteenth century, very few candidates for sanctity were being approved by the papal curia, and then only with intense and extended support from powerful quarters.[60] Still, in this case the effort does not seem to have even been made. Why was there no sustained campaign orchestrated by the nuns of Longchamp, the French court, and the Franciscan Order to have Isabelle's sanctity confirmed by the pope?

For the nuns, one reason may have concerned Blanche of France, the daughter of Philip V. The presence of the king's daughter at Longchamp provided a strong tie to the court that temporarily lessened the need for the nuns to remind themselves and others of their royal founder. Evidence for this shift can be found in the archival inventories. Whereas before 1320 the label "Ma dame" always indicated some legacy of Isabelle of France, after this date the "Dame" of Longchamp is frequently Blanche.[61] Thus, at least until Blanche's death in 1358, the nuns themselves may have felt no pressing reason to stress the memory of their founder.

As for the Capetian court, the canonization of Louis IX in 1297 provided a towering figure of royal sanctity, thus sapping any intentions to begin again the lengthy process that canonization required by this time. If one royal sibling had to be supported, the canonization of the king was of far greater political utility than that of his sister. And if further evidence of royal holiness was necessary, the canonization of Charles of Anjou's grandson Louis of Toulouse (or Anjou) in 1317 supplied a model of piety even more firmly tied to mendicant spirituality than his namesake's.

The Angevin branch of the family (descended from Charles of Anjou) was particularly noted for its promotion of family saints. But the Angevins understandably focused their attention on Louis of Toulouse, who, as the brother of King Robert the Wise of Naples, effectively demonstrated their line's holiness.[62] They also could claim descent from Elizabeth of Hungary, great-aunt of Robert's wife Sancia, a female model of sanctity for the family. Charles of Anjou's initial step of commissioning a life of Isabelle may have been an important catalyst in the Angevin cultivation of dynastic holiness, but there is no evidence that the Angevins afterward actively promoted Isabelle's cult.[63]

The Franciscan Order likewise seems temporarily to have forgotten about Isabelle after the generation of friars who had known her died. The later fourteenth-century *Chronicle of the Twenty-Four Generals*, for instance, contains only a garbled version of the founding of Longchamp.[64] The order had never been particularly comfortable with Isabelle's rule, and, as time passed, it probably had little inclination to publicize its creator.

Nevertheless, interest from these quarters did not entirely disappear, even at what seems to have been the nadir of Isabelle's cult in the middle and later fourteenth century. The court remained actively interested in Isabelle's life, as witnessed by the copy of a *Life of Sister Isabelle of Longchamp, Who Was the Sister of St. Louis, and of Her Miracles*, found in the royal library in 1373. The nuns of Longchamp, for their part, never ceased to honor her memory. For instance, the introduction to the abbey's first necrology, composed in 1325, recounted her role as founder. Moreover, in these years the nuns copied Agnes of Harcourt's *Life of Isabelle* into a now-lost codex, which demonstrates their interest in preserving their record of their founder and her miracles.[65] Little artistic evidence from the abbey in this period survives, but, as noted earlier, Blanche of France's tomb is known to have been decorated with an image of Isabelle as well as of Louis.[66] It is more difficult to determine to what extent Isabelle's own tomb remained an active site of pilgrimage throughout this period. Longchamp suffered from the plagues and wars of the later fourteenth and early fifteenth centuries, and archival documentation from this era is sparse.[67] But evidence from the later fifteenth century shows that the nuns had recorded a number of miracles that had taken place since the time of Agnes's *Life*,[68] and Longchamp probably never entirely ceased to draw pilgrims to its founder's burial site. Other monastic houses, both in the Île-de-France and farther afield, preserved Isabelle's memory by including her date of death in necrologies and martyrologies.[69]

By the fifteenth century, Isabelle's cult began to attract renewed attention. For example, the earliest surviving copy of the *Letter on Louis IX and Longchamp*, which was made around 1446, includes a new preface recalling Isabelle's foundation of Longchamp.[70] More dramatically, in 1461 the Duchess of Étampes and her daughter visited Longchamp and out of devotion requested that Isabelle's tomb be reopened, evidently revealing continuing interest in her cult among noble women.[71] But the first substantial rewriting of her life is found in a vernacular text compiled by the sisters of Longchamp sometime in the late fifteenth century.[72] This "epitaph" is actually a manuscript composed of three enormous pieces of parchment, originally held together with a wooden frame and suspended over Isabelle's tomb,[73] which claims to be based on "the legend of the holy life of [Isabelle] . . . and on certain letters of good testimony that are preserved in this abbey."[74] It draws almost all of its information from Agnes's *Life* and *Letter* but attempts to depersonalize and abbreviate Agnes's testimony. Isabelle is predictably presented as a paragon of charity, chastity, and humility, with several miracles selected from the *Life* to demonstrate her posthumous healing powers.[75] The timeless virtues of healing and compassion are emphasized to promote devotion to Isabelle and to encourage visits to her tomb at Longchamp.

This epitaph also began to add new elements to Isabelle's legend, for instance, by insisting that she was devoted to the Eucharist. Agnes's description of the princess begging forgiveness from her servants when she had spoken harshly to them[76] here becomes a prelude to her reverence for the Eucharist.[77] Similarly, Agnes's account of Isabelle's insistence on daily confession now becomes mingled with a desire for frequent communion.[78] An episode claiming Isabelle's propensity for rapture is also introduced. Although the manuscript is badly mutilated at this point, the epitaph recounts briefly that Isabelle had been up all night praying and was so transported into God that she felt nothing of the world around her and would say only "Illi soli honor et gloria" for the space of a whole day.[79] In addition, the epitaph begins a tradition of describing the tattered state of Isabelle's daily apparel.[80] To the fifteenth-century inhabitants of

Longchamp these omissions in Isabelle's legend needed to be rectified; all of them would be elaborated by later biographers.

Visitors to Isabelle's tomb who perused this prominently displayed epitaph might have expected that more miraculous events were still to come. Nor would they have been disappointed. In 1516 at Longchamp a new miracle involving the healing of a novice named Jeanne Carphaude brought fresh attention to Isabelle's claim to sanctity. According to an account probably written before 1532 by Abbess Katherine Picarde and the nuns of Longchamp, this miracle was promptly publicized by hanging a written description of it at the entrance to the abbey church.[81] Inspired by this miracle, the abbess and sisters of Longchamp wrote to Pope Leo X asking him to enroll Isabelle in the catalogue of saints.[82] Leo did not go that far, but he did have pressing reasons for pleasing the French crown.[83] Perhaps partly on this account, on 11 January 1521 he issued a bull allowing Isabelle's office to be celebrated at the abbey as long as an investigation into the facts recounted by Longchamp's representatives bore them out.[84] After some delay, the bull was carried into the abbey with great ceremony (perhaps on 23 August)[85] by several Franciscans, including Robert Messier, a doctor of theology and the abbey's confessor, subsequently the order's Provincial Minister for France.[86] Since the bull was addressed to Cardinal Legate Adrian of Boissy, Robert sent it on to him, and Adrian in turn dispatched a commission to Longchamp to investigate Isabelle's claims to sanctity.[87] On 11 December the cardinal confirmed the authenticity of miracles recounted by witnesses and found in "ancient books" held at the abbey, and he gave his approval for the celebration of Isabelle's office, newly composed at about this time by Brother Messier, on August 31 of each year.[88]

The readings for this liturgy draw on the *Life* and epitaph while stressing Isabelle's role as part of a saintly royal family. Messier emphasized the way in which her chastity and purity complemented Blanche of Castile's Christian steadfastness, Louis VIII's determination to rout the heretics of Toulouse, and Louis IX's example of temperance, in essence making her part of a perfect, holy, Capetian court.[89]

At about the same time, other Franciscans began to take note of Isabelle. In 1515, Mariano of Florence was referring to her as an "illustrissima madonna" who had led a life as "celibe et sancta" as that of her brother, and in 1587 Francesco Gonzaga could call her "serenissima," "pietissima," and "beata."[90] Isabelle was evidently reemerging with a new level of re-nown, thanks to an alliance between the nuns of Longchamp and Francis-can authors.

The most important catalyst for this renewed publicity was evidently Messier, who not only helped to engineer Isabelle's "beatification" of 1521 and composed her new office but also was almost certainly the author of a vernacular life of the princess.[91] A unique sixteenth-century manuscript of this life, recently purchased by Princeton University, reveals Messier's work as influential in continuing to reshape and augment Isabelle's legend and as a main source for the tradition of later printed biographies of the princess.[92] This life repeats and amplifies the embellishments included in the fifteenth-century epitaph, for instance, greatly expanding the story of Isabelle's "rapture."[93] Moreover, Messier sought to further emphasize Isabelle's humility by waxing poetic about her distaste for drawing attention to her royal lineage, her insistence on performing menial tasks herself and on wearing tattered rags, and her refusal to have noble women serve her.[94] He also retold most of the miracles from Agnes's *Life*, added a number of more recent ones, and concluded with the story of Jeanne Carphaude's healing in 1516. Another new version of Isabelle's life, in turn closely based on Messier's text, was presented to Longchamp by Sister Jeanne of Mailly in 1569.[95] This book repeated and expanded upon many of the recent addi-tions to Isabelle's legend.[96] In this way she was refashioned by the nuns of Longchamp and advisers such as Messier into a figure who could better attract pilgrims and warrant papal approbation by meeting contemporary expectations of Eucharistic devotion and mystical ecstasy.[97]

In 1619 this process culminated in the first published biography of the princess, written by Sébastien Roulliard.[98] Though Roulliard had access to original documents at Longchamp, including Agnes's *Life*, his greater reliance on Isabelle's epitaph and Messier's texts produced a six-hundred-page tome filled with flights of fancy. He also played a significant role in confusing contemporary evidence with later interpolations by attributing directly to Agnes stories and quotations that could only be found in later sources and by adding his own imaginary dialogue and embellishments. Roulliard's was only the first of a long line of printed pious biographies. Nicolas Caussin, for example, a Jesuit and former royal confessor, was com-missioned by the nuns of Longchamp to write a biography of their founder in 1644.[99] This new work began a tradition of deprecating Roulliard's book while relying on it to supplement Agnes's testimony.[100] In fact, the Jesuit's only notable innovation was to add even more fictional dialogue and correspondence where Roulliard seemed to have passed up the opportunity.[101]

The seventeenth century was something of a golden era for Isabelle's cult. Not since the 1280s had so much attention been showered upon her. Roulliard and Caussin both claimed to record the contemporary miracles that continued to occur at her tomb.[102] A new translation of her relics took place in June 1637, marked by papal approval, a large gathering of ecclesiastical officials and noble women, a printed pamphlet, and a further wave of miracles.[103] As Isabelle's seventeenth-century fame grew, a new office was composed in her honor in the 1680s, and by 1696 the Franciscan Order added her feast day to its calendar.[104] The date of August 31 placed her feast six days after her brother's, thus emphasizing Isabelle's pairing with Louis as a saintly, royal couple. Visual imagery of the period often placed the siblings next to each other,[105] and biographies of the princess invariably contained the phrase "soeur de saint Louis" in the titles or subtitles.

Not surprisingly, there was also a new scholarly interest in Isabelle among seventeenth-century *érudits*, just as there was in Louis IX. Sébastien Le Nain de Tillemont wrote a brief life of the princess along with his famous biography of St. Louis.[106] An edition by the Sieur Du Cange in 1668, which appeared as part of a reprinting of Joinville's *Vie de saint Louis*, made a version of Agnes's *Life* more widely available, and a Latin translation of this edition by the Bollandist Johannes Stilting was included in the *Acta sanctorum* in 1743.[107]

The revolutionary years in France destroyed the center of Isabelle's cult and ended the period of easy access to Longchamp's archives. The abbey was torn down stone by stone, its tombs were looted and demolished and its documents scattered. But even after Longchamp's demise, the conservative Catholic segment of nineteenth-century French society found Isabelle's royal sanctity a useful tool for religious instruction and polemic.[108] At least ten biographies of Isabelle were written between 1814 and 1899. One gets a general impression of the tone of these works in Magnier's title, *Les deux saintes du sang royal des Bourbons, ou Esquisse d'un parallèle religieux et historique, entre la bienheureuse Isabelle de France, soeur de Saint Louis, et Madame Elisabeth de France, soeur de Louis XVI* (The Two Female Saints of the Royal

Blood of the Bourbons, or a Sketch of a Religious and Historical Parallel between the Blessed Isabelle of France, Sister of Saint Louis, and Madame Elizabeth of France, Sister of Louis XVI). This pamphlet of 1814 argued that St. Louis I and St. Isabelle I were eventually succeeded by St. Louis II and St. Isabelle II (the names Elizabeth and Isabelle being regarded as interchangeable), who suffered martyrdom during the Revolution. Whatever the merits of this thesis, the book demonstrates Isabelle of France's nineteenth-century guise as a symbol of benevolent Catholic royalty.[109] Thanks to works such as this, she may have been better known to a wider audience in the nineteenth century than ever before.

Thus, there was significant belief in the reality of Isabelle of France's saintly credentials in the decades after her death, as witnessed by the miracle-seekers who came to her tomb, the chroniclers who referred to her "saintly" life, the recollections of Agnes of Harcourt and the nuns of Longchamp, and the words and actions of royal figures such as Marguerite of Provence and Philip IV. Though Isabelle was temporarily eclipsed as a symbol of Capetian sanctity in the era of the Hundred Years War, from the later fifteenth to the seventeenth century her fame was on the rise, promoted especially by Franciscan supporters and authors tied to Longchamp. Nineteenth-century French authors particularly sought to elevate her to the level of popular national saint.

Today this impulse continues. A sleek, glass parish church in Neuilly-sur-Seine is dedicated to "la bienheureuse Isabelle," a recent pious children's book recounts her story for young French readers,[110] and medals proclaiming her a patron saint of the sick are available for purchase on the World Wide Web. Isabelle has even begun to resonate in twenty-first-century imaginations in new ways, since she has recently been refashioned as the heroine of a bizarre but entertaining historical novel.[111]

Conclusion

This book has laid out two related arguments about Isabelle of France's importance. Fundamental to both is my contention that Isabelle was widely regarded as a budding royal saint by the 1250s. This reputation is seen in stories recorded in Agnes of Harcourt's *Life of Isabelle of France*, such as that of the serving girls who collected and preserved Isabelle's hair as relics, of the Cistercian nun Peronnelle of Montfort who tracked down the nightcap that she had knitted and likewise treated it as a relic, and of her childhood nurse, Helen of Buesemont, who was struck by Isabelle's devotion and austerity. It is further apparent in texts such as Alexander IV's bull of 1256, which refers to Isabelle as emulating the Virgin Mary in the pursuit of "spiritual and bodily sanctity." Her list of admirers also included Innocent IV and Franciscans such as Eudes of Rosny and Gilbert of Tournai, who encouraged her to exert her considerable influence in positive and constructive ways. She had every opportunity to leave a mark on the protean institutional structures of the thirteenth-century religious movement.

It is here that my two arguments diverge. One analyses Isabelle's own institutional efforts, arguing that as an active historical agent she made an important impact on the world of female Franciscanism. Through not only her actions, decisions, and negotiations but also by taking advantage of fortuitous political circumstances, she guided her rule and its revision through the papal curia. She had the support and encouragement of Alexander IV as well as the power of Louis IX's court behind her, and thus she was in a strong position from which to negotiate with Bonaventure and the Franciscan Order. In 1263 she succeeded in getting Urban IV to acknowledge more fully her original intentions for her rule, including granting her nuns the controversial title of *Sorores minores*. Isabelle is thus a striking example of the potential for high-status women to shape ecclesiastical institutions in the thirteenth century.

The importance of the rule that resulted from these negotiations should not be underestimated. It offered a number of innovations that appealed to women inspired by Franciscan ideals: guaranteeing a measure of local autonomy greater than previous rules while simultaneously offering a new form of female Franciscan identity and ensuring full incorporation into the Franciscan family. Not only did some Franciscan women in the 1260s demand the option of adopting Isabelle's rule, but over the ensuing decades royal and noble women also often chose it for their houses when founding their own religious communities. Isabelle's actions produced a long-lasting ripple effect, making new structures available for Franciscan women and their patrons across much of Europe for centuries.

On the other hand, through a less clear-cut process, and one that only partly rested on her own agency, Isabelle's life, reputation, and cult helped to cement the idea of Capetian sanctity. This process was in some measure the result of her conscious efforts; she founded Longchamp as a royal abbey, with the close support of her brother and his wife, and exploited ritual moments to highlight the Capetian element of her project. She later promoted Longchamp as a place for royal burial, acquired relics and secured indulgences that would attract pilgrims, and sought to make her own burial the occasion for additional royal ceremonial. Moreover, she played the part of a living saint, at least to some extent, by consenting to pray for supplicants and, on at least one occasion, by publicly laying her hands on an ailing nun. In these ways, she adopted the role of Capetian holy woman.

Her contribution to the development of Capetian sanctity, however, also rested, necessarily, on the views and belief of others. Throughout Isabelle's dossier we find evidence of the perceptions of a wide range of people—the women, popes, and friars who fostered her early reputation, the nuns of Longchamp and others who saw her as a source of divine aid, family members who emulated her, and her brother who laughed at her, supported her, and cried at her tomb.

Observers sometimes linked Isabelle with her brother to form a holy Capetian pair. Thomas of Cantimpré made a point of praising the siblings' pious actions together. Alexander IV joined his praise of Isabelle and Louis to a general statement of the influence of devout princes. In Agnes of Harcourt's *Letter*, Louis and Isabelle appeared as mother and father to the abbey of Longchamp at its very inception, walked together among the nuns at their first chapter meeting, and were linked at the moment of Isabelle's death. In Agnes's *Life*, Isabelle and Louis were remembered in stories together. Indeed, in the dreams of several nuns, Isabelle appeared as Louis's posthumous partner in miracle-working. Agnes's texts themselves, written in 1282 and 1283, connected Isabelle's cult to Louis's canonization process.

To the Capetians, Isabelle stood as welcome proof that the royal family was a *beata stirps*. Louis IX's saintly reputation was an important plank in the Capetian ideological platform, but one individual alone could not constitute a pattern of sanctity. Thus, Charles of Anjou went out of his way in his testimony for Louis's canonization to argue that Louis's brothers and sister were also saintly. There is little reason to think, however, that anyone ever shared Charles's view of Robert of Artois or Alphonse of Poitiers as holy figures. Charles must have known that he was grasping at straws in making this case. But Isabelle was another matter. Here it was only a question of shining new light on an already existing cult. Charles commissioned her biography in order to demonstrate that sanctity really did course through the Capetian line.

Indeed, for some members of the family, Isabelle may have seemed like a better candidate for sainthood than Louis. Because Marguerite of Provence did not testify at Louis IX's canonization proceedings (so far as we know), it has never been clear whether she really regarded her husband as having been a living saint.[1] But by bringing her grandson to Isabelle's tomb in his hour of peril, she publicly demonstrated her belief in her sister-in-law's saintly status. Her choice may be telling—she could have transported the future Philip IV to Louis's tomb, but she chose Isabelle's instead. Philip himself remembered his great-aunt's claims to sanctity, and Philip V, for his part, was ultimately carried to Longchamp to die near the tomb of Isabelle of France.

Isabelle's life also offered proof to the papal curia that the Capetian court was a cradle of saints. Innocent IV at first treated her like any other young girl whose marriage was subject to the dictates of political expediency. But by 1254 he had come to accept her as a holy (if somewhat disconcerting) presence at court as virgin laywoman. Alexander IV rejoiced at finding such an exemplary woman at court; he praised her in lavish terms in 1256 and offered his laudatory appreciation of her life in 1259. Even Clement IV, who had occasion to rebuke her for her audacious claims about relics, praised the unwavering devotion with which she had led her life in granting permission for her family to attend her funeral.

To the Franciscan Order, Isabelle's legacy was more problematic but no less important. Gilbert of Tournai was certainly convinced of her spiritual potential, and we know that Franciscans were singing Isabelle's praises at the papal curia in the 1250s. Her battles with the order may ultimately have left men such as Bonaventure with mixed feelings about the princess, but there can be no doubt that she provided an indispensable connection to the court and was a powerful public convert to Franciscan ideals. Louis IX is often thought of as a "mendicant" king and saint, as a man who brought Franciscan and Dominican influence into the business of government and into his own devout outlook.[2] This is undeniably true, but it was his sister who was most fully linked to the Franciscans, who may have spent the most time and energy in negotiations with the order, and who developed the closest contacts with its leading intellectuals. The Franciscan nuns of Longchamp were, predictably, devoted to their founder's memory. They prayed to her for everything from cures to deliverance from demonic attacks. They also promoted her cult, both by contributing to Agnes of Harcourt's biography and through the public actions of translating Isabelle's body and orienting her tomb in their church in such a manner as to invite veneration.

Finally, in the minds of average people around the Île-de-France and beyond, Isabelle made an impact as a royal saint alongside her brother. Just as one of our best ways of understanding how common people regarded Louis's sanctity is through analysis of the miracles recorded at his tomb,[3] so Agnes of Harcourt's *Life* lets us see women and men approaching Isabelle's burial site in search of comfort and cures. When Agnes "the chest maker" lay in bed in Paris, overwrought at the expected death of her child, it was Isabelle who came to her dreaming mind as a last hope. This anxious mother's pilgrimage to Longchamp provides a poignant example of Isabelle's saintly reputation, its intangible but magnetic pull, and its effects on the lives of others.

NOTES

Introduction

1. For the original Latin of the passages translated in this paragraph see chapter 3, note 54.

2. Daniel H. Weiss, *Art and Crusade in the Age of Saint Louis* (Cambridge: Cambridge University Press, 1998), 200–202.

3. For example, the introduction to Jacques Le Goff et al., eds., *Le sacre royal à l'époque de saint Louis, d'après le manuscrit latin 1246 de la BNF* (Paris: Gallimard, 2001), 15, refers to Louis's reign as a "moment crucial dans l'histoire des rituels royaux et de l'idéologie monarchique." Criticisms of Marc Bloch's *The Royal Touch: Sacred Monarchy and Scrofula in England and France*, trans. J. E. Anderson (London: Routledge & Kegan Paul, 1973), actually tend to focus attention on the reign of St. Louis as a decisive moment in developing the regular custom of touching for scrofula. See Frank Barlow, "The King's Evil," *English Historical Review* 95 (1980): 24–26. On the changing meaning of the thirteenth-century royal touch see also Philippe Buc, "David's Adultery with Bathsheba and the Healing Power of the Capetian Kings," *Viator* 24 (1993): 101–20.

4. Joseph R. Strayer, "France: The Holy Land, the Chosen People, and the Most Christian King," in Theodore K. Rabb and Jerrold E. Seigel, eds., *Action and Conviction in Early Modern Europe: Essays in Memory of E. H. Harbison* (Princeton: Princeton University Press, 1969), 3–16. See also Elizabeth A. R. Brown, "The Religion of Royalty: From Saint Louis to Henry IV," in Marie-Hélène Tesnière and Prosser Gifford, eds., *Creating French Culture: Treasures from the Bibliothèque nationale de France* (New Haven: Yale University Press, 1995), 131–48; and Jacques Le Goff, "Aspects religieux et sacrés de la monarchie française du Xe au XIIIe siècle," in Alain Boureau and Claudio Sergio Ingerflom, eds., *La royauté sacrée dans le monde chrétien* (Paris: Éditions de l'École des Hautes Études en Sciences Sociales, 1992), 19–28. On the full development of these symbols and legends by the fifteenth century see Colette Beaune, *The Birth of an Ideology: Myths and Symbols of Nation in Late Medieval France*, trans. Susan Ross Huston (Berkeley: University of California Press, 1991). On the fleur-de-lis and oriflamme see Anne Lombard-Jourdan, *Fleur de lis et oriflamme: Signes célestes du royaume de France* (Paris: Presses du CNRS, 1991).

5. On the distinction between sacral royalty and dynastic sanctity see the introduction to Gábor Klaniczay, *Holy Rulers and Blessed Princesses: Dynastic Cults in Medieval Central Europe*, trans. Éva Pálmai (Cambridge: Cambridge University Press, 2002).

6. André Vauchez, *Sainthood in the Later Middle Ages*, trans. Jean Birrell (Cambridge: Cambridge University Press, 1997), 177–83; idem, "*Beata Stirps*: Sainteté et lignage en Occident aux XIIIe et XIVe siècles," in Georges Duby and Jacques Le Goff, eds., *Famille et parenté dans l'Occident médiéval* (Rome: École Française de Rome, 1977): 397–406. See also Andrew W. Lewis, *Royal Succession in Capetian France: Studies on Familial Order and the State* (Cambridge, MA: Harvard University Press, 1981), 122–49; and Klaniczay, *Holy Rulers and Blessed Princesses*, 295–304.

7. On the ways in which medieval communities came to recognize living figures in their midst as saints see Aviad M. Kleinberg, *Prophets in Their Own Country: Living Saints and the Making of Sainthood in the Later Middle Ages* (Chicago: University of Chicago Press, 1992).

8. Bloch, *The Royal Touch*, 140.

9. Another "family" saint, Louis of Toulouse (or of Anjou), belongs to a somewhat different context in terms of chronology (died 1297, canonized 1317), geography (a career carried out mainly in Provence, Aragon, and Italy), and descent (from the Capetians through his father, Charles II of Anjou, but also from the royal family of Hungary through his mother). On this Louis as a "dynastic" saint see Jacques Paul, "Louis d'Anjou, un évangélisme dynastique?" in *Évangile et évangélisme (XIIe–XIIIe siècle): Cahiers de Fanjeaux*, vol. 34 (Toulouse: Éditions Privat, 1999), 141–70; and Klaniczay, *Holy Rulers and Blessed Princesses*, 304–10.

10. On later portrayals of Louis IX's sanctity see, most recently, M. Cecilia Gaposchkin, "Boniface VIII, Philip the Fair, and the Sanctity of Louis IX," *Journal of Medieval History* 29 (2003): 1–26; eadem, "*Ludovicus decus regnantium*: The Liturgical Office for Saint Louis and the Ideological Program of Philip the Fair," *Majestas* 10 (2003): 27–89; and eadem, "Philip the Fair, the Dominicans, and the Liturgical Office for Louis IX: New Perspectives on *Ludovicus Decus Regnantium*," *Plainsong and Medieval Music* 13 (2004): 33–61.

11. André Vauchez, *Sainthood in the Later Middle Ages*, 263–84.

12. Gábor Klaniczay, "The Cinderella Effect: Late Medieval Female Sainthood in Central Europe and in Italy," *East Central Europe* 20–23 (1993–1996): 51–68, quotation at 53; idem, *Holy Rulers and Blessed Princesses*, 195–294; idem, "Legends as Life-Strategies for Aspirant Saints in the Later Middle Ages," in *The Uses of Supernatural Power*, trans. Susan Singerman, ed. Karen Margolis (Cambridge: Polity Press, 1990), 95–110. Other recent studies linking gender and royal sanctity include Robert Folz, *Les saintes reines du moyen âge en Occident (VIe–XIIIe siècles)* (Brussels: Société des Bollandistes, 1992); and Patrick Corbet, *Les saints ottoniens: Sainteté dynastique, sainteté royale et sainteté féminine autour de l'an Mil* (Sigmaringen: J. Thorbecke, 1986).

13. The classic survey of Elizabeth's career is Jeanne Ancelet-Hustache, *Sainte Elisabeth de Hongrie* (Paris: Éditions Franciscaines, 1947), trans. Paul J. Oligny and Venard O'Donnell as *Gold Tried by Fire: St. Elizabeth of Hungary* (Chicago: Franciscan Herald Press, 1963); particularly relevant to the present discussion is Raoul Manselli, "Santità principesca et vita quotidiana in Elisabetta d'Ungheria: La testimonianza della ancelle," *Analecta tertii ordinis regularis sancti Francisci* 139 (1985): 23–45, trans. Edward Hagman, "Royal Holiness in the Daily Life of Elizabeth of Hungary: The Testimony of Her Servants," *Greyfriars Review* 11 (1997): 1–20. For a recent examination of Elizabeth's life, the evidentiary problems associated with it, and its interpretation by Franciscan sources see Lori Pieper, "St. Elizabeth of Hungary and the Franciscan Tradition" (Ph.D. diss., Fordham University, 2002). See also Klaniczay, *Holy Rulers and Blessed Princesses*, 202–4 and passim; and Dyan Elliot, *Proving Woman: Female Spirituality and Inquisitional Culture in the Later Middle Ages* (Princeton: Princeton University Press, 2004), 85–116.

14. Klaniczay, *Holy Rulers and Blessed Princesses*, 202–9.

15. Klaniczay, *Holy Rulers and Blessed Princesses*, 237. On this theme see idem, "Legends as Life-Strategies for Aspirant Saints in the Later Middle Ages," in *The Uses of Supernatural Power*, 95–110.

16. For example, Alexander IV's bull *Benedicta filia tu* addresses Isabelle as "Helizabet." See Field, "New Evidence," 129. Isabelle, however, was presumably named after her grandmother, Isabelle of Hainault, and certainly could not have been named after Elizabeth of Hungary in 1225.

17. René Hague, trans., *The Life of St. Louis by John of Joinville* (London: Sheed & Ward, 1955), 48; for original text and modern French translation see Jacques Monfrin, ed., *Joinville, Vie de saint Louis* (Paris: Garnier, 1995), 204 (par. 96). Because Monfrin's edition was issued in several formats, I give paragraph as well as page number when citing it.

18. Further evidence for Elizabeth of Hungary's influence on Isabelle's circle is not lacking. The poet Rutebeuf composed his vernacular life of Elizabeth for Isabelle, the daughter of Louis IX, between 1258 and 1270. See Brigitte Cazelles, *The Lady as Saint: A Collection of French Hagiographic Romances of the Thirteenth Century* (Philadelphia: University of Pennsylvania Press, 1991), 151–71. The Franciscan house at Reims, from which several nuns came to help found Longchamp, was apparently dedicated to St. Elizabeth. See Antoine de Serent, "L'ordre de sainte Claire en France pendant sept siècles," *Études franciscaines* 11 (1953): 133–65, at 133. In 1261 a document referred to Longchamp as of the "Order of St. Damian and St. Elizabeth." See AN L1020 no. 5C, where Longchamp is called the "monasterium sive ecclesiam nuper fundatam iuxta villam Sancti Clodoaldis Ordinis Sancti Damiani et Sancte Helysabeth."

19. For the importance in the thirteenth century of a lay spirituality based on the imitation of Christ through various modes of penance see André Vauchez, *The Laity in*

the Middle Ages: Religious Beliefs and Devotional Practices, ed. Daniel E. Bornstein, trans. Margery J. Schneider (Notre Dame, IN: University of Notre Dame Press, 1993). For a concise summary of Vauchez's view of thirteenth-century developments see his *La spiritualité du Moyen Âge occidental VIIIe–XIIIe siècle*, nouvelle édition augmentée (Paris: Éditions de Seuil, 1994), 131–68.

20. Klaniczay, *Holy Rulers and Blessed Princesses*, 243–79; idem, "From Sacral Kingship to Self-Representation," and "Legends as Life-Strategies for Aspirant Saints," in *The Uses of Supernatural Power*, 79–94 and 95–110.

21. Klaniczay, *Holy Rulers and Blessed Princesses*, 244–45, quotation at 245.

22. On the way that notions of "Capetian sacral mystique" could open up avenues of female influence see Kimberly A. LoPrete, "Historical Ironies in the Study of Capetian Women," in Kathleen D. Nolan, ed., *Capetian Women* (New York: Palgrave, 2003), 271–86.

23. Among recent works on the spread of female Franciscan institutions see *Sainte Claire d'Assise et sa postérité: Actes du Colloque de l'U.N.E.S.C.O. 29 septembre–1er octobre 1994* (Paris: Éditions Franciscaines, 1995); Giancarlo Andenna and Benedetto Vetere, eds., *Chiara e la diffusione delle Clarisse nel secolo XIII: Atti del Convegno di studi in occasione dell'VII centenario della nascita di santa Chiara* (Manduria, 14–15 dicembre 1994) (Manduria: Congedo Editore, 1998); Lezlie Knox, "Audacious Nuns: Institutionalizing the Franciscan Order of Saint Clare," *Church History* 69 (2000): 41–62; Maria Pia Alberzoni, *Clare of Assisi and the Poor Sisters in the Thirteenth Century* (St. Bonaventure, NY: Franciscan Institute Publications, 2004); and Jean François Godet-Calogeras and Roberta McKelvie, eds., *An Unencumbered Heart: A Tribute to Clare of Assisi, 1253–2003* (St. Bonaventure, NY: Franciscan Institute Publications, 2004).

24. Throughout this book I refer to *Soeurs mineures* and *Sorores minores*, and occasionally the ungainly English equivalent "Sisters Minor," interchangeably.

25. Pauline Stafford, "Emma: The Powers of the Queen in the Eleventh Century," in Anne J. Duggan, ed., *Queens and Queenship in Medieval Europe* (Woodbridge: Boydell, 1997), 3–26, quotation at p. 11.

26. For example, Miriam Shadis and Constance Hoffman Berman, "A Taste of the Feast: Reconsidering Eleanor of Aquitaine's Female Descendants," in *Eleanor of Aquitaine: Lord and Lady*, ed. Bonnie Wheeler and John Carmi Parsons (New York: Palgrave, 2003), 177–211; Linda E. Mitchell, *Portraits of Medieval Women* (New York: Palgrave, 2003); Theodore Evergates, ed., *Aristocratic Women in Medieval France* (Philadelphia: University of Pennsylvania Press, 1999). For a nuanced reconsideration of women, power, and agency in the Middle Ages see the introduction to Mary C. Erler and Maryanne Kowaleski, eds., *Gendering the Master Narrative: Women and Power in the Middle Ages* (Ithaca: Cornell University Press, 2003), 1–16. But compare also Jo Ann McNamara, "Women and Power through the Family Revisited," in ibid., 17–30.

27. See Nolan's introduction to *Capetian Women*, 1–7, quotations at 2 and 5.

28. Of the eleven essays in *Capetian Women* that focus on individual women, all but William Chester Jordan's on Isabelle of France ("Isabelle of France and Religious Devotion at the Court of Louis IX," in Nolan, ed., *Capetian Women*, 209–23) concern married women, and all but two concern queens and consorts. As such, the volume has much in common with recent works on queenship, including Marcel Faure, ed., *Reines et princesses au Moyen Âge: Actes du cinquième colloque international de Montpellier, Université Paul-Valéry, 24–27 novembre 1999* (Montpellier: Association CRISIMA, Université Paul-Valéry, 2001); Duggan, ed., *Queens and Queenship in Medieval Europe*; John Carmi Parsons, ed., *Medieval Queenship* (New York: St. Martin's Press, 1993); and Louise Olga Fradenburg, ed., *Women and Sovereignty* (Edinburgh: Edinburgh University Press, 1992).

29. Edited and translated in *Writings of AH*. See the introduction for discussion of the manuscript tradition of Agnes's texts.

30. Raoul held the positions of archdeacon of Coutances and Rouen and founded the College of Harcourt in Paris. Robert became bishop of Coutances in 1291, and Guy was elected bishop of Lisieux in 1303. See *Writings of AH*, 3–5, and the references found there in note 4.

31. For further details on Agnes of Harcourt's career see the introduction to *Writings of AH*. On the dates of the abbesses of Longchamp see Field, "The Abbesses of Longchamp up to the Black Death," *AFH* 96 (2003): 87–93, which refines the table found in Gertrud Mlynarczyk, *Ein Franziskanerinnenkloster im 15. Jahrhundert: Edition und Analyse von Besitzinventaren aus der Abtei Longchamp* (Bonn: Röhrscheid, 1987), 57.

32. Sébastien Roulliard, *La saincte mère, ou vie de M. saincte Isabel de France, soeur unique du roy s. Louys, fondatrice de l'abbaye de Long-champ* (Paris: Taupinart, 1619). For a list of biographies of Isabelle of France see the bibliography to this book. Lives of Isabelle that were written before Roulliard's and remain in manuscript are discussed briefly in chapter 6 and more completely in Field, "The Princess, the Abbess, and the Friars: Isabelle of France (1225–1270) and the Course of Thirteenth-Century Religious History" (Ph.D. diss., Northwestern University, 2002), chapter 1.

33. Albert Garreau, *Bienheureuse Isabelle de France* (Paris: Éditions Franciscaines, 1943); and idem, *Bienheureuse Isabelle de France, soeur de saint Louis* (Paris: Éditions Franciscaines, 1955). Some confusion is possible since the two books have slightly different titles and the 1955 version is not identified as a second edition. All references here are to the 1955 edition unless otherwise stated. The only other twentieth-century biography is a short and pious booklet by Eugène Langevin, *La bienheureuse Isabelle de France, soeur de saint Louis* (Paris: Éditions Albin Michel, 1944).

34. Gaston Duchesne, *Histoire de l'abbaye royale de Longchamp (1255 à 1789)*, 2nd ed. (Paris: Daragon, 1906), 1–9. Though this work is not without value, on the thirteenth century it should be used with care, and its references to Isabelle are often secondhand and inaccurate. A more careful (though equally antiquated) study of the

early evidence for life at Longchamp is Guy Trouillard, *Études sur la discipline et l'état interieur des abbayes de l'ordre des Urbanistes et principalement de l'abbaye de Longchamp du XIIIe siècle au XVIIIe* (Thèse de l'École des chartes, 1896). This work has never been published, but for a summary see *École nationale des chartes, positions des thèses soutenues par les élèves de la promotion de 1896*, 61–67. The original of this thèse is now manuscript F458–459 of the Archives départementales de Loir-et-cher. I consulted the hand-written copy held as ms. 1530 by the Bibliothèque franciscaine provinciale des Capucins in Paris. Two further unpublished thèses bear on Longchamp and less directly on Isabelle. I have not been able to see Joël Audouy's 1949 École des chartes thèse, *Le temporel de l'abbaye de Longchamp des origines à la fin du XVe siècle*. A summary may be found in *École nationale des chartes, positions des thèses soutenues par les élèves de la promotion de 1949*, 19–22. Cécile Geiger, *Deux bibliothèques d'abbayes féminines dans la seconde moitié du XVème siècle*; Mémoire de maîtrise, Université de Paris IV, 1981, is a useful study, though the section on Longchamp has for the most part been incorporated by Mlynarczyk (see n.31 above). Patricia Stirnemann kindly located a copy for me at the Institut de Recherche et d'Histoire des Textes in Paris.

35. Mlynarczyk, *Ein Franziskanerinnenkloster*, 34–40.

36. Beth Lynn, "Clare of Assisi and Isabelle of Longchamp: Further Light on the Early Development of the Franciscan Charism," *Magistra* 3 (1997): 71–98.

37. William Chester Jordan, *Louis IX and the Challenge of the Crusade: A Study in Rulership* (Princeton: Princeton University Press, 1979), 9–12; Miriam Theresa Shadis, *Motherhood, Lineage, and Royal Power in Medieval Castile and France: Berenguela de León and Blanche de Castille* (Ph.D. diss., Duke University, 1994), 245–49; Jacques Le Goff, *Saint Louis* (Paris: Gallimard, 1996), 270–71 and 727–29. See also Philippe Delorme, *Blanche de Castille: Épouse de Louis VIII, mère de saint Louis* (Paris: Pygmalion, 2002), 188–90.

38. William Chester Jordan, "Isabelle of France and Religious Devotion at the Court of Louis IX," in Nolan, ed, *Capetian Women*, 209–23.

39. This characterization continues to apply in large measure to Anne-Hélène Allirot, "Isabelle de France, soeur de saint Louis: La vierge savante. Étude de la *Vie d'Isabelle de France* écrite par Agnès d'Harcourt," *Médiévales* 48 (2005): 55–98, which appeared only after this book had gone to press.

CHAPTER ONE.   *The Princess and the Queen: Negotiating Virginity*

1. Louis VIII left Isabelle 20,000 *livres* in his will, dated June 1225, so she was certainly born before that date. *Layettes*, vol. 2, #1710. The chronicler of Saint-Denis gives her birth as March 1224, in a yearly cycle that began with Easter, or 1225 in modern reckoning. "Chronicon Breve Ecclesiae S. Dionysii ad Cyclos Paschales," in Luc

d'Achery, *Spicilegium sive collectio veterum aliquot scriptorum*, vol. 2 (Paris, 1723), 496. This seems to be the most likely date, though 1223 and 1224 remain possible.

2. Her other brothers died young. Isabelle never knew Philip, who was born as the heir to the throne in 1209 but died in 1218, nor twins born in 1213 who did not long survive. She was probably too young to be much affected by the death of her brother Jean (1219–1227) or of the short-lived Étienne born in 1226, but Philip Dagobert's (1222–1235) early death must have had some impact on her. For basic information on Isabelle's siblings see Gérard Sivéry, *Blanche de Castille* (Paris: Fayard, 1990), 69.

3. The term "regent" is convenient but anachronistic. Blanche was simply given the guardianship of the king. See Sivéry, *Blanche de Castille*, 131–32; and Régine Pernoud, *Blanche of Castile*, trans. Henry Noel (London: Collins, 1975), 301 n. 1.

4. On Blanche, in addition to the works in the previous note, see Élie Berger, *Histoire de Blanche de Castille, reine de France* (Paris: Thorin & fils, 1895); Terryl N. Kinder, "Blanche of Castile and the Cistercians: An Architectural Re-evaluation of Maubuisson Abbey," *Cîteaux: Commentarii cistercienses* 27 (1976): 161–88; Miriam Theresa Shadis, *Motherhood, Lineage, and Royal Power in Medieval Castile and France*; eadem, "Piety, Politics, and Power: The Patronage of Leonor of England and Her Daughters Berenguela of León and Blanche of Castile," in June McCash, ed., *The Cultural Patronage of Medieval Women* (Athens: University of Georgia Press, 1996), 202–27; Elizabeth S. Hudson, "The Psalter of Blanche of Castile: Picturing Queenly Power in Thirteenth Century France" (Ph.D. diss., University of North Carolina at Chapel Hill, 2002); Delorme, *Blanche de Castille*; Shadis, "Blanche of Castile and Facinger's 'Medieval Queenship': Reassessing the Argument," in Nolan, ed., *Capetian Women*, 137–61; and Tracy Chapman Hamilton, "Queenship and Kinship in the French *Bible Moralisée*: The Example of Blanche of Castile and Vienna ÖNB 2554," ibid., 177–208.

5. Albert Garreau summed up the standard characterization of Isabelle's youthful nature when he claimed that "Isabelle n'est que silence, modestie, humilité." *Bienheureuse Isabelle de France, soeur de saint Louis*, 25.

6. Hague, *The Life of St. Louis by John of Joinville*, 179–80; Monfrin, ed., *Joinville, Vie de saint Louis*, 506 (pars. 606–607). On Joinville's picture of Marguerite and Blanche see Afrodesia E. McCannon, "Two Capetian Queens as the Foreground for an Aristocrat's Anxiety in the *Vie de saint Louis*," in Nolan, ed., *Capetian Women*, 163–76.

7. Shadis, *Motherhood, Lineage, and Royal Power*, 245–49.

8. Shadis, *Motherhood, Lineage, and Royal Power*, 247, suggests that "Isabelle's gender was an essential element of her ability to make her own way in regard to marriage."

9. Robert Fawtier, *The Capetian Kings of France*, trans. Lionel Butler and R. J. Adam (London: MacMillan, 1960), 28. For the tangle of shifting alliances and baronial revolts in this period see also Elizabeth M. Hallam and Judith Everard, *Capetian France, 987–1328*, 2nd ed. (New York: Longman, 2001), 267–75; Sivéry, *Blanche de*

Castille, 134–46; and Jean Richard, *Saint Louis*, ed. Simon Lloyd, trans. Jean Birrell (Cambridge: Cambridge University Press, 1992), 41–61.

10. On Isabelle of Angoulême see William Chester Jordan, "Isabelle d'An-goulême, By the Grace of God Queen," *Revue belge de philologie et d'histoire* 69 (1991): 821–52; and Nicholas Vincent, "Isabella of Angoulême: John's Jezebel," in *King John: New Interpretations*, ed. S. D. Church (Woodbridge: Boydell, 1999), 165–219.

11. Edmund Martène and Ursine Durand, *Veterum scriptorum et monumentorum historicorum, dogmaticorum moralium: Amplissima collectio*, vol. 1 (Paris, 1724; reprint, New York: Burt Franklin, 1968), col. 1215: "Ludovicus, etc. Notum, etc. quod nos de ascensu et voluntate carissimae matris nostrae B. reginae Francorum dilecto et fideli nostro Hugoni de Lesignano comiti Marchiae concessimus, quod carissimus frater noster Alfonsus comes Pictavensis Elizabeth filiam dicti comitis Marchiae, si Romana ecclesia concesserit, habeat in uxorem, et Hugo primogenitus ipsius comitis ducat in uxorem Elisabeth carissimam sororem nostram . . . De his quae Hugo primogenitus comitis Marchiae debet habere in maritagium Elisabeth sororis nostrae vult comes quod assignetur ad voluntatem nostram. Si autem Hugo primogenitus comitis forsitan decederet, nondum consummato matrimonio inter ipsum et dictam Isabellam sororem nostram, alius primogenitus comitis duceret in uxorem eamdem Isabellam, si sancta ecclesia consentiret, et assignaretur ei maritagium sicut praedictum est de Hugone. Quando quatuor praedictae personae ad annos nubiles pervenerint, si per nos steterit, quod dicta matrimonia non fiant, et haec matrimonia facienda Romana ecclesia con-cesserit, nos tenebimur praedicto comiti in decem millibus marcharum argenti." See Berger, *Histoire de Blanche de Castille*, 84–87, on these treaties. In a separate document the Countess of La Marche verified that her dowry claims (as widow of King John) were satisfied as well. *Layettes*, vol. 2, #1921.

12. *Layettes*, vol. 2, #1969.

13. Walter W. Shirley, *Royal and Other Historical Letters Illustrative of the Reign of Henry III*, vol. 1, #288 (London: Longman, 1862), 350–51.

14. A letter from Hugh of Lusignan dated 30 May 1230 at Clisson stated that the payments stipulated at Vendôme had been met for the last three years and reaffirmed the continuing commitments on both sides, but it made only a passing reference to the plans for marriage between Isabelle of France and the younger Hugh. Again this understanding was acknowledged by a separate act of Isabelle of Angoulême. *Layettes*, vol. 2, #2052 and #2068.

15. See Berger, *Histoire de Blanche de Castille*, 86 n. 2. Even when Louis was the nominal royal negotiator, his mother's role was generally acknowledged. The Treaty of Vendôme was issued by Louis, "de ascensu et voluntate carissimae matris nostrae B. reginae Francorum"; the barons who swore to observe it pledged themselves "Ludovico illustri regi Franciae et dominae reginae matri ejus"; the Treaty of Clisson notes that Louis acts "de assensu et voluntate domine Blanche illustris regine Francie."

Isabelle of Angoulême sought to slight Blanche's role to the extent possible, but even she included the same formula in endorsing the Treaty of Clisson. On this point see also Shadis, "Blanche of Castile and Facinger's 'Medieval Queenship': Reassessing the Argument," in *Capetian Women*, 141.

16. *Layettes*, vol. 2, 2065. "Noveritis dominum Ludovicum, Dei gratia illustrem regem Francie, tradidisse karissimo viro nostro Hugoni comiti Marchie et nobis castellum suum de Sancto Johanne Angeliaci et quicquid juris habebat in villa et pertinentiis, et Mosterolium in Gastina et quicquid possidebat ibidem et in pertinentiis Petrus de Marliaco, et Langestum cum pertinentiis, sub hac forma quod, si matrimonium possit fieri, tolerante sancta Romana ecclesia, de Elysabet sorore domini regis et Hugone filio nostro primogenito, vel de alio subsequente, si de primogenito contingeret humanitus, rehabebit dominus rex omnia supradicta, tradita nobis sorora sua. Et si non possit fieri matrimonium, sicut predictum est, omnia ista remanebunt predicto viro nostro et nobis et heredibus nostris habenda in perpetuum et pacifice possidenda . . . Et super agendo matrimonio debet dominus rex impetrare dispensationem bona fide, infra duos annos. Quibus elapsis, non tenebimur nos vel filius noster dominum regem ulterius expectare." Clearly these lands were neither a firm grant nor a dowry for Isabelle (Cf. Richard, *Saint Louis*, 58–59) but a surety for the marriage. My reading agrees with that of Edgar Boutaric, who discussed these treaties in detail. See *Saint Louis et Alfonse de Poitiers* (Paris: Henri Plon, 1870), 42–43, 49.

17. *Layettes*, vol. 2, #2065. "Si autem sororem suam infra predictos duos annos traderet in matrimonium alii quam filio nostro, vel etiam, dispensatione habita, per eum staret quominus matrimonium fieret; vel etiam, dispensatione habita, si per eandem sororem domini regis remaneret quin matrimonium fieret quando ad annos nubiles pervenerit, eadem sorore domini regis in sua potestate remanente, ipse teneretur nobis et marito nostro solvere pro pena quinque milia marcarum argenti vel heredibus nostris. Si vero eandem sororem domini regis traderet nobis vel filio nostro dominus rex dispensatione habita, et ipsa in etate nubili contradiceret matrimonio, non teneretur dominus rex ad penam predictam. Et sciendum quod, si non impetraretur dispensatio infra predictos duos annos, dum tamen per dominum regem non staret, quitus et immunis remaneret dominus rex de omnibus convencionibus supradicti matrimonii."

18. For instance, in 1227, Blanche arranged the marriage of her son, Jean, to Yolanda, the daughter of Peter Mauclerc, as part of a second Treaty of Vendôme making peace with Peter. As a condition for this marriage, Peter had to hand over his daughter to a group of barons including Matthew of Montmorency, the constable of France. *Layettes*, vol. 2, #1922. See also Berger, *Histoire de Blanche de Castille*, 85–86. Moreover, in arranging Alphonse's marriage, Blanche ensured that Joan of Toulouse was brought up at the Capetian court. Boutaric, *Saint Louis et Alfonse de Poitiers*, 41. Similarly, Beatrice of Provence was later placed "in the hands of the king and his

people" several months before her marriage to Charles of Anjou. Gérard Sivéry, *Marguerite de Provence: Une reine au temps des cathédrales* (Paris: Fayard, 1987), 86. Claudia Opitz calls this custom of patrilocality "the rule among the aristocracy and many urban patricians in the late Middle Ages." See "Life in the Late Middle Ages," in *A History of Women in the West*, vol. 2: *Silences of the Middle Ages*, ed. Christiane Klapisch-Zuber (Cambridge, MA: Harvard University Press, 1992), 273.

19. Sivéry, *Blanche de Castille*, 92.

20. John Carmi Parsons, "Mothers, Daughters, Marriage, Power: Some Plantagenet Evidence, 1100–1500," in Parsons, ed., *Medieval Queenship*, 63–78. More generally, on medieval mothers and their relationship to their children, see the essays in Parsons and Bonnie Wheeler, eds., *Medieval Mothering* (New York: Garland Publishing, 1996). Especially relevant to Blanche is Miriam Theresa Shadis, "Berenguela of Castile's Political Motherhood: The Management of Sexuality, Marriage, and Succession," in ibid., 335–58.

21. She was selected to marry the future Louis VIII based on her status as the niece of King John of England, to cement a peace concluded in 1200 between that newly crowned monarch and his rival, Philip Augustus. See Berger, *Histoire de Blanche de Castille*, 6–10; Pernoud, *Blanche of Castile*, 14–20 (a rather fanciful account); and Sivéry, *Blanche de Castille*, 9–17. Shadis, *Motherhood, Lineage, and Royal Power*, 89–98 is the most helpful analysis.

22. Consent of the parties involved was considered necessary for a valid marriage in thirteenth-century canon law. See David Herlihy, *Medieval Households* (Cambridge, MA: Harvard University Press, 1985), 80–81.

23. Sivéry, *Blanche de Castille*, 70.

24. Richard, *Saint Louis*, 59.

25. *Layettes*, vol. 2, #2928. The "Conventiones initae inter comitem Marchiae et comitem Pictavensem" contain the following clauses: "Nos autem et regina uxor nostra eidem domino comiti restituimus et quiptavimus Sanctum Johannem de Angeliaco, scilicet castrum et villam, cum ominibus pertinenciis . . . Preterea eidem domino comiti fecimus aliud homagium ligium de Mosterolio in Gastina, cum pertinenciis, contra omnes homines et feminas qui possunt vivere et mori. Quod siquidem Mosterolium, cum pertinenciis, nos et regina uxor nostra et heredes nostri habebamus ex donacione illustris domini regis Ludovici fratris dicti domini comitis Pictavensis."

26. *Writings of AH*, 52 (par. 2).

27. *Writings of AH*, 56 (par. 10).

28. On beauty as a sign of sanctity see Donald Weinstein and Rudolph M. Bell, *Saints and Society: The Two Worlds of Western Christendom, 1000–1700* (Chicago: University of Chicago Press, 1982), 27–28; on Isabelle's beauty specifically, see the remarks of Jordan, "Isabelle of France and Religious Devotion at the Court of Louis IX," 211.

29. *Writings of AH*, 54 (par. 5).

30. Perhaps Agnes or the serving girls in question were familiar with Chrétien de Troyes's *Le chevalier de la charette*, where Lancelot finds a comb that preserves strands of Guenevere's hair, which he removes and adores, even believing that they will ward off illness. See D. D. R. Owen, trans., *Chrétien de Troyes, Arthurian Romances* (London: Dent & Sons, 1987), 203–5. Cecilia Gaposchkin pointed out this parallel to me.

31. For these two anecdotes, *Writings of AH*, 56 (par. 8), and 58 (par. 11).

32. Caroline Walker Bynum, *Holy Feast and Holy Fast: The Religious Significance of Food to Medieval Women* (Berkeley: University of California Press, 1987), esp. 220–27. More generally on conflict between parents and saintly children, especially between girls and their mothers, see Weinstein and Bell, *Saints and Society*, 45–46.

33. *Writings of AH*, 58 (par. 12).

34. *RHGF*, vol. 21, 230, 237, 244, 246. She and Charles seem to have been referred to as "the other children" (*alii pueri*) in these records.

35. She was still referred to here collectively with her future sister-in-law, Joan of Toulouse, as the "*domicellae*." *RHGF*, vol. 22, 582, "Expensa Militiae Comitis Attrebatensis in Penthecoste Anno Domino M. CC. XXX. VII," #32: "Robae pro pueris. De stanno forti ad domicellas." Joan of Toulouse is referred to explicitly as one of the *domicellae*, and Charles of Anjou as one of the *pueri*. It seems safe to assume (with Pernoud, *Blanche of Castile*, 179) that Isabelle was the other *domicella*.

36. *RHGF*, vol. 22, "Itinera, dona, et hernesia anno Domini MCCXXXIX, inter Ascensionem et Omnes Sanctos." "—Pro uno valeto qui custodiebat palefridum domicellae, crucesignato, XX s.," p. 595; "—Soror regis, pro una ceintura argenti, XXII s.," p. 608; "Juvenis regina, pro serico et fillo auri a compoto Candelosae usque ad compotum sanctorum, XIII l. X s. IIII d . . . . —Domicella Ysabella, similiter de eodem termino, pro eodem, IIII l. XV s. VI d.," p. 610. "Item, robae domini Alfonsi, comitissarum, domicellae Ysabellae, de termino Ascensionis, summa LXVII l. XIII s. —Pelleteria ad easdem robas forrandas, summa LXV l. VII s. —Summa de termino Ascensionis, VI. XX. XIIII l. XII d. Item, robae domini Alfonsi, comitissarum, domicellae Ysabellae, de termino Omnium sanctorum, summa, VII. XX. XL l. VI s. VI d. —Pelleteria ad easdem robas forrandas, summa IX. XX. VI l. IX s. Summa istius termini, XVI. XX. XVII l. XV s. VI d.," p. 610. Compare Sivéry, *Blanche de Castille*, 207.

37. Isabelle had probably been too young to attend the wedding of Louis IX to Marguerite of Provence in 1234, since she and Charles seem to be referred to in a record of expenses paid to several townspeople of Paris for watching the "other children" during the court's absence. See *RHGF*, vol. 22, 566, which includes payments for "Burgenses ante pueros jacentes" during the royal wedding. See also Berger, *Blanche de Castille*, 260. We cannot be sure whether she attended other major celebrations in this period, such as the extravagant feast held at Saumur for Alphonse of Poitiers's knighting in 1241. Joinville's description makes no mention of Isabelle, and the surviving royal accounts do not record finery given to her for this event. One would especially

like to know whether Isabelle was present at this feast, since it is here that Joinville records Blanche reverently kissing the forehead of a nephew of Elizabeth of Hungary, hinting at the possibility of Elizabeth as a role model for Isabelle's involvement with the Franciscans. Hague, *The Life of St. Louis*, 47–48; Monfrin, ed., *Joinville, Vie de saint Louis*, 202–6 (pars. 93–97). The accounts for the occasion deal mostly with gifts and clothes for the new knights created along with Alphonse and mention the rest of the royal family in less detail. See *RHGF*, vol. 22, 615–22.

38. *Writings of AH*, 54 (par. 6).

39. On the gendered aspects of medieval education see Anneke B. Mulder-Bakker, ed., *Seeing and Knowing: Women and Learning in Medieval Europe, 1200–1550* (Turnhout: Brepols, 2004). On medieval women as book owners see Susan Groag Bell, "Medieval Women Book Owners: Arbiters of Lay Piety and Ambassadors of Culture," in Mary C. Erler and Maryanne Kowaleski, eds., *Women and Power in the Middle Ages* (Athens: University of Georgia Press, 1988), 149–87; and specifically on book ownership within female monastic communities see David N. Bell, *What Nuns Read: Books and Libraries in Medieval English Nunneries* (Kalamazoo: Cistercian Publications, 1995).

40. Louis Carolus-Barré, *Le procès de canonisation de saint Louis (1272–1297): Essai de reconstitution*, ed. Henri Platelle (Rome: École Française de Rome, 1994), 68.

41. *Writings of AH*, 54 (par. 5).

42. *Writings of AH*, 60 (par. 14).

43. On Longchamp's library see Mlynarczyk, *Ein Franziskanerinnenkloster*, 139–83; Geiger, *Deux bibliothèques d'abbayes féminines*; Ubald d'Alençon, "L'abbaye royale de Longchamp et sa bibliothèque au XVe siècle," *Études franciscaines* 15 (1906): 206–12; and Trouillard's 1896 École des chartes thèse, Appendix II and Pièce justificative III. The latter works are in the main superseded by Mlynarczyk. An error committed by D'Alençon is important enough to warrant mention here. Due to a careless transcription of AN L1028 no. 9, he recorded a book described as "les revelacions saint elysabeth notre Saint mere qui nous funda." "L'abbaye royale de Longchamp et sa bibliothèque," 211. Mlynarczyk's edition gives the correct reading, "les Revelacions sainte Elysabeth de hongrie. Item, deux livres de la Reigle, en l'ung est la Vie sainte Claire, et en l'aultre la Vie sainte Elysabeth nostre sainte mere, qui nous funda." *Ein Franziskanerinnenkloster*, 334. On the prophecies of pseudo-Elizabeth of Hungary see Klaniczay, *Holy Rulers and Blessed Princesses*, 372–73.

44. The first inventory of Longchamp's books, AN L1026 no. 2, dating from Agnes of Harcourt's second term as abbess, 1281–1287, is analyzed (but not edited) in Mlynarczyk, *Ein Franziskanerinnenkloster*. The inventory of 1294 is in AN L1026 no. 5. More extensive is the inventory of 1305 found in AN K37 no. 2, partially edited in *Histoire de la ville et de tout le diocèse de Paris par l'abbé Lebeuf. Nouvelle édition annotée et continuée jusqu'à nos jours par Hippolyte Cocheris*, vol. 4 (Paris: Durand, 1870), 262–64.

45. AN L1027 no. 5. "L'an de grace mil ccc xxv le jour S. Denis qui lors fu au mercredi, suer Jehanne de Gueuz fu [*text cut off*] Jehanne de Vitri y fu esleue. Et lors estoit ou tresor les choses ci empres escriptes: . . . Item en l'eglise avoit . . . le breviaire qui fu ma d[*text cut off*] . . . item .1. donat et .1. alixandre qui furent ma dame. Item .1. petit livre qui comence audi domina qui fu madame . . . item .1. bestiaire qui fu madame qui nous funda." Mlynarczyk does not attribute the breviary cited here to Isabelle (see her chart, *Ein Franziskanerinnenkloster*, 149). Given the damage to the manuscript it is impossible to be absolutely certain about this attribution, but in this and earlier inventories "ma dame" always refers to Isabelle, and I do not see any possible reading for "qui fu ma d" besides "ma dame."

46. AN L1027 no. 9: "Ce sunt les livres que le couvent a presente aus suers pour leurs usages . . . item .1. missel qui fu madame qui nous funda." Mlynarczyk notes this book's presence in the inventory of 1375 but does not realize that it was catalogued earlier; see *Ein Franziskanerinnenkloster*, 150.

47. We cannot be certain whether Isabelle possessed these books before or after 1243. It does seem likely, though, that at least the secular titles must have been in her possession before her move to Longchamp and that she was acquainted with the Donatus at an early age.

48. Cynthia Renée Bland, *The Teaching of Grammar in Late Medieval England* (East Lansing: Colleagues Press, 1991), 22. Of Donatus's original *Ars grammatica*, only the *Ars minor* circulated widely after the eleventh century. Thus, the term *donat* became synonymous with the *Ars minor*, though it was also used generically in the vernacular to refer to any text of grammatical instruction. Ibid., 25 n. 5. On the medieval history of the *Ars minor* see ibid., 22–47; Wayland Johnson Chase, *The Ars Minor of Donatus* (Madison: University of Wisconsin Studies in the Social Sciences and History, Number 11, 1926), 3–26; and Louis Holtz, *Donat et la tradition de l'enseignement grammatical: Étude et édition critique* (Paris: Centre National de la Recherche Scientifique, 1981), 585–602. Longchamp's more detailed inventories of the fifteenth century indicate that this book probably survived in the abbey's library at least to that time. The inventories of 1325, 1339, and 1345 all list only one "donat," identified as having belonged to Isabelle. An inventory of 1448 recorded two "Donas glosés et 1 aultre de petite value" in the section devoted to Latin texts, Mlynarczyk, *Ein Franziskanerinnenkloster*, 299. The inventory of 1467 also broke the abbey's books into Latin and French titles and included two "Donas" in the former category, describing them as "biaux" and "glosés." AN L1028 no. 7, ed. Mlynarczyk, *Ein Franziskanerinnenkloster*, 303–19, here p. 315 number 205.

49. Robert Branner, "Saint Louis et l'enluminure parisienne au XIIIe siècle," in *Septième centenaire de la mort de saint Louis: Actes des colloques de Royaumont et de Paris (21–27 mai 1970)* (Paris: Les Belles Lettres, 1976), 80 n. 4. On manuscripts and texts owned by Louis see ibid., 69–84; on Louis's education see Richard, *Saint Louis*, 9–10.

On royal book ownership and collecting in this period see Patricia Stirnemann, "Les bibliothèques princières et privées aux XIIe et XIIIe siècles," in André Vernet, ed., *Histoire des bibliothèques françaises: Les bibliothèques médiévales du VIe siècle à 1530* (Paris: Promodis, 1989), 173–92.

50. Since the 1448, 1467, and 1483 inventories all list "1 *Alexandre*" under the heading "Item, aultres livres en latin," the possibilities are limited to works in that language. Mlynarczyk, *Ein Franziskanerinnenkloster*, 299, 315, 334.

51. For surveys of the medieval Alexander sources see Gerrit H. V. Bunt, *Alexander the Great in the Literature of Medieval Britain* (Groningen: Forsten, 1994), 3–13; the introduction to Donald Maddox and Sara Sturm-Maddox, eds., *The Medieval French Alexander* (Albany: State University of New York Press, 2002); David J. A. Ross, *Alexander Historiatus: A Guide to Medieval Illustrated Alexander Literature* (Frankfurt am Main: Athenäum, 1988); and George Carey, *The Medieval Alexander* (Cambridge: Cambridge University Press, 1956).

52. Marvin L. Colker, ed., *Galteri de Castellione Alexandreis* (Padua: Antenore, 1978). For translations see R. Telfryn Pritchard, trans., *Walter of Châtillon: The Alexandreis* (Toronto: Pontifical Institute of Mediaeval Studies, 1986); and David Townsend, trans., *The* Alexandreis *of Walter of Châtillon* (Philadelphia: University of Pennsylvania Press, 1996). The latter provides a convenient introduction to the author and a discussion of the date and reception of the text.

53. On the popularity of the work see Colker, *Galteri de Castellione Alexandreis*, xviii–xx. See also Ross, *Alexander Historiatus*, 72; Carey, *The Medieval Alexander*, 63–64; and Townsend, *The* Alexandreis *of Walter of Châtillon*, xi. For manuscripts see Colker, xxxiii–xxxviii.

54. John W. Baldwin, *The Government of Philip Augustus: Foundations of French Royal Power in the Middle Ages* (Berkeley: University of California Press, 1986), 363–67.

55. The sections quoted are found in Townsend, *The* Alexandreis *of Walter of Châtillon*, book ten, lines 68–75, 128–137; and Colker, *Galteri de Castellione Alexandreis*, lines 64–68, 113–120.

56. See, for example, Barbara Newman, "*La mystique courtoise*: Thirteenth-Century Beguines and the Art of Love," in *From Virile Woman to WomanChrist: Studies in Medieval Religion and Literature* (Philadelphia: University of Pennsylvania Press, 1995), 137–67.

57. AN L1027 no. 9, the inventory of 1339, includes "1 livre de la beste en française." Though this inventory does not attribute ownership to Isabelle, presumably it is the same book as the one mentioned in 1325. The 1483 inventory lists "ung aultre petit livre appelle Bestiere" among the "livres en françois."

58. Surviving in at least twenty-three French and English manuscripts from the thirteenth to fifteenth centuries. See Florence McCulloch, *Medieval Latin and French Bestiaries* (Chapel Hill: University of North Carolina Press, 1960), 45–69. For updated

manuscript lists and bibliography see Willene B. Clark and Meradith T. McMunn, eds., *Beasts and Birds of the Middle Ages: The Bestiary and Its Legacy* (Philadelphia: University of Pennsylvania Press, 1989). For a bibliography specific to the French bestiaries see Debra Hassig, *Medieval Bestiaries: Text, Image, Ideology* (Cambridge: Cambridge University Press, 1995), 200–201 n. 50. On bestiaries as moral teaching aids and royal women as their dedicatées see Xenia Muratova, "Bestiaries: An Aspect of Medieval Patronage," in Sarah Macready and F. H. Thompson, eds., *Art and Patronage in the English Romanesque* (London: The Society of Antiquaries, 1986), 120–21. See also Ron Baxter, *Bestiaries and Their Users in the Middle Ages* (Phoenix Mill: Sutton, 1998), 1–22; and Debra Hassig, ed., *The Mark of the Beast: The Medieval Bestiary in Art, Life, and Literature* (New York and London: Garland, 1999).

59. C. Hippeau, ed., *Le bestiaire divin de Guillaume, clerc de Normandie* (Caen, 1852; reprint, Geneva: Slatkine Reprints, 1970), 235–38. For a modern French translation see Gabriel Bainciotto, *Bestiaires du moyen âge* (Paris: Stock, 1980), 92–94. Pierre de Beauvais gives a similar but simpler version (ibid., 38–39), while Phillip de Thaon's version is more remote but does follow the same basic pattern. Philippe de Thaün, *Le bestiaire: Texte critique publié avec introduction, notes et glossaire par Emmanuel Walberg* (Paris, 1900; reprint, Geneva: Slatkine Reprints, 1970), 15–18.

Biblical phrases given in English in this book are based on *The Catholic Bible, Douay-Rheims Version* (New York: Benzinger, 1941), modified after comparison with Alberto Colunga and Laurentio Turrado, eds., *Biblia Sacra iuxta Vulgatam Clementinam*, 10th ed. (Madrid: Biblioteca de Autores Cristianos, 1999). I number Psalms in accordance with these versions as well.

60. *Writings of AH*, 54 (par. 4).

61. On Louis's books see Branner, "Saint Louis et l'enluminure parisienne," 71; and Léopold Delisle, *Le cabinet des manuscrits de la Bibliothèque Impériale*, vol. 1 (Paris: Imprimerie Impériale, 1868), 6–10. The surviving records catalogue only sacred texts, such as Psalters and Bibles, as having been owned by Blanche of Castile. See Hudson, "The Psalter of Blanche of Castile," 144–52; and Hamilton, "Queenship and Kinship in the French *Bible Moralisée*," in Nolan, ed., *Capetian Women*, 177–208, at 180–82. Similarly, another Capetian saint, Louis of Toulouse, left evidence only for the ownership of sacred and religious texts. See Christine Gadrat, "La bibliothèque de saint Louis d'Anjou, évêque de Toulouse," *Revue Mabillion*, n. s. 14 (2003): 179–202. But for evidence that Isabelle's tastes were not unusual, see (on a later Isabelle) Anne Rudloff Stanton, "Isabelle of France and her Manuscripts, 1308–1358," in *Capetian Women*, 225–52; and Margaret Howell, *Eleanor of Provence: Queenship in Thirteenth-Century England* (Oxford: Blackwell, 1998), 82–92.

62. In an article of 1888, Léopold Delisle noted the existence of an anonymous vernacular tract entitled the *Miroir de l'âme* with the Latin incipit *Audi domina et vide*, found in Paris, Bibliothèque Mazarine ms. 870. Delisle demonstrated that it was

composed for Blanche of Castile and edited the prologue and several representative paragraphs. L. Delisle, "Durand de Champagne," *Histoire litteraire de la France* 30 (1888): 302–33, on the *Miroir de l'âme*, pp. 325–29. See also Auguste Molinier, *Catalogue des manuscrits de la Bibliothèque Mazarine*, vol. 1 (Paris, 1885), 408–9. Molinier thought that Marguerite of Provence might have been the dedicatée, but I agree with Delisle that this was clearly an error.

63. Berger, *Histoire de Blanche de Castille*, 316; Pernoud, *Blanche of Castile*, 95–96; Sivéry, *Blanche de Castile*, 226; Delorme, *Blanche de Castille*, 237–39, 312. Most recently, see Hudson, "The Psalter of Blanche of Castile," 137–39; and Hamilton, "Queenship and Kinship in the French *Bible Moralisée*," in Nolan, ed., *Capetian Women*, at 181.

64. I am currently preparing editions of the French and Latin versions of this work, and I intend to treat its authorship, date, composition, and transmission more fully in separate articles.

65. Richard and Mary Rouse have recently pointed out that the French translation presented to Blanche was not, as Delisle thought, a unique copy. At least three other vernacular copies exist, two of which were dedicated to later female patrons. See Richard H. and Mary A. Rouse, *Manuscripts and Their Makers: Commercial Book Producers in Medieval Paris, 1200–1500* (Turnhout: Harvey Miller, 2000), 152–54. But the Latin version seems to have circulated just as widely, since at least three copies survive: BNF ms. lat. 14878, ff. 148rb–154ra; Grenoble, Bibliothèque municipale ms. 271, ff. 28v–36v; and Naples, Biblioteca Nazionale ms. VII.G.15, ff. 241ra–244va. None of these manuscripts can be the copy owned by Isabelle.

66. The book was always catalogued with the Latin works in Longchamp's fifteenth-century inventories. See Mlynarczyk, *Ein Franziskanerinnenkloster*, 299, 315, 334.

67. *PL*, vol. 185, cols. 485–508.

68. The quotation is from Sivéry. Berger's only comment on the *Miroir* was to wonder whether one of the intimates of Blanche's household might have written it. Pernoud, however, argued that "the text could well be the work of a woman. . . . Probably the writer was a nun who had already benefited from the royal open-handedness." See note 63 above for citations.

69. This attribution goes back at least to John Pits, *De illustribus Angliae scriptoribus* (Paris, 1619), #427. I have been unable to examine a copy of this book myself. Luke Wadding simply cited Pits's attribution in his *Scriptores Ordinis Minorum* (Rome, 1650), 217, while A. G. Little's *Initia operum latinorum quae saeculis xiii. xiv. xv. attribuuntur* (Manchester, 1904), 27, in turn attributes the work to Pecham citing Wadding. In 1948, G. Melani investigated the question in the introduction to his *Tractatus de anima Ioannis Pecham* (Florence, 1948), xxiii–xxvi. He correctly determined that the *Speculum anime* with the incipit *Audi domina* was not the same as Pecham's *Tractatus de anime*, incipit *Mirabilis est sibi anima mea*, nor the same as a pseudo-Bonaventurian

Speculum, incipit *Arbor mala*, nor as a work that circulated in Spanish under the same title. Melani did not commit himself on the question of whether the *Audi domina* text was really the work of Pecham, noting that he did not himself know whether any manuscripts of the work survived. But G. E. Mohan, "Initia operum Franciscalium" *Franciscan Studies* 35 (1975): 36, unambiguously credits Pecham with the work citing Pits, Wadding, Little, and Melani. Mlynarczyk followed this attribution as well, *Ein Franziskanerinnenkloster*, 276 n. b[1].

70. See Alain Boureau, *Théologie, science et censure au XIIIe siècle: Le cas de Jean Peckham* (Paris: Les Belles Lettres, 1999), 140. Though Pecham was probably an arts student at Paris earlier in his life, he did not return to begin his theological studies until 1258 or 1259, and it is hardly likely that an obscure arts student would have presented a work of spiritual direction to the queen.

71. For a reconsideration of mothers' roles in promoting their daughters' literacy see Pamela Sheingorn, "The Wise Mother: The Image of St. Anne Teaching the Virgin Mary," in Erler and Kowaleski, eds., *Gendering the Master Narrative*, 105–34.

72. BNF ms. lat. 14878, f. 151rb: "Si cogites quid respondebis cum dicetur de te, 'Ecce, ista fuit Regina Francie!', mirum erit si non timeas, quia tunc reduces ante oculos tuos omnia opera tua, sive bona sint sive mala."

73. Hague, *The Life of St. Louis*, 41; Monfrin, ed., *Joinville, Vie de saint Louis*, 188 (par. 71).

74. Hague, *The Life of St. Louis*, 28–29; Monfrin, ed., *Joinville, Vie de saint Louis*, 158 (par. 28).

75. *Writings of AH*, 68 (par. 26).

76. Carolus-Barré, *Le procès de canonisation de saint Louis*, 75.

77. On Conrad's claims to Jerusalem see Hans Eberhard Mayer, *The Crusades*, 2nd ed., trans. John Gillingham (Oxford: Oxford University Press, 1988), 237–38, 258, and 316–17 n. 126.

78. Élie Berger, *Saint Louis et Innocent IV* (Paris: Thorin & fils, 1893), 10; Richard, *Saint Louis*, 61. It is only in retrospect that we know that these were the final rebellions of the reign.

79. On these events see David Abulafia, *Frederick II: A Medieval Emperor* (Oxford and New York: Oxford University Press, 1988), 350–54; T. C. Van Cleve, *The Emperor Frederick II of Hohenstaufen: Immutator Mundi* (Oxford: Clarendon Press, 1972), 454–62; Berger, *Saint Louis et Innocent IV*, 12–14; and Ernst Kantorowicz, *Frederick the Second*, trans. E. O. Lorimer (London: Constable, 1931), 578–80.

80. Le Goff, *Saint Louis*, 163–68; Richard, *Saint Louis*, 101; Abulafia, *Frederick II*, 344–47.

81. "Ceterum ad tractandam et ordinandam consummationem matrimonialis federis inter Conradum in Romanorum regem electum et regni Ierosolymitani heredem dilectum filium nostrum et Isabellam sororem vestram, venerabilem . . . [*sic*]

Cluniacensem abbatem et magistrum Gualterium de Ocra notarium et fidelem nostrum, excellentie nostre legatos et nuncios speciales, ad vestram presentiam duximus destinandos." J. L. A. Huillard-Bréholles, ed., *Historia diplomatica Friderici secundi*, vol. 6, part 1 (Paris: Henri Plon, 1860), 97–98. The editor also reprints a letter of safe conduct issued by Frederick to Walter of Ocra, increasing the likelihood that these negotiations actually took place. Ibid., 98 n. 1. Walter of Ocra's movements in this period are traced in Ernst Kantorowicz, "Petrus de Vinea in England," in *Selected Studies by Ernst H. Kantorowicz* (Locust Valley, NY: Augustin, 1965), 228 n. 81. I thank Robert E. Lerner for the reference. Kantorowicz describes Walter as "practically the permanent representative of the Emperor in England," but concludes that he was in France in 1243 before returning to England by December of that year. Hugh VI of Rochecorbon (or of Sales), abbot of Cluny from 1235 to 1244, had been sent by Louis to Frederick bearing a letter of protest in 1241, and was part of a delegation sent by the cardinals to Frederick II in May 1243. Le Goff, *Saint Louis*, 164; Berger, *Saint Louis et Innocent IV*, 6 n. 1, 9.

82. *Writings of AH*, 54 (par. 7). See ibid., 102 n. 3, on the translation of *jureé* and *ses amis* in this context.

83. Edited in Field, "New Evidence," and discussed in chapter 2 below.

84. *BU*, 319. On the interpretation of the term *desponsata* as indicating something very like a firm agreement of marriage see Christopher N. L. Brooke, *The Medieval Idea of Marriage* (Oxford: Oxford University Press, 1989), 145–46.

85. Though too late to be definitive in itself, Isabelle's fifteenth-century epitaph demonstrates that the nuns of Longchamp at that date also believed that an agreement had been reached. BNF ms. fr. 6214: "Et quant la royne sa mere et ses nobles parens la vouldrent marier comme ja promise l'avoient et acordee au filz de l'empeure de Rome, qui devoit estre hoir de l'empire apres son pere, et qui moult desiroit et se penoit et efforcoit d'avoir la dicte dame a espouse, au quel elle ne s'y voult acorder." The manuscript is discussed in chapter 6 below.

86. The letter does not seem to have been dated, but Huillard-Bréholles assigns it to June 1243 based on its clear references to Frederick's political and military maneuverings. There is no doubt that it was written before Innocent IV's election. The date is confirmed in J. F. Böhmer, *Regesta Imperii* (Innsbruck: Wagner'schen Universitätis-Buchhandlung, 1881–82), 588, #3366.

87. On negotiations between Frederick and Innocent and their breakdown see Abulafia, *Frederick II*, 355–66; and Berger, *Saint Louis et Innocent IV*, 12–24.

88. Garreau, *Bienheureuse Isabelle de France, soeur de saint Louis*, 33. Compare Innocent's actions as described by Abulafia, *Frederick II*, 366–75.

89. Berger, *Saint Louis et Innocent IV*, 146–47, especially 147 n. 1; Sivéry, *Marguerite de Provence*, 84–85. Garreau's further argument (added between the first and second editions of his book) that Isabelle was presented to Conrad after Louis's return from the crusade is based on an egregious misreading of Joinville, who related that he

saw a silver ship dedicated in thanksgiving to St. Nicholas by Queen Marguerite after her return from the crusade "quant nous menames la sereur le roy a Haguenoe, au roy d'Allemainge." Garreau believed that this phrase must have meant that Joinville went to present Isabelle of France to Conrad at Haguenau some time after 1254. In fact, Joinville was referring to Blanche the sister of Philip the Fair, who married Rudolf, son of the Emperor Albert, in 1300. See Sivéry, *Marguerite de Provence*, 113; Hague, *The Life of St. Louis*, 186–87 (see also note p. 291); and Monfrin, ed., *Joinville, Vie de saint Louis*, 522 (par. 633). The fact that Conrad died on 21 May 1254 seems to have escaped Garreau.

90. Innocent IV's contemporary biographer, Nicholas of Curbio, asserts that Frederick asked for the hand in marriage for Conrad of one of Innocent's nieces at this moment. See Berger, *Saint Louis et Innocent IV*, 23 n. 2. It can be noted in addition that when Frederick wrote to Conrad in April 1244 to announce his (short-lived) peace agreement with Innocent IV, he made no mention of any proposed marriage. See Huillard-Bréholles, *Historia diplomatica Friderici secundi*, vol. 6, part 1, 175–77.

91. For instance, Louis IX's marriage to Marguerite of Provence took place in 1234, when he was twenty-one and she was about thirteen. When Robert of Artois married Matilda of Brabant in 1237, he was also about twenty-one, though I have not been able to determine her age. Alphonse of Poitiers's marriage probably took place in 1241 when he was twenty-one. His bride, Joan of Toulouse, had been at the Capetian court since 1229 and was approximately his own age. Charles of Anjou married Beatrice of Provence in 1246 at probably the age of twenty, when she was about fourteen. Eleanor and Sanchia of Provence, sisters of Marguerite, married Henry III of England and Richard of Cornwall at the ages of twelve and fifteen, respectively. See Sivéry, *Marguerite de Provence*, 56–62, 77–81; and Howell, *Eleanor of Provence*, 1, 9–16. For a broader examination of the question of medieval women's average age at first marriage see Herlihy, *Medieval Households*, 103–7.

92. One wonders, again, about the impact of romance literature. Isabelle and her circle might well have known Jean Renart's *Guillaume de Dole*, in which the Emperor "Conrad" (though he has fallen in love with Guillaume's sister Liénor) is urged to "ask for the hand of the French king's daughter" by his counselors. See Patricia Terry and Nancy Vine Durling, trans., *The Romance of the Rose or Guillaume de Dole* (Philadelphia: University of Pennsylvania Press, 1993), 60. This imagery might have helped to give the proposed marriage a fairy-tale appeal, making Isabelle's rejection all the more definitive.

93. Jordan, *Louis IX and the Challenge of the Crusade*, 9.

94. *Writings of AH*, 56 (par. 9).

95. See *Writings of AH*, 102 n. 4, on the problematic reading of this place name. It seems far more likely that Blanche would have sent to nearby Nanterre than to "Angleterre," as some early modern sources would have it, in a moment of crisis. I have not been able to propose an identity for the holy woman of Nanterre.

96. Jordan assumed that Isabelle's illness occurred before the offer of marriage from Conrad IV in June 1243 (or at least before her rejection of it), and consequently that both episodes preceded Louis's own illness in December 1244. Jordan, *Louis IX and the Challenge of the Crusade*, 9. Pernoud, with no evidence cited, states that Isabelle was twenty when she fell ill. *Blanche of Castile*, 257.

97. For instance, Guillaume of Saint-Pathus's *Vie de saint Louis*, written around 1302, refers to Louis's illness of 1244 as occurring "eu tens de sa jeunece," though Louis was thirty years old. H.-François Delaborde, ed., *Vie de saint Louis par Guillaume de Saint-Pathus, confesseur de la reine Marguerite* (Paris: Picard & fils, 1899), 21. Agnes elsewhere refers to Isabelle in her "enfance," indicating that, for her, "jeunesse" is a more general term extending to a later age. This conclusion seems to be in keeping with Didier Lett's extensive discussion of medieval terminology on childhood in *L'enfant des miracles: Enfance et société au Moyen Âge (XIIe–XIIIe siècle)* (Paris: Aubier, 1997), 19–56. I would like to thank William D. Paden for consulting on this question.

98. *RHGF*, vol. 21, "Index mansionum," 510, and "Additum regum mansionibus et itineribus," p. L. Note that dates are given old-style, so that 17 February 1243 would be 1244 in modern reckoning.

99. Though it should be noted that Marguerite gave birth to the couple's first son, Louis, on 24 February 1244, presumably limiting the potential date for Isabelle's illness to the early part of the month. Louis Carolus-Barré, "Le prince héritier Louis et l'intérim du pouvoir royal de la mort de Blanche de Castille (novembre 1252) au retour de saint Louis (juillet 1254)," in *Académie des inscriptions et belles-lettres: Comptes rendus des séances de l'année 1970*, 588.

100. Hague, *The Life of St. Louis*, 51; Monfrin, ed., *Joinville, Vie de saint Louis*, 210–12 (pars. 106–107). For analysis see Jordan, *Louis IX and the Challenge of the Crusade*, 3–13.

101. Jordan, *Louis IX and the Challenge of the Crusade*, 9.

102. Jordan is not the only scholar to have made this assumption. Cf. De Serent, "L'ordre de saint Claire en France pendant sept siècles," 134; and Elizabeth M. Hallam, "Aspects of the Monastic Patronage of the English and French Royal Houses, c. 1130–1270" (Ph.D. diss., University of London, 1976), 267.

CHAPTER TWO.   Virgo regia: *Fashioning a Royal Reputation*

1. Hans Neumann, ed., *Mechthild von Magdeburg: Das fließende Licht der Gottheit*, vol. 1 (Munich: Artemis, 1990), 104 (III: 21). See Bynum, *Holy Feast and Holy Fast*, 229, for commentary.

2. *Writings of AH*, 60–64 (pars. 14–21). Neither the beginning nor end of this section, however, should be seen as firm. Agnes's final use of the expression "en sa

jeunesse" is easy enough to identify, but it is impossible to be certain how far beyond this point she conceived of the section on Isabelle's youth as extending. Similarly, the foundation of Longchamp in a sense functions as part of Agnes's evidence for Isabelle's adult charity and monetary largess, and from this point of view does not begin an entirely new section.

3. The later nuns of Longchamp preserved this tradition, as seen in Roulliard, *La saincte mère*, 448. It is also possible that Alexander IV's bull of 1256, *Benedicta filia tu*, discussed below, refers to Agnes and places her close to Isabelle in these years.

4. *Writings of AH*, 60 (par. 14). On tears as a form of medieval piety see Piroska Nagy, *Le don des larmes au moyen âge: Un instrument spirituel en quête d'institution, Ve–XIIIe siècle* (Paris: Albin Michel, 2000).

5. Andrew Hughes, *Medieval Manuscripts for Mass and Office: A Guide to Their Organization and Terminology* (Toronto: University of Toronto Press, 1982), 124–59.

6. Hughes, *Medieval Manuscripts for Mass and Office*, 160–244; Pierre Salmon, *L'office divin au moyen âge: Histoire de la formation du bréviaire du IXe au XVIe siècle* (Paris: Éditions du Cerf, 1967).

7. Cambridge, Fitzwilliam Museum, ms. 300. See Francis Wormald and Phyllis M. Giles, *A Descriptive Catalogue of the Additional Illuminated Manuscripts in the Fitzwilliam Museum*, vol. 1 (Cambridge: Cambridge University Press, 1982), 280–81; Wormald and Giles, *Illuminated Manuscripts in the Fitzwilliam Museum: An exhibition to commemorate the 150th anniversary of the death of the founder Richard, 7th Viscount Fitzwilliam of Merrion* (Cambridge: Fitzwilliam Museum, 1966), 21; and S. C. Cockerell, *A Psalter and Hours, executed before 1270 for a lady connected with St. Louis, probably his sister Isabelle of France* (London: Chiswick Press, 1905), 10–36. Cockerell advanced the argument that this book was created for Isabelle of France. However, in the 1970s this conclusion was challenged by Robert Branner, who thought it had probably belonged to either Marguerite of Provence or to her daughter Isabelle. Branner, *Manuscript Painting in Paris during the Reign of Saint Louis: A Study of Styles* (Berkeley: University of California Press, 1977), 132–33; idem, "Saint Louis et l'enluminure parisienne," 80–83. Kathleen S. Schowalter has recently reexamined this question in detail, and argues for Marguerite of Provence on the grounds of the illumination program of the Psalter. "Capetian Women and Their Books: Art, Ideology, and Dynastic Continuity in Medieval France" (Ph.D. diss., Johns Hopkins University, 2005), 145–221.

8. Dyan Elliot, "Women and Confession: From Empowerment to Pathology," in Erler and Kowaleski, eds., *Gendering the Master Narrative*, 31–51; and eadem, *Proving Woman*.

9. *Writings of AH*, 60 (par. 15). The quotation in the final sentence reads "pour nient fut une fame de religion."

10. *Writings of AH*, 60–62 (par. 16).

11. See, for example, the many examples cited in Caroline Walker Bynum, "The Female Body and Religious Practice in the Later Middle Ages," in *Fragmentation and Redemption: Essays on Gender and the Human Body in Medieval Religion* (New York: Zone Books, 1992), 181–238. On the question of whether medieval women actually did understand their own spirituality in terms of bodily suffering see Amy Hollywood, *The Soul as Virgin Wife: Mechthild of Magdeburg, Marguerite Porete, and Meister Eckhart* (Notre Dame, IN: University of Notre Dame Press, 1995), 26–39.

12. A point that I explore further in a forthcoming article.

13. *Writings of AH*, 62 (pars. 17–19).

14. On women's control of food as both literal and symbolic means of religious expression see Bynum, *Holy Feast and Holy Fast*. Many pious royal figures were noted for distributing food and alms to the poor. See, for example, Vauchez's discussion of Charles of Blois in *Sainthood in the Later Middle Ages*, 363–68, and note 18 below on Louis IX.

15. *Writings of AH*, 62–64 (pars. 19–20). Peronelle (or Petronilla or Perronella) of Montfort was the daughter of Simon IV of Montfort and Alice of Montmorency (and thus the sister of Henry III's nemesis), born in 1211. Her mother placed her at Saint-Antoine-des-Champs in 1221 or 1222 to be raised. She eventually took the veil there, became abbess by 1254, and was described as "religiosissima et magne sanctitatis." See J. R. Maddicott, *Simon de Montfort* (Cambridge: Cambridge University Press, 1994), 5, 101–2, 175; Charles Bémont, *Simon de Montfort, Earl of Leicester, 1208–1265*, 2nd ed., trans. E. F. Jacob (Oxford: Clarendon Press, 1930), xxx n. 1; M. Zerner, "L'Épouse de Simon de Montfort et la croisade albigeoise," in *Femmes, mariages, lignages (XIIe–XIVe s.): Mélanges offerts à Georges Duby* (Brussels: De Boeck, 1992), 449–70 at 465–69. I have not been able to identify "Dame Jeanne." Saint-Antoine was the abbey just outside Paris's eastern walls founded by Foulques de Neuilly ca. 1198 and attached to the Cistercian Order by 1208. See Constance Berman, "Cistercian Nuns and the Development of the Order: The Abbey at Saint-Antoine-des-Champs outside Paris," in *The Love of Learning and the Love of God: Studies in Honor of Jean Leclercq* (Kalamazoo: Cistercian Publications, 1995), 121–56; eadem, "Abbeys for Cistercian Nuns in the Ecclesiastical Province of Sens: Foundation, Endowment, and Economic Activities of the Earlier Foundations," *Revue Mabillon* n. s. 8 (1997): 83–113; and eadem, "Dowries, Private Income, and Anniversary Masses: The Nuns of Saint-Antoine-des-Champs (Paris)," *Proceedings of the Annual Meeting of the Western Society for French History* 20 (1993): 3–12.

16. A common ritual for pious royalty in this period, and one advocated by Louis IX. Barlow, "The King's Evil," 14.

17. *Writings of AH*, 64 (par. 21).

18. Delaborde, *Vie de saint Louis par Guillaume de Saint-Pathus*. On serving food to the poor, 79, 105; on abstinence at table and fasts, 119–22; on wearing a hair shirt

and having himself whipped, 122–23. Indeed, Louis is said to have sent a whip for such "disciplines" to his daughter Isabelle, recommending the practice to her. Ibid., 63. This episode has sometimes been twisted into a statement that he sent whips to his sister, an assertion for which there is no evidence. Geoffrey of Beaulieu claimed to have talked Louis into wearing a hair shirt only on Fridays during Advent and Lent. See Richard, *Saint Louis*, 238. See also Joinville in Hague, *The Life of St. Louis*, 27; Monfrin, ed., *Joinville, Vie de saint Louis*, 154 (par. 22), on Louis's eating habits; on the advisability of washing the feet of the poor on Maundy Thursday, Hague, 29, Monfrin, 158 (par. 29); on hearing the hours of the Divine Office every day, Hague, 36, Monfrin, 176 (par. 54); on his charity generally, Hague, 209, Monfrin, 578 (pars. 720–22). On his frequent confession and respect for his confessors see Georges Minois, *Le confesseur du roi: Les directeurs de conscience sous la monarchie française* (Paris: Fayard, 1988), 178.

19. William Jordan remarks that in this relationship "it is hard always to know who was influencing whom." *Louis IX and the Challenge of the Crusade*, 11.

20. Le Goff in particular emphasizes Louis's new determination after 1254 to act as the perfect Christian king. *Saint Louis*, 213.

21. *GC* vol. 9, col. 471 notes that Isabelle was present with Blanche of Castile and Marguerite of Provence at the founding of the chapel at La Barre in 1235. Perhaps this indicates an exception to the picture of narrative indifference described above, but the source for this statement is unclear.

22. J. M. Canivez, *Statuta capitulorum generalium ordinis cisterciensis*, vol. 2 (Louvain: Bibliothèque de la Revue d'Histoire Ecclésiastique, 1934), 276: "Illustribus comitibus Attrebatensi et Pictavensi fratribus domini regis Franciae, et Boloniensi et uxoribus eorum, et dominae Isabellae sororis domini regis Franciae, conceditur plenarium servitium et anniversarium post mortem ipsorum, nihilominus pro quolibet ipsorum dicatur una missa de Spiritu Sancto anno praesenti a singulis sacerdotibus per Ordinem universum." The following year at the General Chapter meeting of 1245 a specific request for masses was granted to the king's sister. See ibid., vol. 2, 292; and in 1254, after Louis's return from the crusade, masses were again granted for the royal family specifically including Isabelle. Ibid., 400–401.

23. Matthew Paris, *Chronica majora*, ed. Henry Richards Luard, vol. 4 (London: Longman, 1877), 391, mentions only "dominus rex Francorum . . . nobilis domina Blanchia mater ejus, quae a domino Papa privilegium impetraverat, ut liceret ei domos religiosas Cisterciensis ordinis cum duodecim mulieribus orandi gratia intrare . . . fratres regis, Atrebatensis et Pictavensis comites, dux Burgundiae et sex comites Francorum cum ipsis." Isabelle was probably one of the twelve women accompanying Blanche.

24. Berger, *Saint Louis et Innocent IV*, 26–27; Richard, *Saint Louis*, 102.

25. Matthew Paris, *Chronica majora*, vol. 4, 484–85, mentions only the king and his mother, as does Guillaume of Nangis, *RHGF*, vol. 20, 352–53. But the late-fifteenth-century *Chronicum clunicense* lists a host of dignitaries including "domnus Ludouicus Rex Franciae, et Regina mater eius, et soror eius" and later, "Domnus Rex Franciae cum matre sua et fratre suo et sorore sua, et cum tota ipsorum familia priuata." See Martinus Marrier and Andreas Quercetanus, eds., *Bibliotheca cluniacensis* (1614, reprint, Mâcon, 1915), col. 1666. Though this source is obviously much later than Matthew Paris or Guillaume of Nangis, it seems unlikely that the monks of Cluny would have included Isabelle here unless her presence had been recorded in some manner. Similarly, accounts of the dedication of the Church of St. Peter at Mâcon, which was attended by the pope and royal family on 8 December, do not record Isabelle's participation, but if she was indeed at Cluny she almost certainly would have been present. Berger, *Saint Louis et Innocent IV*, 162, citing *GC*, vol. 4, col. 1080.

26. Edmond Martène and Ursine Durand, *Thesaurus novus anecdotorum*, vol. 3 (Paris, 1717; reprint, 1968), col. 1863: "Venit ergo primus pius rex Franciae Ludovicus et venerabilis mater ejus regina dicta Blancha, jam nunc blande, ut credimus, in pace sepulta. Venerunt et tres comites fratres regis, videlicet dominus Robertus Attrebatensis, Alfonsus Pictaviensis, et Carolus postmodum factus comes Provinciae, Andegavensis, et soror horum quatuor Isabellis filia regis et soror regis, nec minor quam regina, quia Christo regi virginitatis flore conjuncta." The mention of Blanche's death puts the text after 1252. On the translation see L.-F. Massé, *Vie de saint Edme* (Auxerre: Gallot, 1858), 355–68, 410–11, and *DHGE*, vol. 1, col. 1563 for Albert of Suerbeer's career. On the author, date, and extant thirteenth-century manuscript for this text see Louis Carolus-Barré, "Saint Louis et la translation des corps saints," in *Études d'histoire du droit canonique dédiées à Gabriel Le Bras*, vol. 2 (Paris: Sirey, 1965), 1089, no. 11; and C. H. Lawrence, *St. Edmund of Abingdon: A Study in Hagiography and History* (Oxford: Clarendon Press, 1960), 8, 14–18. Richard of Chichester, another eyewitness, in a letter to Matthew Paris mentions only the king, his mother, and his brothers. Matthew's own account likewise mentions only Louis and Blanche. Matthew Paris, *Chronica majora*, vol. 3, 128–29, 631.

27. There is no modern critical edition or English translation of the *Bonum universale*, though Jacques Berlioz, Pascal Collomb, and Marie Anne Polo de Beaulieu, "La face cachée de Thomas de Cantimpré," *Archives d'histoire doctrinale et litteraire du moyen âge* 68 (2001): 73–94, at 74 n. 2, notes that a new edition is under way, and the introduction to Margot H. King, trans., *The Life of Margaret of Ypres by Thomas de Cantimpré* (Toronto: Peregrina, 1995), 11, indicated that Robert Sweetman was preparing a translation. The best available edition is Georgius Colvenerius, *Thomae Cantimpratani bonum universale de apibus* (Douai: Belleri, 1627). References here are to this edition, abbreviated as *BU*, book.chapter.part. Divisions of books and chapters

represent Thomas's own designations, while the "parts" are Colvenerius's editorial decision. On Thomas's career see A. DeBoutte, "Thomas de Cantimpré," *DS* vol. 15 (1990), cols. 784–792. See also Thomas Walter Grzebien III, "Penance, Purgatory, Mysticism, and Miracles: The Life, Hagiography, and Spirituality of Thomas of Cantimpré (1200–1270)" (Ph.D. diss., University of Notre Dame, 1989), 1–116; T. Kaepelli, *Scriptores Ordinis Praedicatorum medii aevi*, vol. 4 (Rome: Istituto Storico Domenicano, 1993), 344–55; and Robert Sweetman, "Thomas of Cantimpré, *Mulieres Religiosae*, and Purgatorial Piety: Hagiographical Vitae and the Beguine 'Voice,'" in Jacqueline Brown and William P. Stoneman, eds., *A Distinct Voice: Medieval Studies in Honor of Leonard E. Boyle, O.P.* (Notre Dame, IN: University of Notre Dame Press, 1997), 623 n. 13. A partial French translation of the *Bonum universale* is Henri Platelle, trans., *Les exemples du Livre des Abeilles* (Turnhout: Brepols, 1997), 5–56; Berlioz et al., "La face cachée de Thomas de Cantimpré," surveys the *exempla* omitted by Platelle.

28. Scholars have generally assumed that Humbert's 1256 request launched Thomas on his work, but Sweetman (following A. DeBoutte) argues that Thomas's own statements run counter to this assumption (see the references in the previous note). Thomas is thought to have studied in Paris around 1237–1240, but his report cannot stem from this period since it refers to Isabelle's temporary engagement to Conrad of 1243. Thomas was attached to the Dominican house at Louvain in the 1240s before travelling to Cologne to study with Albertus Magnus, probably in 1250–51. After this period he was appointed a Preacher General in the order, which allowed him to travel throughout his province. It seems unlikely that Thomas knew of Isabelle's plans for Longchamp when he wrote, or he would have noted something about them. Therefore, either Thomas was in Paris (presumably on one of his preaching tours) in the early 1250s, or his claim to have "seen" Isabelle was mere poetic license.

29. The argument is made most fully in Robert Sweetman, "Dominican Preaching in the Southern Low Countries, 1240–1260: *Materiae Praedicabiles* in the *Liber de natura rerum* and *Bonum universale de apibus* of Thomas of Cantimpré" (Ph.D. diss., University of Toronto, 1988), 158–65; restated in idem, "Visions of Purgatory and Their Role in the *Bonum universale de apibus* of Thomas of Cantimpré," *Ons geestelijk erf* 67 (1993): 20–33, esp. 20–26; and idem, "Thomas of Cantimpré, *Mulieres Religiosae*, and Purgatorial Piety," 610.

30. For an outline of the entire structure of the *Bonum universale* see Sweetman, "Dominican Preaching," 172–77, and, in more condensed form, idem, "Visions of Purgatory," 22–24.

31. A specific problem with the manuscript transmission of Thomas's text must be mentioned here. The work survives in "long" and "short" versions. Though the difference between the two is relatively minor, most of the additions of the longer one are found in exactly the chapter under consideration here. Hence the long version (found in the 1627 edition) has forty parts, whereas the short version has only thirty-five.

Isabelle's example is thus II.29.34 in the short version and II.29.40 in the long. See Platelle, *Les exemples du Livre des Abeilles*, 7 n. 4, for manuscripts of each version.

32. On Yolanda see Richard H. Lawson, trans., *Brother Hermann's Life of the Countess Yolanda of Vienden* (Columbia, SC: Camden House, 1995); and Herbert Grundmann, *Religious Movements in the Middle Ages*, trans. Steven Rowan (Notre Dame, IN: University of Notre Dame Press, 1995), 100.

33. *BU*, II.29.40: "Vidimus et illam quam minus iuste extremam ponimus, filiam Ludovici Regis Francorum, sororem scilicet devotissimi Regis Ludovici qui felicissime regnat ad praesens. Haec desponsata Conrado filio Frederici Romanorum Imperatoris, in virginitate permanere innuba praeelegit. Quae soli Deo vacans, adeo contemplationi deditur et virtuti, ut nulla ei cura in ullis transitoriis videatur. Sed et ipsius frater, quem diximus, Rex devotissimus Ludovicus, in tantum amplectitur virgineae dignitatis pudicitiam consectantes, ut Parisiis collegerit Beghinarum maximam multitudinem, ut se in humilitatis obsequiis exercea[n]t et salute." I have checked this reading against several manuscripts that were available to me: BNF mss. lat. 3309, f. 68v (short version), 14628, f. 154r–v (long version), and 14535, ff. 59v–60r (long version). Aside from my emendation from "exerceat" to "exerceant" (following ms. lat. 3309) the variations are insignificant.

34. She is thus connected to Thomas of Cantimpré's intense interest in women such as Christina Mirabilis and Marie d'Oignies, who, Sweetman argues, attracted Thomas precisely because their attempts to live a religious life in the world were complementary to the Dominican ideals of the *vita apostolica*. Sweetman, "Dominican Preaching," 72.

35. *Writings of AH*, 64 (par. 21). William Jordan has estimated that five thousand *livres tournois* would pay for the salary, provisions, retinue, and passage to the Holy Land for ten to fifteen knights at this time. *Louis IX and the Challenge of the Crusade*, 67–68. Louis VIII's bequest to his daughter of twenty thousand *livres* would therefore have allowed Isabelle to contribute these funds with a substantial portion of her inheritance left over.

36. Boutaric, *Saint Louis et Alfonse de Poitiers*, 75: "Ge vos faz à savoir que madame la Roine vostre mere et madame Ysabel vostre seuer, et vostre neveu sont saint et haitié." The letter is dated only "le mercredi après les trois semaines de Pâques," but since Philip had received word of Alphonse's safe arrival at Damietta, which occurred on 24 October 1249, but not of the crusaders' subsequent disastrous defeat in spring 1250, it must have been written after Easter 1250 and before news of the crusade's fortunes filtered back to Paris.

37. *Layettes*, vol. 3, #3956. A passage in Joinville has sometimes been cited as evidence that Isabelle had withdrawn from life at court by 1252. While still in the Holy Land, Joinville was surprised to find Queen Marguerite weeping when she heard the news of Blanche's death. She explained that she wept not for the queen herself, but for the sorrow of her husband and for their daughter in France, "who was left to the care

of men." César Pascal argued that this passage showed that Isabelle was no longer at court with Blanche, a supposition that seems highly speculative. "L'hostel royal de Longchamp," *Bulletin de la Société de l'histoire de Paris* 31 (1904): 77. Garreau followed this interpretation, *Bienheureuse Isabelle de France, soeur de saint Louis*, 41. For Joinville's passage see Hague, *The Life of St. Louis*, 179; and Monfrin, ed., *Joinville, Vie de saint Louis*, 506 (par. 605).

38. On Blanche's death see Berger, *Histoire de Blanche de Castille*, 414–16; Pernoud, *Blanche of Castile*, 287–88; and Sivery, *Blanche de Castille*, 253–54.

39. For edition and discussion of this bull see Field, "New Evidence," 120–22 and 128–29. The original of this letter has disappeared, but a copy was made at Longchamp by Antoine Le Maistre in 1653 and is now found in notebook B of Le Nain de Tillemont, BNF ms. fr. 13747, f. 119r–v.

40. Louis Carolus-Barré, "Le prince héritier Louis et l'intérim du pouvoir royal," 588–96; Jordan, *Louis IX and the Challenge of the Crusade*, 116–17.

41. Jordan, *Louis IX and the Challenge of the Crusade*, 118–19 (quotation at 104); Berger, *Saint Louis et Innocent IV*, 393.

42. See *Layettes*, vol. 3, #4042–4047, 4080–4082.

43. *Sancti Gregorii magni liber sacramentorum*, PL vol. 78 col. 173: "Respice, Domine, propitius super hanc famulam tuam, ut sanctae virginitatis propositum, quod te inspirante suscepit, te gubernante custodiat." The *Sacramentarium Gelasianum* and the *Liber sacramentorum ecclesiae Romanae* attributed to Leo I have similar passages. Cf. *PL* vol. 74 col. 1153 and vol. 55 col. 129.

44. Field, "New Evidence," 128.

45. Field, "New Evidence," 128.

46. Field, "New Evidence," 128–29. The *Sacrarium* attributed to Leo I and the *Sacramentarium Gelasianum* both use similar language. Cf. *PL* vol. 55 col. 130; vol. 74 col. 1152.

47. The Provincial Minister is not named in the bull but must be Geoffrey of Brie. See André Callebaut, "Les provinciaux de France au XIIIe siècle," *AFH* 10 (1917): 315–28, and Francesca Joyce Mapelli, *L'amministrazione francescana di Inghilterra e Francia: Personale di governo e strutture dell'Ordine fino al Concilio di Vienne (1311)* (Rome: Antonianum, 2003), 400–401, 427.

48. Luke Wadding, *Annales minorum*, vol. 3, 399–400: " . . . ipsa, quae tamquam praecipua honestatis et sanctimoniae imitatrix quandoque in claustris Monialium dicitur conversari, aliquos ex Fratribus tui Ordinis secum ad decorem honestatis suae, et confitendum eis peccata infirmitatis propriae affectet desideranti animo commorari." The phrase "quandoque in claustris Monialium dicitur conversari" certainly cannot indicate that Innocent thought that Isabelle was living the life of a professed nun. Compare Pascal's rather tortured interpretation of this phrase, "L'hostel royal de Longchamp," 77–78.

49. Leonardo Pisanu, *Innocenzo IV e i francescani (1243–1254)* (Rome: Edizioni Francescane, 1968), 116, places this bull in the context of other grants of Franciscan confessors by Innocent.

50. Xavier de la Selle, *Le service des âmes à la cour: Confesseurs et aumôniers des rois de France du XIIIe au XVe siècle* (Paris: École des chartes, 1995), 37–42, 261.

51. Franciscans Guillaume of Saint-Pathus and Jean of Mons acted as confessors to Marguerite of Provence; Jean of Mons probably also acted as Louis's confessor, and perhaps also that of his daughter Isabelle; Guillaume of St. Pathus became confessor to Louis's daughter Blanche. See De la Selle, *Le service des âmes à la cour*, 41, 71, 110, 310; and Minois, *Le confesseur du roi*, 162–65. Though it is certain that Marguerite of Provence had a confessor at court by 1255, there is no evidence to show exactly when Franciscans took over this role.

52. Though it is often assumed that Bonaventure's *De perfectione vitae ad sorores* was also composed for Isabelle of France, I have argued elsewhere that this assertion is incorrect. To put the matter succinctly, Bonaventure's treatise was demonstrably written for a Franciscan nun. Since Isabelle never took the veil, she was not therefore the work's commissioner or recipient. Moreover, anyone reexamining the discussion in which Bonaventure's Quaracchi editors first suggested Isabelle as a likely recipient will see that there are no manuscript attributions to this effect, that there is no other hard evidence, and that Isabelle was offered only as a tentative hypothesis as the sort of woman likely to have commissioned such a tract. *S. Bonaventurae opera omnia*, vol. 8 (Quaracchi, 1898), lvi–lvii. See further Field, "The Princess, the Abbess, and the Friars," 155–58.

53. For an edition of this text, and my full argument for its date, see Field, "Gilbert of Tournai's Letter to Isabelle of France: An Edition of the Complete Text," *Mediaeval Studies* 65 (2003): 57–97. See also A. de Poorter, "Lettre de Guibert de Tournai, O.F.M. à Isabelle, fille du roi de France," in *Revue d'ascétique et de mystique* 12 (1931): 116–27. My dating of the text is based on three factors: it seems to have been written before Gilbert's regency, putting it before 1259; it refers to Isabelle's "fame," indicating a date around the period of *Sancta virginitatis propositum* when her reputation began to spread; and it includes Isabelle in the category of *adulescens*, indicating a date earlier rather than later in the 1250s.

54. For surveys of Gilbert's career see Benjamin de Troeyer, *Bio-bibliographia Franciscana neerlandica ante saeculum XVI*, vol. 1 (Nieuwkoop, 1974), 15–43; and Boudouin d'Amsterdam, "Guibert de Tournai," in *DS*, vol. 6 (Paris, 1967), cols. 1139–1146.

55. See A. de Poorter, *Le traité "Eruditio Regum et Principum" de Guibert de Tournai, O.F.M.* (Louvain: Institut Supérieur de Philosophie de l'Université, 1914), vi, for justifiable doubt about the reality of Gilbert's participation in the crusade.

56. In addition to the *Eruditio regum et principum* (see previous note) for Louis and the *Epistola* under consideration here, Gilbert wrote his treatise *De pace et animi tran-*

quillitate (c. 1275) for Marie of Dampierre, daughter of William of Dampierre, Count of Flanders; he addressed his *De modo addiscendi* (ca. 1263–1268), in turn part of his *Rudimentum doctrinae*, to Jean the son of Guy of Dampierre, also Count of Flanders. See Ephrem Longpré, *Tractatus de pace, auctore Fr. Gilberto de Tornaco* (Quaracchi: Collegium S. Bonaventurae, 1925); and E. Bonifacio, *Gilberto di Tournai: De modo addiscendi* (Turin: Società Editrice Internazionale, 1953).

57. Field, "Gilbert of Tournai's Letter to Isabelle of France," 83.

58. Field, "Gilbert of Tournai's Letter to Isabelle of France," 85–86: "Et sic calidum dilectionis, secundum beatum Dyonisium, ad accutum promovet cognitionis. In Evvangelio legitur: *Nonne cor nostrum ardens erat* de Ihesu *dum loqueretur nobis in via*? O dilectionis admirabile sacramentum! Amor Ihesu corda rapuerat. Ihesum siciunt, audiunt, aspiciunt, nec cognoscunt. Unde *stulti et tardi* vocati sunt. Sed quoniam sic arserunt, ideo postmodum cognoscere meruerunt; quoniam habuerunt amoris calidum, perceperunt postmodum et accutum. Significat autem acutum impetum quemdam amoris et vehemenciam desiderii ardentis, ferentis se in amatum, intrantis et penetrantis et transeuntis in ipsum." Compare Hugh of St. Victor, *Expositio in hierarchiam coelestem S. Dionysii areopagitae, PL* vol. 175, lib. vi, col. 1037: "Significat enim acutum impetum quemdam amoris, et vehementiam desiderii ardentis, ferentis se in amatum, et intrantis, et penetrantis, ut ibi sit, ubi est ipsum, quod amatur, cum ipso, et in ipso, ut non solum ab ipso calidum sit, sed transeat acutum in ipsum."

59. Field, "Gilbert of Tournai's Letter to Isabelle of France," 97: "Notum enim satis est—benedictus Dominus!—quoniam nullatenus indigetis ut super hiis admoneamini."

60. For these sources see J. Leclercq and H. Rochais, eds., *Sancti Bernardi opera*, vol. 7, *Epistolae* (Rome: Editiones Cistercienses, 1974), Epistola 113, *Ad Sophiam virginem*; J. Fraipont, ed., *Sancti Fulgentii episcopi Ruspensis opera*, CCL 91 (Turnhout: Brepols, 1968), Epistula III, *Ad Probam*; S. Ambrosii liber secundus de virginibus, PL vol. 16; M. Testard, ed., *Sancti Ambrosii Mediolanensis de officiis*, CCL 15 (Turnhout: Brepols, 2000), *Liber I*. For detailed analysis of Gilbert's use of his sources see Field, "Gilbert of Tournai's Letter to Isabelle of France."

61. For edition and discussion of this bull see Field, "New Evidence," 122–25, 129–31. Two originals were sent to Isabelle by Alexander, preserved as AN L250 nos. 78 and 78bis.

62. *Sancti Gregorii magni liber responsalis, PL* vol. 78 col. 799, "In Matutinis" from the "Responsoria sive Antiphonae de Assumptione sanctae Mariae."

63. Field, "New Evidence," 129.

64. Field, "New Evidence," 130.

65. Field, "New Evidence," 130: "Ave igitur virgo regia! Et celestis gratie pinguedine replearis que discreto iudicio partem eligens potiorem, ut penales maledictionis erumpnas quas in mulieres seducta et prevaricatrix Eva produxit procul effugias, bene-

dictionem sectaris integritatis virginee cum Maria, in qua nimirum angelice salutationis Ave participas, dum cum ea pro modulo tuo stabili voto comunicas propositum spiritualis et corporee sanctitatis."

66. Agnes of Harcourt's mother's name is rendered in Latin in *GC*, vol. 11, col. 881. See further Field, "New Evidence," 124 nn. 19 and 20. In addition, a woman named Agnes of Fallouel was referred to in 1261 as having been in the service of Blanche of Castile. See Berger, *Blanche de Castille*, 316.

67. Field, "New Evidence," 130: "In hoc utique non tibi soli sed quam plurimis consulis te velud conspicuum imitationis exemplar ad famulatum Domini emulatione laudabili secuturis, sicque de aliorum etiam meritis tibi surget seges uberior premiorum, horum iam letas primitias in dilecta in Christo filia Agnete Eloidis progressus tuos, sicut audivimus, in virginitatis amore ad sanctioris vite propositum subsequente pregustas, quam velud tue institutionis alumpnam in Domino fovere te convenit, ut ad Deum vite tibi sit semper individua comes vie, et in ipsius consortio iocundior sit spiritualis boni possessio, quod a Domino suscepisti. Serva itaque tam tibi quam illi cauta custodia bonum depositum quod inspiratio divina reposuit in utraque, et humiliter agnosce inmensi huius muneris maiestatem tibi ex sola dei munificentia provenisse."

68. Field, "New Evidence," 131.

69. Field, "New Evidence," 131: "Ceterum, licet pro contemptu glorie mundialis et voto munditie centuplum eterne vite tibi a Domino reservetur in diem illum quo iustitie premia de retributoris affluentissimi habundantia consequeris, ut tamen interim tibi ecclesie sancte suffragia prerogentur, tibi votum virginalis continentie ac famulatus celestis propositum continua instantia prosequenti, ex illa quam nobis Deus ligandi atque solvendi contulit potestate de beatorum apostolorum Petri et Pauli nostraque auctoritate confisi, peccatorum omnium veniam indulgemus."

70. Field, "New Evidence," 125 n. 22.

71. Barbara Newman, "Flaws in the Golden Bowl: Gender and Spiritual Formation in the Twelfth Century," in *From Virile Woman to WomanChrist*, 19–45. The texts considered in this chapter differ from those of Newman's dossier in that they were written about twenty-five years after the cutoff point for her study and concerned a devout laywoman rather than a nun.

72. A point emphasized in R. W. Southern's classic, *The Making of the Middle Ages* (New Haven: Yale University Press, 1953), 230.

73. For reconsiderations of Newman's argument see Elisabeth Bos, "The Literature of Spiritual Formation for Women in France and England, 1080–1180," in Constant J. Mews, ed., *Listen, Daughter: The Speculum Virginum and the Formation of Religious Women in the Middle Ages* (New York: Palgrave, 2001), 201–20; and Janice M. Pinder, "The Cloister and the Garden: Gendered Images of Religious Life from the Twelfth and Thirteenth Centuries," in ibid., 159–79.

74. See *From Virile Woman to WomanChrist*, Appendix A, "Religious Literature of Formation, 1075–1225," 313–16, for a list of the texts considered by Newman.

CHAPTER THREE.   *House Rules: Isabelle of France and Longchamp's Rule of 1259*

1. Denis Diderot, *La religieuse* (Paris: Maxi-poche Classiques Français, 1993), 89.

2. See, for example, Shadis, "Piety, Politics, and Power," 202–27; and more generally Hallam, "Aspects of the Monastic Patronage of the English and French Royal Houses."

3. On women's involvement in writing rules see Maiju Lehmijoki-Gardner, "Writing Religious Rules as an Interactive Process: Dominican Penitent Women and the Making of Their Regula," *Speculum* 79 (2004): 660–87.

4. Scholars have recently preferred to grant Clare's text the more accurate title of "form of life." I nevertheless continue to employ the term "rule" for the sake of consistency.

5. Hence one finds casual references such as June McCash's to "Clare of Assisi, the only woman ever to have written a female monastic rule that was officially approved by the pope." McCash, "The Cultural Patronage of Medieval Women: An Overview," in McCash, ed., *The Cultural Patronage of Medieval Women*, 22. A short summary of Isabelle's rule is found in Mlynarczyk, *Ein Franziskanerinnenkloster*, 36–40. François Berriot, "Les manuscrits de l'abbaye de Longchamp aux Archives de France et la *Vie de sainte Claire* inédite (début XIVe s.)," *AFH* 79 (1986): 329–58, at 330–32, is similarly brief in examining an early fourteenth-century copy of the rule held at Longchamp.

6. Patricia Ranft, "An Overturned Victory: Clare of Assisi and the Thirteenth-Century Church," *Journal of Medieval History* 17 (1991): 123–34, quotation at 132. Along the same lines is Jo Ann Kay McNamara, *Sisters in Arms: Catholic Nuns through Two Millennia* (Cambridge, MA: Harvard University Press, 1996), 306–12. See the perceptive remarks in Lezlie Knox, "Clare of Assisi: Foundress of an Order?" in Godet-Calogeras and McKelvie, eds., *An Unencumbered Heart*, 11–29, esp. 12–13.

7. This success and the need for new attention to the genesis of Isabelle's rule is nicely demonstrated by Nancy Warren's recent analysis of the rules governing Benedictine, Franciscan, and Brigittine female communities in fourteenth- and fifteenth-century England. Warren identifies Isabelle's importance as a woman who worked out influential new ideas about female monastic life, along with Clare of Assisi and Birgitta of Sweden, but she is forced to treat Isabelle's rule as a decontextualized document that seems to have appeared out of thin air. Nancy Bradley Warren, *Spiritual Economies: Female Monasticism in Later Medieval England* (Philadelphia: University of Pennsylvania Press, 2001), 4–25.

8. Limited attention is given to Isabelle's rules in Maria Pia Alberzoni, "*Sorores minores* e autorità ecclesiastica fino al pontificato di Urbano IV," and Giancarlo Andenna, "Urbano IV e l'ordine delle Clarisse," both in Andenna and Vetere, eds.,

Chiara e la diffusione delle Clarisse nel secolo XIII, 165–94 and 195–218. The former is translated in Alberzoni, *Clare of Assisi and the Poor Sisters in the Thirteenth Century.* In spite of its title, Optatus van Asseldonk, " 'Sorores Minores,' una nuova impostazione del problema," *Collectanea franciscana* 62 (1992): 595–634, does not mention Isabelle or her rule.

9. *Writings of AH,* 64 (par. 22).

10. On the thirteenth-century hospitals of Paris, presumably representative of the sort of institution that Isabelle was contemplating, see Sharon Farmer, *Surviving Poverty in Medieval Paris: Gender, Ideology, and the Daily Lives of the Poor* (Ithaca: Cornell University Press, 2002), 86–90; and on Louis IX's foundation and support of hospitals, see Jordan, *Louis IX and the Challenge of the Crusade,* 185–86.

11. Agnes of Bohemia is discussed below.

12. Aymeric, chancellor from 1249 until his death between June 1262 and March 1263, remains a little-known figure. See P. Glorieux, *Répertoire des maîtres en théologie de Paris au XIIIe siècle,* vol. 1 (Paris: J. Vrin, 1933), #149; Astrik L. Gabriel, "The Conflict between the Chancellor and the University of Masters and Students at Paris during the Middle Ages," in Albert Zimmermann, ed., *Die Auseinandersetzungen an der Pariser Universität im XIII. Jahrhundert* (Berlin: Walter de Gruyter, 1976), 106–54, at 114, 148.

13. AN L1020 no. 1 records the sale by "Simon de Valle Grignon de Sancto Lodaldo" of four *arpents* of arable land "in loco qui dicitur Losrengier in censiva Sancte Genovese Parisiensis." The document is edited in Hallam, "Aspects of the Monastic Patronage of the English and French Royal Houses," 404. Hallam, however, did not note that on the back of the document is written "pro domina Ysabelli," in a hand that appears to be contemporary with that of the text. AN L1020 nos. 2 and 3 are also records of land acquired before the abbey's dedication, dated May 1255 and October 1256, respectively.

14. Louis returned to France on 3 July 1254 and arrived back in Paris on 4 September. On the halt to royal building projects during the crusade see Jordan, *Louis IX and the Challenge of the Crusade,* 91–92, 177; and idem, "Cutting the Budget: The Impact of the Crusades on Appropriation for Public Works in France," in *Ideology and Royal Power in Medieval France: Kingship, Crusades, and the Jews* (Aldershot: Variorum, 2001), 307.

15. A reliable and complete study of Longchamp's early years remains to be written. In addition to the bibliography found in the introduction to this book, nn. 33 and 34, see *GC,* vol. 7, 943–50; Gratien de Paris, *Histoire de la fondation et de l'évolution de l'ordre des Frères mineurs au XIIIe siècle* (1928; New edition ed. Mariano d'Altri and Servus Gieben, Rome: Istituto Storico dei Cappuccini, 1982), 609–11; Honoré Champion, *Notice historique sur l'abbaye de Longchamps* [sic] (Extrait de la *Revue Nobiliaire,* 1868) (Paris, 1869); C. Leroux-Cesbron, "L'abbaye de Longchamp," *Bulletin de la*

Commission municipale historique et artistique de Neuilly-sur-Seine 7 (1909): 42–48; and Berriot, "Les manuscrits de l'abbaye de Longchamp aux Archives de France."

16. The date of this ceremonial beginning of the construction of Longchamp is sometimes given in secondary sources without attribution as 10 or 12 June 1256, but I have found no evidence to substantiate this claim. Cf. Garreau, *Bienheureuse Isabelle de France, soeur de saint Louis*, 46; Duchesne, *Histoire de l'abbaye royale de Longchamp*, 2; Lynn, "Clare of Assisi and Isabelle of Longchamp," 78. One also finds the date of Longchamp's foundation given as 1249, which seems to stem ultimately from a passage in AN LL1604, "Registre contenant la Nomenclature des Abbesses" of Longchamp begun by the abbey's treasurer, Denise Costeblanche, around the year 1600, which claimed that Longchamp "fust comensee a bastir mil. ii. xlix." On this manuscript see Berriot, "Les manuscrits de l'abbaye de Longchamp aux Archives de France."

17. *Writings of AH*, 46 (par. 2).

18. First in the fifteenth-century introduction to the *Letter*, edited in *Writings of AH*, 35 n. 68. Cf. Duchesne, *Histoire de l'abbaye royale de Longchamp*, 2, quoting Julien-F. Daniello, *Vie de Mme. Isabelle, soeur de saint Louis, fondatrice de l'abbaye de Longchamp, avec une description historique de la fête de Longchamp* (Paris: Gaume frères, 1840); Garreau, *Bienheureuse Isabelle de France, soeur de saint Louis*, 46.

19. In a similar example of royal solidarity, Louis once had his brothers Alphonse, Robert, and Charles publicly assist him in the building of a wall for the royal abbey of Royaumont. This seems to have been more an example of conspicuous humility, however, and less a ritual moment. See Delaborde, ed., *Vie de saint Louis par Guillaume de Saint-Pathus*, 71, and 110 for similar actions on Louis's part. Cecilia Gaposchkin pointed out this parallel to me.

20. *Layettes*, vol. 3, #4467. The original document is AN J687 no. 93, edited in F. M. Delorme, "En marge du Bullaire franciscain," *La France franciscaine*, 3rd Series, 21 (1938): 19–20. See Bernard Barbiche, *Les actes pontificaux originaux des Archives nationales de Paris*, 2 vols. (Vatican City: Biblioteca Apostolica Vaticana, 1975), #999. For more details on the bulls mentioned here see Field, "New Evidence," 122 n. 16. The document does not specify which daughter Louis had in mind, but the most likely is Blanche, who was born in 1253 and seems to have been intended for the life of a nun, or perhaps Margaret, born in 1255. Louis's oldest living daughter, Isabelle, had already married by 1259.

21. AN L253 no. 204: "Alexander episcopus servus servorum Dei, dilectis in Christo filiabus abbatisse et conventui monasterii humilitatis beate Marie virginis ordinis humilium ancillarum virginis eiusdem Parisiensi diocesis, salutem et apostolicam benedictionem. Cum a nobis petitur quod iustum est et honestum, tam vigor equitatis quam ordo exigit rationis ut id per sollicitudinem officii nostri ad debitum perducatur effectum. Ea propter, dilecte in Christo filie, vestris iustis postulationibus grato concurrentes assensu, sepulturam monasterii vestri liberam esse decernimus, ut eorum

devotioni et extreme volutati qui se illic sepeliri deliberaverint, nisi excommunicati ve interdicti sint aut publice usuraii, nullus obsistat, salva tamen iustitia illarum ecclesiarum a quibus mortuorum corpora assumuntur. Nulli ergo omnino hominum liceat hanc paginam nostre constitutionis infringere, vel ei ausu temerario contrare. Siquis autem hoc attemptare presumpserit indignationem omnipotentis Dei et beatorum Petri et Pauli apostolorum eius se noverit incursurum. Datum Anagnie vi kalendas Martii, pontificatus nostri anno quinto." Manuscript described in Barbiche, *Les actes pontificaux*, #1000. Similar bulls with this incipit were granted to many houses. See Williell R. Thompson, "Checklist of Papal Letters Relating to the Three Orders of St. Francis," *AFH* 64 (1971): 550.

22. The original does not survive, but the early fourteenth-century copy found in AN LL1601, ff. 63r–67r, is edited in Delorme, "En marge," 20–22. Other Franciscan houses received similar bulls. See Thompson, "Checklist of Papal Letters," 558.

23. The original does not survive, but the fifteenth-century copy in BNF ms. fr. 11662, f. 43v, is edited by Delorme, "En marge," 23. This was also a privilege extended to many Franciscan houses. See Thompson, "Checklist of Papal Letters," 556.

24. *Writings of AH*, 64–66 (par. 23).

25. On St. Bonaventure, J. G. Bougerol, *Introduction to the Works of Bonaventure*, trans. José de Vinck (Paterson, NJ: St. Anthony Guild Press, 1964), remains a fundamental starting point. For Bonaventure's sermons to the royal family see J. G. Bougerol, "Saint Bonaventure et le roi saint Louis," in *S. Bonaventura, 1274–1974*, vol. 2 (Grottaferrata: Collegium S. Bonaventurae, 1973), 469–89; but see also the same author's more cautious conclusions on the dates of these sermons in *Saint Bonaventure, Sermons de Tempore: Reportations du manuscrit Milan, Ambrosienne A 11 sup.* (Paris: Éditions Franciscaines, 1990).

26. P. Glorieux, *Répertoire*, vol. 2, 55; Callebaut, "Les provinciaux de France au XIIIe siècle," 328–35; Mapelli, *L'amministrazione francescana di Inghilterra e Francia*, 402. The evidence for William's presence at the nuns' entrance to Longchamp comes from the preface to the abbey's first necrology of 1325 (AN L1027 no. 22).

27. On Eudes of Rosny see Glorieux, *Répertoire*, vol. 2, 52; François-Marie Henquinet, "Eudes de Rosny, O.F.M., Eudes Rigaud et la somme d'Alexandre de Hales," *AFH* 33 (1940): 3–54; A. Teetaert, "Rosny (Eudes de)," in *Dictionnaire de théologie catholique*, vol. 14 (1939), cols. 1–3; Nicole Bériou, *L'avènement des maîtres de la parole: La prédication à Paris au XIIIe siècle* (Paris: Institut d'Études Augustiniennes, 1998), vol. 2, 762–63 and passim; eadem, "La prédication au béguinage de Paris pendant l'année liturgique 1272–1273," *Recherches augustiniennes* 13 (1978): 105–229, at 132 and 174–75; J. G. Bougerol, "Autour de 'La naissance du Purgatoire,'" *Archives d'histoire doctrinale et littéraire du moyen âge* 50 (1983): 7–57, at 52–59; Louis-Jacques Bataillon, "Fragments des sermons de Gérard d'Abbeville, Eudes de Rosny et Thomas

d'Aquine," in *La prédication au XIIIe siècle en France et en Italie* (Aldershot: Variorum, 1993), 257–68, at 266–67.

28. Glorieux, *Répertoire*, vol. 2, 34–36; André Callebaut, "L'année de la mort de Fr. Guillaume de Melitona," *AFH* 19 (1926): 431–34; B. Pergamo, "De quaestionibus ineditis Fr. Odonis Rigaldi, Fr. Gulielmi de Melitona et Codicis Vat. Lat. 782," *AFH* 19 (1936): 3–54; Beryl Smalley, "William of Middleton and Guibert of Nogent," *Recherches de théologie ancienne et médiévale* 16 (1949): 281–91; Antonio Samaritani, "La Quaestio de sanctificatione B. Virginis di Guglielmo di Melitona," *Marianum* 30 (1968): 161–80; Antoine Côté, "William of Melitona on Divine Beatitude," *Franciscan Studies* 60 (2002): 17–38. A good summary and further bibliography may be found in Willibrord van Dijk, "Guillaume de Middletown," in *DS* vol. 6 (1967), cols 1221–1224.

29. Thus the entry in Glorieux, *Répertoire*, vol. 2, 54–55, identifies "Godefroid de Vierzon" as master in theology around 1257–1260 solely on the strength of Agnes's inclusion of him among the other Franciscan masters of the period. It should be noted that another well-known Franciscan master, Eudes Rigaud, is sometimes mistakenly given as one of Isabelle's collaborators. This erroneous attribution goes back to the sixteenth century, presumably the result of confusion with Eudes of Rosny. Eudes Rigaud, however, did preach at Longchamp on 1 June 1265 and so must have known Isabelle. I thank Adam Davis for bringing this fact to my attention. See Th. Bonnin, *Regestrum visitationum archiepiscopi Rothomagensis* (Rouen: Auguste Le Brument, 1852), 519–20, and more generally Adam J. Davis, *The Holy Bureaucrat: Archbishop Eudes Rigaud and the Politics of Reform in Thirteenth-Century Normandy* (Ithaca: Cornell University Press, forthcoming).

30. Callebaut, "L'année de la mort de Fr. Guillaume de Melitona." The evidence for William's death before 23 May 1260 is firm, since on that date the Franciscan General Chapter at Narbonne included him in the list of brothers who had died since the Chapter of 1257. Callebaut's reasoning in fixing his death to shortly after the 1257 Chapter is more speculative, based on the assumption that the brothers were listed in the order of their deaths. I agree with B. Pergamo, "De quaestionibus ineditis Fr. Odonis Rigaldi, Fr. Gulielmi de Melitona et Codicis Vat. Lat. 782," 46 n. 1, that this assumption is questionable.

31. Bougerol, "Saint Bonaventure et le roi saint Louis," 488; idem, *Introduction to the Works of Bonaventure*, 171–77. The most detailed attempts to trace Bonaventure's movements after 1257 are P. Glorieux, "Essai sur la chronologie de saint Bonaventure (1257–1274)," *AFH* 19 (1926): 145–68; and John F. Quinn, "Chronology of St. Bonaventure's Sermons," *AFH* 67 (1974): 145–84.

32. Callebaut, "Les provinciaux de France au XIIIe siècle," 333.

33. *BF* vol. 3, 64–68 note b. This edition was reprinted without fresh recourse to the manuscript in Flaminio Maria Annabali da Latera, *Ad Bullarium Franciscanum . . . Supplementum* (Rome: Typis Archangeli Casaletti, 1780), 122–31. More recently,

Ignacio Omaechevarria has reprinted the rule including obvious corrections and a Spanish translation in *Escritos de Santa Clara y documentos complementarios*, 3rd ed. (Madrid: Biblioteca de Autores Cristianos, 1993), 292–324, hereafter *Escritos*. Though this is the best and most convenient edition available, there has been no reexamination of the unique manuscript found by Sbaralea, if indeed it still exists. Zeffirino Lazzeri, "La 'Forma vitae' di S. Chiara e le regole sue e del suo ordine," in *Santa Chiara d'Assisi.: Studi e cronica del VII centenario (1253–1953)* (Assisi: Comitato Centrale per il VII Centenario Morte S. Chiara, 1953), 79–121, at 116, alluded to the manuscript as "ora nell'Archivio di Stato [di Firenza]," but I have been unable to locate it there. The date of this rule is sometimes given as 1258, following Roulliard, or 2 February 1259, following an error made in Annibal's edition, or 9 February, the date given by Omaechevarria. In fact, the bull concludes, "Datum Anagniae, IV idus februarii, pontificatus nostri anno quinto," or 10 February 1259.

34. *BF* vol. 3, 68: "*Explicit Regula humilium ancillarum Gloriosissimae Mariae Virginis Matris Dei, quam Frater Mansuetus de Ordine Fratrum Minorum de mandato Summi Pontificis et Cardinalium quorumdam diligenti consilio composuit et dictavit*, ita additum legitur in cit. Cod. Floren."

35. René de Nantes made this argument, "Les origines de l'ordre de sainte Claire," *Études franciscaines* 2 (1912): 175–77, as did Walter Seton, in R. W. Chambers and Walter W. Seton, *A Fifteenth-Century Courtesy Book and Two Fifteenth-Century Franciscan Rules*, Early English Text Society No. 148 (Oxford: Oxford University Press, 1914; reprint, 1962), 70–71. Garreau seems to follow these authors, though in general he devotes little attention to Isabelle's rules. *Bienheureuse Isabelle de France, soeur de saint Louis*, 47–50. Micheline de Fontette, *Les religieuses à l'âge classique du droit canon: Recherches sur les structures juridiques des branches féminines des ordres* (Paris: J. Vrin, 1967), 147 n. 17, also seems to subscribe to this view.

36. On Mansuetus see Nicole Bériou, *Les sermons et la visite pastorale de Federico Visconti, archévêque de Pise (1253–1277)* (Rome: École Française de Rome, 2001), 797–803, 1122 (with further bibliography); Louis Carolus-Barré, "Le reliquaire de la sainte Épine d'Assise: Fra Mansueto et le traité de Paris, 1258–1259," *Bulletin de la Société nationale des antiquaires de France* (1989): 121–31; and Callebaut, "L'année de la mort de Fr. Guillaume de Melitona," 432–33.

37. Field, "Annihilation and Perfection in Two Sermons by Gilbert of Tournai for the Translation of St. Francis," *Franciscana* 1 (1999): 243–44 nn. 16 and 21.

38. A supplementary agreement with Richard of Cornwall (brother of Henry III) dated 8 June 1258 at Paris carries Mansuetus's seal. See *Layettes* vol. 3, #4423. For his seal see Louis Douët d'Arcq, *Collection de sceaux*, vol. 2 (Paris: Plon, 1868), #6240. Reproduced in Carolus-Barré, "Le reliquaire de la sainte Épine d'Assise," 129.

39. A *vidimus* of this letter dated 1270 is edited in Carolus-Barré, "Le reliquaire de la sainte Épine d'Assise," 130–31.

40. Callebaut, "L'année de la mort de Fr. Guillaume de Melitona," 432–33.

41. Barbiche, *Les actes pontificaux*, vol. 1, xcix, states simply that Mansuetus was "procureur, en 1259, de l'abbaye de Longchamp." The two bulls are described in ibid. #999 and #1000.

42. Here I am in agreement with Lynn, "Clare of Assisi and Isabelle of Longchamp," 79.

43. Two foundational accounts of the history of the thirteenth-century rules for Franciscan women are L. Oliger, "De origine regularum Ordinis S. Clarae," *AFH* 5 (1912): 181–209, 413–47; and Grundmann, *Religious Movements in the Middle Ages*, 109–24, 130–34. Oliger mistakenly believed that the text of Longchamp's Rule of 1259 did not survive (p. 437). Though this error was pointed out almost immediately (see Walter Seton's comments of 1914, in Chambers and Seton, *A Fifteenth-Century Courtesy Book and Two Fifteenth-Century Franciscan Rules*, 70), Grundmann (342 n. 249) was among those misled by Oliger's oversight. Thus, these two standard accounts have relatively little to say about Isabelle of France, since their authors had never seen the Rule of 1259.

44. A convenient edition of the Rule of 1219 is found in *Escritos*, 217–32. An earlier edition is *BF* vol. 1, 263–67, and an English translation is printed in Regis J. Armstrong, *Clare of Assisi: Early Documents* (New York: Paulist Press, 1988), 87–96.

45. Werner Maleczek has demonstrated that the earlier "Privilege of Poverty" supposedly granted by Innocent III to Clare is not authentic. "Das *Privilegium Paupertatis Innocenz III.* und das Testament der Klara von Assisi: Überlegungen zur Frage ihrer Eichtheit," *Collectanea franciscana* 65 (1995): 5–82; trans. Cyprian Rosen and Dawn Nothwehr, "Questions about the Authenticity of the Privilege of Poverty of Innocent III and of the Testament of Clare of Assisi," *Greyfriars Review* 12, Supplement (1998): 1–80. On Clare's attitude in 1228 see Maria Pia Alberzoni, "San Damiano in 1228: A Contribution to the Clarian Question," in *Clare of Assisi and the Poor Sisters in the Thirteenth Century*, 89–112.

46. My account in this and the two following paragraphs is based on Grundmann, *Religious Movements in the Middle Ages*, 109–24; Andenna, "Urbano IV e l'ordine delle Clarisse"; Maria Pia Alberzoni, *La nascita di un'istituzione: L'ordine di s. Damiano nel XIII secolo* (Milan: Edizioni CUSL, 1996), 3–51; and eadem, "The Papacy and New Women's Religious Orders," in *Clare of Assisi and the Poor Sisters in the Thirteenth Century*, 155–207; Roberto Rusconi, "L'espansione del francescanesimo femminile nel secolo XIII," in *Movimento religioso femminile e francescanesimo nel secolo XIII: Atti del VII Convegno internazionale (Assisi, 11–13 ottobre 1979)* (Assisi: Società Internazionale di Studi Francescani, 1980): 263–313 [trans. Edward Hagman, "The Spread of Women's Franciscanism in the Thirteenth Century," *Greyfriars Review* 12 (1998): 35–73]; De Fontette, *Les religieuses à l'âge classique du droit canon*, 132–36, 142–47; De Nantes, "Les origines de l'ordre de sainte Claire"; and Gratien de Paris, *Histoire de la fondation et de*

l'évolution de l'ordre des Frères mineurs au XIIIe siècle, 596–617. See also Bert Roest, *Franciscan Literature of Religious Instruction before the Council of Trent* (Leiden and Boston: Brill, 2004), 169–90.

47. *Escritos*, 242–64. Earlier editions in Wadding, *Annales minorum*, vol. 3, 545–53; *BF* vol. 1, 476–82; Conrad Eubel, *Bullarii franciscani epitome et supplementum* (Quaracchi: Collegium S. Bonaventurae, 1908), 241–46; English translation in Armstrong, *Clare of Assisi: Early Documents*, 109–21.

48. Good recent editions of Clare's rule are *Escritos*, 271–94, and Marie-France Becker et al., *Claire d'Assise: Écrits* (Paris: Éditions du Cerf, 1985), 120–65; English translation in Armstrong, *Clare of Assisi: Early Documents*, 60–77.

49. Grundmann, *Religious Movements in the Middle Ages*, 130–31.

50. Miriam Shadis has highlighted the way in which this sort of institutional uncertainty could open up space for royal women to exert authority. She argues that the patronage of Blanche of Castile (and her sister Leonor) was designed to take advantage of tension within the Cistercian Order in order to gain a greater degree of control over her foundations of Maubuisson and Lys. See "Piety, Politics, and Power," 202–27. Another useful comparison in Cistercian circles is Isabelle of Arundel (ca. 1226–1279), a noble widow and literary patron who founded the Cistercian house of Marham in 1249, apparently in the face of the order's opposition. See Jocelyn Wogan-Browne, *Saints' Lives and Women's Literary Culture c. 1150–1300* (Oxford: Oxford University Press, 2001), 151–76.

51. Since the Rule of 1247 was in turn modeled on the Rule of 1219 in many places, it is only through a close reading of the entire document that one can determine that Isabelle's rule was based on the 1247 text. Where differences in wording or substance do occur between the rules of 1219 and 1247, however, the Rule of 1259 consistently works from the latter. It is clear that Clare's rule, recently approved by Alexander IV (as Cardinal Rainaldo before his election), with its intensely personal statement of Franciscan poverty, was not taken up as the foundation for Longchamp's new rule. Thus, statements that imply that Isabelle's rule was a "mitigated" version of Clare's are seriously misleading. Cf. A. Blasucci, "Clarisse isabelliane o minoresse," in *Dizionario degli istituti di perfezioni*, vol. 2 (1975), col. 1146; and McNamara, *Sisters in Arms*, 310.

52. Rainaldo had been chaplain to Cardinal Hugolino as early as 1221. The latter, as Gregory IX, named him Cardinal Deacon in 1227 and Cardinal Bishop of Ostia in 1231. Rainaldo was third Cardinal Protector of the Franciscans (after John of St. Paul and Hugolino) from approximately the time of his elevation to cardinal. Armstrong, *Clare of Assisi: Early Documents*, 28–29, speculates that Rainaldo may have had a hand in the composition of Innocent IV's rule of 1247. In general on Alexander IV see Agostino Paravicini Bagliani, *Cardinali di Curia e "Familiae" Cardinalizie dal 1227 al 1254*, vol. 1 (Padua: Antenore, 1972), 41–60; Salvatore Sibilia, *Alessandro IV*

(1254–1261) (Anagni: Cassa Rurale ed Artigiana di Anagni, 1961); Franz Tenckhoff, *Papst Alexander* IV (Paderborn: Schönigh, 1907); Luigi Pellegrini, *Alessandro IV e i francescani (1254–1261)* (Rome: Edizioni Francescane, 1966); and Williell R. Thompson, "The Earliest Cardinal-Protectors of the Franciscan Order: A Study in Administrative History, 1210–1261," *Studies in Medieval and Renaissance History* 9 (1972): 21–80, at 52–75.

53. Compare Jean François Godet-Calogeras's analysis of the structure of Clare's rule as a "double-decker sandwich," with the text wrapped inside approvals by Cardinal Rainaldo and Pope Innocent IV. "Structure of the *Form of Life* of Clare," in Godet-Calogeras and McKelvie, eds., *An Unencumbered Heart*, 1–10, at 2.

54. *Escritos*, 298–300: "Sol ille verus perpetuo fulgore coruscans, lux quidem clarissima summae lucis, et fons luminis defectum vel immutationem penitus nescientis fidelium corda in hac ima et caliginosa valle sub carnis mole degentium infusione invisibili suae admirabilis claritatis illustrat, et saepe reges et principes micantioribus contingens radiis, in eorum mentes lucem ingerit potiorem, per quam iidem, intuitu perspicaciori sublimius contemplantes, altiora liberius comprehendunt, et celsiora etiam de iis subtilius eligunt, et ardentius amplectuntur, adeo quod et ad suavem gustum, et amorem caelestium alios suo salutari exemplo vehementer animant et inducunt. Hac siquidem luce perfusi, princeps ille christianissimus Ludovicus, carissimus in Christo filius noster, rex Francorum illustris, et dilecta in Christo filia nobilis mulier Isabella soror eius, quae virginalis pudicitiae candore nitida et pollens aliarum claritate virtutum, spatioso temporalis regni palatio spreto, in otio dulcis contemplationis divinis perseveranter vacare laudibus ferventi spiritu appetit, nobis devote ac humiliter supplicarunt, ut eidem I[sabellae] ac omnibus Christi ancillis inclitum Christo cum ipsa cupientibus impendere famulatum, aliquam certam Regulam seu vivendi regulariter formulam specialem, sub cuius salubri observantia ipsi Domino magis placere valeant, statuere ac concedere curaremus. Nos autem, licet inhibitum fuerit in concilio generali, ne quis novam religionem inveniat, *sed quicumque ad religionem converti voluerit, unam de approbatis assumat, similiter qui voluerit religiosam domum de novo fundare, Regulam et institutionem accipiat de religionibus approbatis:* volentes tamen regis et Isabellae praedictorum votis annuere favorabiliter in hac parte, infrascriptam Regulam eidem Isabellae ac omnibus mulieribus de saeculo fugere illamque in monasterio Humilitatis Beatae Mariae Virginis, Parisiensis diocesis, volentibus profiteri, et sub ipsa divinis se beneplacitis dedicare, tradimus, in eodem solummodo monasterio perpetuis temporibus observandam, prohibitioni eiusdem concilii generalis obtentu [*sic*] eorumdem regis et Isabellae, in hoc specialiter detrahentes. Quam utique Regulam a praedicto loco volumus sortiri vocabulum, ut quae ipsam professae fuerint, nuncupentur Sorores Ordinis Humilium Ancillarum Beatissimae Mariae Virginis Gloriosae." Omaechivaria justifiably suggests reading "obtutu" for "obtentu." I have added italics to indicate where Alexander is quoting directly from

canon thirteen of the Fourth Lateran Council. See C. J. Hefele, *Histoire des conciles d'après les documents originaux*, vol. 5, part 2, trans. H. Leclercq (Paris: Letouzey & Ané, 1913), 1344. The texts of Isabelle's rules are cited throughout this book from Omaechevarria's edition with modernized capitalization and punctuation but compared to Annibali da Latera's edition of 1780. There are discrepancies between the two, and I occasionally follow the latter.

55. *Escritos*, 242: ". . . beati Francisci Regulam quantum ad tria tantum, videlicet oboedientiam, abdicationem proprii in speciali et perpetuam castitatem, necnon formam vivendi praesentibus annotatam . . . vobis et iis quae successerint concedimus observandam." The English translation is from Armstrong, *Clare of Assisi: Early Documents*, 110.

56. This gesture toward the Rule of St. Francis was new in the Rule of 1247; up to this point the preamble to this rule is largely the same as Hugolino's Rule of 1219. Cf. *Escritos*, 218.

57. *Escritos*, 272: "formam vitae . . . quam vobis beatus pater vester sanctus Franciscus verbo et scripto tradidit observandam."

58. *Escritos*, 328: "Denique huiusmodi praedilectas filias ac sponsas magnifici Regis, monemus et hortamur, attente in Domino Iesu obsecrantes, ut, cum sint huius excelsae religionis et clarissimae vitae sorores, considerent solertia vigili ac diligentia vigilanti se, iam pompa praesentis inopiae spreta, iam floridi saeculi vanitate contempta, iam guadiis vilibus plenis moerore despectis, abnegando propriam voluntatem, super seipsas evolasse sublimius, ut, ad horam corpore in antro salutis constricto, valeant mentes in serenissimis splendoribus dilatare. Nihil igitur ex nunc terrenitatis eis sapiat, nihilque delectet, sed, mortalibus omnibus spretis, solummodo Sponsum integrae puritatis amplectentes ex animo, ei ardenter ex amoris incendio uniri nitantur. Omni namque hora cor earum suspiret ad Ipsum, ac pro universali Ecclesia ex intimo mentis clangore ad Altissimum valida voce clamet."

59. *Escritos*, 328–29: "Nos vero cunctis hanc sacratissimam Regulam profitentibus, de omnipotentis Dei misericordia, et beatorum Petri et Pauli apostolorum eius auctoritate confisi, omnium peccatorum, de quibus corde contritae et ore confessae fuerint, plenam veniam indulgemus; et minora vota, quae unquam in hoc saeculo emiserunt, in hoc perfectionis votum celebre salubriter commutamus; et benedictionem eis adicimus salutarem, ut sic nitore sublimi clarificatae incedant, quousque perveniant ad thalamum claritatis."

60. *Escritos*, 295, notes that the Rule of 1259 "se caracteriza por su tonalidad mística y por las motivaciones espirituales con que frecuentemente enriquece las normas jurídicas."

61. *Escritos*, 301: "Quaelibet, inspirata Divino Flamine, Ordinem hunc assumens, Domini nostri Iesu Christi et eius sacratissimae matris vestigiis inhaerendo, iuxta evangelicae perfectionis consilium, vivat in oboedientia, in castitate ac sine proprio, et, velut thesaurus occultus incliti regis, inclusa moretur toto tempore vitae suae."

Omaechevarria capitalizes "Regis," but it seems that the metaphor is rather to royalty in general than to God.

62. *Escritos*, 302: "Si vero contingeret ex insultu hostilis incursus, aut ex aquarum inundantium impetu monasterii muros dirui, aut ipsum monasterium incendio concremari, vel ex aliqua huiusmodi causa taliter dissipari vel destrui, seu domibus eius ruinam minantibus, aut terrore hostium irruentium, locum tali dispositione constitui quod sine manifesto et grave periculo personae ibidem manere nequeant, nec suprascripti ministri licentiam et consilium expectare, de consilio et consensu totius conventus et abbatissae mandato, ad alium locum tutum se transferant sorores, in quo, si possint, clausae morentur, donec plena deliberatione praehabita, quid agere debeant, decernatur. Si autem conventus vellet ex alia causa evidenti totum earum monasterium alibi aedificare, sorores tunc de generalis ministri licentia possint ad alium locum se transferre."

63. *Escritos*, 303–4: "Tunc etiam prudens magistra concedatur eisdem ex devotioribus sororibus una, quae ipsas seorsum [*sic*] in sanctis moribus instruat et in fervore devotionis inflammet, ac ea, quae sunt secundum hanc sacram religionem ferenda, in suavitate caritatis ferre doceat, et in corrigendis corrigat diligenter." The word "seorum" appears as "sorores" in Isabelle's revised Rule of 1263. It seems likely that this is the correct reading for the Rule of 1259 as well.

64. *Escritos*, 244: "Ego talis soror promitto Deo et beatae Mariae semper Virgini, beato Francisco et omnibus Sanctis, servare perpetuam oboedientiam secundum Regulam et Formam Vivendi a Sede Apostolica Ordini nostro traditam, vivendeo toto tempore vitae meae sine proprio et in castitate." My translation follows Armstrong, *Clare of Assisi: Early Documents*, 111, with small changes.

65. *Escritos*, 304: "Ego talis soror promitto Deo et beatae Mariae semper Virgini et omnibus Sanctis in manibus vestris, Mater, vivere sub Regula a Domino Alexandro Papa IV Ordini nostro concessa, toto tempore vitae meae in obedientia, castitate ac sine proprio, et etiam sub clausura, secundum quod per eandem Regulam ordinatur."

66. For the Rule of 1247 see *Escritos*, 259–60. Cf. Clare's rule, ibid., 288–89.

67. *Escritos*, 305 (Cf. ibid., 248–49): "Vittis autem, aut peplis omnino albis, non tamen pretiosis, capita sua cooperiant uniformiter et honeste, ita quod frons, genae, et collum sint, sicut convenit, cooperta. Nec aliter coram personis extraneis audeant apparere;" only the Rule of 1259 then proceeds: "non enim decet sponsam Regis aeterni alicui alteri se exponere, nec etiam in aliquo alio delectari."

68. *Escritos*, 307–8: "Sorores vero horis et locis statutis, prout ordinatum fuerit, utilibus et honestis laboribus sub illa providentia occupentur, *quod, excluso otio animae inimico, sanctae orationis et devotionis spiritum non exstinguant, cui debent cetera temporalis deservire*; et cui se debet sponsa Christi mancipare totaliter, ut ibi Sponsi sui colloquiis et consolationibus perfruatur." The passage I have placed in italics is found in Francis's and Clare's rules. For Clare's rule cf. ibid., 284; for the *Regula bullata*, Kajetan Esser,

Die Opuscula des Hl. Franziskanus von Assisi (Grottaferrata: Editiones Collegii S. Bonaventurae ad Claras Aquas, 1976), 368.

69. *Escritos*, 308: "Sacratissimum autem Corpus Domini nostri Iesu Christi sorores, confessione praemissa, cum fuerit necesse, cum reverentia et devotione duabus vicibus quolibet mense recipiant. In quadragesima vero et in adventu Domini, si eis expedire videbitur, omni die dominico, nisi ex causa rationabili aliqua ipsarum de abbatissae licentia praetermittat." For Clare's rule cf. ibid., 278.

70. *Escritos*, 308: " . . . ut earum pectora Sancti Spiritus charismatibus foecundentur."

71. *Escritos*, 310: "Abbatissa vero, quantum potest, studeat continuare conventum et vitam communem ducere, cum debeat esse speculum charitatis ceteris et omnibus suis sororibus in exemplum. Abbatissa tamen, quae communem vitam ducere non potuerit, vel noluerit, sine mora aut dispendio a suo regimine per ministrum, seu per visitatores Ordinis absolvatur, nisi de sua mora in officio nullum dispendium domus esset, sed grandis valde necessitas et evidens utilitas appareret." Omaechevarria reads "speculum claritatis." I have preferred the reading in Annibali da Latera, *Ad Bullarium Franciscanum . . . Supplementum*, 126.

72. *Escritos*, 312: "Verum cum aliqua soror confiteri voluerit, per locutorium sola soli confessionem faciat sacerdoti."

73. *Escritos*, 314: "Et simili modo ingressum omnibus aliis inhibemus, exceptis generali et provinciali ministris Ordinis Fratrum Minorum, et illis quos de abbatissae mandato, consilio et consensu conventus, pro aliquo opere valde necessario faciendo evidens necessitas exegerit introire. . . . Super hoc etiam Provincialis Ministri requiratur assensus, quando fieri poterit congruenter, ut in omnibus famae claritas conservetur." Omaechevarria inadvertently omits "Super . . . congruenter." Supplied from Annibali da Latera, *Ad Bullarium Franciscanum . . . Supplementum*, 126.

74. *Escritos*, 321: "Visitator sit semper ex Ordine Fratrum Minorum, et per ministrum generalem Ordinis transmittatur. Omni autem anno, quo per visitatorem a generali transmissum visitari non poterit, si necesse fuerit, per ministrum illius provinciae secundum formam visitationis praesentis Regulae visitentur."

75. *Escritos*, 321: "Cum autem visitatur aliqua ex sororibus, vel etiam abbatissa, suae visitationi non intersit, sed tunc extra capitulum commoretur; contra quam nihil in publico ab aliqua proponatur omnino, quod non possit probari factum fuisse, vel per publicam famam."

76. *Escritos*, 321–22: "Caveant autem omnes sorores, et considerent diligenter praecipue in visitatione sororum, ut nihil aliud quam amor divinus et suarum sororum correctio eas moveat ad loquendum. Illis autem, quae noluerint recognoscere culpam quae ipsis impingitur, si excusare se voluerint, praesertim si gravia fuerint, audientia non negetur. Accusantes autem in gravibus, si in probatione defecerint, pro culpae impositae modo legitime puniantur. Excessus qui fuerit sufficienter correctus a visitatore, iterum nullatenus corrigatur."

77. *Escritos*, 322: "... infra octo vel novem dies ad plus omnino visitatio terminetur. Nec postmodum monasterium ingrediendi habeant facultatem."

78. *Escritos*, 323–24: "Et si fratres aliquando ibidem steterint, vel etiam si, non ibidem morantes, audierint confessiones earum, et visitator contra ipsos aliquid notabile invenerit, teneatur illud ministro provinciae nunciare, qui ipsos mox corrigere debeat, vel etiam de loco amovere."

79. *Escritos*, 324: "Visitatori vero districte iniungimus, ut celanda, quae in sua visitatione invenerit, nulli aliquo modo scienter revelet; sed, lectis excessibus et iniunctis poenitentiis, omnia scripta corum conventu comburat, nisi essent talia, quae ex consilio discretarum sororum conventus omnino essent ministro generali referenda. Si vero provincialis minister aliquid notabile contra visitatorem aut socios suos post visitationem invenerit, id teneatur ministro generali Ordinis indicare."

80. *Escritos*, 325–26: "De cura vero, dispositione ac dispensatione possessionum et rerum temporalium, generalis vel provincialis minister aut alii fratres Ordinis se nullatenus intromittant."

81. *Escritos*, 326: "Ad haec, propter discursum indecentem praetextu temporalium evitandum, et ut quietius possint sorores praedictae Domino deservire, liceat eis in communi redditus et possessiones recipere, ac eas libere retinere."

82. *Escritos*, 326: "Pro quibus possessionibus modo debito pertractandis procurator unus prudens et fidelis in singulis huius Ordinis monasteriis habeatur, qui per abbatissam, de consilio et consensu conventus, constitui debeat, et etiam, quandocumque eis videbitur, amoveri." Cf. the Rule of 1247, ibid., 260–61: "Pro quibus possessionibus modo debito pertractandis procurator unus prudens pariter ac fidelis in singulis monasteriis vestri Ordinis habeatur, quandocumque expedire videbitur, qui per visitatorem constitui et amoveri debeat, sicut viderit expedire."

83. *Escritos*, 326: "Cum igitur sit alibi illa perennis habitatio patriae huius religionis sororum, curiositatem, quae Deo est in omnibus odibilis ac valde pietati contraria, et aedificiorum superfluitatis excessum, modis omnibus eas volumus evitare."

84. On these final two clauses compare Clare's rule, *Escritos*, 286 (VIII. 7), and 280 (IV. 15–18).

85. See Caroline Walker Bynum, "Women Mystics and Eucharistic Devotion in the Thirteenth Century," in *Fragmentation and Redemption*, 119–50.

86. Clare's rule stresses mutual confession of sins among the abbess and sisters, *Escritos*, 280: "Semel in hebdomada ad minus abbatissa sorores suas teneatur ad capitulum convocare. Ubi tam ipsa quam sorores de communibus et publicis offensis et negligentiis humiliter debeant confiteri." Isabelle's rule is more straightforward in calling on the abbess to issue correction, *Escritos*, 327: "Abbatissa autem de correctione, monitione, ac ordinatione sororum capitulum teneat qualibet hebdomada semel."

87. De Nantes, "Les origines de l'ordre de sainte Claire," 124–28.

88. Dominican Master General Humbert of Romans railed in 1274 against "certain poor religious women . . . who, occasionally seeking necessities, run about to and fro through villages and camps." Quoted in Edward Tracey Brett, *Humbert of Romans: His Life and Views of Thirteenth-Century Society* (Toronto: Pontifical Institute of Mediaeval Studies, 1984), 193. On growing suspicion concerning semi-religious and Beguines in this era see Walter Simons, *Cities of Ladies: Beguine Communities in the Medieval Low Countries, 1200–1565* (Philadelphia: University of Pennsylvania Press, 2001), 118–37; and Elizabeth Makowski, *"A Pernicious Sort of Woman": Quasi-Religious Women and Canon Lawyers in the Later Middle Ages* (Washington, DC: Catholic University of America Press, 2005). For a more wide-ranging argument about increasing clerical suspicion of women's religiosity see Elliot, *Proving Woman*.

89. Elizabeth Makowski, *Canon Law and Cloistered Women: Periculoso and Its Commentators, 1298–1545* (Washington, DC: Catholic University of America Press, 1997). See pages 34–37 on the importance of rules for Franciscan women as precursors of *Periculoso*. Makowski does not mention Isabelle's rules, but see the short analysis in De Fontette, *Les religieuses à l'âge classique du droit canon*, 147–48. Also useful is the discussion of later nuns' complex attitudes toward strict enclosure in Anne Winston-Allen, *Convent Chronicles: Women Writing about Women and Reform in the Late Middle Ages* (University Park: Pennsylvania State University Press, 2004), 152–67.

90. My discussion follows Alfonso Marini, *Agnese di Bohemia* (Rome: Istituto Storico dei Cappuccini, 1991); see also Joan Mueller, "Agnes of Prague and the Juridical Implications of the Privilege of Poverty," *Franciscan Studies* 58 (2000): 261–87; Jaroslav Nemec, *Agnese di Boemia: La vita, il culto, la "Legenda"* (Padua: Edizioni Messaggero, 1987); Petr Pitha, "Agnes of Prague: A New Bohemian Saint," *Franziskanische Studien* 72 (1990): 325–40; and Klaniczay, *Holy Rulers and Blessed Princesses*, 204–5, 225–26, 238–40, 257–59, 278–79. Barbara Newman's study, "Agnes of Prague and Guglielma of Milan," is forthcoming in Alistair J. Minnis and Rosalynn Voaden, eds., *Yale Guide to Medieval Holy Women in the Christian Tradition*. I thank her for sending me a pre–publication copy.

91. Agnes's fourteenth-century *vita* claimed that she had rejected the role of abbess, but see Gregory IX's bull of 18 May 1235, *Cum relicta seculi*, cited by Mueller, "Agnes of Prague and the Juridical Implications of the Privilege of Poverty," 271, where she is clearly referred to as abbess.

92. Marini, *Agnese di Bohemia*, 76–77.

93. The claim that Agnes's community eventually was allowed to follow Clare's Rule of 1253 relies on her early fourteenth-century *vita*, not on any surviving papal documents. See Marini, *Agnese di Bohemia*, 95–96. On the reissuance of the Rule of 1219 to Agnes's house in 1238 see ibid., 76.

94. My summary draws on D. L. Douie, *The Conflict between the Seculars and the Mendicants at the University of Paris in the Thirteenth Century* (London: Blackfriars,

1954); idem, "St. Bonaventure's Part in the Conflict between Seculars and Mendicants at Paris," in *S. Bonaventura, 1274–1974*, vol. 2, 585–612; Lester K. Little, "Saint Louis's Involvement with the Friars," *Church History* 33 (1964): 125–48; and Michel-Marie Dufeil, "Le roi dans la querelle des mendiants et des séculiers," in *Septième centenaire de la mort de saint Louis* (Paris: Les Belles Lettres, 1976), 280–89. More generally see Dufeil, *Guillaume de Saint-Amour et la polémique universitaire parisienne, 1250–1259* (Paris: Picard, 1972).

95. Little, "Saint Louis's Involvement with the Friars," 139.

96. Dufeil, "Le roi dans la querelle des mendiants et des séculiers," 284–85.

97. Cited by Little, "Saint Louis's Involvement with the Friars," 141, 147–48 n. 52.

98. Little, "Saint Louis's Involvement with the Friars," 143.

99. If the traditional, but unsubstantiated, date of 10 June 1256 is accepted for the laying of the foundations of Longchamp. This date is followed by Dufeil without proof of its veracity. Cf. *Guillaume de Saint-Amour et la polémique universitaire parisienne*, 275 n. 173, referring to *Layettes, #4266*, which does not concern Longchamp; and "Le roi dans la querelle des mendiants et des séculiers," 288, where no evidence is cited.

100. Hallam, "Aspects of the Monastic Patronage of the English and French Royal Houses," 381. On Louis and Franciscan houses more generally see ibid., 266–69. According to Hallam's analysis, of the thirty-two royal foundations established during Louis IX's reign, thirteen were for mendicants but only four (including Longchamp) were Franciscan, and one of these was at Jaffa in the Holy Land. See also Appendix Two in Jordan, *Louis IX and the Challenge of the Crusade*, 232–35; and, for a recent assessment of Louis's patronage patterns, M. Cecilia Gaposchkin, "The King of France and the Queen of Heaven: The Iconography of the Porte Rouge of Notre-Dame of Paris," *Gesta* 39 (2000): 58–72.

101. Most notably the construction of the Grand Couvent des Cordeliers in Paris. See Gaposchkin, "The King of France and the Queen of Heaven," 65; and Jérôme Poulenc, "Une histoire du Grand Couvent des Cordeliers de Paris des origines à nos jours," *AFH* 49 (1976): 474–95, at 493–95.

CHAPTER FOUR.   *A Minor Triumph: The Revised Rule of 1263 and Its Impact*

1. Jacques Dalarun, *François d'Assise ou le pouvoir en question: Principes et modalités du gouvernement dans l'ordre des Frères mineurs* (Paris and Brussels: De Boeck, 1999), 22.

2. Isabelle's Rule of 1263 is edited in Wadding, *Annales minorum*, vol. 4, 573–82; *BF* vol. 2, 477–86; Eubel, *Bullarii franciscani epitome et supplementum*, 269–75; *Escritos* uses the Rule of 1259 as a base and notes changes implemented in 1263. All editions of the 1263 rule are from Urban IV's register and not from the copy that was held at

Longchamp, which is today Paris, Bibliothèque de l'Arsenal, ms. 1240. My examination of this manuscript, however, did not reveal any important discrepancies with the aforementioned editions.

3. AN L1027, no. 22: "L'an de grace mil .cc. lx. la veille s. Jehan Baptistre qui fu au mecredi, le convent des sereurs meneurs de l'Humilite Nostre Dame de Lonc Champ fu vestu et mis en la clouture, present mon seigneur Saint Looys qui lors estoit rois de France, madame Ysabel sa suer qui funda la dicte eglise de son avoir, et frere Guillame de Hardenbourt qui lors estoit ministre de France, et presentes moult de grant persones qui ne sont pas y nommees." Ed. Auguste L. Molinier, *Les obituaires de la province de Sens*, vol. 1, part 2 (Paris: Imprimerie Nationale, 1902), 664. The document was drawn up by Abbess Jeanne of Vitry with the aid of a list written by Sister Jeanne of Quitry (who had been at Longchamp for forty-seven years before she died in 1325), which recorded the nuns by the order of their deaths.

4. Salimbene is cited by Little, "Saint Louis's Involvement with the Friars," 130. For Guillaume of St. Pathus see Delaborde, *Vie de saint Louis par Guillaume de Saint-Pathus*, 85–86, 102, 109 (eating in the refectories of Royaumont, Compiègne, Orléans, Chaalis); and 108–9 (listening to sermons while seated with the monks of Chaalis and Royaumont).

5. Quotations in this paragraph are from *Writings of AH*, 46–48 (par. 3).

6. Darleen N. Pryds, *The King Embodies the Word: Robert d'Anjou and the Politics of Preaching* (Leiden: Brill, 2000), 15 n. 56, says that Louis "did not himself preach." On Louis as a crusade "preacher" in an informal sense see Christopher T. Maier, "*Civilis ac pia regis Francorum deceptio*: Louis IX as Crusade Preacher," in Michael Balard, Benjamin Z. Kedar, and Jonathan Riley-Smith, eds., *Dei gesta per Francos: Études sur les croisades dédiées à Jean Richard* (Burlington, VT: Ashgate, 2001), 57–63. Even here, Louis "preaches" more by deed than by word.

7. For Agnes's record of his gifts see *Writings of AH*, 48 (par. 5). Fifteenth-century inventories confirm that the abbey continued to treasure these relics. See Mlynarczyk, *Ein Franziskanerinnenkloster*, 289–90, 310, 328. Louis's donations of rents, money, and firewood are well documented. See AN K32 no. 7 (later copies nos. 7b and 7c, AN L1020 no. 28), Jules Tardif, *Monuments historiques* (Paris: Cayce, 1866), #848, original with seal of donation of 400 *livres* of rent dated February 1267; AN J148 no. 6, somewhat confusingly, is a renunciation dated February 1267 by Abbess Agnes of Harcourt and the nuns of Longchamp of 100 out of the 500 *livres* in annual rents that they say were given by Louis, in exchange for a cash payment of 2,000 *livres*, ed. *Layettes*, vol. 4, #5253. The following grants are all dated March 1270 when Louis seems to have given a flurry of gifts on the eve of his departure on crusade: AN L1020 no. 35 (later copy no. 36), grant of rights to firewood; AN K33 no. 5 (Tardif #864), another grant of firewood; AN K33 no. 10 (Tardif #863), "amortissement" of Longchamp's rents; AN K33 no. 11 (Tardif #859), grant of "droit du quint" to Longchamp. Many of these grants

are summarized and confirmed in documents issued by Philip III, for instance, AN L1020 nos. 39 and 49.

8. The original of this bull is lost, though it was still in the treasury of Longchamp in 1472, according to AN LL1600, f. iv. The French version given here is Pierre Perrier's seventeenth–century translation, the only surviving copy I am aware of, found in his unpublished biography of Isabelle of France, BNF ms. fr. 24950, pp. 103–4: "Urbain, evéque, serviteur des serviteurs de Dieu, a notre bien aimé fils le gardien des freres mineurs de Paris, salut et apostolique benediction. Il a été proposé devant nous de la part de nostre tres cher fils en Christ l'illustre Roi de France, que quelques seurs du monastére des seurs cloistrées de la ville de Reims sont venue au monastére de l'humilité Notre Dame du diocese de Paris, pour y instruire les seurs de ce lieu, qui ne sont encore que nouvelles plantés aux institutions regulieres. Pour accorder au roi ce qu'il demande, nous vous donnons par ces presentes lettres l'authorité necc[essaire] pour absoudre les dites seurs de leur engagement au dit monastére de Reims, et les attacher a celui de la sainte vierge susdit, pour y demeurer toujours et y servir le Dieu tres ha[ut]. Donné a Viterbe, le 12 des kalendes de decembre, c'est le 20 novembre, l'an 1 de notre pontificat, c'est 1261." Where Perrier's other translations can be checked against extant Latin originals, they are substantially faithful.

9. The first name on the list is Sister Lore "la novice," who presumably died in the first year of the abbey's existence. The four women who are known to have been abbesses before 1275—Agnes of Anery, Mahaut of Guyencourt, Agnes of Harcourt, and Julianne of Troyes—were probably all among the original nuns. The very last of the original nuns was Alice of Mucedent, the eighty-first to die, who was more than 101 years old, had lived at Longchamp for sixty-three years, and died in 1323 (new style). See Molinier, *Les obituaires de la province de Sens*, vol. 1, part 2, 666. AN L1020 no. 5C mentions the gifts of three nuns in May 1261—Jeanne of Harcourt (the aunt of Agnes), Mahaut of Scotland, and Desirée—to the abbey. Since they were all described as being in their probationary year, they must have been among the first group to take the veil. In 1282, five sisters added their names to Agnes of Harcourt's as witnesses of Queen Marguerite's story about the three doves appearing at the abbey's groundbreaking. In addition to names already mentioned, Sister Mahaut of Gondarville's inclusion in this list probably marks her as one of the surviving original nuns. Finally, although Peronnelle of Pontoise was not among the initial group, she took the veil during the abbey's first year and was the first nun to do so actually inside the monastery, on 24 July 1260 ("le veille S. Jaques et S. Christofle l'an [mil] CCLX"). She lived at Longchamp for sixty-seven years and died on 17 March 1327/28. Molinier, *Les obituaires de la province de Sens*, vol. 1, part 2, 667.

10. Certainly the Harcourt family, who contributed two of these fifteen, had become one of France's more illustrious noble houses by the later thirteenth century. Only two of the first nuns, Sisters Lore and Desirée, receive no family or place name.

Agnes of Harcourt was mostly likely part of Isabelle's household before Longchamp's foundation, and Mahaut of Gondarville was identified by Agnes as having been in Isabelle's service. *Writings of AH*, 46 (par. 2), 58 (par. 11).

11. Duchesne, *Histoire de l'abbaye royale de Longchamp*, 137–42.

12. In 1904, César Pascal argued that the royal residence at Longchamp actually predated the construction of the abbey. This claim seems to be founded on very tenuous evidence and is to my mind unconvincing. César Pascal, "L'hostel royal de Longchamp," 71–78. Cf. Duchesne, *Histoire de l'abbaye royale de Longchamp*, 3–4; Garreau, *Bienheureuse Isabelle de France, soeur de saint Louis*, 33–34. These sources frequently say that Isabelle "retired" to Longchamp only in 1263. I know of no evidence that makes this date more likely than 1260.

13. See Garreau passim for reproductions of early-modern artwork and maps depicting Longchamp. For the abbey's buildings see Duchesne, *Histoire de l'abbaye royale de Longchamp*, 10–22. For a brief assessment of Longchamp's architectural significance see Robert Branner, *St. Louis and the Court Style in Gothic Architecture* (London: Swemmer, 1965), 89–90. Today on the northern edge of the modern Hippodrome of Longchamp is a re-creation of the abbey's windmill. Across the road stands a circular tower, which was treated by Duchesne (p. 17) as an architectural remnant of Longchamp. Its authenticity, however, seems dubious. On the royal residence at Longchamp, Marguerite of Provence and her daughter Blanche each lived there for a time in the thirteenth century, and in the early fourteenth century both Philip IV and Philip V dated documents from Longchamp. On Philip IV see Tardif, *Monuments historiques*, #1002, 1004, 1005; for Philip V see ibid., #1133, 1134, 1144, 1146, and Elizabeth A. R. Brown, "The Ceremonial of Royal Succession in Capetian France: The Funeral of Philip V," in *The Monarchy of Capetian France and Royal Ceremonial* (Aldershot: Variorum, 1991), VIII, 289, Appendix I. Duchesne edited a letter that gives some information on these residences in 1341. See *Histoire de l'abbaye royale de Longchamp*, 4.

14. AN Q*[1] 1072[1], f. 38r (letter 68): "A noble dame et saige, Madame Ysabel seur le Roy, et a religieuse dame et honneste humble abbeesse des cordellieres, Je, Emeline humble abbeesse de Mont Martre, salut et oroisones en Notre Seigneur." Dated "en l'an de l'incarnation Notre Seigneur mil. cc. soixante et ung, le lundi devant pasque fleuries." The date must be 1262 in modern reckoning. AN Q*[1] 1072[1] is a late-fourteenth- or early-fifteenth-century cartulary that contains copies of eighty-three letters from 1260 to 1270, all, however, in French translation. Many of the Latin originals are found in AN L1020, but the original of letter sixty-eight is lost. It is probably substantially faithful, however, since a spot check of letters fourteen (f. 7r) and seventeen (f. 8v), also from Emeline de Fleury and also dated September 1262, with the Latin originals in AN L1029 nos. 10 and 11, reveals a basic level of fidelity.

15. AN L1020, no. 12: "Universis presentes litteras inspecturis . . . [*sic*] Th . . . [*sic*] Abbas ste. Genovese Par[isiensis] totusque eiusdem ecclesie conventus humilis eternam in Domino salutum. Notum facimus quod, cum nos et ecclesia nostra haberemus, teneremus, et possideremus super nova abbacia Illustrissime Domine Isabellis sororis Excellentissimi Regis Francie sita iuxta Sanctum Clodoaldium et in territorio eidem abbacie adiacenta viginti et octo denarios census annui capitalis, nos ad preces et instanciam dictorum domini Regis et domine Isabellis eidem nove abbacie et sororibus de eadem abbacia quittavimus in perpetuum et remisimus in manu mortua dictos viginti et octo denarios pro decem libris turon[ensis] iam nobis solutis in pecunia numerata. In cuius rei testimonium presentibus litteris sigilla nostra duximus apponenda. Datum anno Domini millesimo ducentesimo sexagesimo secondo, mense septemb."

16. After 1262 Isabelle is not mentioned again in extant documents of this sort. This change might have been due either to Isabelle's consciously retiring to the background or to the natural tendency of ecclesiastics to address the abbess and sisters directly once Longchamp became a fixture on the monastic landscape. Louis's influence, by contrast, continued to be cited as a contributing factor whenever abbots of major houses made concessions to Longchamp during the rest of his reign. In addition to Thomas of Sainte-Geneviève and his successor Odo, Girard of Saint-Germain-des-Prés (AN L1020 no. 23, dated 1266, see also *Layettes*, vol. 3, #4806), Matthew of Saint-Denis (AN L1020 no. 27, dated September 1266), and Peter of Saint-Victor (AN L1020 no. 30, dated January 1267/68) all bowed to Louis's will in making concessions to Longchamp.

17. *Escritos*, 300–301: "Nos igitur . . . Regulam ipsam, per dilectum filium nostrum Simonem tituli Sanctae Caeciliae Cardinalem corrigi facientes." On Simon of Brie (Martin IV) see Richard Kay, "Martin IV and the Fugitive Bishop of Bayeux," *Speculum* 40 (1965): 460–83; E. Jordan, *Les origines de la domination Angevine en Italie*, vol. 2 (Paris, 1909; reprint, New York: Burt Franklin, 1960), 297–309 and passim; idem, "Les promotions de cardinaux sous Urbain IV," *Revue d'histoire et de littérature religieuses* 5 (1900): 322–34; and Nikolaus Backes, *Kardinal Simon de Brion (Papst Martin IV)* (Berlin: Hermann Blanke, 1910).

18. Kay, "Martin IV and the Fugitive Bishop of Bayeux," 464.

19. Jordan, *Les origines de la domination Angevine en Italie*, 297–303.

20. Simon was in Italy in August 1263, before being sent back to Paris to negotiate further with Charles of Anjou in early 1264. Jordan, *Les origines de la domination Angevine en Italie*, 351, 488.

21. Kay, "Martin IV and the Fugitive Bishop of Bayeux," 473, 465; the last quotation is from J. N. D. Kelly, *The Oxford Dictionary of Popes* (Oxford: Oxford University Press, 1986), 203.

22. *Escritos*, 300–3: "Urbanus episcopus, servus servorum Dei. Dilectis in Christo filiabus . . . [*sic*] abatissae et conventui sororum Minorum Monasterii

Humilitatis Beatae Mariae Parisiensis Dioecesis. Salutem et Apostolicam Benedictionem. Religionis augmentum eo libentius procuramus, quo per hoc amplius dilatatur Divini Nominis cultus et salus proficit animarum. Sane felicis recordationis Alexander Papa praedecessor noster, carissimi in Christo filii nostri . . . [*sic*] regis Franciae supplicationibus condescendens, omnibus Christi ancillis e saeculo fugientibus et in vestro monasterio Humilitatis Beatae Mariae vocabulo insignito, in quo, tunc de novo constructo, nemo adhuc, ut dicitur, morabatur, professionem facientibus, Regulam infra scriptam in eodem monasterio perpetuis temporibus observandam, cum *Sororum Inclusarum* vocabulo nuncupandam, concessit. Porro ex parte dicti regis nobis fuit humiliter supplicatum, ut dictam Regulam, in aliquibus capitulis corrigi facientes, nominationis eius *Minorum* vocabulum adicere de benignitate Apostolica dignaremur. Nos igitur, eiusdem regis precibus inclinati, Regulam ipsam, per dilectum filium nostrum Simonem tituli Sanctae Caeciliae cardinalem corrigi facientes, et ut, sicut re ita et nomine, praesertim cum idem monasterium, sicut praemittitur, titulum Humilitatis Beatae Mariae sibi ascripserit, eiusdem humilitatis possit profectibus insigniri, nuncupationi eiusdem Regulae dictum *Minorum* adicientes vocabulum, duximus statuendum ut Regula ipsa *Sororum Minorum Inclusarum* de cetero nominetur, et servetur perpetuo in praetacto monasterio, et in aliis monasteriis de cetero fundandis seu plantandis, in quibus sorores eandem Regulam profiteri contigerit, sic correcta."

23. *Writings of AH*, 66 (par. 25).

24. In a letter of 1238. See Maria Pia Alberzoni, "Le congregazioni monastiche: Le Damianite," in Giancarlo Andenna, ed., *Dove va la storiografia monastica in Europa? Temi e metodi di ricerca per lo studio della vita monastica e regolare in età medievale alle soglie del terzo millennio: Atti del Convegno internazionale Brescia-Rodengo, 23–25 marzo 2000* (Milan: Vita e Pensiero, 2001), 379–401, at 396 n. 64.

25. On Urban IV see Philippe Levillain, ed., *The Papacy: An Encyclopedia* (New York and London: Routledge, 2002), 1554–55; Steven Runciman, *The Sicilian Vespers* (Cambridge: Cambridge University Press, 1958), 53–54; and Jordan, *Les origines de la domination Angevine en Italie*, 291 and following. It is possible that Urban could have met Isabelle of France at some point, since he was resident in France for much of the 1240s.

26. Runciman, *The Sicilian Vespers*, 68–70.

27. This task is facilitated by Omaechevarria's edition, which uses the Rule of 1259 as a base text but tries to indicate wherever the Rule of 1263 made changes. It should be noted, however, that some of the smaller changes go unremarked.

28. *Escritos*, 316 n. 26: "Cum viris autem discretis et maturis, ac honestis confessoribus suis, vel etiam aliis, locis et temporibus congruis, ad consolationem earum, et aedificationem animarum, de licentia generalis ministri, seu provincialis, vel abbatissae aliquando loqui possint." This section replaced the clause in the Rule of 1259 that

threatened excommunication to anyone who entered against the terms laid out in the rule.

29. *Escritos*, 327–28. The Rule of 1259 reads: "Insuper abbatissae et ceteris sororibus districtius inhibemus, ut nullam auctoritatem seu laxationem directe vel indirecte contra praesentem Regulam, per se vel per alium, ab Apostolica Sede obtinere procuret sine licentia generalis ministri, ac etiam consilio et consensu totius conventus; quin, si forte aliquando fuerit per aliquem aliquid huiusmodi procuratum, vel sine procuratione concessum, decernimus illud nihil valoris, vel roboris obtinere." Compare to the Rule of 1263 (ibid., n. 42): "Ad haec penitus prohibemus, ne in monasterio praetacto aliquis visitator aut minister auctoritate sua Constitutiones faciat aliquas ultra formam ipsam et Regulam, quae sorores ad aliquod culpae vel poenae obligent, sine consensu et voluntate omnium sororum. Quod si forte aliquis fecerit, eas non teneantur aliquatenus observare. Volumus etiam et attente monemus, ne aliquid eis praecipiant, seu praecipiatur sine magna utilitate, et valde evidenti et manifesta necessitate."

30. *Escritos*, 303–4: "Omnibus autem hanc religionem *in praetacto monasterio, et in aliis de novo fundandis, in quibus hanc regulam contigerit profiteri,* assumere cupientibus . . . Omnes vero volentes *in hoc monasterio, et in aliis in posterum fundandis, in quibus haec Regula professa fuerit,* hanc sacram religionem assumere." I have added italics to indicate words that were newly added in the Rule of 1263.

31. *Escritos*, 317. The Rule of 1259 reads: "Porro ad exsequias circa sepulturas agendas capellanus non ingrediatur in claustrum, sed exterius in ecclesia, indutus sacerdotalibus, ante altare maneat, et quod ad illud officium pertinet cum sociis exsequatur." Compare the Rule of 1263 (ibid., n. 30): "Porro ad exequias circa sepulturas agendas sororum vel aliorum, duo vel tres fratres minores sacerdotes, quando corpus portatur ad sepulturam, ingredi valeant cum sacerdotalibus indumentis; qui, quod ad illud officium pertinet exequentes, semper simul stent quandiu morabuntur ibidem; et completo opere, sepulturae exeant sine more."

32. *Escritos*, 323–24. The Rule of 1259 reads: "Et si fratres aliquando ibidem steterint, vel etiam si, non ibidem morantes, audierint confessiones earum." Compare the Rule of 1263 (ibid., n.37): "Confessores vero earum ac socii eorumdem sint de Ordine fratrum minorum ibi commorantes, qui eis Eucharistiam, et alia sacramenta ministrent, nisi forte in aliquo loco a ministro generali vel provinciali, ex causa rationabili et honesta, fuerit aliter ordinatum." The modifying final clause with its reference to "in aliquo loco" seems intended to guard against potential problems at houses other than Longchamp.

33. *Escritos*, 312: "Confessores vero ipsarum, eis per ministrum generalem, seu provincialem illius provinciae assignati solummodo, *secundum quod ipsi, vel ipsorum alter duxerit ordinandum,* eas a peccatis omnibus absolvant." My italics indicate words that were deleted from the revised Rule of 1263.

34. A claim that goes back at least to Roulliard, *La saincte mère*, 166.

35. See Lezlie Knox, "Audacious Nuns," 41–62, building on the fundamental work by Grundmann, *Religious Movements in the Middle Ages*, 131–33. Most of the documents that detail this conflict of 1261–63 are edited in Zephyrinus Lazzeri, "Documenta controversiam inter Fratres Minores et Clarissas spectantia (1262–1297)," *AFH* 3 (1910): 664–79, and 4 (1911): 74–94.

36. In his bull *Inter personas, BF* vol. 2, 574–75.

37. Lazzeri, "Documenta," 672: "Gravia siquidem inter alia, dispendiosum posset emergere scandalum, si Regum et aliorum Magnatum filias, quae sub eiusdem Ordinis observantia Domino famulantur, contingeret absque debita custodia derelinqui." Since Isabelle was not actually a nun, Urban is more likely to have had Agnes of Bohemia in mind. It is still possible, however, that Urban was reminding Bonaventure of his own relationship with Isabelle of France.

38. Lazzeri, "Documenta," 671–72; Knox, "Audacious Nuns," 49–50.

39. Knox, "Audacious Nuns," 51–52; *BF*, vol. 2, 474–75.

40. Lazzeri, "Documenta," 77–83.

41. All quotations here are taken from Dominic Monti, *St. Bonaventure's Writings Concerning the Franciscan Order* (St. Bonaventure, NY: Franciscan Institute, 1994), 192–95. For the original Latin see "Lletra de Sant Bonaventura al Ministre Provincial d'Aragó," *Etudis Franciscans* 37 (1926): 112–14.

42. The authorship of the rule was attributed to Cardinal Orsini, though it was closely modeled on the Rule of 1247. Omaechevarria includes only excerpts of this rule, *Escritos*, 330–42. For the entire text see Eubel, *Bullarii franciscani epitome et supplementum*, 276–84; *BF* vol. 2, 509–21; and *Regulae et constitutiones generales monialium Ordinis sanctae Clarae* (Rome: Curia Generalitia Ordinis Fratrum Minorum, 1941), 27–69. I cite the latter for the sake of availability.

43. *Regulae et constitutiones*, 38.

44. *Regulae et constitutiones*, 31: "inevitabilis et periculosa necessitas, sicut exustionis ignis, vel incursus hostilis."

45. *Regulae et constitutiones*, 34.

46. *Regulae et constitutiones*, 36–37.

47. *Regulae et constitutiones*, 41–42.

48. *Regulae et constitutiones*, 61.

49. *Regulae et constitutiones*, 59. Isabelle's Rules of 1259 and 1263 read: "qui [the Procurator] per Abbatissam de consilio et consensu Conventus constitui debeat et etiam quandocumque eis videbitur amoveri." Urban's rule reads: "qui per Abbatissam et Conventum constitui et amoveri debeat."

50. On the repeated papal attempts to get Franciscan nuns to accept Urban's rule see Knox, "Audacious Nuns," 56–58.

51. *BF* vol. 3, p. 82: 31 May 1266, Clement IV's bull *De statu tuo audivimus prospera*: "Dilecto filio J[oanni] Sancti Nicolae in Carcere Tullianen. Diacono Cardinali Sal., et

apostol. benedictionem . . . Verum Sorores Ordinis S. Clarae venerunt Viterbium pro multarum terrarum Sororibus; quarum mora in Curia nec olim tibi placuit, nec hodie Nobis placet. Sunt omnes in hoc proposito, quod tuam Regulam non recipiant; sed vel statum observent pristinum; vel si ille videbitur dubius, vivendi formam, quam habet dilecta in Christo filia soror Regis Francia, acceptabunt. Super quo intentionem tuam ad plenum Nobis per tuas intimes litteras; aut si mavis, ad tuam eas mittemus praesentiam, ut celeriter eas expedias, tua ipsis saltem per alium exposita volunte; super quorum alterutra tuam scire volumus voluntatem. Datum Viterbii II kalendas Junii, Pontificatus Nostri Anno Secundo." On this episode see Knox, "Audacious Nuns," 54–61.

52. *BF* vol. 3, 82, note b, indicates that the letter is actually mutilated at the point that might have revealed exactly who these women were and which houses from what "lands" they claimed to represent.

53. On the history of this title see Maria Pia Alberzoni, "*Sorores minores* and Ecclesiastical Authority to the Pontificate of Urban IV," in *Clare of Assisi and the Poor Sisters in the Thirteenth Century*, 113–54; eadem, *La nascita di un'istituzione*, 34–40; Luigi Pellegrini, "Female Religious Experience and Society in Thirteenth-Century Italy," in Sharon Farmer and Barbara H. Rosenwein, eds., *Monks and Nuns, Saints and Outcasts: Religion in Medieval Society. Essays in Honor of Lester K. Little* (Ithaca: Cornell University Press, 2000), 97–122, at 119–22; Optatus van Asseldonk, " 'Sorores minores,' una nuova impostazione del problema," 595–634; idem, "Sorores minores e Chiara d'Assisi a San Damiano, una scelta tra clausura e lebbrosi?" *Collectanea franciscana* 63 (1993): 399–421; C. Gennaro, "Il Francescanesimo femminile nel XIII secolo," *Rivista di storia e letteratura religiosa* 25 (1989): 281–84; and Oliger, "De origine regularum Ordinis S. Clarae," 438 n. 1.

54. Grundmann, *Religious Movements in the Middle Ages*, 113–14 n. 149. This evidence for Francis's rejection of the term comes from a story told by Thomas of Pavia (d. 1278/1279) in the 1260s or 1270s. See L. Oliger, "Descriptio codicis S. Antonii de Urbe unacum appendice textuum de S. Francisco," *AFH* 12 (1919): 321–401, at 382–83. It may therefore reflect later struggles more than Francis's own words. See Jacques Dalarun, *François d'Assise, un passage: Femmes et féminité dans les écrits et les légendes franciscaines*, trans. Catherine Dalarun-Mitrovitsa (Arles: Actes Sud, 1997), 65; and Robert Rusconi, "The Spread of Women's Franciscanism in the Thirteenth Century," *Greyfriars Review* 12 (1998): 35–73, at 48; Alberzoni, "*Sorores Minores* and Ecclesiastical Authority to the Pontificate of Urban IV," 113–14.

55. In his bull *Ad audientiam nostram*, 21 February 1241, *BF* vol. 1, 290. Alberzoni suggests that it was only after the deposition of Brother Elias as Minister General of the Franciscans that this title became so odious to Franciscan authority. *La nascita di un'istituzione*, 35–36. See also Giulia Barone, *Da frate Elia agli spirituali* (Milan: Edizione Biblioteca Francescana, 1999), 29–86. Jacques de Vitry's use of the term (see below) and his statement that the *Fratres* and *Sorores minores* were held in

high esteem by the pope and cardinals also indicate that the term was inoffensive at first.

56. In the bull *Cum harum rector*. A copy dated 20 April 1250 is printed in *BF* vol. 1, 541. Translated in Luigi Pellegrini, "Female Religious Experience and Society in Thirteenth-Century Italy," 120. See also Rusconi, "The Spread of Women's Franciscanism in the Thirteenth Century," 69; and Alberzoni, "*Sorores minores* and Ecclesiastical Authority," 127.

57. Agathange de Paris, "L'origine et la fondation des monastères de Clarisses en Aquitaine au XIIIe siècle," *Collectanea franciscana* 25 (1955): 5–52, at 7 n. 7. For the bull of 14 March 1261 see Van Asseldonk, "Sorores minores e Chiara d'Assisi a San Damiano," 417, citing *BF* vol. 2, 417.

58. R. B. C. Huygens, ed., *Lettres de Jacques de Vitry* (Leiden: Brill, 1960), 75: "Vnum tamen in partibus illis inveni solatium, multi enim utriusque sexus divites et seculares omnibus pro Christo relictis seculum fugiebant, qui *Fratres minores* et *Sorores minores* vocantur. A domno papa et cardinalibus in magna reverentia habentur, hii autem circa temporalia nullatenus occupantur, sed ferventi desiderio et vehementi studio singulis diebus laborant ut animas que pereunt a seculi vanitatibus retrahant et eas secum ducant." For commentary see Van Asseldonk, " 'Sorores minores,' una nuova impostazione del problema."

59. Pellegrini, "Female Religious Experience and Society in Thirteenth-Century Italy," 108 n. 33; Alberzoni, "*Sorores Minores* and Ecclesiastical Authority," 132–33; eadem, "*Nequaquam a Christi sequela in perpetuum absolvi desiderio*," trans. Nancy Celashi, "Clare between Charism and Institution," *Greyfriars Review* 12, Supplement (1998): 81–121, see 117–18 n. 118, citing *BF* vol. 1, 330; Giancarlo Andenna, "Le Clarisse nel novarese (1252–1300)," *AFH* 67 (1974): 185–267 (pp. 236–37, letters from Bishop Sigebaldo Cavallazzi referring to the "religio sororum minorum" of Novara).

60. A. F. C. Bourdillon, *The Order of Minoresses in England* (Manchester: University of Manchester Press, 1926), 11.

61. *Layettes*, vol. 3, #4387.

62. The most recent edition is Kathryn Betts Wolfkiel, "*The Life of the Blessed Saint Doucelina* (d. 1274): An Edition and Translation with Commentary" (Ph.D. diss., Northwestern University, 1993), 60. For English translation see Kathleen Garay and Madeleine Jeay, trans., *The Life of Saint Douceline, a Beguine of Provence* (Rochester: D. S. Brewer, 2001), 7. Since this text was not written until the end of the thirteenth century, however, the label is not definitive evidence of usage at midcentury.

63. See, for instance, Oliger, "De origine regularum Ordinis S. Clarae," 438 n. 1. Geneviève Brunel-Lobrichon says that Franciscan women were usually called "minorettes ou menoretas en occitan dans le midi," but it is not clear how early this label was applied. "Diffusion et spiritualité des premières clarisses méridionales," in *La*

femme dans la vie religieuse du Languedoc (XIIIe–XIVe siècles) (Toulouse: Privat, 1988), 261–80, quotation at 263. The name sometimes continued to be applied indiscriminately to Franciscan women. For example, a fourteenth-century copy of the 1263 "Urbanist" Rule that created the Order of St. Clare (discussed below), today Uppsala, University Library ms. C 65, ff. 81–89, is labeled "Regula Sororum Minorum." See Margarete Andersson-Schmitt and Monica Hedlund, *Mittelalterliche Handschriften der Universitätsbibliothek Uppsala*, vol. 2 (Stockholm: Almquist & Wiksell, 1989), 41. Robert E. Lerner brought this manuscript to my attention.

64. AN L1020 no. 5C: " . . . ad monasterium sive ecclesiam nuper fundatam iuxta villam Sancti Clodoaldis Ordinis Sancti Damiani et Sancte Helysabeth." A 1265 ratification of this document (AN L1020 no. 6) changed this nomenclature to "Ordinis Sororum Minorum Inclusarum."

65. AN L1020 nos. 8–11. The consistent addition of the word "inclusarum" before 1263 suggests to me that Isabelle of France may have settled on this formal title in consultation with Simon of Brie before he traveled to Rome in March 1262.

66. I draw here upon the remarks of Dalarun, *François d'Assise, un passage*, 59.

67. Clare's Rule of 1253 might seem to be the most likely candidate to embody this imagined "pristine state," since it declared itself to be based on the first oral form of life given by Francis to Clare and her house. But a simple desire to follow Clare's model cannot fully account for the dynamic at work here since, as Lezlie Knox has noted, the women would then have been demanding to be allowed either to adhere to Clare's vision of absolute poverty or to Isabelle's rule that rejected it. Knox, "Audacious Nuns," 59.

68. A conversation with Jacques Dalarun helped to clarify this point for me.

69. Urban IV's bull approving Longchamp's revised Rule of 1263 recognized as much by saying that he was granting the title *Sorores minores* so that the rule should be "distinguished with the advances of . . . humility, especially since this monastery . . . has taken to itself the title of the Humility of the Blessed Mary."

70. Though there is no evidence that Isabelle designed the abbey's seal herself, it seems likely that it would have been acceptable to her, especially since the imagery of the seal clearly evokes the abbey's name.

71. AN L1020 no. 26A. On women's use of seals see Brigitte Bedos-Rezak, "Medieval Women in French Sigillographic Sources," in Joel T. Rosenthal, ed., *Medieval Women and the Sources of Medieval History* (Athens: University of Georgia Press, 1990), 1–36; and on seals as a catalyst for and representation of medieval identity, eadem, "Medieval Identity: A Sign and a Concept," *American Historical Review* 105 (2000): 1489–1533.

72. The sermon is from Gilbert's *de sanctis* collection, quoted here from BNF ms. lat. 15942, f. 39ra, "Sermo de beata Elizabeth": "*Quesivit lanam et linum et operata est consilio manuum suarum*, proverbiorum ultimum. Verbum hoc allegorice potest exponi

de beata Elizabeth, que pro Christo paupertatem sustinuit et de labore manuali vixit." And in the conclusion to the sermon: "Et sic patet quomodo nobilis hec mulier *quesivit linum et operata est* in eo *consilio manuum suarum.*"

73. Nicole Bériou, "Les sermons sur sainte Claire dans l'espace française," in *Sainte Claire d'Assise et sa postérité*, 119–54; 137–38 for edition of sermon, 138 for quotation: "Ex caritate enim Christo desponsata est . . . Hec enim desponsacio iniciata fuit in eius virginitate, rata autem fuit in religionis paupertate, et consumpmata in humilitate."

74. For Bonaventure's sermons see Bougerol, *Saint Bonaventure, Sermons de tempore*; to Franciscan women stressing humility, 103–4 #54 and 338 #244. Bonaventure gave at least one sermon at Longchamp for which Isabelle presumably would have been present, but the outline of the text that survives reveals nothing that explicitly connects this sermon to her. See ibid., 274–75 #200. The rubric reads: "Sabbato quattuor temporum post primam dominicam Quadragesimae sermo fratris Bonaventurae Parisius in monasterio monialium Sanctae Clarae." Longchamp was the only "monastery of St. Clare" near Paris that could have been referred to in Bonaventure's lifetime. However, the possible date proposed by Bougerol, 3 March 1257, cannot be correct since Longchamp was not yet in existence. I would propose 19 March 1261 as the most likely date, with other possibilities including 20 February 1266, 12 March 1267, and 25 February 1268. Sermon #171 (pp. 238–39) may also have been preached at Longchamp, but the rubric does not allow certainty. Bonaventure is also known to have preached twenty-seven sermons to members of the French royal family in the period 1254–1270. Though none of the rubrics to these sermons explicitly mentions Isabelle of France's presence, it is likely that she would have heard a number of sermons that were preached to the king and his "whole household" (*coram rege Franciae et tota familia*) before Longchamp's foundation in 1260. But again, the extant *reportationes* of these sermons do not preserve any passages that obviously pertain to Isabelle.

75. Kenneth Baxter Wolf, *The Poverty of Riches: St. Francis of Assisi Reconsidered* (Oxford: Oxford University Press, 2003), 39–46 and passim. Wolf's argument will probably not be universally accepted, but this distinction is worth considering.

76. *Writings of AH*, 62 (par. 18).

77. On humility as a specifically royal saintly virtue see Corbet, *Les saints ottoniens*, 96–99, 174–80.

78. As Jacques Dalarun remarks regarding St. Francis's stress on submission, obedience, and humility, "[l]a 'minorité' n'est pas un des aspects parmi d'autres de la vocation franciscaine, elle en est la définition." *François d'Assise ou le pouvoir en question*, 13–14. David Burr has also noted that humility would be a better word than poverty to describe the original goal for which Francis was striving. See *The Spiritual Franciscans: From Protest to Persecution in the Century after Saint Francis* (University Park: Pennsylvania State University Press, 2001), 2. Of course, Clare stressed the virtue of humility as well, but she did not place it on quite the same level as poverty as an ideal.

79. Luigi Pellegrini has argued that poverty ceased to be the defining goal of most Italian women's communities in the second half of the thirteenth century, with even many communities that had originally been inspired by the ideal of poverty accepting communal possessions. See "Female Religious Experience and Society in Thirteenth-Century Italy."

80. Alberzoni, "*Sorores minores* and Ecclesiastical Authority"; eadem, "Le congregazioni monastiche"; eadem, "*Nequaquam a Christi sequela in perpetuum absolvi desidero*"; eadem, *La nascita di un'istituzione*. See also Knox, "Clare of Assisi: Foundress of an Order?"

81. In this connection, it is no coincidence that neither of Isabelle's rules mentions St. Clare in its vows. Alberzoni remarks on this absence in "*Sorores minores* and Ecclesiastical Authority," 135. See similar observations concerning Filippa Mareri and Margherita Colonna in Lezlie Knox, "Clare of Assisi: Foundress of an Order?" 11–12.

82. Alberzoni, "*Nequaquam a Christi sequela in perpetuum absolvi desidero*," 100; eadem, "San Damiano in 1228," 100.

83. The rule spread in its revised form of 1263, but it should also be noted that in later years it underwent modifications that are beyond the scope of the present investigation. See, for example, the fifteenth-century Middle English translation in Seton, *A Fifteenth-Century Courtesy Book*, 84, where the vows now mention "myne ladi seint Clare" and the "rule of myne lorde the apostole Boneface the eytith correctid and approuid."

84. Urban's bull is edited in *BF* vol. 2, 563–64: "Urbanus etc. Dilectis in Christo filiabus . . [*sic*] Abbatissae, et Conventui Sororum Minorum Inclusarum Monasterii Beatae Caterinae juxta Provinum Senonen. Dioecesis Salutem, et Apostol. Benedictionem. Carissimi in Christo filii . . [*sic*] Regis Navarrae illustris precibus inclinati Regulam et vitae formulam, quam fel. record. Alexander Papa praedecessor noster ad preces carissimi in Christo filii nostri Franciae Regis illustris Abbatissae, et Conventui Monasterii Humilitatis Beatae Mariae Parisien. Dioecesis perpetuis observandam temporis, et Regulam Sororum inclusarum nuncupandam concessit; quamque Nos postmodum ad ipsius Regis Franciae precum instantiam in aliquibus capitulis per dilectum filium nostrum S. tit. Sanctae Ceciliae Presbyterum Cardinalem corrigi facientes Sororum Minorum Inclusarum Regulam statuimus nuncupandam; vobis juxta correctionem, et nuncupationem hujusmodi perpetuo in vestro Monasterio concessimus observandam. Quia vero dilectus filius noster J., S. Nicolai in Carcere Tulliano Diaconus Cardinalis, Regulam seu formulam, Sororum Ordinis Sancti Damiani, cujus curam sibi commisimus, in aliquibus de mandato nostro correxit, et a personis ipsius Ordinis observari mandavit: Nos attendentes, quod eaedem vivendi Formulae in substantialibus parum differre noscuntur, vestris precibus annuentes devotioni vestrae assumendi, et servandi perpetuo illam et praedictis Formulis, quae magis secundum Deum concordaverit votis vestris, plenem, et liberam auctoritate Apostolica

concedimus facultatem. Datum apud Urbem veterem x kal. Julii, pontificatus Nostri anno tertio." See also Knox, "Audacious Nuns," 59 n. 70; Seton, *A Fifteenth-Century Courtesy Book*, 71; Molinier, *Les obituaires de la province de Sens*, vol. 1, part 2; *GC* vol. 12, col. 255; Félix Bourquelot, *Histoire de Provins* (Provins and Paris, 1839–40; reprint, Marseille: Lafitte Reprints, 1976), 183–86, 218; and *Layettes*, vol. 3, #4387.

85. On Saint-Marcel see Théobald (de Courtomer), "Les cordelières de Saint-Marcel-lez-Paris," *Études franciscaines* 20 (1908): 561–621 (p. 564 for date of 1268 and Louis's involvement); Jean-Pierre Willesme, "Les cordelières de la rue de Lourcine, des origines à l'implantation du nouvel Hôpital Broca," *Paris et Ile-de-France: Mémoires* 43 (1992): 207–48; *GC* vol. 7, cols. 950–952; Cocheris, *Histoire de la ville et de tout le diocèse de Paris par l'abbé Lebeuf*, vol. 2, 740–42; and Marcel Lecoq, *Les cordelières de Lourcine au faubourg Saint-Marcel-lez-Paris* (Paris: Éditions Municipales, 1969).

86. On sisters from Longchamp coming to Saint-Marcel see Théobald, "Les cordelières de Saint-Marcel-lez-Paris," 565. The evidence for this claim, however, comes only from early modern narratives compiled by the nuns.

87. See Ghislain Brunel, "Un italien en France au XIIIe siècle: Galien de Pise, chanoine de Saint-Omer et fondateur du couvent des Cordelières de Lourcine à Paris, d'après son testament de 1287," in *Histoire d'archives: Recueil d'articles offert à Lucie Favier par ses collègues et amis* (Paris: Société des amis des Archives de France, 1997), 249–76, where Galien's will is edited and the significant documentation for Saint-Marcel in AN L1050 is inventoried. L1050 no. 4 is dated July 1284 and shows Galien negotiating details of his bequest by that date.

88. AN L1050 no. 12 is a grant from Marguerite of Provence to Saint-Marcel, dated February 1295, of the residence she has had constructed for herself, with the stipulation that the sisters not sell it and that its use be reserved for her daughter Blanche during her lifetime. No. 13 is a ratification of this act by Philip IV dated September 1296. Marguerite was acting as a patron of the abbey as early as 1271. See Théobald, "Les cordelières de Saint Marcel-lez-Paris," 564; on Blanche see ibid., 573–74.

89. A letter from Honorius IV to Cardinal Orsini of 9 January 1287, in *BF* vol. 3, p. 592, describes the "Sorores Minores Ordinis Sanctae Clarae" of Saint-Marcel as already "viventes sub observantia Regulae, quae servatur in Monasterio Humilitatis Beatae Mariae prope Sanctum Clodoaldum Parisien. dioecesis." See also *BF* vol. 4, p. 5

90. Original is AN L1050 no. 8. The bull, addressd "filiabus Abbatisse et conventui Sororum Minorum Inclusarum Monasterii Sancte Clare iuxta Parisius," grants them the rule given to ". . [*sic*] Abbatisse et Conventui Sororum Monasterii Humilitatis Beate Marie prope Sanctum Clodoaldum," at the request "carissimi in Christo filii nostri Philippi Regis et carissimarum in Christo filiarum nostrarum Margarete, Marie ac Johanne Reginarum Francie illustruum."

91. *BF* vol. 3, 528.

92. *GC* vol. 8, cols. 1404–1407, and (in the same volume) "Instrumenta" cols. 434–436, 437–439, 440–442. The latter columns print Nicholas IV's bull of 1288, which makes Julianne of Troyes's identity certain. See also *BF* vol. 4, 11–15, 33–36.

93. See Jacques Coquelle, *Les cordelières en Picardie* (Amiens: Dalmanio, 1994), 56–60; *GC* vol. 9, cols. 504–507, vol. 10, "Instrumenta," cols. 139–141; Jackie Lusse, "Les religieuses en Champagne jusqu'au XIIIe siècle," in Michel Parisse, ed., *Les religieuses en France au XIIIe siècle* (Nancy: Presses Universitaires de Nancy, 1985), 11–26, at 24; and Edmund Wauer, *Entstehung und Ausbreitung des Klarissenordens* (Leipzig: J. C. Hinrichs'sche, 1906), 90.

94. Henry the Fat's own ties to Franciscan women's houses are shown by the fact that he requested that his heart be buried at Provins. Bourdillon, *The Order of Minoresses in England*, 17.

95. The house's existence before 1335 is shadowy, but there is no doubt as to Philip IV's role in founding the abbey ca. 1309. See *GC* vol. 9, cols. 852–856, and vol. 10, "Instrumenta," cols. 270–73; Mya Pereira et al., "Un espace monastique royal: L'abbaye du Moncel (Pontpoint, Oise)," *Archéologie médiévale* 19 (1989): 131–72; Coquelle, *Les cordelières en Picardie*, 61–64; and L. Meister, "Quelques chartes inédites relatives à l'acquisition du Moncel par Philippe le Bel (1309–1310)," *Mémoire de la Société academique de l'Oise* 17 (1900): 593–611. Elizabeth Hallam, "Philip the Fair and the Cult of Saint Louis," in Stuart Mews, ed., *Religion and National Identity* (Oxford: Basil Blackwell, 1982), 201–14, speculates that Moncel may have been planned as early as 1298.

96. Wadding, *Annales minorum*, vol. 7, 557–58. Other documents concerning Moncel are found in ibid., 553–62. Longchamp's first necrology (ed. Molinier, *Les obituaires de la province de Sens*, 668) mentions that Mary of Lyons "fu au Moncel V ans pour funder." Since she became a nun at Longchamp around 1307 and was abbess from 1339 to her death in 1345, these five years could have begun anytime between 1309 (when Moncel was founded) and 1334 (leaving five years before her term as abbess of Longchamp). See Field, "The Abbesses of Longchamp up to the Black Death."

97. Compare, however, Germain Delorme, "Supplément au Bullaire franciscain: À-propos du monastère de Sainte-Claire de Toulouse," *La France franciscaine* 3 (1914): 11–44, 129–66; and Agathange de Paris, "L'origine et la fondation des monastères de Clarisses en Aquitaine au XIIIe siècle," 5–21. Neither of these authors says that Toulouse ever followed Isabelle's rule. Bulls of John XXII dated 1332, however (edited by Delorme, pp. 146–52), refer to the "conventus sororum Minorissarum" of Toulouse. This seems to be the basis for Toulouse's inclusion in Oliger's list of houses adhering to Longchamp's rule, "De origine regularum Ordinis S. Clarae," 438, following Wauer, *Entstehung und Ausbreitung des Klarissenordens*, 63, 84.

98. Mlynarczyk, *Ein Franziskanerinnenkloster*, 38 n. 31; Paris, Bibliothèque franciscaine provinciale des Capucins, ms. 1530 (Trouillard, *Études sur la discipline*), p. 39; Wauer, *Entstehung und Ausbreitung des Klarissenordens*, 83 n. 1.

99. On England see Bourdillon, *The Order of Minoresses in England*; Seton, *A Fifteenth-Century Courtesy Book*, 63–124; Warren, *Spiritual Economies*, 58–62 and passim; Michael Hicks, "The English Minoresses and Their Early Benefactors," in Judith Loades, ed., *Monastic Studies: The Continuity of Tradition* (Bangor, Wales: Headstart History, 1990), 158–70; and David Parker, "Three Models of Self-Government: Medieval English Translations of Latin Rules for Nuns," *Magistra* 7 (2001): 100–125.

100. Jens Röhrkasten has shown that the London community of Franciscan women left traces in the records as early as 1281, indicating that perhaps Blanche of Navarre should be seen as refounding, rather than founding, the house in 1293. See "The Origin and Early Development of the London Mendicant Houses," in T. R. Slater and Gervase Rosser, eds., *The Church in the Medieval Town* (Aldershot: Ashgate, 1998), 76–99, at 80, and *The Mendicant Houses of Medieval London, 1221–1539* (Münster: Lit, 2004), 64–66.

101. Bourdillon, *The Order of Minoresses in England*, 17–18. In support of this assertion see Field, "The Abbesses of Longchamp up to the Black Death."

102. See Hilary Jenkinson, "Mary de Sancto Paulo, Foundress of Pembroke College, Cambridge," *Archaeologia* 66 (1914–15): 401–46.

103. *BF* vol. 3, 544–45, 549–50; Oliger, "De origine regularum Ordinis S. Clarae," 438–39; on Margherita and her foundation see further Robert Brentano, *Rome before Avignon: A Social History of Thirteenth-Century Rome* (New York: Basic Books, 1974), 173–79, 229–47; G. Furitano, "Una santa donna del Duecento: Margherita Colonna," in Renato Lefevre, ed., *Fatti et figure del Lazio medievale* (Rome: Gruppo Culturale di Rome e del Lazio, 1979), 387–96; Giulia Barone, "Margherita Colonna e le Clarisse di S. Silvestro in Capite," in Angiola Maria Romanini, ed., *Roma anno 1300: Atti della IV settimana di studi di storia dell'arte medievale dell'Università di Roma "La Sapienza" (19–24 maggio 1980)* (Rome: L'Erma di Bretschneider, 1983), 799–805; Barone, "Le due vite di Margherita Colonna," in Marilena Modica Vasta, ed., *Esperienza religiosa e scritture femminili tra medioevo ed età moderna* (Palermo: Bonanno, 1992), 25–32; and L. Oliger, *B. Margherita Colonna: Le due vite scritte dal fratello Giovanni Colonna senatore di Roma e da Stefania monaca di S. Silvestro in Capite* (Rome: Facultas Theologica Pontificii, 1935).

104. *Escritos*, 294–95. I am uncertain upon what evidence this claim is based. Blasucci, "Clarisse isabelliane o minoresse," in *Dizionario degli istituti di perfezioni*, vol. 2 (1975), col. 1146, also lists S. Lorenzo in Panisperna as following Isabelle's rule.

105. Peter Linehan, *The Ladies of Zamora* (Manchester: Manchester University Press, 1997), 137–40. Charles de Miremon brought this book to my attention.

106. See Lezlie S. Knox, "*The True Daughters of Francis and Clare*: The Formation of the Order of Saint Clare in Late Medieval Italy" (Ph.D. diss., University of Notre Dame, 1999), 54–55 n. 100. Indeed, after St. Clare's death the nuns of

San Damiano moved to a richly appointed new abbey inside the city walls of Assisi and adopted Urban IV's Rule of 1263. A list drawn up by the General Chapter of the Franciscan Order in 1316 numbered 372 female monasteries (forty-seven in France), so those following either Isabelle's or Clare's rules were in a distinct minority. Rusconi, "The Spread of Women's Franciscanism in the Thirteenth Century," 39, 57.

CHAPTER FIVE.   *Between Court and Cloister: Life and Death at Longchamp*

1. *Writings of AH*, 70–72 (mir. 3).

2. Perhaps the most notable recent example is in an otherwise outstanding article by Nicole Bériou that referred to Isabelle as the first abbess of Longchamp. "Sermons sur sainte Claire dans l'espace française," 120. Professor Bériou herself graciously pointed out this error to me. Among other influential works, Isabelle is also referred to as abbess of Longchamp in Glorieux, *Répertoire*, vol. 2, 56; and Bougerol, *Introduction to the Works of Bonaventure*, 161.

3. See Field, "The Abbesses of Longchamp up to the Black Death."

4. Emphasis added. *Writings of AH*, 54 (par. 6): "... ele me dit de sa bouche qu'ele avoit ausi boen quer et ausi devot a Notre Segneur quant ele avoit ces riches aournements en son chief et en son quors comme ele avoit quant ele ot abit plus religieus." It would be an error to translate "quant ele ot abit plus religieus," with Pernoud, as "when she wore the nun's habit." Pernoud, *Blanche of Castile*, 256. In the original French version of her book, Pernoud made a silent and misleading emendation (from the seventeenth-century edition of Agnes's *Vie* published by Du Cange) to "quand elle eut habits *de* religieuse." My emphasis. Pernoud, *La reine Blanche* (Paris: Éditions Albin Michel, 1972), 307.

5. Emphasis added. *Writings of AH*, 60 (par. 15): "et mout estoit obediens a lui pour nient fut une fame de religion."

6. *Writings of AH*, 48 (par. 4).

7. Printed edition H. Géraud, ed., *Chronique latine de Guillaume de Nangis de 1113 à 1300 avec les continuations de cette chronique*, vol. 1 (Paris: Jules Renouard, 1843), 219. On manuscripts of the two redactions see Gabrielle M. Spiegel, *The Chronicle Tradition of Saint-Denis: A Survey* (Brookline, MA, and Leyden: Classical Folia Editions, 1978), 98–108. My transcription of the first redaction is from BNF ms. fr. 5703, f. 154r. My reading of the second redaction is based on BNF mss. lat. 4917, f. 229v; 4918, f. 382v; 4919, f. 395r; and 4920, f. 220r. The variants in these four manuscripts are not significant.

8. *RHGF*, vol. 23, 171: "Domum etiam Sororum Minorum juxta Sanctum Clodoaldum prope Parisius, tam in forma quam in materia praecellentem, aedificavit egregie cum multimodis sumptibus expensarum, cum sufficencia reddituum terrenorum et

multarum numero personarum, ubi memoriae venerabilis soror ipsius unica praedilecta, nomine Elizabeth, ob cujus reverenciam et amorem aedificaverat illud claustrum, ut contemplationi vacaret liberius elegerat ad mandendum. Ibi tandem in fine sororis habitum induit, et sicut sancte vixerat, vitam in Christo sanctissime terminavit."

9. *RHGF*, vol. 21, 81: " . . . la damoiselle [Isabelle] fu cordelière; de quoi li rois Looys, son frère, fonda une abeye à Longchamp, desouz Saint Clout, sous la rivière de Sainne."

10. *Writings of AH*, 32 n. 59.

11. See Beaune, *The Birth of an Ideology*, 102. For an investigation into a similar bit of early-modern Franciscan fabrication see Jacques Dalarun, *Claire de Rimini: Entre sainteté et hérésie* (Paris: Peyot, 1999), 9–30.

12. For instance, in 1515, Mariano of Florence claimed that Isabelle "entered the monastery of Longchamp, in which she led a celibate and saintly life like that of her brother." See his *Libro delle degnità et excellentie del Ordine della seraphica madre delle povere donne Sancta Chiara da Asisi*, ed. Giovanni Boccali (Florence: Edizioni Studi Francescani, 1986), 167, #271. I thank Lezlie Knox for the reference. Leo X's bull of 1521 "beatifying" Isabelle (discussed in chapter 6) assumed that Isabelle had been a nun as well. The seventeenth-century Franciscan, Luke Wadding, held the same opinion. See Wadding, *Annales minorum*, vol. 3, 316 and 399. The Jesuit J. Stilting's more thorough eighteenth-century exposé on Isabelle in the *Acta sanctorum* considered the question to be open. See *AS*, August, vol. 6, 789–90. More recently, John Moorman's standard work stated that "in 1252 [Isabelle] joined the Order of Damianites." *A History of the Franciscan Order from Its Origins to the Year 1517* (Oxford: Clarendon Press, 1968), 210. Moorman cites A. de Serent, who relies on "tradition," and the Franciscan breviary, in "L'ordre de sainte Claire en France pendant sept siècles," 134.

13. *Writings of AH*, 68 (par. 26).

14. *Writings of AH*, 68 (par. 27).

15. *Writings of AH*, 68 (par. 28).

16. On the dates of the first abbesses of Longchamp see Field, "The Abbesses of Longchamp up to the Black Death."

17. *Writings of AH*, 70 (mir. 2).

18. *Writings of AH*, 70–72 (mirs. 1–3).

19. AN L1026 no. 2, "Inventaire Seur Agnes d'Harcourt abbesse la second fois": "en tressor avoit ces chosces . . . ii. saffirs assis en or qui furent madame." AN L1026 no. 5, an inventory of 1289, has the same entry. AN K37 no. 2, inventory of 1305 (ed. Cocheris, *Histoire de la ville et de tout le diocèse de Paris par l'abbé Lebeuf*, 262–64), and AN L1027 no. 5, inventory of 1325, record "ii pierres assises en or, qui furent ma dame." By 1339 the nuns seem to have decided that more of their jewels had once belonged to Isabelle. The inventory of that year, AN L1027 no. 9, reads: "Ce sunt les pierres precieuses qui furent madame Ysabel la suer monseigneur S. Looys roy de France qui

funderent l'eglise. Premieres ii safiers assis en or et une aultre pierre en argent et i annes d'or." Descriptions of twelve more stones follow. These stones continued to be inventoried in 1448 (AN L1028 no. 5), 1467 (AN L1028 no. 7), and 1483 (AN L1028 no. 9). See Mylnarczyk, *Ein Franziskanerinnenkloster*, 294, 310–11, 329.

20. AN K37 no. 2 (ed. Cocheris, *Histoire de la ville et de tout le diocèse de Paris par l'abbé Lebeuf*, 262–64), "En l'office du Tresor avoit . . . 1 [hanap] a pie d'argent qui fu madame qui nous funda." AN L1027, no. 5 reads virtually identically.

21. AN L1027 no. 5: "C'est les choses qui estoient en la segreteinere . . . Item .i. blanc escrin diuyze qui furent madame qui nous funda . . . Une chauce et .i. orillier de duvet qui furent ma dicte dame . . . Item une vinronique qui fu madame et une pomme d'ambre et .i. agnus dei." Elsewhere in this manuscript the word here rendered as "diuyze" generally appears as "diuuyze" and should probably be read as "d'ivuise" or "d'ivoire" in more modern orthography. According to legend, Veronica, a woman of Jerusalem, wiped the sweat from the Savior's face with her veil on his way to Calvary, and the image remained fixed on the cloth.

22. AN K37 no. 2 (ed. Cocheris, *Histoire de la ville et de tout le diocèse de Paris par l'abbé Lebeuf*, 262–64), "Item, .iii. estoles et .iii. fanons de l'oevre Madame." AN L1027 no.5: "Item des vestemens par les prestres . . . Item uns vestemens blans de soie de tans madame qui nous funda . . . Item .iii. estoles, .iiii. fanons de l'ouvre madame."

23. *Writings of AH*, 54 (par. 5).

24. Some of Isabelle's possessions and relics are said to be extant. For instance, a woolen tunic and a chemise were exhibited in 1960, along with a tube containing some of her hair. See *Saint Louis: Exposition organisée par la direction générale des Archives de France* (Paris, 1960), 71–72, #128–130. On the dispersal and history of Longchamp's relics see Garreau, *Bienheureuse Isabelle de France, soeur de saint Louis*, 112–15. In 1699, Pierre Perrier made a list of the abbey's relics, which included "relics of St. Isabelle of France," "vestments of the same saint," "hairs of this saint, ten of her teeth, and one of her bones," "bones of St. Louis and of St. Isabelle," "an apple or egg covered with circles of gold and garnished with turquoise and rubies, which was one of the *joyaux* of the saint," and "two rings of the same saint." My paraphrases and translations are from AN L1029 no. 37 (unnumbered inventory at end of manuscript). In the era after Isabelle's beatification the number of her "relics" evidently mushroomed.

25. See Jeffrey F. Hamburger, "Vision and the Veronica," in *The Visual and the Visionary: Art and Female Spirituality in Late Medieval Germany* (New York: Zone Books, 1998), 317–82. I thank Anne Clark for the reference and for sharing her knowledge of Veronicas.

26. AN L260 no. 92: "Clemens episcopus servus servorum Dei, dilectis in Christo filiabus. .[sic] Abbatisse et conventui monasterii humilitatis beate Marie parisiensis diocesis, salutem et apostolicam benedictionem. Devotionis vestre

promeretur affectus, ut quod a nobis suppliciter petitis ad exauditionis gratiam quantum cum Deo possumus favorabiliter admittamus. Vestris itaque supplicationibus inclinati, ut quosvis heredes carissimi in Christo filii nostri. .[*sic*] Regis Francorum Illustris vel successorum eius qui pro tempore fuerint, causa devotionis apud monasterium vestrum ecclesiasticam elegerint sepulturam, cum abierint huiusmodi sepulture tradere libere valeatis, vobis auctoritate presentium indulgemus. Nulli ergo omnino hominum liceat paginam nostre concessionis infringere vel ei ausu temerario contraire. Siquis autem hoc attemptare presumpserit indignationem omnipotentis Dei et beatorum Petri et Pauli apostolorum eius se noverit incursurum. Datum Viterbii vi Idus Novembris, pontificatus nostri anno secundo." Described in Barbiche, *Les actes pontificaux*, #1411.

27. As a former adviser to Louis IX (as Guy Foucois) and Alphonse of Poitiers, Clement may have been sympathetic to requests from the Capetian court and could have known Isabelle of France personally. See Levillain, ed., *The Papacy: An Encyclopedia*, 332–33.

28. AN L261 no. 100. The manuscript is described in Barbiche, *Les actes pontificaux*, #1435, and edited in Field, "New Evidence," 131.

29. AN LL1600 f. 1r: "[C]y commence ung papier ou registre que l'en peult appeler et nommer Repertoire ou Inventoire des lettres tiltres et enseignemens que les dames Religieuses abbesse et couvent de Longchamp pres Saint Cloud de l'ordre Ste Clere ont en leur tresor. . . . fait et escript en l'an mil. IIII. lxxii."

30. AN LL1600 f. 10r: "Une bulle scellee en plonb sur laz de soye jaune et vermeille donnee de pape Clement quart on tiers an de son pontificat. Par laquelle appert que iceluy pape, a la requeste de madame Ysabel de France, donna et octroya a tous ceulx et celles vrays confes et repentans qui devotement visiteroient l'eglise et monastere de l'Umilite Notre Dame de Longchamp le jour qu'elle seroit dedye et par huyt jours apres ensuyvans pour chacun jour troys ans et troys Xlnes de pardon. Et a ceulx et a celles qui par chacun an d'illec apres ensuyant le jour de la dedycace visiteroient ladite eglise, il donna ung an et XL jours de pardon. Laquelle bulle est on tresor de ladite eglise avecque les autres bulles papaulx, signee au dos X." This bull was also recorded in the eighteenth-century inventory found in AN L1029, unnumbered document before no. 1. It refers to the bull (p. 14) as issued "a la suplication de Madame Isabel de France." Several sources attest that the anniversary of the church's dedication was celebrated on November 17. BNF ms. lat 9376, folios 21–33 of which form a calendar probably used at Longchamp in the thirteenth century, gives that date for the feast for the "dedicatio ecclesie sororum minorum in longo campo." See François Avril and Patricia Danz Stirnemann, *Manuscrits enluminés d'origine insulaire VIIe–XXe siècle*, 26–27 (Paris: Bibliothéque nationale, 1987), no. 38. Longchamp's fifteenth-century calendar in BNF ms. fr. 11662, f. 12r, corroborates this date, as does Bibliothèque Mazarine ms. 443 (fifteenth-century), the

latter according to Molinier, *Catalogue des manuscrits de la Bibliothèque Mazarine*, vol. 1, 172–73.

31. For example Delorme, "En marge du Bullaire franciscain," records similar privileges granted to the Franciscans of Arles and Aquitaine (pp. 15, 18) and the Clares of La Roquette (p. 29). Nikolaus Paulus, *Geschichte des Ablasses im Mittelalter*, vol. 2 (Paderborn: Schöningh, 1923), 1–24, confirms that indulgences of three years and three forty-day periods for church dedications in the 1260s were not uncommon with royal patrons or in special circumstances. For instance, the new church of St. Clare at Assisi was granted such a privilege by Clement IV in 1265 (p. 12).

32. *BF* vol. 3, 155: "Carissimae in Christo Filiae Isabellae Francorum Regis germanae Salutem et Apostol. Benedictionem. Scias, filia, Apostolorum capita Romae indubitanter haberi, quae felicis recordationis Gregorius Papa nonus praedeces- sor noster, de sanctis sanctorum suis manibus extrahens, Romano populo patenter exhibuit, et in locum suum restituit cum debita reverentia, praesentibus et sci- entibus universis. Quod si forsitan caput B. Pauli Apostoli apud te esse putas, depone conscientiam, ne fallaris, nec proponas scandalum matri tuae Romanae ecclesiae, quae deceptionem hujusmodi non posset aequanimiter tolerare. Si vero Graeci aliquo tem- pore se illud habere dixerunt, ne mireris: nam odio Latinos habentes, facile tibi formaverunt mendacium, qui de fide mentiri Catholica, quod est majus, minime dubitarent. Bene igitur facies, si, quod habes, dilecto filio nostro Simoni S. Caeciliae presbytero Cardinali, apostolicae Sedis legato, nomine nostro reddideris, nobis per eun- dem mittendum: ne, si ad alias manus devenerit, possit inde cum erroris periculo scandalum suscitari. Dat. Viterbii xiv kal. Mai pontificatus nostri anno IV."

33. Paul Riant included it in his list of such relics on the strength of Clement's bull. See Paul Le Comte Riant, *Des dépouilles religieuses enlevées à Constantinople au XIIIe siècle, et des documents historiques nés de leur transport en Occident*, Mémoires de la Société nationale des antiquaires de France, 4th series, vol. 4 (Paris: Dumoulin, 1875), 202. I thank Alfred J. Andrea for the reference.

34. One might note also Isabelle's continued contact with Simon of Brie, Cardinal of S. Cecilia, a collaborator on Longchamp's Rule of 1263 and the future Pope Martin IV.

35. *Writings of AH*, 48 (par. 5).

36. This attraction may also have been among the factors that led to Longchamp's success with new recruits, since on 20 April 1268 Clement's bull *Licet cultum divini* lim- ited Longchamp to sixty inhabitants, thus revealing a thriving abbey that was in danger of overcrowding. AN L262 no. 112 and no. 112 bis. Described in Barbiche, *Les actes pontificaux*, vol. 2, 161, #1447. The text can be found in Field, "The Princess, the Abbess, and the Friars," Appendix C.

37. The evidence for Isabelle's date of death has generally been said to rest on Roulliard, who cites Longchamp's now-lost martyrology as giving it as "sur la mi-

nuicte du 23. Feburier, selon qu'il est cotté au Martyrologe de Longchamp, la veille de S. Mathias 1269." This would be the early morning hours of 23 February 1270 in modern reckoning. *La saincte mère*, 401. Several other unremarked sources confirm Roulliard's evidence. In 1244 the Cistercians had promised to pray for Isabelle on her death. This charge was carried out when the order's General Chapter met in September 1270, and the wording of the official resolution leaves no doubt as to the date of her demise: "Item, pro domina Isabella sorore illustris regis Franciae iam defuncta, ab universis personis Ordinis plenarium servitium persolvatur, et fiat de cetero eius anniversarium solemniter in conventu per universum Ordinem VII° kalendas martii, sicut eidem dominae olim promissum fuit per litteras Capituli generalis." Canivez, *Statuta capitulorum generalium Ordinis Cisterciensis*, vol. 3, 92. The calendar of obituaries compiled in the fifteenth century at Longchamp and now in BNF ms. fr. 11662, f. 22v (ed. Molinier, *Les obituaires de la province de Sens*, vol. 1 part 2, 660) reads: "Le xxii iour du dit mois [February] on doibt chanter vespres de mors et apres commoncer le Invitatoire, *Regem cui omnia vivunt*, et le *Venite*, et vegiles tres reveranment chantees pour ma dame Ysabel de France, laquelle fonda ceste eglise." Since it is clear from the description in the *Life* that Isabelle died at night, the question of whether she died before midnight on February 22 or in the early morning of 23 February is trivial. The *obituaires* of the abbeys of Barbeaux (thirteenth- or fourteenth-century) and Vauluisant also recorded Isabelle's death as 23 February. See Molinier, *Les obituaires de la province de Sens*, vol. 1 part 1, 33 note 3, and 53. Several other sources give differing dates. The necrology of Port-Royal-des-Champs, compiled c. 1450, gives 24 February, while the martyrology of the Abbaye-de-Val (c. 1275) has 17 February. See ibid., vol. 1 part 2, 637, and part 1, 627.

38. *Writings of AH*, 72 (mir. 4).

39. *Writings of AH*, 72 (mirs. 5–7).

40. Elizabeth A. R. Brown, "Death and the Human Body in the Later Middle Ages: The Legislation of Boniface VIII on the Division of the Corpse," in *The Monarchy of Capetian France and Royal Ceremonial* (Aldershot: Variorum, 1991), VI, 221–70, at 228–35 (articles in this series are reprinted with their original pagination and designated by Roman numeral). Louis VIII was disemboweled and his intestines buried where he died in Clermont in Auvergne, before the rest of his corpse was brought back to Saint-Denis. Blanche of Castile directed that her heart be buried at the abbey of Lys while the rest of her remains were to go to Maubuisson. After his death in 1270 near Carthage, Louis IX's heart was taken by Charles of Anjou to Monreale, while the rest of his body was returned to Saint-Denis. See "Philippe le Bel and the Remains of Saint Louis," in ibid., III, 175–82. On their return from this crusade Louis's daughter Isabelle, her husband Thibaud of Champagne, and Philip III's wife Isabelle all died and had their bodies divided in various ways. When Alphonse of Poitiers died in 1271 near Siena, his entrails were buried there while his body was sent

back to Saint-Denis. Charles of Anjou's body was buried in Naples in 1285, but his heart went to the Dominicans in Paris. Louis's son Pierre of Alençon wished on his death in 1283 that his heart should go to the Dominicans and his body to the Franciscans in Paris. On Philip III see "Death and the Human Body in the Later Middle Ages," in ibid., VI, 235–46. Philip IV destined his body for Saint-Denis but his heart for the Dominican nunnery at Poissy. See "Persona et Gesta: The Image and Deeds of the Thirteenth-Century Capetians: The Case of Philip the Fair," in ibid., V, 219–46, at 225, and Alexandre Bande, "Philippe le Bel, le coeur, et le sentiment dynastique," *Micrologus* 11 (2003): 267–78. On changes in royal burial practices in general see Brown, "Burying and Unburying the Kings of France," in *The Monarchy of Capetian France and Royal Ceremonial*, IX, 241–66.

41. On earlier Capetian women's burial and memorial choices see Kathleen D. Nolan, "The Tomb of Adelaide of Maurienne and the Visual Imagery of Capetian Queenship," in Nolan, ed., *Capetian Women*, 45–76.

42. On Louis's reactions to the death of his family members see William Chester Jordan, "The Case of Saint Louis," *Viator* 19 (1988): 209–17, at 210–12.

43. *Writings of AH*, 48 (par. 4).

44. *Writings of AH*, 48 (par. 4). Agnes relates this request directly after her report of Louis's presence at his sister's burial and seems to connect the two events.

45. 72, 74–75 (mirs. 4, 9). Miracle nine refers to "Icis freres de cui nous avons dessus parlé," which seems to mean Denis of Étampes.

46. If Isabelle had originally been buried immediately on Sunday 23 February 1270, which seems overly hasty, nine days later would place her translation on Tuesday 4 March. More likely the event took place slightly later, perhaps only a week before Louis left Paris for his ill-fated final crusade. The quotations in this paragraph are from *Writings of AH*, 72–74 (par. 8).

47. Vauchez, *Sainthood in the Later Middle Ages*, 19–20.

48. Vauchez, *Sainthood in the Later Middle Ages*, 26–32.

49. Vauchez, *Sainthood in the Later Middle Ages*, 94 (though here referring to the fourteenth and fifteenth centuries).

50. Francis of Assisi, for example, died in 1226, was canonized in 1228, and was translated in 1230. Clare of Assisi died in 1253, was canonized in 1255, and translated in 1260. These cases differ from Isabelle's in that Francis and Clare were speedily canonized, and it was thought necessary to build impressive new tombs for their reburials.

51. *Writings of AH*, 72–74 (mir. 8).

52. The "Lady of Audenarde" may refer to Alix of Rosoit, a lady-in-waiting to Blanche of Castile, who married Arnould IV of Audenarde (d. 1242) and founded the Hôpital Notre-Dame-à-la-Rose at Lessines. Some sources, however, give her date of death as 1265, in which case Agnes's reference might be to Alix and Arnould's daughter Marie. Marguerite (d. 1280) "of Constantinople" was the daughter of Baldwin IX of

Flanders and Marie of Champagne. Brought up at the court of Philip Augustus, after her early marriage to Burchard of Avesnes was annulled she married William of Dampierre in 1223 and was Countess of Flanders from 1244 to 1278, when she abdicated in favor of their son Guy. See David Nichols, *Medieval Flanders* (London and New York: Longman, 1992), 156–57, 440–41; and Karen S. Nichols, "Countesses as Rulers in Flanders," in Evergates, ed., *Aristocratic Women in Medieval France*, 111–37. Marie of Flanders was a daughter of Marguerite of Flanders and William of Dampierre. She became a Cistercian nun at Flines by 1252 (though apparently not a very firmly cloistered one) and died around 1302. See Longpré, *Tractatus de pace, auctore Fr. Gilberto de Tornaco*, xxxvii. The "daughter of the Count of Flanders who was the Duchess of Brabant" is probably another Marguerite, daughter of Guy of Dampierre and his first wife, Matilda of Béthune. She married Jean I of Brabant in 1273 and died in 1285. William of Quitry, Giles of Sally, Pierre of Meureville, and Thomas of Plexi are otherwise obscure figures.

53. Isabelle's late fifteenth-century epitaph records that the tomb was already in this position at that time. Paris, BNF ms. fr. 6124: "Et pour ce que les pelerins qui venoient requirir ceste saincte dame et ly faire leurs offrandes ne povoient veoir la place de sa sepulture, pour son corps qui gisoit ou meillieu de ceste eglise dedens la cloture des religieuses, pour quoy dudit lieu fut le corps leve, translate et mis au lieu et en la maniere que on peut veoir; moytie dedens la cloture des religieuses et moitie dehors." Since there is no evidence that Isabelle's body was moved between 1270 and 1461, this passage probably refers to the initial translation of 1270. If the epitaph was written after 1461, however, it is possible that when Isabelle's tomb was opened in that year another translation took place, but there is no hard evidence for this. See the diagram and description of Isabelle's tomb in *AS*, August, vol. 6, 791, provided by the Jesuit Souciet when he visited Longchamp in the mideighteenth century. He describes a *gisant* (recumbent) with Isabelle wearing a Franciscan habit. Roulliard, *La saincte mère*, 407, records Latin and French inscriptions at her tomb, translated in *AS*. Images of Isabelle and Louis appeared as part of her monument as well, but it is not clear from what century these inscriptions and images date, and it is likely that most of them were later additions. Garreau also reprints a drawing of a funerary statue, which shows Isabelle in a nun's habit with two sisters at her feet and which he believed to be from approximately 1521. *Bienheureuse Isabelle de France, soeur de saint Louis*, following p. 65 for representation and 94–95 for date.

54. *Writings of AH*, 74–78 (mirs. 10–13).

55. On early declarations of Louis's sanctity see Le Goff, *Saint Louis*, 301–2.

CHAPTER SIX.   Notre Sainte Mère: *Making a Capetian Saint*

1. BNF lat. 16481, f. 7r: "Habui talem filiam spiritualem que non respiceret faciem suam in speculo pro centum libris, vel pro magno aliquo." On this manuscript, the context of this sermon, and Raoul of Châteauroux's *reportationes* see Bériou, *L'avènement des maîtres de la parole*. On the location of sermons preached "in campellis," see ibid., 221, and map, 745. I thank Professor Bériou for discussing this passage with me.

2. See Baldwin, *The Government of Philip Augustus*, 390–92; and Jacques Le Goff, "Le dossier de sainteté de Philippe Augustus," *L'Histoire* 100 (1987): 22–29.

3. Blanche of Castile, for example, was certainly regarded as a pious woman, but not as a saint. See Klaniczay, *Holy Rulers and Blessed Princesses*, 235–36. To the best of my knowledge, Klaniczay is mistaken when he says that "Blanche was eventually beatified." Isabelle of France's grandmother, Isabelle of Hainault (first wife of Philip Augustus), as well as Philip Augustus's second wife, Ingeborg of Denmark, were also known for their piety but were not treated as saints before or after their deaths. See Aline G. Hornaday, "A Capetian Queen as Street Demonstrator: Isabelle of Hainault," and Kathleen S. Schowalter, "The Ingeborg Psalter: Queenship, Legitimacy, and the Appropriation of Byzantine Art in the West," in Nolan, ed., *Capetian Women*, 77–97 and 99–135. On Ingeborg see also George Conklin, "Ingeborg of Denmark, Queen of France, 1193–1223," in Duggan, ed., *Queens and Queenship in Medieval Europe*, 39–52. Moreover, each of these women, as members of the royal family only by marriage, could contribute to, but not truly embody, the concept of a Capetian *beata stirps*.

4. This miracle can be dated more precisely, since Julienne is described as having been well for more than ten years after her cure. The *Life of Isabelle* was composed about 1283, so the cure must have taken place between 1270 and 1273.

5. Compare a similar miracle told of an earlier literate, royal, and saintly woman, Margaret of Scotland (ca. 1046–1093), cited by Richard Gameson, "The Gospels of Margaret of Scotland and the Literacy of an Eleventh-Century Queen," in *Women and the Book: Assessing the Visual Evidence*, ed. Lesley Smith and Jane H. M. Taylor (London: The British Library, 1996), 149, 160. See 160–61 for other examples of early-medieval miracles involving manuscripts that survived a dunking.

6. *Writings of AH*, 86 (mir. 27).

7. William Jordan is surely correct to include Longchamp in a list of shrines in the Île-de-France where Louis's cult was promoted. William Chester Jordan, "Honoring Saint Louis in a Small Town," *Journal of Medieval History* 30 (2004): 263–77, at 270. It should be stressed, however, that veneration of Louis at Longchamp generally seems to have been paired with attention to Isabelle, unlike at other sites such as Saint-Denis.

8. *Writings of AH*, 88 (mir. 32). William D. Paden suggested to me the importance of this shift in tense.

9. Robert Bartlett has recently considered some of these cases in *The Hanged Man: A Story of Miracle, Memory, and Colonialism in the Middle Ages* (Princeton: Princeton University Press, 2004), esp. 148–52.

10. The interest of this passage was pointed out by Christopher K. Gardner in a review of *Writings of AH* that appeared in the electronic forum H-France.

11. The queen referred to here could have been Marguerite of Provence; or her daughter Blanche (widow of Ferdinand of Castile, who retired for a time to Longchamp); or the current queen of France, Marie of Brabant.

12. These figures are only approximate, for several reasons. First, they do not include some of the children who were cured (often of indeterminate sex), only their parents. Second, they refer only to people who appear in the "miracles" section of the *Life*, though clearly others saw Isabelle as a saintly figure as well. Finally, some of the noble women and Franciscans were merely present at Isabelle's translation. It seems legitimate to include them as witnesses to Isabelle's saintly status, however, since they must have gone out of their way to attend this event.

13. Le Goff gives the numbers as thirty-four men and boys compared to twenty-nine women and girls. *Saint Louis*, 848. These numbers refer only to the sex of the recipients of cures and do not include other witnesses or the parents of children who were cured (in contrast to my tally for Isabelle's miracles).

14. See Percival B. Fay, ed., *Guillaume de Saint-Pathus: Les miracles de saint Louis* (Paris: Champion, 1932), miracles twelve and forty-six (pp. 39, 140) on the healing power of items of Louis's clothing, miracle thirty-one (pp. 94–96) on the return to sanity of a young girl, and miracle nineteen (p. 66) on vowing a candle of the height of a sick child to the saint.

15. For recent scholarly approaches to distinguishing the voices of saints from those of their biographers see Catherine M. Mooney, ed., *Gendered Voices: Medieval Saints and Their Interpreters* (Philadelphia: University of Pennsylvania Press, 1999), especially Mooney's introduction, 1–15; and, among other recent studies, Anne M. Schuchmann, "Literary Collaboration in the Life of Umiliana dei Cerchi," *Magistra* 7 (2001): 5–22.

16. See my introduction to *Writings of AH*, 11–15.

17. On the date of Agnes's *Life of Isabelle* see *Writings of AH*, 9–10. On the context of the ongoing inquiry into Louis's sanctity see Carolus-Barré, *Le procès de canonisation de saint Louis*, 2–23. Because Anne-Hélène Allirot's "Isabelle de France, soeur de saint Louis: La vierge savante" appeared only after this book was in press, I have not been able to engage fully with it here. To the extent that Professor Allirot highlights the theme of dynastic sanctity, her ideas would seem to complement the argument that I make here (and first suggested in my 2002 doctoral dissertation, which was available to Professor Allirot). I would note, however, that her dating of the text to 1279–1281 cannot be supported by a close examination of all the evidence.

18. Vauchez, *Sainthood in the Later Middle Ages*, 182; idem, "*Beata Stirps*: Sainteté et lignage en Occident aux XIIIe et XIVe siècles," 397–406. See also Gábor Klaniczay, "The Cult of Dynastic Saints in Central Europe: Fourteenth-Century Angevins and Luxemburgs," in *The Uses of Supernatural Power*, 111–28; and idem, *Holy Rulers and Blessed Princesses*, 299–301. For more general recent assessments of Charles see Jean Dunbabin, *Charles I of Anjou: Power, Kingship, and State-Making in Thirteenth-Century Europe* (London and New York: Longman, 1998); David Abulafia, "Charles of Anjou Reassessed," *Journal of Medieval History* 26 (2000): 93–114; and Chris Jones, ". . . *mais tot por le servise Deu*? Philippe III le Hardi, Charles d'Anjou, and the 1273/74 Imperial Candidature," *Viator* 34 (2003): 208–28.

19. Carolus-Barré, *Le procès de canonisation de saint Louis*, 68–70, 75.

20. Charles's movements are traced in Paul Durrieu, *Les archives Angevines de Naples: Étude sur les registres du roi Charles Ier (1265–1285)*, vol. 2 (Paris: Libraire des Écoles Françaises d'Athènes et de Rome, 1887), 165–89.

21. Joseph Strayer, "The Crusade against Aragon," in *Medieval Statecraft and the Perspectives of History* (Princeton: Princeton University Press, 1971), 110.

22. Runciman, *The Sicilian Vespers*, 236. The duel turned out to be something of a farce with the combatants contriving to arrive on the field at different times of the day and so miss each other entirely.

23. Durrieu, *Les archives Angevines de Naples*, 188–89.

24. For Charles's interest in demonstrating divine sanction for his rule see Pryds, *The King Embodies the Word*, 22–25, and Jean-Paul Boyer, "La 'Foi monarchique': Royaume de Sicile et Provence (mi-XIIIe-mi-XIVe siècle)," in Paolo Cammarosano, ed., *Le forme della propaganda politica nel due e nel trecento* (Rome: École Française de Rome, 1994): 85–110.

25. *Writings of AH*, 54 (par. 6).

26. Vauchez, *Sainthood in the Later Middle Ages*, 40–43.

27. *Writings of AH*, 54 (par. 5), 56 (par. 9), on not playing with her brothers' wives and on illness.

28. *Writings of AH*, 46 (par. 2) for quotation on doves; 70 (mir. 1), 78 (mir. 17) on miracles.

29. *Writings of AH* 46–48 (pars. 3–4), 58 (par. 11), 62–64 (par. 20).

30. A donation made in 1265 by Alfonse "aux Nonnes fondées par la soeur du seigneur comte" is noted by Boutaric, *Saint Louis et Alfonse de Poitiers*, 46; in his will of June 1270 Alphonse left one hundred *livres* to the "sereurs Meneuretes de l'Umilité Nostre Damme lez Saint Clot." *Layettes*, vol. 4, #5712. Louis IX bequeathed fifty *livres* to Longchamp. *Layettes*, vol. 4, #5638.

31. Cited by Carolus-Barré, *Le procès de canonisation de saint Louis*, 162. I owe the reference to William Jordan.

32. *BF*, vol. 3, 582–83.

33. The importance of this miracle to Philip is discussed by Elizabeth A. R. Brown in "The Prince Is Father of the King: The Character and Childhood of Philip the Fair of France," in *The Monarchy of Capetian France and Royal Ceremonial*, II, 327.

34. Among other gifts, AN K52, 54 and 55 (Tardif, *Monuments historiques* #1002, 1004, 1005) are dated at Longchamp, indicating that Philip returned as king to the site of his cure.

35. Klaniczay, *Holy Rulers and Blessed Princesses*, 301–3; Hallam, "Philip the Fair and the Cult of Saint Louis," 201–14; Elizabeth A. R. Brown, "Philippe le Bel and the Remains of Saint Louis," in *The Monarchy of Capetian France and Royal Ceremonial*, III, 175–82; Gaposchkin, "Boniface VIII, Philip the Fair, and the Sanctity of Louis IX," 1–26; eadem, "*Ludovicus decus regnantium*"; eadem, "Philip the Fair, the Dominicans, and the Liturgical Office for Louis IX."

36. Bloch, *The Royal Touch*, 61–64, 74–75.

37. See Brown, "The Ceremonial of Royal Succession in Capetian France: The Funeral of Philip V," in *The Monarchy of Capetian France and Royal Ceremonial*, VIII, 271 nn. 16 and 17. See also AN L1026 no. 1, which notes that "madame Blanche fu vestue la veille de la chandeleur l'an mil ccc xviii." This date would correspond to the beginning of February 1319 in modern reckoning. This information is repeated and expanded upon in BNF ms. fr. 11662 (ed. Molinier, *Les obituaires de la province de Sens*, vol. 1 part 2, 669–70); see also Duchesne, *Histoire de l'abbaye royale de Longchamp*, 139–42.

38. Duchesne, *Histoire de l'abbaye royale de Longchamp*, 142.

39. Brown, "Death and the Human Body in the Later Middle Ages," in *The Monarchy of Capetian France and Royal Ceremonial*, VI, 258, and "The Ceremonial of Royal Succession in Capetian France: The Funeral of Philip V," in ibid., VIII, 271–72 n. 17, citing AN J404A, no. 23. Queen Jeanne died on 21 January 1330. According to Garreau, in 1787 the tomb of her entrails was still visible at Longchamp. *Bienheureuse Isabelle de France, soeur de saint Louis*, 103.

40. In the eighteenth century, it was mistakenly claimed that Louis IX's sons Louis and Jean had their tombs at Longchamp. For the claim see Garreau, *Bienheureuse Isabelle de France, soeur de saint Louis*, 102; for refutation see Richard, *Saint Louis*, 79. Garreau also believed that Robert, son of Philip III, was buried there (p. 110).

41. Brown, "The Ceremonial of Royal Succession in Capetian France: The Funeral of Philip V," in *The Monarchy of Capetian France and Royal Ceremonial*, VIII, 269.

42. The final official document of his reign, a codicil to his will, is dated 2 January at Longchamp. Brown, "The Ceremonial of Royal Succession in Capetian France: The Funeral of Philip V," in *The Monarchy of Capetian France and Royal Ceremonial*, VIII, 269–72; 289–90 for edition of the codicil from AN J404A no. 27. See also Garreau, *Isabelle de France, soeur de saint Louis*, 90–91.

43. *Writings of AH*, 64 (par. 23) on Franciscan advisers; 72–74 (mir. 8) on Isabelle's translation; 72 (mir. 4) and 74 (mir. 9) on Denis; 74–76 (mir. 10) on Giles.

44. *Writings of AH*, 68 (par. 26).

45. John Coakley's work on mendicant confessors and their relationship to female saints and penitents has been especially influential. See Coakley, "A Marriage and Its Observer: Christine of Stommeln, the Heavenly Bridegroom, and Friar Peter of Dacia," in Mooney, ed., *Gendered Voices*, 99–117; idem, "Friars, Sanctity and Gender: Mendicant Encounters with Saints, 1250–1325," in *Medieval Masculinities: Regarding Men in the Middle Ages*, ed. Clare A. Lees (Minneapolis: University of Minnesota Press, 1994), 91–110; idem, "Gender and the Authority of Friars: The Significance of Holy Women for Thirteenth-Century Franciscans and Dominicans," *Church History* 60 (1991): 445–60; and idem, "Friars as Confidants of Holy Women in Medieval Dominican Hagiography," in Renate Blumenfeld-Kosinski and Timea Szell, eds., *Images of Sainthood in Medieval Europe* (Ithaca: Cornell University Press, 1991), 222–46. His book *Women, Men, and Spiritual Power* is forthcoming from Columbia University Press.

46. Nicole Leapley explored similar issues in a paper read at the 2005 International Congress on Medieval Studies at Kalamazoo, Michigan, entitled "Royal Hagiography's New Voice: Agnes de Harcourt's *Vie de nostre saincte et benoite dame et mere madame Yzabeau de France*." I thank her for sending me a copy of this paper.

47. *Writings of AH*, 64 (par. 22).

48. *Writings of AH*, 64–66 (par. 23).

49. *Writings of AH*, 66 (par. 24).

50. *Writings of AH*, 66 (par. 25).

51. *Writings of AH*, 62–64 (par. 20), 66 (par. 24).

52. *Writings of AH*, 54 (par. 6), 60 (par. 15), 68 (par. 26).

53. For instance, contemporary female hagiographers Felipa of Porcellet and Marguerite of Oingt did not employ this sort of confident first-person voice. See Garay and Jeay, trans., *The Life of Saint Douceline, a Beguine of Provence*; Renate Blumenfeld-Kosinski, trans., *The Writings of Margaret of Oingt: Medieval Prioress and Mystic* (Newburyport, MA: Focus, 1990). Many better-known male hagiographers such as Thomas of Celano and St. Bonaventure also avoided it. See also the comments about authorial reticence in Gertrud Jaron Lewis, *By Women, For Women, About Women: The Sister-Books of Fourteenth-Century Germany* (Toronto: Pontifical Institute of Mediaeval Studies, 1996), 32–35.

54. A point made by Leapley, "Royal Hagiography's New Voice" (note 46 above), but also in Field, "The Princess, the Abbess, and the Friars," ch. 8.

55. *Writings of AH*, 46 (pars. 1–2).

56. *Writings of AH*, 52 (pars. 1–2), 56 (par. 8).

57. *Writings of AH*, 56–62 (pars. 10, 11, 14, 18).

58. *Writings of AH*, 68 (par. 27).

59. *Writings of AH*, 70, 76, 80 (mirs. 2, 12, 20).

60. Vauchez, *Sainthood in the Later Middle Ages*, 61–84.

61. Often referred to somewhat redundantly as "ma dame Madame Blanche." See, for example, Molinier, *Les obituaires de la province de Sens*, vol. 1 part 2, 669.

62. Samantha Kelly, *The New Solomon: Robert of Naples (1309–1343) and Fourteenth-Century Kingship* (Leiden and Boston: Brill, 2003), 97–98. Robert's court was also supporting the canonization causes of Nicholas of Tolentino and Thomas Aquinas.

63. This is not to say that evidence of Angevin promotion, or at least awareness, of Isabelle's cult may not emerge from future research. At the present time, however, scholars studying Angevin dynastic sanctity have not pointed to any relevant evidence. See, particularly, Kelly, *The New Solomon*, 119–29; Pryds, *The King Embodies the Word*, 47–50 and passim; Klaniczay, *Holy Rulers and Blessed Princesses*, 295–331; and idem, "The Cult of Dynastic Saints in Central Europe: Fourteenth-Century Angevins and Luxemburgs," in *The Uses of Supernatural Power*, 111–28. Figures such as Robert and Sancia, though devoted to Franciscan ideals, patrons of female Franciscan houses, and adherents to the notion of their family's sanctity, do not seem to have made mention of Isabelle. On Robert and Sancia's support of female Franciscan houses see Darleen N. Pryds, "Clarisses, Franciscans, and the House of Anjou: Temporal and Spiritual Partnership in Early Fourteenth-Century Naples," in *Clare of Assisi: A Medieval and Modern Woman. Clarefest, Selected Papers*, ed. Ingrid Peterson (St. Bonaventure, NY: Franciscan Institute, 1996), 99–114. On Sancia in particular see Ronald G. Musto, "Queen Sancia of Naples (1286–1345) and the Spiritual Franciscans," in *Women of the Medieval World: Essays in Honor of John H. Mundy*, ed. Julius Kirshner and Suzanne F. Wemple (Oxford: Blackwell, 1985), 179–214. Musto translates a letter from Sancia to the Franciscan General Chapter of 1334 in which the queen explicitly lays out the sanctity and connections to the Franciscans of her own and her husband's families. This would have been an obvious place to include Isabelle, but she does not. Ibid., 208. Further study of Angevin artistic patronage might be productive. For example, Isabelle of France, among others, has been proposed as one of the five saints in an Angevin-inspired project, the "St. Elizabeth" chapel of the lower basilica of San Francesco, Assisi, but more recently Adrian S. Hoch has identified the figure in question as Agnes of Bohemia. See "*Beata Stirps*, Royal Patronage, and the Identification of the Sainted Rulers in the St. Elizabeth Chapel at Assisi," *Art History* 15 (1992): 279–95. See note 14 for T. M. Gallino's earlier identification of Isabelle. Hoch's claim seems plausible, but I see no reason why Agnes is a more compelling candidate than Isabelle.

64. See *Analecta franciscana* 3 (1897): 370. The *Chronicle* author's lack of familiarity with Isabelle and her house is demonstrated by the fact that he mistakenly places the foundation of Longchamp around 1279.

65. On these two now-lost books see *Writings of AH*, 32 n. 59; Field, "The Princess, the Abbess, and the Friars," 22–23; and Jean-Luc Deuffic, ed., *La bibliothèque royale du Louvre* (Saint-Denis: Pecia, 2004), 76 #356. I thank Robert E. Lerner for the latter reference.

66. Duchesne, *Histoire de l'abbaye royale de Longchamp*, 141–42. Since this citation is to a later description of her tomb, however, its reliability for the fourteenth century is suspect.

67. For detail on the abbey in the fifteenth century see Mlynarczyk, *Ein Franziskanerinnenkloster*; Duchesne, *Histoire de l'abbaye royale de Longchamp*, passim; and Garreau, *Isabelle de France, soeur de saint Louis*, 93–94. The nuns had to flee Longchamp several times during the course of the Hundred Years War.

68. Isabelle's late-fifteenth-century epitaph (BNF ms. fr. 6214) records four miracles. Three are easily identified as miracles number eleven, thirteen, and thirty-four of Agnes's *Life*. Since the fourth does not seem to be drawn from Agnes's *Life*, miracles at the tomb were probably recorded in the fourteenth and fifteenth centuries. Moreover, Princeton ms. 188, f. 26r, refers to a register of miracles and relates several that might date from the end of the thirteenth or early fourteenth century. These manuscripts are discussed below.

69. See chapter 5, note 37.

70. See *Writings of AH*, 35 n. 68.

71. This incident was first detailed in Princeton ms. 188, ff. 29v–30v, and subsequently retold in BNF ms. n.a.fr. 10871, f. 55v (see below), and by Roulliard.

72. BNF ms. fr. 6214. A Latin translation of this epitaph is given in *AS*, August vol. 6, 792–94. A fragmentary copy is preserved as part of Perrier's catalogue of Longchamp's archives ca. 1699 in AN L1029 no. 37. The text was certainly composed before Isabelle's "beatification" in 1521, and probably before 1516, since it does not mention the well-publicized miracle involving Jeanne Carphaude.

73. The sheets measure 740 by 540 mm. In 1699, Pierre Perrier noted: "Ce tableau etoit attaché au dessus du tombeau, mais il est a présent derrière le grand autel dans la sacristie des pères." AN L1029 no. 37, edited as Appendix F to Field, "The Princess, the Abbess, and the Friars."

74. BNF ms. fr. 6214: ". . . la legende de la saincte vie de la dicte dame . . . et de certainnes lettres de bon tesmoingnage qui sont guardees en ceste abbaye."

75. See note 68 above.

76. *Writings of AH*, 68 (par. 27).

77. BNF ms. fr. 6214: "Et quant elle devoit recevoir le precieux corps de Nostre Seigneur Iehsu Crist elle disoit tres humblement sa coulpe a genoulz a ses servans."

78. BNF ms. fr. 6214: "Et chascun iour se confessoit et recevoit souvent tres devotement le corps de nostre seigneur Iehsu Crist."

79. BNF ms. fr. 6214: "Et [avint une] fois come elle avoit este presque toute la nuit en oroison que elle y fut par contemplacion si trans[. . . .]it en Dieu qu'elle ne sentoit ne entendoit riens de ceste mortele vie, car pour chose que on ly feist ne pour parole que on ly deist elle ne mouvoit ne parloit, fors seulement cest parole: 'Illi soli [hono]r et gloria.' C'est a dire, a yceluy seul honneur et gloire. Et avoit la face et la chair si tres esperituele de si tres merveilleuse doulceur, beaute, et clarte, que c'estoit grant admiration a veoir. En ce point elle fut de l'eure du bien matin dusques a [vespres, et ces choses vir]ent plusieurs personnes digne de foy." Text within brackets represents lacunae in the manuscript supplied from other indications. Stories about a rapture experienced by St. Louis also circulated after his death. See Jordan, "Cutting the Budget: The Impact of the Crusades on Appropriation for Public Works in France," in *Ideology and Royal Power in Medieval France*, 307. The episode was related by a Flemish chronicler before 1294.

80. BNF ms. fr. 6214: "Elle estoit moult humble en vesture et estoient ses robes de gros drap de burel et les vestoit dusques a tant qu'elles fussent usees et percees."

81. The account is in BNF ms. fr. 11662, f. 15r–17r. On Katherine Picarde see Duchesne, *Histoire de l'abbaye royale de Longchamp*, 124.

82. The text of Leo's answering bull makes it clear that this was what was requested of him. The only complete copy of Leo's bull that I have been able to locate is edited in Aubertus Miraeus (Aubert le Mire), *Isabellae sanctae* (Brussels: Ioannem Pepermanum, 1622), ff. 8r–10r (no page numbers given). The incipit there is "Piis omnium praesertim devoti feminei sexus personarum sub suavi religionis iugo Altissimo famulantium."

83. The so-called Conciliabulum of Pisa had threatened Pope Julius II with a renewed conciliarism, supported by the French crown. Leo X, upon his ascension in 1513, neutralized this threat by convoking the Fifth Lateran Council and then reaching the Concordat of Bologna with Francis I of France in 1516, which granted extended French control over the Gallican church in exchange for a repudiation of the Pragmatic Sanction of Bourges of 1438, in which the French crown had supported the idea of conciliar supremacy. See Francis Oakley, *The Western Church in the Later Middle Ages* (Ithaca: Cornell University Press, 1979), 73, 78–79. Good relations with the French crown were thus at the heart of papal objectives at this time. There is no evidence that Francis I had a hand in requesting Isabelle's canonization, but Leo may nevertheless have realized that it would be flattering to honor a member of the French royal family.

84. The nuns' account in BNF ms. fr. 11662 dates the bull 19 January 1521, while Garreau and others give 3 January (Duchesne's version is garbled). But Miraeus's printed edition of the bull is dated "III Idus Ienuarii pontificatus nostri anno octavo."

85. The nuns recounted that a man named Franc de Spinolle carried the request to Rome. He sent the bull back to Longchamp by way of a banker named Fristobaldi,

who demanded a large sum of money before he would hand it over. The transfer of funds was finally arranged by Robert Messier. The date of 23 August is from the nuns' account in BNF ms. fr. 11662.

86. Oliger, citing the seventeenth-century necrology of the Franciscans of Auxerre, says that Messier was guardian of Troyes and of the Grand Couvent at Paris, and twice Provincial Minister of France (1523–1526 and 1529–1532); in his old age he retired to Longchamp as confessor and died there on 23 July 1546. He was buried close to the tomb of Isabelle. Livier Oliger, "Le plus ancien office liturgique de la B.se Isabelle de France," in *Miscellanea Giovanni Mercati*, vol. 2 (Vatican City: Biblioteca Apostolica Vaticana, 1946), 484–508, at 492.

87. According to BNF ms. fr. 11662.

88. The cardinal's confirmation is printed in Miraeus, *Isabellae sanctae*, ff. 10v–12v. The date given here is from this edition, where Adrian refers to himself as "informatus luculenter et clare tam testium depositionibus quam exemplaribus, sive extractis antiquorum liberum dicti monasterii de Longo Campo, de veritate contentorum in eodem rescripto, quodque ipsa Elisabetha beata pluribus coruscat in dies miraculis." BNF ms. fr. 11662, ff. 15v–16r, gives the date as 21 December, and ff. 17v–20r give a French translation of Adrian of Boissy's letter.

89. The office is preserved in a sixteenth–century copy as BNF ms. lat. 912. Edited in Oliger, "Le plus ancien office liturgique de la B.se Isabelle de France."

90. Mariano of Florence, *Libro delle degnità et excellentie del Ordine della seraphica madre delle povere donne Sancta Chiara da Asisi*, 167; Francesco Gonzaga, *De origine seraphicae religionis franciscanae* (Rome, 1587), 576.

91. Internal evidence from this life points to a Franciscan close to Longchamp. Messier is the most likely candidate. Most concretely, BNF ms. n.a.fr. 10871, a life composed in 1569 and discussed below, notes on ff. 5r–v that Isabelle's biography was written once in the thirteenth century and "depuis a este mise en langue vulgaire comme il sensuit a la requeste de les filles du dict lieu de Longchamp par ung devot et notable docteur en theologie confesseur de dict mesme lieu nomme frere Robert Messier, lequel la feit approuver par la court de Romme et auctoritee papal avec l'office par luy composee a l'honneur de la saincte dame pour satisfaire a la devotion des dictes religieuses." Thus we have clear evidence that Messier did, in fact, write a life of Isabelle around 1521.

92. Princeton ms. 188 (Manuscripts Division, Department of Rare Books and Special Collections, Princeton University Library). I thank Sandra Hindman for first bringing this manuscript to my attention, and Don Skemer for information on its new shelf number. The incipit reads: "A la louenge de Nostre Seigneur Dieu et de la tres sacree mere de Iehsu Crist et a l'honneur de madame notre saincte mere Ysabel de France aussy a la promocion de la devocion des vener-

ables dames et devottes religieuses du sainct monastere de Longchamp, s'ensuit la declaracion de la saincte vie de la dicte notre saincte mere Ysabel divisee en douze chapitres."

93. Princeton ms. 188, ff. 10v–12r. Messier adds the characters of her confessor Eudes of Rosny and chaplain Thomas "of Provins" to provide realistic details and has Agnes present to ask Isabelle where she had been.

94. Princeton ms. 188, ff. 12r–13r. He was also the first to include (mistakenly) Eudes Rigaud in the list of Franciscan masters who helped Isabelle to compose her rule for Longchamp, f. 9r.

95. BNF ms. n.a.fr. 10871. On the book's front and back covers reads: "donné l'an 1569 par Seur Jehanne de Mailly, pour l'abbaye et monastere de Longchamp." Perhaps Jeanne of Mailly herself refashioned Messier's earlier text. At least ff. 10v ("Ci commence la vie de madame saincte Ysabel de France . . .") to 46v appear to be based on Messier's life, though the text has been rearranged and expanded. The manuscript contains also, in the same hand throughout, the "Passio des V freres martirs" (f. 68r), "La legende de S. Anthoine de Pade" (f. 89r), "La vie de Monsieur sainct Bonaventure cardinal et docteur seraphique" (f. 117v), and "Le Legende de saint Loys de Marseille" (f. 135r). Folios 146r–148v contain a later miracle of Isabelle's, added in 1587. According to this addition Henry III wanted to evict the nuns of Longchamp and replace them with nuns from Toulouse, but he changed his mind after Isabelle's miraculous intervention. Roulliard and others retold this episode.

96. On her ecstasy, ff. 34v–36v; Eudes Rigaud, f. 25v; on dislike for her royal blood, on being served by noble girls, on her performance of menial tasks and her tattered clothes, ff. 33r–34v.

97. On the manipulations of St. Louis's cult in somewhat different but nonetheless instructive ways in this period see Beaune, *The Birth of an Ideology*, 90–125.

98. Roulliard, *La saincte mère.*

99. Nicolas Caussin, *La vie de Ste Isabelle, soeur du roy saint Louis et fondatrice du monastère royal de Long-champ, Qui a donné un parfait exemple de la vie neutre des personnes non mariées ny religieuses* (Paris: Sonnius, Bechet, Bray, 1644).

100. Caussin referred to Roulliard as "un author de grande lecture, qui n'oublie rien à dire, & qui passe souvent son sujet par le fecondité de son esprit." *La vie de Ste Isabelle*, 2.

101. Caussin claimed to give a French version of the letter written from Innocent IV to Isabelle that urged her to marry Conrad, the son of Frederick II, mentioned by Agnes in the *Life*. His version is clearly the product of his imagination, as is Isabelle's response, which he purports to record as well. On Caussin's work see Thomas Worcester, "Neither Married nor Cloistered: Blessed Isabelle in Catholic Reformation France," *Sixteenth Century Journal* 30 (1999): 457–72. On

Caussin's biography and literary output see Robert Bireley, *The Jesuits and the Thirty Years War: Kings, Courts, and Confessors* (Cambridge: Cambridge University Press, 2003), 183–99; and Stephen Campbell, "Nicholas Caussin's *Spirituality of Communication*: A Meeting of Divine and Human Speech," *Renaissance Quarterly* 46 (1993): 44–70.

102. For miracles in this period see BNF ms. fr. 11662, ff. 15r–20r; Princeton ms. 188, ff. 25r–35r; BNF ms. n.a.fr. 10871, ff. 43r–67v; Roulliard, *La saincte mère*, 446 and following; and Caussin, *La vie de Ste Isabelle*, 197–225.

103. See the narrative compiled by several nuns of Longchamp in AN LL1604, "Registre contenant la Nomenclature des Abbesses," ff. 36r–40r; also, *L'abrégé de la vie et miracle fait à l'abbaye de Long-champ sur le tombeau de la bienheureuse Isabel de France, fille du roy Louys VIII & soeur du bon roy S. Louys* (Longchamp, 1637); Caussin, *La vie de Ste Isabelle*, 226–27; and *AS*, August, vol. 6, 797.

104. *AS*, August, vol. 6, 798. The Bibliothèque Mazarine in Paris holds a copy of an *Office de notre B. mère et fondatrice St. Isabelle vièrge, soeur de S. Louis, roy de France*, dated Paris, 1681, bound together with other similar contemporary pamphlets.

105. The earliest surviving image of Isabelle of which I am aware is found on f. 1v of BNF ms. n.a.fr. 10871, the book given by Jeanne of Mailly to Longchamp in 1569, and shows Isabelle and Louis offering the abbey of Longchamp to God. Roulliard's book included an engraving by Iaspar Isaac (reprinted in Garreau, *Bienheureuse Isabelle de France, soeur de saint Louis*, following page 64) that is nearly identical and must have taken the image from BNF ms. n.a.fr. 10871 as its exemplar. For other seventeenth-century images of Isabelle dedicating Longchamp to God see Garreau, following pages 32 and 80. In general on Isabelle's iconography see ibid., 127–36.

106. BNF ms. fr. 13753, ff. 89–102. I am preparing an edition of this unpublished text. Pierre Perrier also wrote an unpublished life of Isabelle at the request of the nuns of Longchamp in 1699. Partial copies are preserved in AN L1029 no. 37 and BNF ms. fr. 24950. Further evidence of interest in Isabelle in this century is the copy of Agnes of Harcourt's life made by Antoine Le Maistre in 1653, which subsequently made its way into the papers of Tillemont (BNF ms. fr. 13747, ff. 127–141) and formed the basis of my recent edition of the text.

107. In *Histoire de S. Louys, IX du nom roy de France, écrite par Jean Sire de Joinville*, ed. Charles Du Fresne, Sieur Du Cange (Paris: Mabre-Cramoisy, 1668), 169–81. The *Acta sanctorum* translation is J. Stilting, ed., "Vita B. Elisabethae seu Isabellae Virginis," in *AS*, August, vol. 6 (Antwerp, 1743): 787–809. Stilting also edited Isabelle's fifteenth-century epitaph for the first time, but in a Latin translation.

108. For the parallel revival of St. Louis as a name to conjure with in nineteenth-century French political discourse see Adam Knoble, "Saint Louis and French Political Culture," *Studies in Medievalism* 8 (1996): 156–73, and William Chester Jordan, "Saint Louis in French Epic and Drama," ibid.: 174–94.

109. The most influential nineteenth-century biography of Isabelle was Danielo, *Vie de Mme. Isabelle, soeur de saint Louis, fondatrice de l'abbaye de Longchamp,* a work of romantic excess that revels in the least likely quotations from Roulliard and Caussin. Duchesne's reliance on Danielo is ultimately behind many twentieth-century scholarly errors concerning Isabelle and Longchamp.

110. Gilles Mauger's *La bienheureuse Isabelle, soeur de saint Louis* (Paris: Éditions Paulines, 1982), which appeared in the series L'histoire dorée pour nos enfants. This work continues a nineteenth-century tradition of books aimed at children, such as Gabrielle d'Étampes's *L'Enfance de saint Louis et de sa soeur Isabelle de France* (Tours: Alfred Cattier, 1892).

111. Fiona Avery, *The Crown Rose* (Amherst, NY: Pyr, 2005).

Conclusion

1. Carolus-Barré, *Le procès de canonisation de Saint Louis,* 300–3, isolates several remarks by Guillaume de St.-Pathus and asserts that they could only have come from Marguerite's recollections. Of these, however, only one actually records words or ideas expressly attributed to Marguerite. In a sermon composed for Louis's canonization, Guillaume quoted her on Louis's refusal even to look at her on nights when he intended to observe marital continence. The wry humor it attributes to Louis has the ring of authenticity, yet even here Marguerite does not make it completely clear whether she equates her husband's sexual renunciation with sanctity.

2. Little, "Saint Louis's Involvement with the Friars"; Le Goff, *Saint Louis,* 746–50.

3. Farmer, *Surviving Poverty in Medieval Paris;* eadem, "Down and Out and Female in Thirteenth-Century Paris," *American Historical Review* 103 (1998): 345–72; Le Goff, *Saint Louis,* 844–53; and S. Chennaf and O. Redon, "Les miracles de saint Louis," in *Les miracles, miroirs des corps,* ed. Jacques Gélis, Odile Redon, and Michel Bouvier (Saint-Denis: Université de Paris VIII—Vincennes à Saint-Denis, 1983), 53–85.

BIBLIOGRAPHY

Archival and Manuscript Sources Cited

Bruges, Openbare Bibliotheek, ms. 490 (*Epistola ad dominam Isabellam*)
Grenoble, Bibliothèque municipale, ms. 271 (*Speculum anime*)
Madrid, Biblioteca Nacional, ms. 9731 (*Epistola ad dominam Isabellam*)
Naples, Biblioteca Nazionale, ms. G. VII. 15 (*Speculum anime*)
Paris, Archives nationales de France (royal privileges and archives of Longchamp)
    J148
    K31–37
    L250, 253, 260–262
    L1020–1029
    LL1600–1604
    Q*[1] 1072[1] (registers)
Paris, Bibliothèque de l'Arsenal, ms. 1240 (Longchamp's rule of 1263)
Paris, Bibliothèque franciscaine provinciale des Capucins, ms. 1530 (Trouillard's École des chartes thèse)
Paris, Bibliothèque Mazarine, ms. 870 (*Miroir de l'âme*)
Paris, Bibliothèque nationale de France
    ms. fr. 5703 (Guillaume de Nangis)
    ms. fr. 6214 (Isabelle's epitaph)
    ms. fr. 11662 (*Letter on Louis IX and Longchamp* and other documents)
    ms. fr. 13747 (Notebook B of Le Nain de Tillemont)
    ms. fr. 13753 (Tillemont's life of Isabelle)
    ms. fr. 24950 (Perrier's life of Isabelle)
    ms. n.a.fr. 10871 (1569 life of Isabelle)
    ms. lat. 912 (Messier's 1521 Office for Isabelle)
    ms. lat. 3309 (Thomas of Cantimpré)
    mss. lat. 4917–4920 (Guillaume de Nangis, later redaction)
    ms. lat. 9376 (Longchamp's calendar)
    ms. lat. 14535 (Thomas of Cantimpré)
    ms. lat. 14628 (Thomas of Cantimpré)
    ms. lat. 14878 (*Speculum anime*)

ms. lat. 15942 (Gilbert of Tournai, *Sermones de sanctis*)
ms. lat. 16481 (*Reportationes*, Eudes de Rosny and others)
Princeton, NJ, Princeton University Library, ms. 188 (Robert Messier's life of Isabelle of France)

Chronological List of Biographies of Isabelle of France

ca. 1283   Agnes of Harcourt, *Vie d'Isabelle*. Edited in Sean L. Field, *The Writings of Agnes of Harcourt*.

ca. 1500   *Epitaph*. BNF ms. fr. 6214. Edited in Field, "The Princess, the Abbess, and the Friars," Appendix D.

ca. 1521   Messier, Robert. Princeton ms. 188 (Unedited).

1569   *Vie de ste. Isabelle*. BNF ms. n.a.fr. 10871, ff. 1–67r. (Unedited).

1619   Roulliard, Sébastien. *La saincte mère, ou vie de M. saincte Isabel de France, soeur unique du roy s. Louys, fondatrice de l'abbaye de Long-champ*. Paris: Taupinart, 1619.

1622   Miraeus, Aubertus (Aubert Le Mire). *Isabellae sanctae*. Brussels: Ioannem Pepermanum, 1622.

1637   *L'abrégé de la vie et miracle fait à l'abbaye de Long-champ sur le tombeau de la bienheureuse Isabel de France, fille du roy Louys VIII & soeur du bon roy S. Louys*. Longchamp, 1637.

1644   Caussin, Nicolas. *La vie de Ste Isabelle, soeur du roy saint Louis et fondatrice du monastère royal de Long-champ, Qui a donné un parfait exemple de la vie neutre des personnes non mariées ny religieuses*. Paris: Sonnius, Bechet, Bray, 1644.

ca. 1680   Tillemont, Sébastien Le Nain de. *La bienheureuse Isabelle de France, soeur de S. Louis et fondatrice de l'abbaye de Longchamp*. BNF ms. fr. 13753, ff. 89r–102r. (My edition of this text is forthcoming in *Revue Mabillon*).

ca. 1690   de la Brière, Fauval. (Lost, mentioned by Perrier).

ca. 1699   Perrier, Pierre. *Vie de Ste. Isabelle*. BNF ms. fr. 24950 and AN L1029 no. 37. (Unedited)

1743   Stilting, Johannes. "Commentarius Praevius," in *Acta sanctorum*, August VI. Antwerp, 1743: 787–98.

1772   Couturier, L'abbé. *La vie d'Isabelle de France, soeur de Saint Louis*. Saint-Quentin: Hautoy; and Paris: Brocas, 1772.

1814   Magnier. *Les deux saintes du sang royal des Bourbons, ou Esquisse d'un parallèle religieux et historique, entre la bienheureuse Isabelle de France, soeur de saint Louis, et Madame Elisabeth de France, soeur de Louis XVI*. Paris: Laurent-Beaupré, 1814.

1840   Danielo, Julien-F. *Vie de Mme Isabelle, soeur de saint Louis, fondatrice de l'abbaye de Longchamp, avec une description historique de la fête de Longchamp.* Paris: Gaume frères, 1840.
1848   Martonne, Alfred de. *Isabelle de France.* Paris, 1848.
1852   Lebon, Hubert. *Vie de sainte Isabelle, aussi appelée Élisabeth de France, vierge soeur de saint Louis, fondatrice du monastère de Long-Champ l'an 1270.* Tours: Alfred Mame & fils, 1852.
1855   André, Jean-Franc. *Histoire de Ste Isabelle de France.* Carpentras, 1855.
1872   La Richardays, Mme Renée de. *Isabelle de France et la cour de saint Louis.* Paris: Lecoffre Fils & Cie, 1872.
1892   d'Étampes, Gabrielle. *L'Enfance de saint Louis et de sa soeur Isabelle de France.* Tours: Alfred Cattier, 1892.
1896   *Histoire poétique de la bienheureuse Isabelle de France, soeur de saint Louis.* Par une pauvre Clarisse de Sainte-Claire de l'Ave-Maria de Bordeaux-Talence. Bourg: J.-M. VilleFranche, 1896.
ca. 1897   Avoine, L'abbé. "La bienheureuse Isabelle de France." In *La charité dans les saints.* Paris, no date: 165–78.
1899   Berguin, Mme M. *Isabelle de France, soeur de saint Louis.* Grenoble, 1899.
1943   Garreau, Albert. *Bienheureuse Isabelle de France.* Paris: Éditions Franciscaines, 1943.
1943   Langevin, Eugène. *La bienheureuse Isabelle de France, soeur de saint Louis.* Paris: Éditions Albin Michel, 1944.
1955   Garreau, Albert. *Bienheureuse Isabelle de France, soeur de saint Louis.* Paris: Éditions Franciscaines, 1955.
1982   Mauger, Gilles. *La bienheureuse Isabelle, soeur de saint Louis.* L'histoire dorée pour nos enfants. Paris: Éditions Paulines, 1982.

Printed Primary Sources

Agnes de Harcourt. "La vie d'Isabelle soeur de S. Louys, fondatrice de l'abbaye de Longchamp." In *Histoire de S. Louys, IX du nom roy de France, écrite par Jean Sire de Joinville.* Edited by Charles Du Fresne, Sieur Du Cange. Paris: Mabre-Cramoisy, 1668: 169–81.
———. "Vita b. Elisabethae seu Isabellae virginis." Translated by J. Stilting. In *Acta sanctorum*, August, vol. 6, 787–809. Antwerp, 1743.
———. "Life of Isabelle of France." In *The Writings of Agnes of Harcourt.* Edited and translated by Sean L. Field. Notre Dame, IN: University of Notre Dame Press, 2003.
Annibali da Latera, Flaminio Maria. *Ad Bullarium Franciscanum . . . Supplementum.* Rome: Typis Archangeli Casaletti, 1780.

Armstrong, Regis J., trans. *Clare of Assisi: Early Documents*. New York: Paulist Press, 1988.

Armstrong, Regis J., and Ignatius Brady. *Francis and Clare: The Complete Works*. New York: Paulist Press, 1982.

Becker, Marie-France, et al. *Clare d'Assise: Écrits*. Paris: Éditions du Cerf, 1985.

Blumenfeld-Kosinski, Renate, trans. *The Writings of Margaret of Oingt: Medieval Prioress and Mystic*. Newburyport, MA: Focus, 1990.

Bonifacio, E. *Gilberto di Tournai: De modo addiscendi*. Turin: Società Editrice Internazionale, 1953.

Bonnin, Th. *Regestrum visitationum archiepiscopi Rothomagensis*. Rouen: Auguste Le Brument, 1852.

Bouquet, M., et al. *Recueil des historiens des Gaules et de la France*. 24 vols. Paris, 1738–1904.

Canivez, J. M. *Statuta capitulorum generalium ordinis cisterciensis*. Louvain: Bibliothèque de la Revue d'Histoire Ecclésiastique, 1934.

Cazelles, Brigittte. *The Lady as Saint: A Collection of French Hagiographic Romances of the Thirteenth Century*. Philadelphia: University of Pennsylvania Press, 1991.

Chambers, R. W., and Walter W. Seton. *A Fifteenth-Century Courtesy Book and Two Fifteenth-Century Franciscan Rules*. Early English Text Society No. 148. 1914. Reprint, Oxford: Oxford University Press, 1962.

"Chronica XXIV generalium." *Analecta franciscana* 3 (1897).

Colker, Marvin L., ed. *Galteri de Castellione Alexandreis*. Padua: Antenore, 1978.

D'Achery, Luc. *Spicilegium sive collectio veterum aliquot scriptorum*. 3 vols. Paris, 1723.

Delaborde, H.-François. *Vie de saint Louis par Guillaume de Saint-Pathus, confesseur de la reine Marguerite*. Paris: Picard & fils, 1899.

Delorme, F. M. "En marge du Bullaire franciscain." *La France franciscaine*. 3rd Series. 21 (1938): 1–45.

Delorme, Germain. "Supplément au Bullaire franciscain: À-propos du monastère de Sainte-Claire d' Toulouse." *La France franciscaine* 3 (1914): 11–44, 129–66.

De Poorter, A. *Le traité "Eruditio Regum et Principum" de Guibert de Tournai, O.F.M.* Louvain: Institut Supérieur de Philosophie de l'Université, 1914.

———. "Lettre de Guibert de Tournai, O.F.M. à Isabelle, fille du roi de France." *Revue d'ascetique et de mystique* 12 (1931): 116–127.

Doctoris seraphici S. Bonaventurae S.R.E. episcopi cardinalis opera omnia. 10 vols. Quaracchi: Collegium S. Bonaventurae, 1882–1902.

Esser, Kajetan. *Die Opuscula des Hl. Franziskanus von Assisi*. Grottaferrata: Editiones Collegii S. Bonaventurae ad Claras Aquas, 1976.

Eubel, Conrad. *Bullarii franciscani epitome et supplementum*. Quaracchi: Collegium S. Bonaventurae, 1908.

Fay, Percival B., ed. *Guillaume de Saint-Pathus: Les miracles de saint Louis*. Paris: Champion, 1932.

Field, Sean L., ed. and trans. *The Writings of Agnes of Harcourt: The Life of Isabelle of France and the Letter on Louis IX and Longchamp*. Notre Dame, IN: University of Notre Dame Press, 2003.

Fraipont, J., ed. *Sancti Fulgentii episcopi Ruspensis opera*. CCL 91. Turnhout: Brepols, 1968.

Garay, Kathleen, and Madeleine Jeay, trans. *The Life of Saint Douceline, a Beguine of Provence*. Rochester: D. S. Brewer, 2001.

Géraud, H. *Chronique latine de Guillaume de Nangis*. 2 vols. Paris: Jules Renouard, 1843.

Hague, René, trans. *The Life of St. Louis by John of Joinville*. London: Sheed & Ward, 1955.

Hippeau, C., ed. *Le bestiaire divin de Guillaume, clerc de Normandie*. Caen, 1852. Reprint, Geneva: Slatkine Reprints, 1970.

Huillard-Bréholles, J. L. A., ed. *Historia diplomatica Friderici secundi*. 6 vols. Paris: Henri Plon, 1860.

Huygens, R. B. C., ed. *Lettres de Jacques de Vitry*. Leiden: Brill, 1960.

King, Margot H., trans. *The Life of Margaret of Ypres by Thomas de Cantimpré*. Toronto: Peregrina, 1995.

Lawson, Richard H. trans. *Brother Hermann's Life of the Countess Yolanda of Vienden*. Columbia, SC: Camden House, 1995.

Lazzeri, Zephyrinus. "Documenta controversiam inter Fratres Minores et Clarissas spectantia (1262–1297)." *AFH* 3 (1910): 664–79; 4 (1911): 74–94.

Leclercq, J., and H. Rochais, eds. *Sancti Bernardi opera*, vol. 7. Rome: Editiones Cistercienses, 1974.

"Lletra de Sant Bonaventura al Ministre Provincial d'Aragó." *Etudis Franciscans* 37 (1926): 112–14.

Longpré, Ephrem. *Tractatus de pace, auctore Fr. Gilberto de Tornaco*. Quaracchi: Collegium S. Bonaventurae, 1925.

Mariano of Florence. *Libro delle degnità et excellentie del Ordine della seraphica madre delle povere donne Sancta Chiara da Asisi*. Edited by Giovanni Boccali. Florence: Edizioni Studi Francescani, 1986.

Marrier, Martinus, and Andreas Quercetanus, eds. *Bibliotheca cluniacensis*. 1614. Reprint, Mâcon, 1915.

Martène, Edmund, and Ursine Durand. *Veterum scriptorum et monumentorum historicorum, dogmaticorum moralium: Amplissima collectio*. 8 vols. Reprint, New York: Burt Franklin, 1968.

———. *Thesaurus novus anecdotorum*. Vol. 3. Paris, 1717; reprint, 1968.

Matthew Paris, *Chronica majora*. Edited by Henry Richards Luard. London: Longman, 1877.

Melani, G. *Tractatus de anima Ioannis Pecham*. Florence: Edizioni Studi Francescani, 1948.

Molinier, Auguste L., ed. *Les obituaires de la province de Sens.* 2 vols. Paris: Imprimerie Nationale, 1902.

Monfrin, Jacques, ed. *Joinville, Vie de saint Louis.* Paris: Garnier, 1995.

Monti, Dominic. *St. Bonaventure's Writings Concerning the Franciscan Order.* St. Bonaventure, NY: Franciscan Institute, 1994.

Neumann, Hans, ed. *Mechthild von Magdeburg: Das fließende Licht der Gottheit.* 2 vols. Munich: Artemis, 1990–1993.

Oliger, L. B. *Margherita Colonna: Le due vite scritte dal fratello Giovanni Colonna senatore di Roma et da Stefania monaca di S. Silvestro in Capite.* Rome: Facultas Theologica Pontificii, 1935.

———. "Le plus ancien office liturgique de la B.se Isabelle de France." In *Miscellanea Giovanni Mercati.* Vol. 2. Vatican City: Biblioteca Apostolica Vaticana, 1946: 484–508.

Omaechevarria, Ignacio. *Escritos de Santa Clara y documentos complementarios.* 3rd edition. Madrid: Biblioteca de Autores Cristianos, 1993.

Owen, D. D. R., trans. *Chrétien de Troyes, Arthurian Romances.* London: Dent & Sons, 1987.

Philippe de Thaün. *Le bestiaire: Texte critique publié avec introduction, notes et glossaire par Emmanuel Walberg.* Paris, 1900. Reprint, Geneva: Slatkine Reprints, 1970.

Platelle, Henri, trans. *Les exemples du Livre des Abeilles.* Turnhout: Brepols, 1997.

Pritchard, R. Telfryn, trans. *Walter of Châtillon: The Alexandreis.* Toronto: Pontifical Institute of Mediaeval Studies, 1986.

Regulae et constitutiones generales monialium Ordinis sanctae Clarae. Rome: Curia Generalitia Ordinis Fratrum Minorum, 1941.

Sbaralea, J.-H. *Bullarium franciscanum.* 4 vols. Rome, 1759–1768.

Shirley, Walter W. *Royal and Other Historical Letters Illustrative of the Reign of Henry III.* London: Longman, 1862.

Tardif, Jules. *Monuments historiques.* Paris: Cayce, 1866.

Terry, Patricia, and Nancy Vine Durling, trans. *The Romance of the Rose or Guillaume de Dole.* Philadelphia: University of Pennsylvania Press, 1993.

Testard, M., ed. *Sancti Ambrosii Mediolanensis de officiis.* CCL 15. Turnhout: Brepols, 2000.

Teulet, A., et al. *Layettes du tresor des chartes.* 5 vols. Paris, 1863–1909.

Thomas de Cantimpré. *Bonum universale de apibus.* Edited by Georgius Colvenerius. Douai: Belleri, 1627.

Townsend, David, trans. *The Alexandreis of Walter of Châtillon.* Philadelphia: University of Pennsylvania Press, 1996.

Wadding, Luke. *Annales minorum.* 3rd edition. 25 vols. Reprint, Quaracchi: Collegium S. Bonaventurae, 1931–1934.

Wolfkiel, Kathryn Betts. "*The Life of the Blessed Saint Doucelina* (d. 1274): An Edition and Translation with Commentary." Ph.D. diss., Northwestern University, 1993.

Secondary Works

Abulafia, David. *Frederick II: A Medieval Emperor*. Oxford and New York: Oxford University Press, 1988.

———. "Charles of Anjou Reassessed." *Journal of Medieval History* 26 (2000): 93–114.

Alberzoni, Maria Pia. *Chiara e il papato*. Milan: Edizioni Biblioteca Francescana, 1995. Translated in Alberzoni, *Clare of Assisi and the Poor Sisters in the Thirteenth Century*.

———. "*Nequaquam a Christi sequela in perpetuum absolvi desidero*: Chiara tra carisma e istituzione." In *Chiara d'Assisi e la Memoria di Francesco: Atti del convegno per l'VIII centenario della nascità di s. Chiara*. Edited by Alfonso Marini and Maria Beatrice Mistretta. Città del Castello: Petruzzi, 1995: 41–65. Translated by Nancy Celaschi as "Clare between Charism and Institution." *Greyfriars Review* 12, Supplement (1998): 81–121.

———. *La nascita di un'istituzione: L'ordine di s. Damiano nel XIII secolo*. Milan: Edizioni CUSL, 1996.

———. "San Damiano nel 1228: Contributo alla 'Questione clariana.'" *Collectanea franciscana* 67 (1997): 459–76. Translated in Alberzoni, *Clare of Assisi and the Poor Sisters in the Thirteenth Century*.

———. "Papato e nuovi Ordini religiosi femminili." In *Il papato duecentesco e gli Ordini mendicanti: Atti del XXV Convegno internazionale (Assisi, 13–14 febbraio 1998)*. Spoleto: Centro Italiano di Studi sull'Alto Medioevo, 1998: 207–61. Translated in Alberzoni, *Clare of Assisi and the Poor Sisters in the Thirteenth Century*.

———. "*Sorores minores* e autorità ecclesiastica fino al pontificato di Urbano IV." In *Chiara e la diffusione delle Clarisse nel secolo XIII: Atti del Convegno di studi in occasione dell'VII centenario della nascita di santa Chiara* (Manduria, 14–15 dicembre 1994). Edited by Giancarlo Andenna and Benedetto Vetere. Manduria: Congedo Editore, 1998: 165–94. Translated in Alberzoni, *Clare of Assisi and the Poor Sisters in the Thirteenth Century*.

———. "Le congregazioni monastiche: Le Damianite." In *Dove va la storiografia monastica in Europa? Temi e metodi di ricerca per lo studio della vita monastica e regolare in età medievale alle soglie del terzo millennio: Atti del Convegno internazionale Brescia-Rodengo, 23–25 marzo 2000*. Edited by Giancarlo Andenna. Milan: Vita e Pensiero, 2001: 379–401.

———. *Clare of Assisi and the Poor Sisters in the Thirteenth Century*. St. Bonaventure, NY: Franciscan Institute Publications, 2004.

Allirot, Anne-Hélène. "Isabelle de France, soeur de saint Louis: La vierge savante. Étude de la *Vie d'Isabelle de France* écrite par Agnès d'Harcourt." *Médiévales* 48 (2005): 55–98.

Ancelet-Hustache, Jeanne. *Sainte Elisabeth de Hongrie*. Paris: Éditions Franciscaines, 1947. Translated by Paul J. Oligny and Venard O'Donnell, *Gold Tried by Fire: St. Elizabeth of Hungary*. Chicago: Franciscan Herald Press, 1963.

Andenna, Giancarlo. "Le Clarisse nel novarese (1252–1300)." *AFH* 67 (1974): 185–267.

———. "Urbano IV e l'ordine delle Clarisse." In *Chiara e la diffusione delle Clarisse nel secolo XIII*. Edited by Andenna and Benedetto Vetere. 195–218.

———, ed. *Dove va la storiografia monastica in Europa? Temi e metodi di ricerca per lo studio della vita monastica e regolare in età medievale alle soglie del terzo millennio: Atti del Convegno internazionale Brescia-Rodengo, 23–25 marzo 2000*. Milan: Vita e Pensiero, 2001.

Andenna, Giancarlo, and Benedetto Vetere, eds. *Chiara e la diffusione delle Clarisse nel secolo XIII: Atti del Convegno di studi in occasione dell'VII centenario della nascita di santa Chiara* (Manduria, 14–15 dicembre 1994). Manduria: Congedo Editore, 1998.

Avril, François, and Patricia Danz Stirneman. *Manuscrits enluminés d'origine insulaire VIIe–XXe siècles*. Paris: Bibliothéque nationale, 1987.

Backes, Nikolaus. *Kardinal Simon de Brion (Papst Martin IV)*. Berlin: Hermann Blanke, 1910.

Bainciotto, Gabriel. *Bestiaires du moyen âge*. Paris: Stock, 1980.

Baldwin, John W. *The Government of Philip Augustus: Foundations of French Royal Power in the Middle Ages*. Berkeley: University of California Press, 1986.

Bande, Alexandre. "Philippe le Bel, le coeur, et le sentiment dynastique." *Micrologus* 11 (2003): 267–78.

Barbiche, Bernard. *Les actes pontificaux originaux des Archives nationales de Paris*. 2 vols. Vatican City: Biblioteca Apostolica Vaticana, 1975.

Barlow, Frank. "The King's Evil." *English Historical Review* 95 (1980): 3–28.

Barone, Giulia. "Margherita Colonna e le Clarisse di S. Silvestro in Capite." In *Roma anno 1300: Atti della IV settimana di studi di storia dell'arte medievale dell'Università di Roma "La Sapienza" (19–24 maggio 1980)*. Edited by Angiola Maria Romanini. Rome: L'Erma di Bretschneider, 1983: 799–805.

———. "Le due vite di Margherita Colonna." In *Esperienza religiosa e scritture femminili tra medioevo ed età moderna*. Edited by Marilena Modica Vasta. Palermo: Bonanno, 1992: 25–32.

———. *Da frate Elia agli spirituali*. Milan: Edizione Biblioteca Francescana, 1999.

Bartlett, Robert. *The Hanged Man: A Story of Miracle, Memory, and Colonialism in the Middle Ages*. Princeton: Princeton University Press, 2004.

Bataillon, Louis-Jacques. "Fragments des sermons de Gérard d'Abbeville, Eudes de Rosny et Thomas d'Aquine." In *La prédication au XIIIe siècle en France et en Italie*. Aldershot: Variorum, 1993: 257–68.

Baxter, Ron. *Bestiaries and Their Users in the Middle Ages*. Phoenix Mill: Sutton, 1998.

Beaune, Colette. *The Birth of an Ideology: Myths and Symbols of Nation in Late Medieval France*. Translated by Susan Ross Huston. Berkeley: University of California Press, 1991.

Bedos-Rezak, Brigitte. "Medieval Women in French Sigillographic Sources." In *Medieval Women and the Sources of Medieval History*. Edited by Joel T. Rosenthal. Athens: University of Georgia Press, 1990: 1–36.

———. "Medieval Identity: A Sign and a Concept." *American Historical Review* 105 (2000): 1489–1533.

Bell, David N. *What Nuns Read: Books and Libraries in Medieval English Nunneries*. Kalamazoo: Cistercian Publications, 1995.

Bell, Susan Groag. "Medieval Women Book Owners: Arbiters of Lay Piety and Ambassadors of Culture." In *Women and Power in the Middle Ages*. Edited by Mary C. Erler and Maryanne Kowaleski. Athens: University of Georgia Press, 1988: 149–87.

Bémont, Charles. *Simon de Montfort, Earl of Leicester, 1208–1265*. 2nd edition. Translated by E. F. Jacob. Oxford: Clarendon Press, 1930.

Berger, Élie. *Saint Louis et Innocent IV: Étude sur les rapports de la France et du Saint-Siège*. Paris: Thorin & fils, 1893.

———. *Histoire de Blanche de Castille, reine de France*. Paris: Thorin & fils, 1895.

Bériou, Nicole. "La prédication au béguinage de Paris pendant l'année liturgique 1272–1273." *Recherches augustiniennes* 13 (1978): 105–229.

———. "Les sermons sur sainte Claire dans l'espace française." In *Sainte Claire d'Assise et sa postérité: Actes du Colloque de l'U.N.E.S.C.O. 29 septembre–1er octobre 1994*. Paris: Éditions Franciscaines, 1995: 119–54.

———. *L'avènement des maîtres de la parole: La prédication à Paris au XIIIe siècle*. 2 vols. Paris: Institut d'Études Augustiniennes, 1998.

———. *Les sermons et la visite pastorale de Federico Visconti, archévêque de Pise (1253–1277)*. Édition critique par Nicole Bériou et Isabelle le Masne de Chermont avec la collaboration de Pascale Bourgain et Marina Innocenti. Rome: École Française de Rome, 2001.

Berlioz, Jacques, Pascal Collomb, and Marie Anne Polo de Beaulieu. "La face cachée de Thomas de Cantimpré." *Archives d'histoire doctrinale et litteraire du moyen âge* 68 (2001): 73–94.

Berman, Constance. "Dowries, Private Income, and Anniversary Masses: The Nuns of Saint-Antoine-des-Champs (Paris)." *Proceedings of the Annual Meeting of the Western Society for French History* 20 (1993): 3–12.

———. "Cistercian Nuns and the Development of the Order: The Abbey at Saint-Antoine-des-Champs outside Paris." In *The Love of Learning and the Love of God: Studies in Honor of Jean Leclercq*. Kalamazoo: Cistercian Publications, 1995.

———. "Abbeys for Cistercian Nuns in the Ecclesiastical Province of Sens: Foundation, Endowment, and Economic Activities of the Earlier Foundations." *Revue Mabillon* n. s. 8 (1997): 83–113.

Berriot, François. "Les manuscrits de l'abbaye de Longchamp aux Archives de France et la *Vie de sainte Claire* inédite (début XIVe S.)." *AFH* 79 (1986): 329–58.

Bireley, Robert. *The Jesuits and the Thirty Years War: Kings, Courts, and Confessors.* Cambridge: Cambridge University Press, 2003.

Bland, Cynthia Renée. *The Teaching of Grammar in Late Medieval England.* East Lansing: Colleagues Press, 1991.

Bloch, Marc. *The Royal Touch: Sacred Monarchy and Scrofula in England and France.* Translated by J. E. Anderson. London: Routledge & Kegan Paul, 1973.

Blumenfeld-Kosinski, Renate, and Timea Szell, eds. *Images of Sainthood in Medieval Europe.* Ithaca: Cornell University Press, 1991.

Blumenfeld-Kosinski, Renate, Duncan Robertson, and Nancy Bradley Warren, eds. *The Vernacular Spirit: Essays on Medieval Religious Literature.* New York: Palgrave, 2002.

Bonaventuriana: Miscelanea in onore de Jacques Guy Bougerol ofm, a cura di Francisco de Asís Chavaro Blanco. 2 vols. Rome: Edizioni Antonianum, 1988.

Bos, Elisabeth. "The Literature of Spiritual Formation for Women in France and England, 1080–1180." In *Listen, Daughter: The Speculum Virginum and the Formation of Religious Women in the Middle Ages.* Edited by Constant J. Mews. New York: Palgrave, 2001: 201–20.

Bougerol, J. G. *Introduction to the Works of Bonaventure.* Translated by José de Vinck. Paterson, NJ: St. Anthony Guild Press, 1964.

———. "Saint Bonaventure et le roi saint Louis." In *S. Bonaventura 1274–1974*, vol. 2. Grottaferrata: Collegium S. Bonaventurae, 1973: 469–89.

———. "Autour de 'La naissance du Purgatoire.'" *Archives d'histoire doctrinale et littéraire du moyen âge* 50 (1983): 7–57.

———. *Saint Bonaventure, Sermons de Tempore: Reportations du manuscrit Milan, Ambrosienne A 11 sup.* Paris: Éditions Franciscaines, 1990.

Bourdillon, A. F. C. *The Order of Minoresses in England.* Manchester: University of Manchester Press, 1926.

Boureau, Alain. *Théologie, science et censure au XIIIe siècle: Le cas de Jean Peckham.* Paris: Les Belles Lettres, 1999.

Boureau, Alain, and Claudio Sergio Ingerflom, eds. *La royauté sacrée dans le monde chrétien.* Paris: Éditions de l'École des Hautes Études en Sciences Sociales, 1992.

Bourquelot, Felix. *Histoire de Provins.* Provins and Paris, 1839–40; reprint, Marseille: Lafitte Reprints, 1976.

Boutaric, Edgar. *Saint Louis et Alfonse de Poitiers: Étude sur la réunion des provinces du Midi et de l'ouest à la couronne.* Paris: Henri Plon, 1870.

Boyer, Jean-Paul. "La 'Foi monarchique': Royaume de Sicile et Provence (mi-XIIIe–mi-XIVe siècle)." In *Le forme della propaganda politica nel due e nel trecento*. Edited by Paolo Cammarosano. Rome: École Française de Rome, 1994: 85–110.

Branner, Robert. *St. Louis and the Court Style in Gothic Architecture*. London: Swemmer, 1965.

———. "Saint Louis et l'enluminure parisienne au XIIIe siècle." In *Septième centenaire de la mort de saint Louis: Actes des colloques de Royaumont et de Paris (21–27 mai 1970)*. Paris: Les Belles Lettres, 1976: 69–84.

———. *Manuscript Painting in Paris during the Reign of Saint Louis: A Study of Styles*. Berkeley: University of California Press, 1977.

Brentano, Robert. *Rome before Avignon: A Social History of Thirteenth-Century Rome*. New York: Basic Books, 1974.

Brett, Edward Tracey. *Humbert of Romans: His Life and Views of Thirteenth-Century Society*. Toronto: Pontifical Institute of Mediaeval Studies, 1984.

Brooke, Christopher N. L. *The Medieval Idea of Marriage*. Oxford: Oxford University Press, 1989.

Brown, Elizabeth A. R. *The Monarchy of Capetian France and Royal Ceremonial*. Aldershot: Variorum, 1991.

———. "The Religion of Royalty: From Saint Louis to Henry IV." In *Creating French Culture: Treasures from the Bibliothèque nationale de France*. Edited by Marie-Hélène Tesnière and Prosser Gifford. New Haven: Yale University Press, 1995: 131–48.

Brown, Jaqueline, and William P. Stoneman, eds. *A Distinct Voice: Medieval Studies in Honor of Leonard E. Boyle, O.P.* Notre Dame, IN: University of Notre Dame Press, 1997.

Brunel, Ghislain. "Un italien en France au XIIIe siècle: Galien de Pise, chanoine de Saint-Omer et fondateur du couvent des Cordelières de Lourcine à Paris, d'après son testament de 1287." In *Histoire d'archives: Recueil d'articles offert à Lucie Favier par ses collègues et amis*. Paris: Société des amis des Archives de France, 1997: 249–76.

Brunel-Lobrichon, Geneviève. "Diffusion et spiritualité des premières clarisses méridionales." In *La femme dans la vie religieuse du Languedoc (XIIIe–XIVe siècles)*. Toulouse: Privat, 1988: 261–80.

Buc, Philippe. "David's Adultery with Bathsheba and the Healing Power of the Capetian Kings." *Viator* 24 (1993): 101–20.

Bunt, Gerrit H. V. *Alexander the Great in the Literature of Medieval Britain*. Groningen: Forsten, 1994.

Burr, David. *The Spiritual Franciscans: From Protest to Persecution in the Century after Saint Francis*. University Park: Pennsylvania State University Press, 2001.

Bynum, Caroline Walker. *Jesus as Mother: Studies in the Spirituality of the High Middle Ages*. Berkeley: University of California Press, 1982.

———. *Holy Feast and Holy Fast: The Religious Significance of Food to Medieval Women*. Berkeley: University of California Press, 1987.

———. *Fragmentation and Redemption: Essays on Gender and the Human Body in Medieval Religion*. New York: Zone Books, 1992.

Callebaut, André. "Les provinciaux de France au XIIIe S." *AFH* 10 (1917): 289–356.

———. "L'année de la mort de Fr. Guillaume de Melitona." *AFH* 19 (1926): 431–34.

Carey, George. *The Medieval Alexander*. Cambridge: Cambridge University Press, 1956.

Carolus-Barré, Louis. "Saint Louis et la translation des corps saints." In *Études d'histoire du droit canonique dédiées à Gabriel Le Bras*, vol. 2. Paris: Sirey, 1965: 1087–1112.

———. "Le prince héritier Louis et l'intérim du pouvoir royal de la mort de Blanche de Castille (novembre 1252) au retour de saint Louis (juillet 1254)." In *Académie des inscriptions et belles-lettres: Comptes rendus des séances de l'année 1970*: 588–96.

———. "Les franciscains et le procès de canonisation de Saint Louis." *Les amis de saint François*, n. s. 11 (1971): 3–6.

———. "Le reliquaire de la sainte Épine d'Assise: Fra Mansueto et le traité de Paris, 1258–1259." *Bulletin de la Société nationale des antiquaires de France* (1989): 121–31.

———. *Le procès de canonisation de saint Louis (1272–1297): Essai de reconstitution*. Edited by Henri Platelle. Rome: École Française de Rome, 1994.

Champion, Honoré. *Notice historique sur l'abbaye de Longchamps* [*sic*]. Extrait de la *Revue Nobiliaire*. Paris, 1869.

Chase, Wayland Johnson. *The Ars Minor of Donatus*. Madison: University of Wisconsin Studies in the Social Sciences and History, 1926.

Chennaf, S., and O. Redon. "Les miracles de saint Louis." In *Les miracles, miroirs des corps*. Edited by Jacques Gélis, Odile Redon, and Michel Bouvier. Saint-Denis: Université de Paris VIII—Vincennes à Saint-Denis, 1983: 53–85.

Chiara di Assisi: Atti del XX Convegno internazionale (Assisi, 15–17 ottobre 1992). Spoleto: Centro Italiano di Studi sull'Alto Medioevo, 1993.

Clark, Willene B., and Meradith T. McMunn, eds. *Beasts and Birds of the Middle Ages: The Bestiary and Its Legacy*. Philadelphia: University of Pennsylvania Press, 1989.

Coakley, John. "Friars as Confidants of Holy Women in Medieval Dominican Hagiography." In *Images of Sainthood in Medieval Europe*. Edited by Renate Blumenfeld-Kosinski and Timea Szell. Ithaca: Cornell University Press, 1991: 222–46.

———. "Gender and the Authority of Friars: The Significance of Holy Women for Thirteenth-Century Franciscans and Dominicans." *Church History* 60 (1991): 445–60.

———. "Friars, Sanctity, and Gender: Mendicant Encounters with Saints, 1250–1325." In *Medieval Masculinities: Regarding Men in the Middle Ages*. Edited by Clare A. Lees with the assistance of Thelma Fenster and Jo Ann McNamara. Minneapolis: University of Minnesota Press, 1994.

———. "A Marriage and Its Observer: Christine of Stommeln, the Heavenly Bridegroom, and Friar Peter of Dacia." In *Gendered Voices: Medieval Saints and Their Interpreters*. Edited by Catherine M. Mooney. Philadelphia: University of Pennsylvania Press, 1999: 99–117.

Cocheris, Hippolyte. *Histoire de la ville et de tout le diocèse de Paris par l'abbé Lebeuf. Nouvelle édition annotée et continuée jusqu'à nos jours par Hippolyte Cocheris*. 4 vols. Paris: Durand, 1863–1870.

Cockerell, S. C. *A Psalter and Hours, executed before 1270 for a lady connected with St. Louis, probably his sister Isabelle of France*. London: Chiswick Press, 1905.

Conklin, George. "Ingeborg of Denmark, Queen of France, 1193–1223." In *Queens and Queenship in Medieval Europe*. Edited by Anne J. Duggan. Woodbridge: Boydell, 1997: 39–52.

Coquelle, Jacques. *Les cordelières en Picardie*. Amiens: Dalmanio, 1994.

Corbet, Patrick. *Les saints ottoniens: Sainteté dynastique, sainteté royale et sainteté féminine autour de l'an Mil*. Sigmaringen: J. Thorbecke, 1986.

Côté, Antoine. "William of Melitona on Divine Beatitude." *Franciscan Studies* 60 (2002): 17–38.

Dalarun, Jacques. *François d'Assise, un passage: Femmes et féminité dans les écrits et les légendes franciscaines*. Translated by Catherine Dalarun-Mitrovitsa. Arles: Actes Sud, 1997.

———. *François d'Assise ou le pouvoir en question: Principes et modalités du gouvernement dans l'ordre des Frères mineurs*. Paris and Brussels: De Boeck, 1999.

———. *Claire de Rimini: Entre sainteté et hérésie*. Paris: Peyot, 1999.

———. *The Misadventure of Francis of Assisi: Toward a Historical Use of the Franciscan Legends*. Translated by Edward Hagman. St. Bonaventure, NY: Franciscan Institute, 2002.

D'Alençon, Ubald. "L'abbaye royale de Longchamp et sa bibliothèque au XVe siècle." *Études franciscaines* 15 (1906): 206–12.

De Fontette, Micheline. *Les religieuses à l'âge classique du droit canon: Recherches sur les structures juridiques des branches féminines des ordres*. Paris: J. Vrin, 1967.

De la Selle, Xavier. *Le service des âmes à la cour: Confesseurs et aumôniers des rois de France du XIIIe au XVe siècle*. Paris: École des chartes, 1995.

Delisle, Léopold. *Le cabinet des manuscrits de la Bibliothèque Impériale*. Vol. 1. Paris: Imprimerie Impériale, 1868.

———. "Durand de Champagne." *Histoire littéraire de la France* 30 (1888): 302–33.

Delorme, Philippe. *Blanche de Castille: Épouse de Louis VIII, mère de saint Louis*. Paris: Pygmalion, 2002.

De Nantes, René. "Les origines de l'ordre de sainte Claire." *Études franciscaines* 2 (1912): 103–85.

De Paris, Agathange. "L'origine et la fondation des monastères de Clarisses en Aquitaine au XIIIe siècle." *Collectanea franciscana* 25 (1955): 5–52.

De Paris, Gratien. *Histoire de la fondation et de l'évolution de l'Ordre des Frères mineurs au XIIIe siècle*. New edition with updated bibliography by Mariano d'Altri and Servus Gieben. Rome: Istituto Storico dei Cappuccini, 1982.

De Serent, Antoine. "L'ordre de sainte Claire en France pendant sept siècles." *Études franciscaines* 11 (1953): 133–65.

Deuffic, Jean-Luc, ed. *La bibliothèque royale du Louvre*. Saint-Denis: Pecia, 2004.

Dimier, Anselme. *Saint Louis et Cîteaux*. Paris: Letouzey & Ané, 1954.

Doucet, Victorin. "Maîtres franciscains de Paris: Supplement au 'Répertoire des Maîtres en théologie de Paris au XIIIe siècle' de M. Le Chan. P. Glorieux." *AFH* 27 (1934): 531–64.

Douët d'Arcq, Louis. *Collection de sceaux*. Paris: Plon, 1868.

Douie, D. L. *The Conflict between the Seculars and the Mendicants at the University of Paris in the Thirteenth Century*. London: Blackfriars, 1954.

Duchesne, Gaston. *Histoire de l'abbaye royale de Longchamp (1255 à 1789)*. 2nd edition. Paris: Daragon, 1906.

Dufeil, Michel-Marie. *Guillaume de Saint-Amour et la polémique universitaire parisienne, 1250–1259*. Paris: Picard, 1972.

———. "Le roi dans la querelle des mendiants et des séculiers." In *Septième centenaire de la mort de saint Louis: Actes des colloques de Royaumont et de Paris (21–27 mai 1970)*. Paris: Les Belles Lettres, 1976: 280–89.

Duggan, Anne J., ed. *Queens and Queenship in Medieval Europe*. Woodbridge: Boydell, 1997.

Dunbabin, Jean. *Charles I of Anjou: Power, Kingship, and State-Making in Thirteenth-Century Europe*. London and New York: Longman, 1998.

Durrieu, Paul. *Les archives Angevines de Naples: Étude sur les registres du roi Charles Ier (1265–1285)*. 2 vols. Paris: Libraire des Écoles Françaises d'Athènes et de Rome, 1886–87.

Elliot, Dyan. *Proving Woman: Female Spirituality and Inquisitional Culture in the Later Middle Ages*. Princeton: Princeton University Press, 2004.

Erler, Mary C., and Maryanne Kowaleski, eds. *Women and Power in the Middle Ages*. Athens: University of Georgia Press, 1988.

———. *Gendering the Master Narrative: Women and Power in the Middle Ages*. Ithaca: Cornell University Press, 2003.

Evergates, Theodore, ed. *Aristocratic Women in Medieval France*. Philadelphia: University of Pennsylvania Press, 1999.

Farmer, Sharon. "Down and Out and Female in Thirteenth-Century Paris." *American Historical Review* 103 (1998): 345–72.

———. *Surviving Poverty in Medieval Paris: Gender, Ideology, and the Daily Lives of the Poor*. Ithaca: Cornell University Press, 2002.

Farmer, Sharon, and Barbara H. Rosenwein, eds. *Monks and Nuns, Saints and Outcasts: Religion in Medieval Society. Essays in Honor of Lester K. Little*. Ithaca: Cornell University Press, 2000.

Faure, Marcel, ed. *Reines et princesses au Moyen âge: Actes du cinquième Colloque international de Montpellier, Université Paul-Valéry, 24–27 novembre 1999*. Montpellier: Association CRISIMA, Université Paul-Valéry, 2001.

Fawtier, Robert. *The Capetian Kings of France: Monarchy and Nation (987–1328)*. Translated by Lionel Butler and R. J. Adam. London: MacMillan, 1960.

Field, Sean L. "Annihilation and Perfection in Two Sermons by Gilbert of Tournai for the Translation of St. Francis." *Franciscana* 1 (1999): 237–74.

———. "New Evidence for the Life of Isabelle of France." *Revue Mabillon* n. s. 13 (2002): 109–23.

———. "The Princess, the Abbess, and the Friars: Isabelle of France (1225–1270) and the Course of Thirteenth-Century Religious History." Ph.D. diss., Northwestern University, 2002.

———. "Gilbert of Tournai's Letter to Isabelle of France: An Edition of the Complete Text." *Mediaeval Studies* 65 (2003): 57–97.

———. "The Abbesses of Longchamp up to the Black Death." *AFH* 96 (2003): 87–93.

Folz, Robert. *Les saintes reines du moyen âge en Occident (VIe–XIIIe siècles)*. Brussels: Société des Bollandistes, 1992.

Fradenburg, Louise Olga, ed. *Women and Sovereignty*. Edinburgh: Edinburgh University Press, 1992.

Furitano, G. "Una santa donna del Duecento: Margherita Colonna." In *Fatti et figure del Lazio medievale*. Edited by Renato Lefevre. Rome: Gruppo Culturale di Rome e del Lazio, 1979: 387–96.

Gabriel, Astrik L. "The Conflict between the Chancellor and the University of Masters and Students at Paris during the Middle Ages." In *Die Auseinandersetzungen an der Pariser Universität im XIII. Jahrhundert*. Edited by Albert Zimmermann. Berlin: Walter de Gruyter, 1976: 106–54.

Gadrat, Christine. "La bibliothèque de saint Louis d'Anjou, évêque de Toulouse." *Revue Mabillion* n. s. 14 (2003): 179–202.

Gallia Christiana, in provincias ecclesiasticas distributa. 16 vols. Paris, 1715–1865.

Gameson, Richard. "The Gospels of Margaret of Scotland and the Literacy of an Eleventh-Century Queen." In *Women and the Book: Assessing the Visual Evidence*. Edited by Lesley Smith and Jane H. M. Taylor. London: The British Library, 1996: 149–71.

Gaposchkin, M. Cecilia. "The King of France and the Queen of Heaven: The Iconography of the Porte Rouge of Notre-Dame of Paris." *Gesta* 39 (2000): 58–72.

———. "The Sanctification and Memorialization of Louis IX of France, 1270–1350." Ph.D. diss., University of California, Berkeley, 2001.

———. "Boniface VIII, Philip the Fair, and the Sanctity of Louis IX." *Journal of Medieval History* 29 (2003): 1–26.

———. "*Ludovicus decus regnantium*: The Liturgical Office for Saint Louis and the Ideological Program of Philip the Fair." *Majestas* 10 (2003): 27–89.

———. "Philip the Fair, the Dominicans, and the Liturgical Office for Louis IX: New Perspectives on *Ludovicus Decus Regnantium*." *Plainsong and Medieval Music* 13 (2004): 33–61.

Geiger, Cécile. *Deux bibliothèques d'abbayes féminines dans la seconde moitié du XVème siècle*. Mémoire de maîtrise, Université de Paris IV, 1981.

Gennaro, C. "Il Francescanesimo femminile nel XIII secolo." *Rivista di storia e letteratura religiosa* 25 (1989): 281–84.

Glorieux, P. "Essai sur la chronologie de saint Bonaventure (1257–1274)." *AFH* 19 (1926): 145–68.

———. *Répertoire des maîtres en théologie de Paris au XIIIe siècle*. 2 vols. Paris: J. Vrin, 1933.

———. "Maîtres franciscains régents à Paris: Mis au point." *Recherches de Théologie ancienne et médiévale* 18 (1951): 324–32.

Godet-Calogeras, Jean François, and Roberta McKelvie, eds. *An Unencumbered Heart: A Tribute to Clare of Assisi, 1253–2003*. St. Bonaventure, NY: Franciscan Institute Publications, 2004.

Gonzaga, Francesco. *De origine seraphicae religionis franciscanae*. Rome, 1587.

Grundmann, Herbert. *Religious Movements in the Middle Ages: The Historical Links between Heresy, the Mendicant Orders, and the Women's Religious Movement in the Twelfth and Thirteenth Century, with the Historical Foundations of German Mysticism*. Translated by Steven Rowan. Introduction by Robert E. Lerner. Notre Dame, IN: University of Notre Dame Press, 1995.

Grzebien, Thomas Walter, III. "Penance, Purgatory, Mysticism, and Miracles: The Life, Hagiography, and Spirituality of Thomas of Cantimpré (1200–1270)." Ph.D. diss., University of Notre Dame, 1989.

Hallam, Elizabeth M. "Aspects of the Monastic Patronage of the English and French Royal Houses, c. 1130–1270." Ph.D. diss., University of London, 1976.

———. "Philip the Fair and the Cult of Saint Louis." In *Religion and National Identity*. Edited by Stuart Mews. Oxford: Basil Blackwell, 1982: 201–14.

Hallam, Elizabeth M., and Judith Everard. *Capetian France, 987–1328*. 2nd edition. New York: Longman, 2001.

Hamburger, Jeffrey F. "Vision and the Veronica." In *The Visual and the Visionary: Art and Female Spirituality in Late Medieval Germany*. New York: Zone Books, 1998: 317–82.

Hamilton, Tracy Chapman. "Queenship and Kinship in the French *Bible Moralisée*: The Example of Blanche of Castile and Vienna ÖNB 2554." In *Capetian Women*. Edited by Kathleen D. Nolan. New York: Palgrave, 2003: 177–208.

Hassig, Debra. *Medieval Bestiaries: Text, Image, Ideology*. Cambridge: Cambridge University Press, 1995.

———. *The Mark of the Beast: The Medieval Bestiary in Art, Life, and Literature*. New York and London: Garland, 1999.

Hefele, C. J. *Histoire des conciles d'après les documents originaux*, vol. 5 part 2. Trans. H. Leclercq. Paris: Letouzey et Ané, 1913.

Henquinet, François-Marie. "Eudes de Rosny, O.F.M., Eudes Rigaud et la somme d'Alexandre de Hales." *AFH* 23 (1940): 3–54.

Herlihy, David. *Medieval Households*. Cambridge, MA: Harvard University Press, 1985.

Heysse, Albanus. "De die obitus Fr. Gilberti Tornacensis." *AFH* 26 (1933): 557–58.

Hicks, Michael. "The English Minoresses and Their Early Benefactors." In *Monastic Studies: The Continuity of Tradition*. Edited by Judith Loades. Bangor, Wales: Headstart History, 1990: 158–70.

Hoch, Adrian S. "*Beata Stirps*, Royal Patronage, and the Identification of the Sainted Rulers in the St. Elizabeth Chapel at Assisi." *Art History* 15 (1992): 279–95.

Hollywood, Amy. *The Soul as Virgin Wife: Mechthild of Magdeburg, Marguerite Porete, and Meister Eckhart*. Notre Dame, IN: University of Notre Dame Press, 1995.

Holtz, Louis. *Donat et la tradition de l'enseignement grammatical: Étude et édition critique*. Paris: Centre National de la Recherche Scientifique, 1981.

Hornaday, Aline G. "A Capetian Queen as Street Demonstrator: Isabelle of Hainault." In *Capetian Women*. Edited by Kathleen D. Nolan. New York: Palgrave, 2003: 77–97.

Howell, Margaret. *Eleanor of Provence: Queenship in Thirteenth-Century England*. Oxford: Blackwell, 1998.

Hudson, Elizabeth S. "The Psalter of Blanche of Castile: Picturing Queenly Power in Thirteenth-Century France." Ph.D. diss., University of North Carolina at Chapel Hill, 2002.

Hughes, Andrew. *Medieval Manuscripts for Mass and Office: A Guide to Their Organization and Terminology*. Toronto: University of Toronto Press, 1982.

Jenkinson, Hilary. "Mary de Sancto Paulo, Foundress of Pembroke College, Cambridge." *Archaeologia* 66 (1914–15): 401–46.

Jones, Chris. ". . . *mais tot por le servise Deu*? Philippe III le Hardi, Charles d'Anjou, and the 1273/74 Imperial Candidature." *Viator* 34 (2003): 208–28.

Jordan, E. *Les origines de la domination Angevine en Italie*. 2 vols. Paris, 1909. Reprint, New York: Burt Franklin, 1960.

———. "Les promotions de cardinaux sous Urbain IV." *Revue d'histoire et de littérature religieuses* 5 (1900): 322–34.

Jordan, William Chester. *Louis IX and the Challenge of the Crusade: A Study in Rulership.* Princeton: Princeton University Press, 1979.

———. "The Case of Saint Louis." *Viator* 19 (1988): 209–17.

———. "Isabelle d'Angoulême, By the Grace of God Queen." *Revue belge de philologie et d'histoire* 69 (1991): 821–52.

———. "Saint Louis in French Epic and Drama." *Studies in Medievalism* 8 (1996): 174–94.

———. *Ideology and Royal Power in Medieval France: Kingship, Crusades, and the Jews.* Aldershot: Variorum, 2001.

———. "Isabelle of France and Religious Devotion at the Court of Louis IX." In *Capetian Women.* Edited by Kathleen D. Nolan. New York: Palgrave, 2003: 209–23.

———. "Honoring Saint Louis in a Small Town." *Journal of Medieval History* 30 (2004): 263–77

Kaepelli, T. *Scriptores Ordinis Praedicatorum medii aevi,* vol. 4. Rome: Istituto Storico Domenicano, 1993.

Kantorowicz, Ernst. *Frederick the Second.* Translated by E. O. Lorimer. London: Constable, 1931.

———. "Petrus de Vinea in England." In *Selected Studies by Ernst H. Kantorowicz.* Locust Valley, NY: Augustin, 1965: 213–46.

Kay, Richard. "Martin IV and the Fugitive Bishop of Bayeux." *Speculum* 40 (1965): 460–83.

Kelly, J. N. D. *The Oxford Dictionary of Popes.* Oxford: Oxford University Press, 1986.

Kelly, Samantha. *The New Solomon: Robert of Naples (1309–1343) and Fourteenth-Century Kingship.* Leiden and Boston: Brill, 2003.

Kinder, Terryl N. "Blanche of Castile and the Cistercians: An Architectural Reevaluation of Maubuisson Abbey." *Cîteaux: Commentarii cistercienses* 27 (1976): 161–88.

Klaniczay, Gábor. *The Uses of Supernatural Power: The Transformation of Popular Religion in Medieval and Early Modern Europe.* Translated by Susan Singerman. Edited by Karen Margolis. Cambridge: Polity Press, 1990.

———. "The Cinderella Effect: Late Medieval Female Sainthood in Central Europe and in Italy." *East Central Europe* 20–23 (1993–1996): 51–68.

———. *Holy Rulers and Blessed Princesses: Dynastic Cults in Medieval Central Europe.* Translated by Éva Pálmai. Cambridge: Cambridge University Press, 2002.

Klapisch-Zuber, Christiane, ed. *A History of Women in the West,* vol. 2: *Silences of the Middle Ages.* Cambridge, MA: Harvard University Press, 1992.

Kleinberg, Aviad M. *Prophets in Their Own Country: Living Saints and the Making of Sainthood in the Later Middle Ages.* Chicago: University of Chicago Press, 1992.

Knoble, Adam. "Saint Louis and French Political Culture." *Studies in Medievalism* 8 (1996): 156–73.

Knox, Lezlie S. *"The True Daughters of Francis and Clare*: The Formation of the Order of Saint Clare in Late Medieval Italy." Ph.D. diss., University of Notre Dame, 1999.

———. "Audacious Nuns: Institutionalizing the Franciscan Order of Saint Claire." *Church History* 69 (2000): 41–62.

———. "Clare of Assisi: Foundress of an Order?" In *An Unencumbered Heart: A Tribute to Clare of Assisi, 1253–2003*. Edited by Jean François Godet-Calogeras and Roberta McKelvie. St. Bonaventure, NY: Franciscan Institute Publications, 2004: 11–29.

Lawrence, C. H. *St. Edmund of Abingdon: A Study in Hagiography and History*. Oxford: Clarendon Press, 1960.

Lazzeri, Zeffirino. "La 'Forma vitae' di S. Chiara e le regole sue e del suo ordine." In *Santa Chiara d'Assisi: Studi e cronica del VII centenario (1253–1953)*. Assisi: Comitato Centrale per il VII Centenario Morte S. Chiara, 1953: 79–121.

Lecoq, Marcel. *Les cordelières de Lourcine au faubourg Saint-Marcel-lez-Paris*. Paris: Éditions Municipales, 1969.

Le Goff, Jacques. "Le dossier de sainteté de Philippe Augustus." *L'Histoire* 100 (1987): 22–29.

——— "Aspects religieux et sacrés de la monarchie française du Xe au XIIIe siècle." In *La royauté sacrée dans le monde chrétien*. Edited by Alain Boureau and Claudio Sergio Ingerflom. Paris: Éditions de l'École des Hautes Études en Sciences Sociales, 1992: 19–28.

———. *Saint Louis*. Paris: Gallimard, 1996.

Le Goff, Jacques, et al., eds. *Le sacre royal à l'époque de saint Louis, d'après le manuscrit latin 1246 de la BNF*. Paris: Gallimard, 2001.

Lehmijoki-Gardner, Maiju. "Writing Religious Rules as an Interactive Process: Dominican Penitent Women and the Making of Their Regula." *Speculum* 79 (2004): 660–87.

Leroux-Cesbron, C. "L'abbaye de Longchamp." *Bulletin de la commission municipale historique et artistique de Neuilly-sur-Seine* 7 (1909): 42–48.

Lett, Didier. *L'enfant des miracles: Enfance et société au Moyen Âge (XIIe–XIIIe siècle)*. Paris: Aubier, 1997.

Levillain, Philippe, ed. *The Papacy: An Encyclopedia*. New York and London: Routledge, 2002.

Lewis, Andrew W. *Royal Succession in Capetian France: Studies on Familial Order and the State*. Cambridge, MA: Harvard University Press, 1981.

Lewis, Gertrud Jaron. *By Women, For Women, About Women: The Sister-Books of Fourteenth-Century Germany*. Toronto: Pontifical Institute of Mediaeval Studies, 1996.

Linehan, Peter. *The Ladies of Zamora*. Manchester: Manchester University Press, 1997.

Little, A. G. *Initia operum latinorum quae saeculis xiii. xiv. xv. attribuuntur*. Manchester, 1904.

Little, Lester K. "Saint Louis's Involvement with the Friars." *Church History* 33 (1964): 125–48.

Lombard-Jourdan, Anne. *Fleur de lis et oriflamme: Signes célestes du royaume de France*. Paris: Presses du CNRS, 1991.

LoPrete, Kimberly A. "Historical Ironies in the Study of Capetian Women." In *Capetian Women*. Edited by Kathleen D. Nolan. New York: Palgrave, 2003: 271–86.

Lusse, Jackie. "Les religieuses en Champagne jusqu'au XIIIe siècle." In *Les religieuses en France au XIIIe siècle*. Edited by Michel Parisse. Nancy: Presses Universitaires de Nancy, 1985: 11–26.

Lynn, Beth. "Clare of Assisi and Isabelle of Longchamp: Further Light on the Early Development of the Franciscan Charism." *Magistra* 3 (1997): 71–98.

Maddicott, J. R. *Simon de Montfort*. Cambridge: Cambridge University Press, 1994.

Maddox, Donald, and Sara Sturm-Maddox, eds. *The Medieval French Alexander*. Albany: State University of New York Press, 2002.

Maier, Christopher T. "*Civilis ac pia regis Francorum deceptio: Louis IX as* Crusade Preacher." In *Dei gesta per Francos: Études sur les croisades dédiées à Jean Richard*. Edited by Michael Balard, Benjamin Z. Kedar, and Jonathan Riley-Smith. Burlington, VT: Ashgate, 2001: 57–63.

Makowski, Elizabeth. *Canon Law and Cloistered Women: Periculoso and Its Commentators, 1298–1545*. Washington, DC: Catholic University of America Press, 1997.

———. *"A Pernicious Sort of Woman": Quasi-Religious Women and Canon Lawyers in the Later Middle Ages*. Washington, DC: Catholic University of America Press, 2005.

Maleczek, Werner. "Das *Privilegium Paupertatis Innocenz III.* und das Testament der Klara von Assisi: Überlegungen zur Frage ihrer Eichtheit." *Collectanea franciscana* 65 (1995): 5–82. Translated by Cyprian Rosen and Dawn Nothwehr as "Questions about the Authenticity of the Privilege of Poverty of Innocent III and of the Testament of Clare of Assisi." *Greyfriars Review* 12, Supplement (1998): 1–80.

Manselli, Raoul. "Santità principesca et vita quotidiana in Elisabetta d'Ungheria: La testimonianza della ancelle." *Analecta tertii ordinis regularis sancti Francisci* 139 (1985): 23–45. Translated by Edward Hagman as "Royal Holiness in the Daily Life of Elizabeth of Hungary: The Testimony of Her Servants." *Greyfriars Review* 11 (1997): 1–20.

Mapelli, Francesca Joyce. *L'amministrazione francescana di Inghilterra e Francia: Personale di governo e strutture dell'Ordine fino al Concilio di Vienne (1311)*. Rome: Antonianum, 2003

Marini, Alfonso, with the collaboration of Paola Ungarelli. *Agnese di Boemia*. Rome: Istituto Storico dei Cappuccini, 1991.

Massé, L.-F. *Vie de saint Edme*. Auxerre: Gallot, 1858.

Mayer, Hans Eberhard. *The Crusades*. 2nd edition. Translated by John Gillingham. Oxford: Oxford University Press, 1988.

McCannon, Afrodesia E. "Two Capetian Queens as the Foreground for an Aristocrat's Anxiety in the *Vie de saint Louis*." In *Capetian Women*. Edited by Kathleen D. Nolan. New York: Palgrave, 2003: 163–76.

McCash, June, ed. *The Cultural Patronage of Medieval Women*. Athens: University of Georgia Press, 1996.

McCulloch, Florence. *Medieval Latin and French Bestiaries*. Chapel Hill: University of North Carolina Press, 1960.

McNamara, Jo Ann Kay. *Sisters in Arms: Catholic Nuns through Two Millennia*. Cambridge, MA: Harvard University Press, 1996.

———. "Women and Power Through the Family Revisited." In *Gendering the Master Narrative: Women and Power in the Middle Ages*. Edited by Mary C. Erler and Maryanne Kowaleski. Ithaca: Cornell University Press, 2003: 17–30.

Meister, L. "Quelques chartes inédites relatives à l'acquisition du Moncel par Philippe le Bel (1309–1310)." *Mémoire de la Société académique de l'Oise* 17 (1900): 593–611.

Merrilees, Brian. "Teaching Latin in French: Adaptations of Donatus' *Ars minor*." *Fifteenth-Century Studies* 12 (1986): 87–98.

———. "*L'Art Mineur* français et le curriculum grammatical." *Histoire, Épistémologie, Langage* 12 (1990): 15–29.

Mews, Constant J., ed. *Listen, Daughter: The Speculum Virginum and the Formation of Religious Women in the Middle Ages*. New York: Palgrave, 2001.

Minois, Georges. *Le confesseur du roi: Les directeurs de conscience sous la monarchie française*. Paris: Fayard, 1988.

Mitchell, Linda E. *Portraits of Medieval Women*. New York: Palgrave, 2003.

Mlynarczyk, Gertrud. *Ein Franziskanerinnenkloster im 15. Jahrhundert: Edition und Analyse von Besitzinventaren aus der Abtei Longchamp*. Bonn: Röhrscheid, 1987.

Mooney, Catherine M., ed. *Gendered Voices: Medieval Saints and Their Interpreters*. Philadelphia: University of Pennsylvania Press, 1999.

Moorman, John. *A History of the Franciscan Order from Its Origins to the Year 1517*. Oxford: Clarendon Press, 1968.

Movimento religioso femminile e francescanesimo nel secolo XIII: Atti del VII Convegno internazionale (Assisi, 11–13 ottobre 1979). Assisi: Società Internazionale di Studi Francescani, 1980.

Mueller, Joan. "Agnes of Prague and the Juridical Implications of the Privilege of Poverty." *Franciscan Studies* 58 (2000): 261–87.

Mulder-Bakker, Anneke B., ed. *Seeing and Knowing: Women and Learning in Medieval Europe, 1200–1550*. Turnhout: Brepols, 2004.

Muratova, Xenia. "Bestiaries: An Aspect of Medieval Patronage." In *Art and Patronage in the English Romanesque*. Edited by Sarah Macready and F. H. Thompson. London: The Society of Antiquaries, 1986: 118–44.

Musto, Ronald G. "Queen Sancia of Naples (1286–1345) and the Spiritual Franciscans." In *Women of the Medieval World: Essays in Honor of John H. Mundy*. Edited by Julius Kirshner and Suzanne F. Wemple. Oxford: Blackwell, 1985: 179–214.

Nagy, Piroska. *Le don des larmes au moyen âge: Un instrument spirituel en quête d'institution, Ve–XIIIe siècle*. Paris: Albin Michel, 2000.

Nemec, Jaroslav. *Agnese di Boemia: La vita, il culto, la "Legenda."* Padua: Edizioni Messaggero, 1987.

Newman, Barbara. *From Virile Woman to WomanChrist: Studies in Medieval Religion and Literature*. Philadelphia: University of Pennsylvania Press, 1995.

Nichols, David. *Medieval Flanders*. London and New York: Longman, 1992.

Nichols, Karen S. "Countesses as Rulers in Flanders." In *Aristocratic Women in Medieval France*. Edited by Theodore Evergates. Philadelphia: University of Pennsylvania Press, 1999: 111–37.

Nolan, Kathleen D., ed. *Capetian Women*. New York: Palgrave, 2003.

Oakley, Francis. *The Western Church in the Later Middle Ages*. Ithaca: Cornell University Press, 1979.

Oliger, L. "De origine regularum Ordinis S. Clarae." *AFH* 5 (1912): 181–209, 413–47.

———. "Descriptio codicis S. Antonii de Urbe unacum appendice textuum de S. Francisco." *AFH* 12 (1919): 321–401.

Omaechevarria, Ignacio. "Regla y las reglas de la Orden de Santa Clara." *Collectanea franciscana* 46 (1976): 93–119.

Opitz, Claudia. "Life in the Late Middle Ages." In *A History of Women in the West*, vol. 2: *Silences of the Middle Ages*. Edited by Christiane Klapisch-Zuber. Cambridge, MA: Harvard University Press, 1992.

Paravicini Bagliani, Agostino. *Cardinali di Curia e "Familiae" Cardinalizie dal 1227 al 1254*. 2 vols. Padua: Antenore, 1972.

Parisse, Michel, ed. *Les religieuses en France au XIIIe siècle*. Nancy: Presses Universitaires de Nancy, 1985.

Parker, David. "Three Models of Self-Government: Medieval English Translations of Latin Rules for Nuns." *Magistra* 7 (2001): 100–125.

Parsons, John Carmi, ed. *Medieval Queenship*. New York: St. Martin's Press, 1993.

Parsons, John Carmi, and Bonnie Wheeler, eds. *Medieval Mothering*. New York: Garland Publishing, 1996.

Pascal, César. "L'hostel royal de Longchamp." *Bulletin de la Société de l'histoire de Paris* 31 (1904): 71–78.

Paul, Jacques. "Louis d'Anjou, un évangélisme dynastique?" In *Évangile et évangélisme (XIIe–XIIIe siècle): Cahiers de Fanjeaux*, vol. 34. Toulouse: Éditions Privat, 1999: 141–70.

Paulus, Nikolaus. *Geschichte des Ablasses im Mittelalter, vom Ursprung bis zur Mitte des 14. Jahrhunderts.* 2 vols. Paderborn: Schöningh, 1923.

Pellegrini, Luigi. *Alessandro IV e i francescani (1254–1261).* Rome: Edizioni Francescane, 1966.

———. "Female Religious Experience and Society in Thirteenth-Century Italy." In *Monks and Nuns, Saints and Outcasts: Religion in Medieval Society. Essays in Honor of Lester K. Little.* Edited by Sharon Farmer and Barbara H. Rosenwein. Ithaca: Cornell University Press, 2000: 97–122.

Pereira, Mya, et al. "Un espace monastique royal: L'abbaye du Moncel (Pontpoint, Oise)." *Archéologie médiévale* 19 (1989): 131–72.

Pergamo, B. "De quaestionibus ineditis Fr. Odonis Rigaldi, Fr. Gulielmi de Melitona et Codicis Vat. Lat. 782." *AFH* 19 (1936): 3–54.

Pernoud, Régine. *La reine Blanche.* Paris: Éditions Albin Michel, 1972. Translated by Henry Noel as *Blanche of Castile.* London: Collins, 1975.

Pieper, Lori. "St. Elizabeth of Hungary and the Franciscan Tradition." Ph.D. diss., Fordham University, 2002.

Pinder, Janice M. "The Cloister and the Garden: Gendered Images of Religious Life from the Twelfth and Thirteenth Centuries." In *Listen, Daughter: The Speculum Virginum and the Formation of Religious Women in the Middle Ages.* Edited by Constant J. Mews. New York: Palgrave, 2001: 159–79.

Pisanu, Leonardo. *Innocenzo IV e i francescani (1243–1254).* Rome: Edizioni Francescane, 1968.

Pitha, Petr. "Agnes of Prague: A New Bohemian Saint." *Franziskanische Studien* 72 (1990): 325–40.

Poulenc, Jérôme. "Une histoire du Grand Couvent des Cordeliers de Paris des origines à nos jours." *AFH* 49 (1976): 474–95.

Pryds, Darleen N. *The King Embodies the Word: Robert d'Anjou and the Politics of Preaching.* Leiden: Brill, 2000.

———. "Clarisses, Franciscans, and the House of Anjou: Temporal and Spiritual Partnership in Early Fourteenth-Century Naples." In *Clare of Assisi: A Medieval and Modern Woman. Clarefest, Selected Papers.* Edited by Ingrid Peterson. St. Bonaventure, NY: Franciscan Institute, 1996: 99–114.

Quinn, John F. "Chronology of St. Bonaventure (1217–1257)." *Franciscan Studies* 32 (1972): 168–86.

———. "Chronology of St. Bonaventure's Sermons." *AFH* 67 (1974): 145–84.

Ranft, Patricia. "An Overturned Victory: Clare of Assisi and the Thirteenth-Century Church." *Journal of Medieval History* 17 (1991): 123–34.

Rhein, André. *La seigneurie de Montfort en Iveline, depuis son origine jusqu'à son union au duché de Bretagne (Xe–XIVe siècles).* Versailles, 1910.

Riant, Paul le Comte. *Des dépouilles religieuses enlevées à Constantinople au XIIIe siècle, et des documents historiques nés de leur transport en Occident.* Mémoires de la Société nationale des antiquaires de France, 4th series, vol. 4. Paris: Dumoulin, 1875.

———. "Déposition de Charles d'Anjou pour la canonisation de saint Louis." In *Notices et documents publiés par la Société de l'histoire de France à l'occasion du cinquantième anniversaire de sa fondation.* Paris, 1884.

Richard, Jean. *Saint Louis.* Edited by Simon Lloyd. Translated by Jean Birrell. Cambridge: Cambridge University Press, 1992.

Roest, Bert. *Franciscan Literature of Religious Instruction before the Council of Trent.* Leiden and Boston: Brill, 2004.

Röhrkasten, Jens. "The Origin and Early Development of the London Mendicant Houses." In *The Church in the Medieval Town.* Edited by T. R. Slater and Gervase Rosser. Aldershot: Ashgate, 1998: 76–99.

———. *The Mendicant Houses of Medieval London, 1221–1539.* Münster: Lit, 2004.

Rosenthal, Joel T., ed. *Medieval Women and the Sources of Medieval History.* Athens: University of Georgia Press, 1990.

Ross, David J. A. *Alexander Historiatus: A Guide to Medieval Illustrated Alexander Literature.* Frankfurt am Main: Athenäum, 1988.

Rouse, Richard H., and Mary A. *Manuscripts and Their Makers: Commercial Book Producers in Medieval Paris, 1200–1500.* Turnhout: Harvey Miller, 2000.

Rousseau, Constance M., and Joel T. Rosenthal, eds. *Women, Marriage, and Family in Medieval Christendom: Essays in Memory of Michael M. Sheehan, C.S.B.* Kalamazoo: Medieval Institute Publications, 1998.

Runciman, Steven. *The Sicilian Vespers.* Cambridge: Cambridge University Press, 1958.

Rusconi, Roberto. "L'espansione del francescanesimo femminile nel secolo XIII." In *Movimento religioso femminile e francescanesimo nel secolo XIII: Atti del VII Convegno internazionale (Assisi, 11–13 ottobre 1979).* Assisi: Società Internazionale di Studi Francescani, 1980: 263–313. Translated by Edward Hagman as "The Spread of Women's Franciscanism in the Thirteenth Century." *Greyfriars Review* 12 (1998): 35–73.

S. Bonaventura, 1274–1974. 2 vols. Grottaferrata: Collegium S. Bonaventurae, 1973.

Sainte Claire d'Assise et sa postérité: Actes du Colloque de l'U.N.E.S.C.O. 29 septembre–1er octobre 1994. Paris: Éditions Franciscaines, 1995.

Saint Louis: Exposition organisée par la direction générale des Archives de France. Paris, 1960.

Salmon, Pierre. *L'office divin au moyen âge: Histoire de la formation du bréviaire du IXe au XVIe siècle.* Paris: Éditions du Cerf, 1967.

Samaritani, Antonio. "La Quaestio de sanctificatione B. Virginis di Guglielmo di Melitona." *Marianum* 30 (1968): 161–80.

Schowalter, Kathleen S. "The Ingeborg Psalter: Queenship, Legitimacy, and the Appropriation of Byzantine Art in the West." In *Capetian Women*. Edited by Kathleen D. Nolan. New York: Palgrave, 2003: 99–135.

———. "Capetian Women and Their Books: Art, Ideology, and Dynastic Continuity in Medieval France." Ph.D. diss., Johns Hopkins University, 2005.

Schuchmann, Anne M. "Literary Collaboration in the Life of Umiliana dei Cerchi." *Magistra* 7 (2001): 5–22.

Septième centenaire de la mort de saint Louis: Actes des colloques de Royaumont et de Paris (21–27 mai 1970). Paris: Les Belles Lettres, 1976.

Shadis, Miriam Theresa. *Motherhood, Lineage, and Royal Power in Medieval Castile and France: Berenguela de León and Blanche de Castille*. Ph.D. diss., Duke University, 1994.

———. "Piety, Politics, and Power: The Patronage of Leonor of England and Her Daughters Berenguela of León and Blanche of Castile." In *The Cultural Patronage of Medieval Women*. Edited by June McCash. Athens: University of Georgia Press, 1996: 202–27.

———. "Berenguela of Castile's Political Motherhood: The Management of Sexuality, Marriage, and Succession." In *Medieval Mothering*. Edited by John Carmi Parsons and Bonnie Wheeler. New York: Garland Publishing, 1996: 335–58.

———. "Blanche of Castile and Facinger's 'Medieval Queenship': Reassessing the Argument." In *Capetian Women*. Edited by Kathleen D. Nolan. New York: Palgrave, 2003: 137–61.

Shadis, Miriam, and Constance Hoffman Berman. "A Taste of the Feast: Reconsidering Eleanor of Aquitaine's Female Descendants." In *Eleanor of Aquitaine: Lord and Lady*. Edited by Bonnie Wheeler and John Carmi Parsons. New York: Palgrave, 2003: 177–211.

Sheingorn, Pamela. "The Wise Mother: The Image of St. Anne Teaching the Virgin Mary." In *Gendering the Master Narrative: Women and Power in the Middle Ages*. Edited by Mary C. Erler and Maryanne Kowaleski. Ithaca: Cornell University Press, 2003: 105–34.

Sibilia, Salvatore. *Alessandro IV (1254–1261)*. Anagni: Cassa rurale ed artigiana di Anagni, 1961.

Simons, Walter. *Cities of Ladies: Beguine Communities in the Medieval Low Countries, 1200–1565*. Philadelphia: University of Pennsylvania Press, 2001.

Sivéry, Gérard. *Marguerite de Provence: Une reine au temps des cathédrales*. Paris: Fayard, 1987.

———. *Blanche de Castille*. Paris: Fayard, 1990.

Smalley, Beryl. "William of Middleton and Guibert of Nogent." *Recherches de théologie ancienne et médiévale* 16 (1949): 281–91.

Smith, Lesley, and Jane H. M. Taylor, eds. *Women and the Book: Assessing the Visual Evidence*. London: The British Library, 1996.

Southern, R. W. *The Making of the Middle Ages*. New Haven: Yale University Press, 1953.

Spiegel, Gabrielle M. *The Chronicle Tradition of Saint-Denis: A Survey*. Brookline, MA, and Leyden: Classical Folia Editions, 1978.

Stafford, Pauline. "Emma: The Powers of the Queen in the Eleventh Century." In *Queens and Queenship in Medieval Europe*. Edited by Anne J. Duggan. Woodbridge: Boydell, 1997: 3–26.

Stanton, Anne Rudloff. "Isabelle of France and Her Manuscripts, 1308–1358." In *Capetian Women*. Edited by Kathleen D. Nolan. New York: Palgrave, 2003: 225–52.

Stirnemann, Patricia. "Les bibliothèques princières et privées aux XIIe et XIIIe siècles." In *Histoire des bibliothèques françaises: Les bibliothèques médiévales du VIe siècle à 1530*. Edited by André Vernet. Paris: Promodis, 1989: 173–92.

Strayer, Joseph R. "France: The Holy Land, the Chosen People, and the Most Christian King." In *Action and Conviction in Early Modern Europe: Essays in Memory of E. H. Harbison*. Edited by Theodore K. Rabb and Jerrold E. Seigel. Princeton: Princeton University Press, 1969: 3–16.

———. *Medieval Statecraft and the Perspectives of History*. Princeton: Princeton University Press, 1971.

Sweetman, Robert. "Dominican Preaching in the Southern Low Countries, 1240–1260: *Materiae Praedicabiles* in the *Liber de natura rerum* and *Bonum universale de apibus* of Thomas of Cantimpré." Ph.D. diss., University of Toronto, 1988.

———. "Visions of Purgatory and Their Role in the *Bonum universale de apibus* of Thomas of Cantimpré." *Ons geestelijk erf* 67 (1993): 20–33.

———. "Thomas of Cantimpré, *Mulieres Religiosae*, and Purgatorial Piety: Hagiographical Vitae and the Beguine 'Voice.'" In *A Distinct Voice: Medieval Studies in Honor of Leonard E. Boyle, O.P.* Edited by Jacqueline Brown and William P. Stoneman. Notre Dame, IN: University of Notre Dame Press, 1997: 606–28.

———. "Thomas of Cantimpré: Performative Reading and Pastoral Care." In *Performance and Transformation: New Approaches to Late Medieval Spirituality*. Edited by Mary A. Suydam and Joanna E. Ziegler. New York: St. Martin's Press, 1999: 133–67.

Tenckhoff, Franz. *Papst Alexander IV*. Paderborn: Schönigh, 1907.

Tesnière, Marie–Hélène, and Prosser Gifford, eds. *Creating French Culture: Treasures from the Bibliothèque nationale de France*. New Haven: Yale University Press, 1995.

Théobald (de Courtomer). "Les cordelières de Saint-Marcel-lez-Paris." *Études franciscaines* 20 (1908): 561–621.

Thompson, Williell R. "Checklist of Papal Letters Relating to the Three Orders of St. Francis-Innocent III-Alexander IV." *AFH* 64 (1971): 367–580.

———. "The Earliest Cardinal-Protectors of the Franciscan Order: A Study in Administrative History, 1210–1261." *Studies in Medieval and Renaissance History* 9 (1972): 21–80.

Timelli, Maria Colombo. *Traductions françaises de l'* Ars Minor *de Donat au Moyen Âge.* Florence: La Nuova Italia, 1996.

Van Asseldonk, Optatus. " 'Sorores minores,' una nuova impostazione del problema." *Collectanea franciscana* 62 (1992): 595–634.

———. "Sorores minores e Chiara d'Assisi a San Damiano, una scelta tra clausura e lebbrosi?" *Collectanea franciscana* 63 (1993): 399–421.

Van Cleve, T. C. *The Emperor Frederick II of Hohenstaufen: Immutator Mundi.* Oxford: Clarendon Press, 1972.

Vauchez, André. *"Beata Stirps*: Sainteté et lignage en Occident aux XIIIe et XIVe siècles." In *Famille et parenté dans l'Occident médiéval.* Edited by Georges Duby and Jacques Le Goff. Rome: École Française de Rome, 1977.

———. *The Laity in the Middle Ages: Religious Beliefs and Devotional Practices.* Edited and introduced by Daniel E. Bornstein, translated by Margery J. Schneider. Notre Dame, IN: University of Notre Dame Press, 1993.

———. *La spiritualité du Moyen Âge occidental, VIIIe–XIIIe siècle.* Nouvelle édition augmentée. Paris: Éditions de Seuil, 1994.

———. *Sainthood in the Later Middle Ages.* Translated by Jean Birrell. Cambridge: Cambridge University Press, 1997.

Vernet, André, ed. *Histoire des bibliothèques françaises: Les bibliothèques médiévales du VIe siècle à 1530.* Paris: Promodis, 1989.

Vincent, Nicholas. "Isabella of Angoulême: John's Jezebel." In *King John: New Interpretations.* Edited by S. D. Church. Woodbridge: Boydell, 1999: 165–219.

Warren, Nancy Bradley. *Spiritual Economies: Female Monasticism in Later Medieval England.* Philadelphia: University of Pennsylvania Press, 2001.

Wauer, Edmund. *Entstehung und Ausbreitung des Klarissenordens.* Leipzig: J. C. Hinrichs'sche, 1906.

Weinstein, Donald, and Rudolph M. Bell. *Saints and Society: The Two Worlds of Western Christendom, 1000–1700.* Chicago: University of Chicago Press, 1982.

Weiss, Daniel H. *Art and Crusade in the Age of Saint Louis.* Cambridge: Cambridge University Press, 1998.

Wheeler, Bonnie, and John Carmi Parsons, eds. *Eleanor of Aquitaine: Lord and Lady.* New York: Palgrave, 2003.

Willesme, Jean-Pierre. "Les cordelières de la rue de Lourcine, des origines à l'implantation du nouvel Hôpital Broca." *Paris et Île-de-France: Mémoires* 43 (1992): 207–48.

Winston-Allen, Anne. *Convent Chronicles: Women Writing about Women and Reform in the Late Middle Ages.* University Park: Pennsylvania State University Press, 2004.

Wogan-Browne, Jocelyn. *Saints' Lives and Women's Literary Culture c. 1150–1300.* Oxford: Oxford University Press, 2001.

Wolf, Kenneth Baxter. *The Poverty of Riches: St. Francis of Assisi Reconsidered.* Oxford: Oxford University Press, 2003.

Worcester, Thomas. "Neither Married nor Cloistered: Blessed Isabelle in Catholic Reformation France." *Sixteenth Century Journal* 30 (1999): 457–72.

Zerner, M. "L'Épouse de Simon de Montfort et la croisade albigeoise." In *Femmes, mariages, lignages (XIIe-XIVe s.): Mélanges offerts à Georges Duby.* Brussels: De Boeck, 1992: 449–70.

INDEX

Abbaye-de-Val, 235n37

Ade of Reims, nun of Longchamp,
98, 135

Adrian of Boissy, cardinal, 162, 247n88

Agnes "daughter of Heloise," 55

Agnes of Anery, abbess of Longchamp,
55, 127, 217n9

Agnes of Bohemia, 5, 64, 90–91, 222n37,
244n63

Agnes of Fallouel, 200n66

Agnes of Harcourt, abbess of
Longchamp, 8–11, 14, 18–23, 26,
28–35, 38–42, 46, 49, 55, 63–68,
86, 88–89, 97, 100–101, 113–14,
121, 123, 125–29, 131–37, 140–52,
165, 167–70, 216n7, 217nn9–10
portrayal of Isabelle of France, 152–59

Agnes of Paris, nun of Longchamp, 142

Agnes "the chest maker," 144, 170

Agnes, townswoman of Suresnes, 144

Albert of Suerbeer, 43–44, 46, 53,
56–57

Albertus Magnus, 195n28

Alberzoni, Maria Pia, 115

Aldgate, female Franciscan abbey of, 119

Alexander IV, pope, 1, 3, 7, 53, 56–59,
69, 71, 74, 92–94, 96, 100–102,
104, 106, 110, 168, 170,
208nn51–52, 209n53
bulls
—*Benedicta filia tu*, 54–56, 78, 89, 92,
101, 167, 173n16, 191n3
—*Cum a nobis*, 66, 72

—*Devotionis vestre precibus*, 66
—*Etsi universe orbis*, 66
—*Inter alia sacra*, 66, 72, 104
—*Sol ille verus*, 66, 70–72, 75–78
and foundation of Longchamp,
65–66
and rule of 1259, 75–78, 85, 88

Alexander the Great, romances of,
21–23, 35

Alice of Montmorency, 191n15

Alice of Mucedent, nun of Longchamp,
127, 141, 158, 217n9

Alix de Beaumont, 55

Alix, wife of Jean of Châtillon, 117

Allariz, female Franciscan abbey of, 120

Alphonse of Poitiers, 5, 13, 15–16, 44,
46–47, 150, 169, 179n18, 181n37,
189n91, 196n36, 203n19, 234n27,
236n40, 241n30

Ambrose of Milan, saint, 52–53

Andrew of Hungary, king, 4

Angre of Reims, nun of Longchamp,
98, 157

Aquitaine, Franciscans of, 235n31

Arles, Franciscans of, 235n31

Arnold IV of Audenard, 237n52

Ars minor. See Donatus

Audenard, the Lady of, 134, 237n52

Augustine of Hippo, saint, 24

Aveline of Hainault, nun of
Longchamp, 132

Aymeric of Veire, 40, 49, 63–65, 67,
92, 153

279

SEAN L. FIELD

is assistant professor of history, University of Vermont.